Optimizing Research Techniques and Learning Strategies With Digital Technologies

J. Sadhik Basha
Department of Process Engineering, National University of Science and Technology, Oman

Taofeek Olanrewaju Alade
National University of Science and Technology, Oman

Mitha Obaid Amur Al Khazimi
National University of Science and Technology, Oman

Ranjit Vasudevan
National University of Science and Technology, Oman

Jahanzeb Bahadur Khan
National University of Science and Technology, Oman

IGI Global
Scientific Publishing
Publishing Tomorrow's Research Today

Vice President of Editorial Melissa Wagner
Managing Editor of Acquisitions Mikaela Felty
Managing Editor of Book Development Jocelynn Hessler
Production Manager Mike Brehm
Cover Design Phillip Shickler

Published in the United States of America by
IGI Global Scientific Publishing
701 East Chocolate Avenue
Hershey, PA, 17033, USA
Tel: 717-533-8845
Fax: 717-533-8661
Website: https://www.igi-global.com E-mail: cust@igi-global.com

Library of Congress Cataloging-in-Publication Data

Names: Basha, J. Sadhik, 1977- editor. | Alade, Taofeek, 1983- editor. | Al-Khazimi, Mitha, 1990- editor. | Vasudevan, Ranjit, 1978- editor. | Bahadur, Jahanzeb Khan, 1979- editor.
Title: Optimizing research techniques and learning strategies with digital technologies / edited by Sadhik Basha J, Taofeek Alade, Mitha Al-Khazimi, Ranjit Vasudevan, Jahanzeb Khan Bahadur.
Description: Hershey, PA : IGI Global Scientific Publishing, [2025] | Includes bibliographical references and index. | Summary: "This book seeks to enhance learning strategies by transforming education by using digital tools and technologies to give students individualized, dynamic, and exciting learning opportunities"-- Provided by publisher.
Identifiers: LCCN 2024055202 (print) | LCCN 2024055203 (ebook) | ISBN 9798369378632 (hardcover) | ISBN 9798369378649 (paperback) | ISBN 9798369378656 (ebook)
Subjects: LCSH: Educational technology--Case studies. | Education--Effect of technological innovations on--Case studies.
Classification: LCC LB1028.3 .O58 2025 (print) | LCC LB1028.3 (ebook) | DDC 371.33/4--dc23/eng/20250211
LC record available at https://lccn.loc.gov/2024055202
LC ebook record available at https://lccn.loc.gov/2024055203

British Cataloguing in Publication Data
A Cataloguing in Publication record for this book is available from the British Library.

To the Almighty and to our adored families, who have inspired us the most with their unending love and support.

Editorial Advisory Board

Table of Contents

Detailed Table of Contents

The present study has tried to investigate the impact of Investment in education, Research and Development, amid Gross Fixed Capital Formation, Tertiary Education Enrolment, Unemployment, Corruption Control and Proportion of internet users on Economic Growth of selected developing nations. The data was sourced from World Data Bank, Our World in data and UNDP for the period from 2000 to 2021. The short run and the long run impact of these variables on economic growth of the selected economies was estimated using Panel ARDL. All the preliminary tests including unit root test, cross sectional dependence, cointegration test, etc. were performed before using Panel ARDL. The results indicated that, in developing countries, government expenditure on education, gross capital formation, tertiary studies, internet facilities and effective corruption control have become one of the key drivers of long-term growth and increasing productivity, as all these variables have positive and significant relationship with economic growth.

In maritime domain, interactive and authentic learning environments are needed for competency development of seafarers. This study aims to propose and pilot test

will analyze platforms like Microsoft Teams and Zoom, assessing their effectiveness in English language learning.

Learning strategies with digital technologies have revolutionized educational practices, offering new opportunities for personalized, adaptive, and engaging learning experiences. The integration of digital tools, such as Artificial Intelligence (AI), machine learning, and digital platforms, enables educators to tailor learning strategies to individual student needs, promoting more effective and efficient learning. This study explores the potential of digital technologies in enhancing learning strategies, focusing on the role of Artificial Neural Networks (ANNs) in personalizing learning pathways for students. By leveraging data such as student performance, learning styles, and engagement, digital technologies can create adaptive learning environments that continuously evolve based on real-time feedback. The study investigates how these technologies can improve learner outcomes by providing targeted support, personalized content delivery, and dynamic feedback mechanisms.

The integration of Artificial Intelligence (AI), Virtual Reality (VR), and Augmented Reality (AR) in education is reshaping the learning landscape by providing immersive and personalized learning experiences. Immersive learning through VR and AR allows for practical simulations and experiential learning, bridging the gap between theoretical knowledge and real-world application. However, challenges such as ethical considerations, data privacy, and the digital divide need to be addressed to ensure inclusive and equitable access to these advanced learning tools. The chapter explores the benefits of AI-driven immersive learning, including improved student motivation, engagement, and retention, while also discussing scalability and the potential for widespread adoption across diverse educational settings. It emphasizes the importance of incorporating ethical frameworks and continuous research to align AI, VR, and AR applications with the evolving needs of modern education, ensuring that these technologies contribute positively to student outcomes and lifelong learning.

This book chapter explores the integration of AI tools into higher educational institutions and uncovers the current trends in utilizing AI tools by educators and educational leaders. Via an interview, the research data was collected from six higher education leaders. Five themes emerged answering the three research questions. The themes highlighted the current practices of AI in Omani higher educational institutions, explained the perceived effects of AI tools on learning, teaching and educational leaderships, and pointed to AI-related challenges. Additionally, the interviewees proposed some strategies to overcome the challenges and recommendations for future implementations of AI. In light of the findings, it becomes clear that AI use in education is unavoidable. Thus, it is recommended that educational leaders offer on-going training to all concerned staff, encourage the participation of educators in making decisions regarding the appropriate application of AI as well as developing guidelines to address the ethical concerns.

This chapter, titled “Integration of Digital Technologies in Entrepreneurship Education in Nigeria,” explores how digital technologies can transform and enhance entrepreneurship education in Nigeria. It addresses key issues such as accessibility, content quality, the digital divide, and the need for ongoing professional development for educators. The chapter highlights the shift from traditional classroom methods to more experiential learning, driven by technological advancements. Furthermore, it discusses the benefits and challenges of digital learning, presents case studies, and provides recommendations for stakeholders to foster an innovative and inclusive entrepreneurial ecosystem in Nigeria.

Foreword

The ways in which we conduct research and learn have changed significantly in a world where technology is driving development. For anybody attempting to navigate this changing environment, Optimizing Research Techniques and Learning Strategies with Digital Technologies is a pertinent and indispensable resource.

We now have unparalleled access to knowledge, simplified collaboration, and a more effective method of tackling challenging research problems thanks to the convergence of digital tools and education, which has completely changed the learning process and results. This book offers helpful tips and techniques for utilizing these tools to improve research speed and quality. It goes beyond only knowing how to use the tools; it explores how to best apply them in a way that promotes deeper learning, critical thinking, and creative approaches.

Educators, researchers, and students may find the incorporation of digital technologies daunting. From choosing the appropriate software to handling enormous volumes of data, the sheer number of options can be intimidating. Nonetheless, this book acts as a manual to assist readers in comprehending not just which instruments to employ but also how to do so efficiently in their research procedures and educational settings. By means of well-crafted methods and well-considered approaches, it enables readers to unleash the possibilities of digital tools in research.

Whether you are a student trying to succeed in the digital age or an academic trying to improve your research techniques, this book will be a great resource. For people who are committed to staying ahead of the curve in a fast-paced, digital world where success depends on one's capacity for learning and adaptation, it is an essential read.

R. B. Anand

National Institute of Technology, Trichy, India

Preface

INTRODUCTION

The integration of digital technologies has ushered in a new era of efficiency and innovation in research methodologies and learning strategies across engineering, physical sciences, and other educational paradigms. These technologies have redefined how academics address complex challenges and how students engage with fundamental concepts. From computational modeling to advanced data analytics, digital tools have revolutionized both research and education.

The convergence of research techniques and digital technologies has empowered scientists, technocrats, educators, and engineers to expand the frontiers of knowledge and capability. Through the use of simulations, remote sensing technologies, and computational algorithms, researchers can model real-world scenarios with unprecedented precision and depth. This not only accelerates discovery but also enhances the reliability and robustness of experimental results. Concurrently, digital technologies have transformed learning strategies in engineering, physical sciences, and foundational education. Students now benefit from interactive simulations, virtual laboratories, and online collaboration platforms that deepen their understanding and practical skills. These digital resources complement traditional instruction and create immersive learning experiences that prepare students for contemporary scientific, educational, and engineering challenges.

This book explores the transformative impact of digital technologies on optimizing research techniques and learning strategies. By presenting case studies and practical examples, it delves into how these technologies are reshaping methodologies, improving productivity, and fostering interdisciplinary collaboration. Additionally, it addresses the evolving role of digital literacy and the ethical considerations in employing advanced technologies in scientific research.

As we navigate this rapidly evolving digital landscape, the fusion of technology with engineering, physical sciences, and education is set to redefine the future of research and learning. Educators, researchers, technocrats, and engineers have pioneered various digital approaches to tackle contemporary challenges. This book serves as a clarion call for both the technical and educational communities to engage with recent breakthroughs and innovations in research techniques and learning strategies empowered by digital technologies.

Objectives of This Book

1. **Enhanced Learning Experiences:** The goal is to leverage digital tools and technologies to offer students personalized, dynamic, and engaging learning experiences.
2. **Optimized Research Methodologies:** This book aims to improve data collection and analysis processes, accelerate discovery, promote interdisciplinary collaboration, and address complex societal challenges more effectively.
3. **Promotion of Access and Inclusivity:** By integrating digital technologies and open access principles, we seek to ensure that diverse populations have equal access to learning resources, research findings, and academic opportunities.
4. **Encouraging Innovation and Creativity:** Providing students and researchers with the necessary tools and platforms fosters an environment where new ideas flourish, breakthroughs occur, and knowledge expands.
5. **Ethical and Responsible Use of Technology:** The responsible application of digital technologies in research and education is crucial. Stakeholders must navigate ethical concerns related to privacy, security, intellectual property, and digital citizenship to ensure technology serves as a force for positive transformation and empowerment.

Target Audience

This book is intended for a diverse audience, including:

- **Teachers and Educators:** Professionals in education and instructional design seeking to enhance student learning outcomes through digital technologies.
- **Researchers and Scholars:** Academics across various disciplines looking to optimize their research processes and accelerate discovery through digital tools.
- **Education Administrators:** Policymakers, curriculum developers, and school administrators interested in understanding the impact of digital advancements on education.

- **Students:** Undergraduate and graduate students eager to enrich their research projects and learning experiences with digital innovations.
- **Corporate Trainers:** Professionals in workforce development aiming to implement digital strategies for more effective training programs.
- **Technology Enthusiasts:** Individuals keen on exploring the intersection of technology and education, as well as staying informed about emerging trends and best practices in digital learning and research.

This book serves as a comprehensive guide to the evolving role of digital technologies in research and education, equipping readers with the knowledge and tools to navigate this ever-changing landscape effectively.

ORGANIZATION OF THE BOOK

Chapter 1: Modelling the Impact of Education, Research, and Digitalization on Economic Growth: Evidence from Developing Economies

Education, research, and digitalization are key drivers of economic growth in developing nations. This chapter presents an empirical study analyzing the impact of investment in education, research and development, and digital infrastructure on economic growth. Using data from global sources spanning two decades, the study employs econometric modeling to assess short- and long-term effects. The findings demonstrate the critical role of government expenditure on education, technological adoption, and corruption control in fostering sustainable economic development. This chapter provides policymakers with actionable insights for optimizing national strategies to enhance economic productivity and innovation.

Chapter 2: Proposing a Serious Game Design Model Towards Maritime Competency Development: A Case Study

The maritime industry requires interactive and authentic learning environments to develop competency among seafarers. This chapter introduces the Serious Game Design for Maritime (SGDM) model, which supports the creation of maritime training simulations. Using the SGDM framework, the Maritime Leaders at Sea (ML@S) game was developed to enhance leadership and teamwork skills among maritime students. The study demonstrates how serious games can meet industry standards and improve maritime education. This chapter provides a foundation for further research and development in digital game-based learning for the maritime sector.

Chapter 3: Understanding Student Perceptions in Digital Education through Deep Learning Stacking Approach

As digital education continues to evolve, understanding student perceptions is crucial for optimizing learning experiences. This chapter employs a deep learning stacking approach to analyze student feedback and engagement in digital education environments. The study examines how AI-driven analytics can enhance course design, instructional strategies, and student satisfaction.

Chapter 4: AI-Driven Research Methodologies: Revolutionizing Data-Driven Discoveries in Engineering and Physical Sciences

The advent of artificial intelligence (AI) has significantly transformed research methodologies across engineering and physical sciences. This chapter explores how AI-driven technologies, including machine learning, deep learning, and predictive analytics, are revolutionizing traditional research approaches by enabling the rapid processing and analysis of vast datasets with unprecedented accuracy. The integration of AI into domains such as materials science, renewable energy, aerospace engineering, and manufacturing has led to groundbreaking discoveries. Additionally, the chapter highlights AI's potential to enhance interdisciplinary collaboration, improve predictive accuracy, and increase research efficiency. However, challenges such as the need for transparent algorithms, ethical considerations, and data biases must be addressed. Through case studies of successful AI applications, this chapter provides a comprehensive overview of AI's transformative role in modern scientific research.

Chapter 5: Optimizing Research Techniques and Learning Strategies with Digital Technologies: The Digital Renaissance at the Workplace

The digital transformation of the workplace is reshaping research methodologies and learning strategies. This chapter examines how businesses can leverage digital tools to enhance productivity, creativity, and problem-solving. The concept of the "digital renaissance" is explored, highlighting the shift from traditional work ethics to technology-driven flexibility and innovation. By understanding employee needs and business constraints, organizations can develop tailored digital solutions that drive efficiency and value creation. This chapter serves as a guide for businesses seeking to maximize the potential of digital technologies in the evolving workplace landscape.

Chapter 6: Exploring the Benefits of Online English Language Programs in Higher Education

The COVID-19 pandemic accelerated the adoption of online learning platforms in higher education, particularly for English language instruction. This chapter examines the effectiveness of digital English language programs in improving literacy and language proficiency. Through student and instructor surveys, the study evaluates platforms such as Microsoft Teams and Zoom, assessing their role in overcoming literacy challenges. The findings highlight the advantages of virtual language learning, including accessibility, personalized instruction, and enhanced engagement. This chapter provides recommendations for integrating online language programs into higher education curricula to optimize learning outcomes.

Chapter 7: Personalized Learning in the Digital Era: Unlocking Potential through AI and Data Analytics

AI and data analytics are revolutionizing personalized learning by enabling adaptive and student-centered educational experiences. This chapter explores the use of Artificial Neural Networks (ANNs) to tailor learning pathways based on student performance, engagement, and learning styles. The study highlights how digital technologies provide real-time feedback, personalized content delivery, and targeted support. By examining case studies and best practices, this chapter offers valuable insights into the future of education, where technology-driven personalization enhances learning outcomes and fosters lifelong learning.

Chapter 8: Leveraging AI to Enhance Teaching and Learning in Education: The Role of Artificial Intelligence in Modernizing Classroom Practices

The integration of AI, Virtual Reality (VR), and Augmented Reality (AR) is revolutionizing education by offering immersive and personalized learning experiences. This chapter explores how these technologies enhance student motivation, engagement, and retention through experiential learning. It also addresses challenges such as ethical considerations, data privacy, and the digital divide. By highlighting best practices and scalable solutions, the chapter underscores the need for ethical frameworks and ongoing research to align AI-driven educational tools with modern learning objectives. The insights presented in this chapter pave the way for the widespread adoption of AI-enhanced learning environments.

Chapter 9: Incorporating AI in Educational Leadership: Trends and Innovations

The integration of AI into educational leadership is reshaping higher education institutions worldwide. This chapter examines current trends in AI adoption by educational leaders through insights gathered from interviews with higher education administrators in Oman. The study identifies key themes, including AI's impact on teaching, learning, and institutional management. Additionally, the chapter discusses challenges associated with AI implementation, such as ethical considerations and staff training needs. Recommendations for future AI adoption emphasize the necessity of continuous professional development, faculty involvement in decision-making, and the establishment of ethical guidelines. This chapter provides a roadmap for educational leaders seeking to harness AI for institutional improvement.

Chapter 10: Integration of Digital Technologies in Entrepreneurship Education in Nigeria

Digital technologies are transforming entrepreneurship education in Nigeria by increasing accessibility, improving content quality, and addressing the digital divide. This chapter explores the shift from traditional classroom-based learning to technology-driven experiential education. It highlights the benefits and challenges of digital learning, offering case studies that illustrate successful implementations. The chapter also provides strategic recommendations for educators, policymakers, and stakeholders to foster an innovative and inclusive entrepreneurial ecosystem. By leveraging digital tools, Nigeria can cultivate a new generation of entrepreneurs equipped with the skills necessary for success in a rapidly evolving global economy.

Chapter 11: Analyzing Linguistic Differences in Academic English: A Graph-Based Machine Learning Approach

Understanding linguistic variations in academic English is crucial for effective global communication and collaboration. This chapter employs graph-based machine learning techniques to analyze the differences between English used by Indian and British academicians. By constructing language graphs from academic texts, the study identifies unique syntactic structures, semantic variations, and writing patterns. Advanced community detection algorithms and semantic network analysis are utilized to uncover key linguistic clusters and contextual nuances. The findings provide valuable insights into regional writing styles, contributing to cross-cultural communication, education, and academic discourse. This research highlights the potential of AI-driven linguistic analysis in refining academic writing and fostering international academic collaboration.

Chapter 12: Using AI-Powered Grammar Correction Tools to Support ESL Students' Writing Skills Development

In this last chapter, the authors explore the role of AI-powered grammar correction tools in enhancing the writing skills of General Foundation Program (GFP) students at the University of Technology and Applied Sciences-Suhar. Through a combination of focus group discussions and classroom observations, the study examines how students interact with these tools in both traditional classroom settings and computer labs. The findings highlight that while AI-assisted grammar correction can significantly boost student engagement, the most effective learning occurs when it is integrated with traditional instruction. Students initially relied on AI-generated corrections passively but gradually developed critical engagement with the suggestions provided, leading to improved writing confidence and independence. However, technical challenges and the necessity of teacher guidance were noted as key factors in ensuring the effective implementation of AI tools. The study underscores that while AI-driven grammar tools hold great promise for ESL education, their success depends on structured support and training to maximize their benefits.

Chapter 13: Effects of the Animation Infographic on Learning Retention and Motivation

Despite the abundance of technological resources in higher education, limited research exists on the effectiveness of animation infographics as pedagogical tools. This chapter addresses the growing challenge of communicating complex technical concepts to students in an era dominated by information and communication technology (ICT). By exploring the role of animation infographics in enhancing learning retention and motivation, this study underscores the importance of innovative educational tools. The chapter provides insights into how visual learning aids can bridge gaps in understanding and improve knowledge retention among students in Information Technology courses, ultimately leading to more effective teaching strategies.

CONCLUSION

As the chapters in this volume illustrate, the integration of artificial intelligence into education is transforming the landscape of learning, assessment, and instructional strategies. From AI-powered grammar correction tools to adaptive learning systems, these innovations offer significant potential to enhance student engagement, support individualized learning, and bridge educational gaps. However, our contributors also highlight the importance of maintaining a balanced approach—where technology serves as a complement rather than a replacement for human instruction. The findings across these studies underscore the necessity of teacher guidance, structured training, and critical engagement to ensure that AI tools are used effectively and ethically.

While challenges such as technical limitations, accessibility concerns, and the need for digital literacy persist, the insights presented in this book provide valuable frameworks for navigating these complexities. As educators, researchers, and policymakers continue to explore the evolving role of AI in education, it is imperative to foster an environment where technology enhances pedagogical best practices while preserving the essential human elements of learning. Ultimately, the future of AI in education lies not in automation alone, but in its ability to support meaningful, thoughtful, and dynamic learning experiences for all students.

J. Sadhik Basha
Department of Science Cluster, National University of Science & Technology, Oman

Taofeek Olanrewaju Alade
Department of Science Cluster, National University of Science and Technology, Oman

Mitha Obaid Amur Al Khazimi
Department of Science Cluster, National University of Science and Technology, Oman

Ranjit Vasudevan
Department of Science Cluster, National University of Science and Technology, Oman

Jahanzeb Bahadur Khan
Department of Science Cluster, National University of Science and Technology, Oman

Acknowledgments

Without the help, advice, and encouragement of numerous people, this book would not have been possible.

First and foremost, we want to sincerely thank our family and friends for their constant support and faith in us, which laid the groundwork for our adventure. Their understanding and patience were crucial, particularly during the difficult writing periods. We are grateful to our loved ones for always being an inspiration.

Additionally, we are grateful to the professionals, educators, and researchers whose work served as inspiration for a large portion of the material in this book. We are privileged to expand on your expertise in the fields of digital technologies and education, which have opened up new avenues for ideas and opportunities.

We would especially want to thank our mentors and coworkers for sharing their knowledge, advice, and helpful criticism. Your wise counsel guaranteed this book's academic integrity and usefulness while also assisting in determining its course. We especially appreciate Dr. Anteneh, Dr. Abdul Hameed, Dr. Rommel, Mr. Patrick McDaid, and Dr. Zouhair for their thorough reviews and the time they took to share their priceless thoughts with us.

We want to express our gratitude to the publishing team for their professionalism, encouragement, and hard work during the publishing process. We appreciate your meticulousness and dedication to making this book a reality.

Lastly, we would like to thank the innumerable scholars, researchers, and educators worldwide who are consistently expanding the frontiers of study and learning using digital technology. This book is devoted to individuals who endeavor to maximize these resources in their quest for understanding and exploration.

We wholeheartedly appreciate the encouragement and support from everyone who helped with this effort, whether directly or indirectly. Many thanks to all of you.

Chapter 1
Modelling the Impact of Education, Research, and Digitalization on Economic Growth:
Evidence From Developing Economies

Devishi Raina
Shri Mata Vaishno Devi University, India

Meenakshi Gupta
https://orcid.org/0000-0002-7866-4961
Shri Mata Vaishno Devi University, India

ABSTRACT

The present study has tried to investigate the impact of Investment in education, Research and Development, amid Gross Fixed Capital Formation, Tertiary Education Enrolment, Unemployment, Corruption Control and Proportion of internet users on Economic Growth of selected developing nations. The data was sourced from World Data Bank, Our World in data and UNDP for the period from 2000 to 2021. The short run and the long run impact of these variables on economic growth of the selected economies was estimated using Panel ARDL. All the preliminary tests including unit root test, cross sectional dependence, cointegration test, etc. were performed before using Panel ARDL. The results indicated that, in developing countries, government expenditure on education, gross capital formation, tertiary

DOI: 10.4018/979-8-3693-7863-2.ch001

studies, internet facilities and effective corruption control have become one of the key drivers of long-term growth and increasing productivity, as all these variables have positive and significant relationship with economic growth.

INTRODUCTION

In today's world when all the major economies are rattling on about sustainable economic growth and to achieve this, UNDP has already defined 17 SDGs. Out of these 17 SDGs, the SDG no.4, focuses on achieving inclusive and equitable, quality education and promoting life-long learning opportunities for everyone. Education, digitalization and economic growth are interwoven drivers of development, particularly in today's rapidly evolving global landscape. In an amassed digital world, education systems are being transformed to prepare individuals for a tech-centric future, where digital literacy is as crucial as traditional skills. Developing nations, where digital infrastructure is still seasoning, are working to bridge gaps in access to digital tools and internet connectivity, as these are essential for modern education and economic participation. Digitalization not only enhances learning by enabling remote and interactive methods but also empowers economies by fostering a skilled workforce ready for a digital economy. Countries embracing this shift see accelerated economic growth as new skills fuel innovation and entrepreneurship, giving rise to job creation and global competitiveness. Yet, without universal access to digital resources and quality education, as the inequality risks deepen, we run a risk of leaving under-connected communities and nations behind. To drive inclusive growth, global collaboration is essential to expand digital infrastructure, support educational reforms and foster policies that prioritize equitable access to these crucial tools for development.

In the past, it was observed that a positive trend in public spending on education causes a positive trend in government spending on education causes a positive effect on economic development (Besime Fekri Ziberi et al.,2022) (Girma Mulugeta Emeru, 2023) (Nura Aliyu Kabuga, 2015) (Paravee Maneejuk & Woraphon Yamaka, 2021) (Chinedu Uchenna Okerekeoti 2022) etc. It is observed that inflation impacts education spending, negatively (Mohamed Maher et al., 2022). Investment in education at all levels aids the growth (Victor Owusu-Nantwi, 2015). Corruption impacts government spending, by interfering with the expenditure needs of a nation, inversely (Agung Suwandaru et al, 2021) (Girma Mulugeta Emeru, 2023). GFCF is positively related to growth of an economy (Agung Suwandaru et al, 2021) (Shikha Pokhrel and Chakra Bahadur Khadka, 2019). Unemployment affects the GDP negatively (Victor Owusu-Nantwi, 2015). Enrolment in tertiary education, mainly, helps economic growth positively (Paravee Maneejuk et al, 2021) (Fadila Kabir

Usman et al, 2019) (Strike Mbulawa et al, 2016) (Muhammad Afzal et al, 2010), etc. All of this forms the basis of our bias towards the selection of the variables for our model. Mentionable, to understand the dynamics of economic growth, selecting variables that capture educational, technological, governance and infrastructural factors is essential. Here, GDP acts as the dependent variable, while the independent variables each offer insights into how different aspects drive growth. Expenditure on R&D (% of GDP) reflects a country's commitment to innovation and technological advancement. High R&D spending often correlates with increased productivity, competitive industries and sustainable economic development. Countries investing in R&D are better positioned to foster groundbreaking technologies, which can transform industries and boost a nation's GDP.

Government Expenditure on education represents the priority given to human capital development. By investing in education, governments equip the workforce with essential skills, fostering higher productivity and encouraging the advancement of industries. This, in turn, fuels economic growth by creating a skilled labor force and attracting foreign investment.

Gross Fixed Capital Formation (% of GDP) measures investment in machinery, infrastructure and other physical assets that are foundational for productivity. Higher capital formation indicates hearty infrastructural growth, supporting economic expansion by enhancing production capacity, facilitating smoother business operations and fostering long-term growth.

Population using the internet as a variable, serves as a proxy for digital inclusion and access to information. A higher internet penetration rate signals increased access to knowledge, e-commerce, global connectivity and digital services, which empowers individuals and businesses alike. Digital connectivity enhances GDP growth by enabling digital economies, expanding markets and supporting remote education and work.

Enrolment in Tertiary Education provides insight into the country's focus on higher education, which is essential for cultivating specialized skills. A higher enrolment rate in tertiary education often correlates with a more qualified labor pool that can drive innovation, research and complex economic activities, thus ultimately increasing GDP.

Unemployment indicates labor market conditions and economic health. Lower unemployment suggests a productive economy with copious job opportunities, whereas higher unemployment can lead to underutilized human resources, restraining the economic growth potential.

Corruption Control is a vital indicator of governance transparency, quality and investor confidence. Effective corruption control ensures efficient allocation of resources, promotes fair competition and fosters a stable economic environment conducive to growth. Low corruption is linked to reduced wasteful spending, higher foreign investments and improved institutional trust, all of which support GDP growth.

Each variable offers a distinct lens through which to analyze the factors that drive economic growth, allowing for a comprehensive exploration of GDP determinants. By investigating these variables in tandem, we can gain richer insights into the interplay between education, digitalization, capital investment, governance and labor market dynamics, revealing how they collectively influence economic performance. This multifaceted approach not only deepens our understanding of growth mechanisms but also highlights the importance of synergistic relationships among these elements in fostering sustainable economic development.

Remarkably, Digitalization has transformed education by expanding access to resources, reshaping learning methods and fostering personalized learning experiences. With digital tools like online courses, e-books and virtual classrooms, students now have more flexibility in when and how they learn, breaking down traditional barriers. This shift enables learners, especially those in remote or underserved regions, to access high-quality educational materials and engage with diverse academic communities. Moreover, digital platforms allow for tailored educational experiences that can adapt to individual learning speeds and styles, promoting more effective learning outcomes. Teachers also benefit from digitalization, using analytics to track student progress in real-time and adjust teaching methods accordingly.

Various economies have already taken steps towards the achievement of this goal. Against this backdrop, the present study is an attempt to evaluate the initiatives taken by the selected developing economies towards sustainable development. The education sector varies in these economies that can be attributed to some factors such as history, economy, politics, culture, tradition, the impact of globalization, progress, economic development, social justice, etc. It is due to these factors together, that influence the importance of education, the creation of educational materials, the distribution of resources and educational outcomes, creating unique characteristics of each country's education system.

In our study, we have considered the developing economies of India, Indonesia, Mauritius, Malaysia, Sri Lanka, Nepal and Pakistan. The reason for this being, the similarity in the dynamics, governance, history and conditions of these nations. India's educational landscape has evolved from the ancient sites of Taksha-shila and Nalanda to modern systems that emphasize national development and international competition. With rapid growth, especially in STEM, management, science and IT, Indian universities have made a priority for research, technical education businesses and leaders to improve education and performance across the country. First influenced by Dutch colonialism, the education system in Indonesia has changed to focus on accessibility, vocational training and technical education. The country is expanding its higher education, particularly in vocational education, technical education and business, which is encouraging international cooperation to improve educational standards. Influenced by the British model, Malaysia emphasizes technology, international expansion and higher education and has the best education, business and hotel management. Malaysian universities actively participate in international collaborations to promote education through cultural exchange, research collaboration and business. With British and French influence, Mauritius has become a regional education hub providing quality education in various fields such as business, economics and innovation. Mauritius has a bilingual environment and a good study environment that attracts students from Africa and Asia. Historically known for its religious Hindu-Buddhist education, Nepal is currently reforming its education system to increase access, effectiveness and relevance, especially in rural areas. Their efforts have focused on teacher training, curriculum reform and meeting agriculture, tourism and technology needs. Pakistan has an education system that has adapted to many challenges in terms of STEM education, research and innovation to support economic growth. Pakistani universities are important for research, international collaboration and quality development in STEM, business education and IT fields. Influenced by the British model, Sri Lanka has invested in higher education, research and international cooperation, especially in fields such as business, engineering, medicine and information technology.

The educational diversity of these countries underscores the importance of international knowledge exchange, innovation and workforce development. Strategic change is essential to overcome challenges and leverage resources to increase the quality, effectiveness, accessibility and impact of global education.

DIGITALIZATION AND ITS IMPEDANCE ON ECONOMIC GROWTH

Digital transformation has become essential as businesses rethink models to stay competitive, but realizing full benefits remains a challenge, with many capturing only a third of their expected revenue gains. Some of the key trends are shaping this evolution like, artificial intelligence and machine learning that enhance productivity and decision-making. Automation streamlines repetitive tasks, especially in customer support and inventory management. Cloud computing reduces the need for in-house data centers and cybersecurity adapts with proactive "shift-left" practices and blockchain for better data security.

IoT and edge computing allow for real-time insights in areas like predictive maintenance, while industry-specific transformations such as telemedicine in healthcare require robust security investments. Low-code and no-code platforms make development more accessible, fostering collaboration and remote work drives the need for secure, adaptable digital tools. Success depends on aligning technology with organizational culture. For those who effectively integrate these trends gain a stronger competitive edge ('Top digital transformation trends' article by IBM, 2024).

Digitalization drives economic growth by accelerating productivity, fostering innovation and creating new market opportunities. As businesses incorporate digital tools—such as automation, data analytics and e-commerce, they streamline operations, reduce costs and reach global markets more efficiently. Digitalization enables small and medium-sized enterprises (SMEs) to compete alongside larger corporations, boosting competition and enhancing consumer choice. Moreover, the demand for digital skills has spurred job creation in tech fields, from software development to cybersecurity. Additionally, as industries adopt new technologies, there's a ripple effect across supply chains, fueling growth in related sectors. Digitalization also makes it easier to measure and optimize resource usage, supporting sustainable business models that appeal to eco-conscious markets. Overall, by enhancing connectivity, digitalization stimulates economies, encourages entrepreneurship and creates a more inclusive global marketplace.

Digitalization in India

The 'Deloitte Tech Trends 2024' report spotlights cutting-edge technologies reshaping India's digital landscape, emphasizing advancements in areas like spatial computing, Generative AI (GenAI) and core modernization. By balancing elevating forces, such as interactive and computing technologies, with grounding ones like cybersecurity and DevOps, Indian industries are aligning innovation with sustainability for maximizing growth. Tech Landscape of India's tech sector revenue is projected at \$254 billion for FY2024, with exports nearing \$200 billion. The domestic tech sector is forecasted to exceed \$54 billion, showing a 5.9% year-over-year growth. Global Capability Centers (GCCs) and Engineering Research and Development (ER&D) hubs are pivotal, with the GCC market expected to reach \$100 billion by 2030, creating 2,500 centers and 4.5 million jobs. Deloitte estimates India's economy to grow by 6.9–7.2% in 2024. Digital adoption, supported by government initiatives, has seen 90% of businesses embrace AI and IoT, although 62% express the need for clearer regulations.

India has over 70 GenAI startups and received \$590 million in funding. GenAI has significant growth potential with an anticipated CAGR of 24.4% from 2023 to 2030. By 2030, GenAI could add \$359–\$438 billion to India's GDP. The Indian cloud market is expected to reach \$10 billion by 2028. By 2026, cloud tech could constitute 8% of India's GDP, generating 14 million jobs.

India’s National Quantum Mission, with a $730 million fund, targets quantum advancements by 2031. Enterprise adoption is projected to rise from 12% to 35-45% over the decade. India’s DPI model, which includes Aadhaar and UPI, has achieved 80% financial inclusion. Eight countries have adopted India's DPI, fostering international tech partnerships.

India’s digitalization approach stands out in the G20 for leveraging Digital Public Infrastructure (DPI) rather than solely relying on the private sector, as in the U.S. or government dominance, like in China. India Stack’s components—Aadhaar (identity), UPI (payments) and Account Aggregators (data sharing)—drive its DPI model. This framework, endorsed by the G20, uses open standards, public-private partnerships and interoperability to provide large-scale, secure digital access and equitable service delivery. Aadhaar, the world’s second-largest digital ID network, currently enrolls 1.4 billion citizens, with a 94% enrolment rate, enhancing welfare programs. Aadhaar-based authentication saved Rs. 2.7 lakh crore in government benefit disbursements worth Rs. 34 lakh crores. However, studies highlight a risk of exclusion, as seen in Jharkhand’s MGNREGS program, where 57% of deleted job cards were genuine. Implementation issues also threaten the eligibility of 34.8% of registered MGNREGS workers. Low Aadhaar coverage in northeastern states has prompted calls to accelerate enrolment efforts. India leads G20 countries in digital payments, reporting 117 billion UPI transactions worth Rs. 182 trillion in 2023. Between 2022 and 2023, Account Aggregators grew from 3.2 million to 38.96 million linked accounts, providing secure financial data-sharing options. Digital financial inclusion for informal workers expanded through the Aadhaar-linked e-Shram portal, recording over 290 million workers by 2023.

India's “whole-of-government” approach to DPI includes sectors like health (ABHA), taxation (GSTN), education (DIKSHA), social protection (e-Shram) and over 4,200 e-services with 160 billion e-transactions recorded in 2023-24. Although UPI is the world’s largest real-time payment system, India’s cybercrime rate is the highest among G20 countries, with UPI constituting 47% of cybercrimes. Security gaps, limited grievance redressal and connectivity issues emphasize the need for resilient regulatory systems and digital infrastructure.

The CHIPS framework measures India’s digitalization and is expanding its focus to include gender, privacy and sustainability. Future editions will add new data on gender gaps, privacy and green technologies, as well as subnational metrics to compare India’s digital progress with other countries. (Centre for internet and digital economy, ‘The state of India’s Digital Economy Report’, 2024).

Launched on July 1, 2015, by the Indian government, the Digital India initiative builds on earlier e-governance efforts from the mid-1990s, addressing their lack of coherence and interactivity. Its primary objectives are to bridge the digital divide, promote digital participation, stimulate economic development and improve living standards for all citizens. The program aims to reduce disparities between tech-savvy individuals and those with limited access to technology, ensuring equitable benefits across sectors like education, healthcare and government services.

To achieve these goals, Digital India is structured around nine foundational pillars. Broadband Highways focus on constructing a vast network of high-speed broadband to enhance connectivity and empower citizens digitally. Universal Access to Mobile Connectivity aims to extend mobile services to remote areas, enabling everyone to participate in the digital economy. The Public Internet Access Programme establishes Common Service Centres in underserved regions to provide affordable internet access, promoting digital literacy and addressing the digital divide. The initiative emphasizes E-Governance, utilizing technology to streamline government services, improving accessibility and transparency while fostering citizen engagement. Platforms like E-Kranti (such as MyGov.in) enable the electronic delivery of services, prioritizing operational efficiency. Furthermore, 'Information for All' seeks to digitize government records for easy online access and support open data initiatives to encourage innovation and development.

Digital India also prioritizes Electronics Manufacturing by fostering local production to reduce imports, create jobs and support economic growth through manufacturing clusters and investment incentives. The Information Technology (IT) for Jobs pillar enhances the IT skills of youth to meet industry demands through initiatives like the Digital Literacy Mission and Skill India, focusing on skill development and employment in the IT sector. Lastly, Early Harvest Programs address immediate digital needs, providing online access to school certificates, facilitating digital attendance and ensuring Wi-Fi availability in public spaces. Together, these components create a comprehensive framework for leveraging technology to drive economic growth, enhance living standards and foster a digitally inclusive society in India. ('Nine years of Digital India Initiative, 2024).

The Digital Economy Report 2024 by UNCTAD[1] highlights the critical need for environmentally sustainable and inclusive digitalization strategies, recognizing that digital technology and infrastructure are increasingly straining the planet's resources. As the digital economy grows, with smartphone shipments doubling since 2010 and Internet of Things (IoT) devices set to surge to 39 billion by 2029, the environmental toll is mounting. Producing and disposing of digital devices, data centers and ICT networks now account for approximately 6%-12% of global electricity use. This demand for resources, including critical minerals like cobalt, lithium and graphite, is projected to rise by 500% by 2050, largely impacting developing countries that supply these materials yet gain limited economic benefit from digitalization. For instance, in 2023, countries such as the Democratic Republic of the Congo and Australia produced a significant share of the world's cobalt and lithium waste, while China handles most of the global processing for many critical minerals. This dependency fuels global competition and geopolitical tensions, especially as the developed world reaps the technological rewards while developing countries face the brunt of ecological costs, including environmental degradation and inadequate digital waste management systems.

The environmental costs of digitalization extend throughout the entire lifecycle of devices. The production phase is particularly impactful, with about 80% of smartphone greenhouse gas emissions generated at this stage. Digital waste continues to rise, with e-waste from screens and IT equipment increasing by 30% between 2010 and 2022. Despite rising waste, global collection rates remain low, particularly in developing countries where only 7.5% of digital waste is formally collected. Energy consumption could double by 2026. The water footprint is also substantial, as technologies like AI and cryptocurrency mining intensify resource demands and Google's data centers alone consumed over 21 million cubic meters of water in 2022. To address these challenges, the report advocates for a global transition to a circular digital economy based on sustainable practices throughout the entire lifecycle of devices, from design and production to disposal. A shift towards circularity, emphasizing durability, repairability, reuse and recycling, could minimize waste and optimize resource use. Although the circular economy comprises only 7.2% of the global economy, its potential is vast, with the global electronics recycling market projected to grow to $108 billion by 2030. By embracing sustainable practices, we can advance technological innovation that benefits both people and the planet, facilitating a fairer distribution of digital benefits across developed and developing countries alike. The report calls for diverse, collaborative efforts among policymakers, businesses and consumers to curb consumption, especially in overdeveloped regions, to ensure equitable digital access and environmental sustainability on a global scale.

PROBLEM STATEMENT

The focus of our study is to analyze the possible effect of public expenditure on education, expenditure on research, internet facilities, total capital flows, unemployment, corruption control and tertiary education enrolment on the growth of developing nations. The analysis arises from the current economy, where many challenges hinder growth, especially from lack of education, network development, foreign investment, unemployment and lack of skillful graduates. The education system faces challenges such as inadequate funding, outdated curriculums and limited access to quality education, hindering the development of skilled workers necessary for innovation and productivity. Additionally, disparity in network access and connectivity leads to greater isolation and inhibits the use of broad technologies that are important for the advancement of the economy. Foreign investment may face restrictions due to global economic uncertainty or regulatory issues that limit investment opportunities and hinder growth. At the same time, rising unemployment leads to economic instability, harming consumers and the economy as a whole. Additionally, the gap in education has led to inequality, social barriers and further economic barriers. Addressing such challenges requires comprehensive reforms, including greater investment in education, infrastructure, policies that encourage innovation and measures to stimulate business growth. This research seeks the solutions as a suggestion from the past data trend analysis, for increasing the efficiency of the government expenditure and policy suggestions to bring fruitful results that might be visible through growth statistics in the future.

LITERATURE REVIEW

A literature review is essential because it provides a comprehensive understanding of existing research, establish context, allowing us to identify gaps and build on the knowledge base of a specific field. It synthesizes diverse perspectives, thus helping us to frame new research within the scope of conventional findings, highlight the unresolved questions and avoid redundancy.

This extensive body of research across several studies, highlights the pivotal role education spending plays in fostering economic growth and sustainable development.

In Ghana, Victor Owusu N. (2015) highlights the government's substantial investment in education, reaching 8.1% of GDP in 2011 and aligning with global educational expenditure goals by 2012. Using a log-linear model, this study demonstrates that funding education, capital formation and labor participation significantly boost Ghana's GDP and suggest strategies for reducing youth unemployment.

Indonesia's education expenditure analysis by Agung Suwandaru et al. (2021) reveals a mixed impact on economic growth, with short-term benefits but no lasting long-term effect. Their findings, based on the Cobb-Douglas function and ARDL bounds testing, recommend reforms to address inefficiencies, emphasizing the importance of the quality of spending.

In North Macedonia, Besime Fekri Ziberi et al. (2022) find a strong link between educational investments and economic growth. Uniquely, the study notes a positive relationship between unemployment and growth but a negative effect on wages, suggesting the need to align education with labor market skills.

For Ethiopia, Girma Mulugeta Emeru (2023) identifies education and healthcare as key drivers of growth despite infrastructure and governance issues. Employing error correction methods, the study reveals that defence spending has a negligible impact on long-term growth and advocates optimizing resources for agriculture and human capital.

In Nigeria, Nura Aliyu Kabuga (2015) confirms a positive correlation between education spending and GDP growth from 1981 to 2013, using econometric models. The findings provide evidence to support increased education funding as a national growth strategy.

Mohamed Maher et al. (2022) examined the effect of inflation on Egypt's education spending and GDP. They find inflation reduces education investment per student while increasing GDP per capita, emphasizing the need for economic reforms to shield educational funding from inflation. In ASEAN countries, Paravee Maneejuk and Woraphon Yamaka (2021) demonstrated that educational investment boosts enrolment and economic stability but disparities like income inequality necessitate targeted policies for effective development outcomes. Eastern Europe, as analysed by Alina CC et al. (2022), similarly shows positive effects from government educational expenditure (GEE) on GDP, though results differ by country. Estonia, for example, benefits initially before it observed diminishing returns, whereas Hungary experienced steady positive effects, highlighting the need for adaptable, long-term strategies to address regional issues like workforce aging.

In Sub-Saharan Africa, Elizabeth N. Appiah (2017) found that education spending has a positive yet modest effect on economic growth, with greater benefits linked to secondary education and workforce development. In low- and middle-income countries, Ibrahim Abubakarr Bah (2023) observed a strong, growth-promoting influence from educational investment, essential for productivity and sustainability in resource-limited settings. Studies in West Africa's ECOWAS region (Fadila KU et al., 2019) emphasized human development investment, advocating for public-private partnerships and policy measures to enhance economic resilience.

In Central Africa's CEMAC, Douanla Tayo et al. (2015) noted the need for coordinated fiscal discipline and regional cooperation to address economic instability. Research by Strike Mbulawa and Piyush Mehta (2016) in Botswana highlights the role of education spending in rural development and enrolment, supporting the importance of evidence-based policies to harness education's potential for sustainable growth across varied economic landscapes.

Muhammad Afzal et al. (2010), explored the complex interactions between growth, education, poverty and macroeconomic stability in Pakistan. By applying root cause analysis, Autoregressive Distributed Lag (ARDL) models and Error Correction Methods (ECM), the study identifies a multifaceted relationship where poverty hampers educational access and inflation affects GDP growth. To promote economic stability and growth, the study suggests targeted policy interventions that reduce poverty, increase educational access and foster human capital development. Shikha Pokhrel and Chakra Bahadur Khadka (2019), focused on Nepal, analyzing the macroeconomic determinants of education and their influence on GDP. Utilizing ARDL models and cointegration analysis, the study finds that gross fixed capital formation (GFCF) and GEE are primary drivers of long-term GDP growth, while human capital investment, foreign aid and trade openness have varied effects. The authors recommend policies that encourage investment in GFCF, GEE and human capital to sustain economic growth while acknowledging the limitations of their data and models.

Ronaldo R. Cabauatan, Ronaldo A. Manalo and Chin Uy (2016), examines the effects of education spending and economic reforms on national development in the Philippines, focusing on population growth and unemployment rates. Using regression analysis and Granger causality tests, they found a positive relationship between education expenditure, employment quality and GDP growth. The study advocates for enhanced investment in primary education, infrastructure and teacher salaries to improve national productivity and support economic expansion. Mohd Yahya Mohd Hussin et al. (2012), investigates the role of public expenditure in Malaysia's economic growth from 1970 to 2010. Employing vector autoregressive (VAR) analysis, they highlight a long-term relationship between GDP, sustainable capital investment, labor relations and public education spending. The study underscores the importance of aligning education funding with national economic goals and suggests that increased public investment in education can drive Malaysia's economic progress and global competitiveness.

The study by Zita Chika Obi et al. (2020) provides an in-depth analysis of Nigeria's educational expenditure and its impact on economic growth, dissecting relationships between variables like population growth, energy consumption, financial use, Gross Fixed Capital Formation (GFCF) and GDP. Their model reveals that both educational expenditure (GEE) and population growth have a positive influence on Nigeria's GDP, although the detrimental effects of inadequate energy infrastructure somewhat constrain these gains. The study also highlights how human capital investments, such as GEE and population growth, support GDP growth but have mixed impacts on employment and human development outcomes in Nigeria. While education expenditure boosts human capital, it indirectly limits employment, indicating nuanced short-term impacts that vary by economic condition, as confirmed through qualitative analysis. Furthermore, the research links workforce education and national literacy improvements with positive outcomes on economic growth and underscores the minor negative effects of underperformance in certain areas.

Similarly, P. Fernando and D. Rajapakshe (2018) examined the influence of foreign direct investment (FDI) on GDP across East Asian countries and Sri Lanka. They found that FDI positively impacts GDP in higher-income and middle-income countries, where solid education, housing development and effective financial management enhance FDI's benefits. However, in middle-income countries, factors like corruption and education limitations hinder this impact. Wijeweera et al. (2010) underscores the critical role of skilled labor in attracting high-tech FDI, while Borensztein et al. (1998) show that FDI correlates positively with GDP, especially in nations with high human capital levels. Studies from Fan and Dickie (2000) and Ahmad and Hamdani (2003) echo these findings, emphasizing the significance of both domestic and foreign investments in fostering growth, with the ARDL model commonly employed to capture short- and long-term economic trends.

For India's Perspective, Pravesh Tamang (2011) explored the effects of education funding on India's economic development. While historical economists like Adam Smith and modern scholars like Romer, Lucas and Solow underscore education's essential role in economic growth, Tamang's study suggests that in India, the impact is less straightforward. Applying the human capital-enhanced growth model through the Cobb-Douglas function and rigorous regression analysis, Tamang revealed that while education expenditures positively influence growth, the effect is relatively modest compared to physical capital investments. The findings indicate the necessity of a balanced approach that combines both theoretical and empirical insights, integrating educational investment with physical capital to promote more robust economic development in India. Sushil Mohan and Monojit Chatterji (2013) critically, through literature studies, examined the ambiguous link between public education spending and economic growth in India. The study highlighted factors like tax policy, school infrastructure, labor market dynamics and resource allocation, which may undermine the potential growth benefits of educational investments. They suggested that a more integrated approach to educational and economic policies, along with targeted investments, could maximize the impact of education spending in India's unique economic landscape. Similarly, Neeraj Kumar and Pooja Choudhary (2019) examined India's education sector, underscoring its foundational role in economic and human development. Their study traced the evolution of educational goals from purely productive endeavors to a broader focus on knowledge and technology-driven growth. They argued that primary education is critical for laying a strong learning foundation, while higher education advances business knowledge crucial for economic success. The study asserts that in an open economy, the benefits of increased education spending are substantial, offering advantages such as skilled labor supply, competitiveness and economic resilience. Plabita Bhattacharyya (2019), conducted a macroeconomic analysis on the role of public education expenditure in growth within India, using ARDL models and Pedroni and Kao correlation analyses across 28 states. The research revealed that while public education spending has a short-term impact on GDP, its long-term influence aligns with Wagner's law, which states that economic growth fuels increased government spending on public services like education. The study provides actionable insights for regional economic development and encourages policy measures that account for India's diverse economic landscapes.

In the field of development of digital world, some others research studies were skimmed, which are mentioned below.

Abdulkarim A. Oloyede et al (2023), examine the definition, measurement and impact of the digital economy, focusing on developing countries like Nigeria. Using a systematic literature review with the PRISMA model, it highlights the challenges such as inconsistent definitions and data scarcity. The study emphasizes the vital role of governments and regulatory agencies in facilitating digital transformation by enhancing infrastructure and promoting internet access. It advocates for a flexible definition of the digital economy tailored to local contexts and proposes establishing a Digital Economy Advisory Board (DEAB) to inform policy decisions.

Yong Seong Foo et al (2024), explore the impact of digitalization on economic growth across 120 countries (2000 to 2020), utilizing generalized method of moments (GMM) estimators. The results indicate a U-shaped relationship, while digitalization initially hampers economic growth, it begins to enhance growth after reaching a certain threshold. The study also finds that globalization negatively affects economic growth but digitalization helps alleviate this adverse impact. These insights suggest that promoting digitalization can harness advanced technologies to foster economic development. Policymakers are encouraged to adopt a global perspective, leveraging digitalization to improve workplace integration and enhance digital infrastructure, which will support better economic performance in the digital era and contribute to achieving Sustainable Development Goals (SDGs).

Xiaoli Hao et al (2023), emphasize the importance of integrating green economic growth within the digital economy. It develops an evaluation index system and utilizes the System of Environmental and Economic Accounting (SEEA) to assess the levels of digitalization (Digi) and green economic growth (GEG) in China, analyzing panel data of 2013 to 2019 time period. The study says that both digitalization and green economy growth are on a steady upward trajectory, with digitalization significantly enhancing green economy growth, exhibiting a marginal effect of 1.648. The study also highlights positive local (0.556; 0.574) and neighboring effects (1.382; 1.415) of digitalization on GEG, indicating simultaneous resonance effects within spatial contexts. The paper concludes with policy recommendations, including the development of new digital infrastructure and promotion of green energy utilization.

Overall, these studies illustrate how educational and FDI investments can collectively stimulate economic growth, human capital development and literacy improvements. These studies emphasize that investing in education, healthcare, digitalization and human capital is vital for driving sustained economic growth. Across different regions, they show that strategic public spending in these areas, along with private sector partnerships, contributes to economic resilience and development.

A consistent theme is that while education supports economic growth globally, its true impact hinges on a nuanced approach tailored to each region's specific needs and resources. This includes policies that ensure high-quality, accessible education and access to digitalization, which can help bridge disparities and optimize the returns on investment. By aligning educational spending with broader economic strategies, nations can bolster workforce productivity, innovation and competitiveness in a globalized economy.

However, the studies reveal that outcomes from education investment and digitalization vary significantly based on unique national contexts, such as governance quality, inflation rates, FDI utilization, developmental stage and labor market dynamics. As a result, adopting liberal policies could further strengthen these positive effects, as seen in countries like Nigeria and Sri Lanka, where such strategies are suggested to bolster economic progress and resilience. These findings advocate for continued research on refining education and innovative' investments, especially in developing regions, to secure sustained national development and long-term economic success.

Given below is the review of literature, in concise form.

Table 1. Literature review

S.no.	Author(s) (publishing year)	Area/country of study	Time-period	Econometric Modelling	Literature findings
1	Victor Owusu-Nantwi (2015)	Ghana	1970-2012	Co-integration and VECM	EE[2], GFCF[3] and labor force participation =+ve[4] on GDP, long run. Bidirectional, EE and GDP, short run
2	Agung Suwandaru et al (2021)	Indonesia	1988-2018	Panel ARDL	EE=+ve on GDP, long term. EE=-ve[5] on GDP, short term. Bureaucratic inefficiencies, corruption, and challenges in policy implementation=-ve on GDP
3	Besime Fekri Ziberi et al (2022)	North Macedonia	1997-2020	IV 2SLS model	EE= +ve on GDP Unemployment= direct relation to GDP GFCF =+ve on GDP
4	Girma Mulugeta Emeru (2023)	Ethiopia	1980-2018	cointegration and VECM	GFCF=-ve on GDP, short term, no effect in long run EE=+ve on GDP, on both short and long term
5	Nura Aliyu Kabuga (2015)	Nigeria	1980-2019	ARDL, CUSUM test	EE=+ve on GDP, on both short and long term GFCF=-ve on GDP
6	Mohamed Maher et al (2022)	Egypt	1976-2019	GMM	EE=+ve on GDP, on both short and long term Inflation=-ve on GDP GFCF= no effect on GDP
7	Pravesh Tamang (2011)	India	1980-2008	ECM	EE=+ve on GDP Labor affects GDP better
8	Paravee Maneejuk et al (2021)	ASEAN-5	2000-2018	Kink regression	EE= non-linear on GDP Enrolment[6] =+ve on GDP
9	Alina Cristina Coman (2022)	Central and Eastern Europe	1990-2020	ARDL	Few countries, EE= +ve effect on GDP Others, no effect
10	Elizabeth N. Appiah (2017)	Developing nations	1975-2015	GMM	EE=+ve on GDP GFCF =+ve on GDP Labor force= diminishing returns on GDP

continued on following page

Table 1. Continued

S.no.	Author(s) (publishing year)	Area/country of study	Time-period	Econometric Modelling	Literature findings
11	Ibrahim Abubakarr Bah (2023)	189 countries (low, middle, high income)	2002-2020	OLS and GMM	EE=+ve on GDP, In low- and middle-income countries No effect in high income countries
12	Neeraj Kumar et al (2019)	India	1951-2014	Unit root, Regression analysis	EE=+ve on GDP EE=+ve on Labor quality
13	Sayantan Ghosh Dastidar et al (2013)	India	–	Econometric methods, Historical, Qualitative analysis	EE= +ve/-ve mixed links Policy factors, institutional factors affect EE and GDP
14	Salwa Trabelsi (2018)	Various countries	1980-2013	Threshold building (TR and STR)	Above threshold, EE=+ve on GDP Below it, diminishing effect
15	Chinedu Uchenna Okerekeoti (2022)	Nigeria	1999-2020	Empirical analysis, Regression analysis	EE=+ve on GDP
16	Dilan Prasanga Rajapakshe (2018)	Sri Lanka	1998-2009	ARDL	GFCF= +ve on GDP, both short & long run
17	Fadila Kabir Usman et al (2019)	ECOWAS nations	1980-2016	FMOLS, DOLS	EE=+ve on GDP Enrolment=+ve on GDP
18	Douanla Tayo et al(2016)	Cameroon	1994-2009	Carree and Klomp test, Sigma Convergence analysis	EE has not been kept consistent to fit into the CEMAC zone category
19	Strike Mbulawa et al(2016)	Botswana	1980-2014	VECM, VAR	EE=+ve on GDP Enrolment=+ve on GDP GFCF/FDI=+ve on GDP Inflation=-ve on GDP
20	M. Afzal (2013)	South Asia	1995-2011	FEM	EE= +ve on GDP GFCF= +ve on GDP Poverty= -ve on GDP
21	Dr. Dil Nath Dangal (2022)	Nepal	1989-2019	ARDL, ECM, CUSUM, CUSUMQ	Enrolment =+ve on GDP (more) EE= +ve on GDP GFCF=+ve on GDP (less)

continued on following page

Table 1. Continued

S.no.	Author(s) (publishing year)	Area/country of study	Time-period	Econometric Modelling	Literature findings
22	Muhammad Afzal et al (2010)	Pakistan	1970-2009	ARDL, ECM	Enrolment= +ve on GDP EE=+ve on GDP
23	Shahriyar Mukhtarov et al (2020)	Azerbaijan	1995-2018	ARDL, DOLS, CCR	EE=+ve on GDP GFCF= +ve on GDP
24	Shikha Pokhrel et al (2019)	Nepal	1975-2016	ADF, ARDL	EE=+ve on GDP GFCF= +ve on GDP
25	Ronaldo R. Cabauatan et al (2016)	Philippines	1991-1998	Regression	Unp =-ve on EE EE=+ve on GDP Human Capital= +ve on GDP
26	Mohd Yahya Mohd Hussin et al (2012)	Malaysia	1970-2010	VAR, VECM	EE= +ve on GDP GFCF= +ve on GDP Labor participation= +ve on GDP
27	Plabita Bhattacharyya (2019)	India (28 states)	2008-2015	VECM	EE=+ve on GDP
28	Zita Chika Obi et al (2020)	Nigeria	1990-2018	ADF, ARDL	EE= +ve on GDP GFCF= mixed affect
29	P. Fernando, et al (2018)	Sri Lanka	1978-2016	ARDL	GFCF=+ve on GDP
30	Abdulkarim A. Oloyede et al(2023)	Nigeria	-	PRISMA	Digitalization=+ve effect on GDP
31	Yong Seong Foo et al (2024)	Global	2000-2020	GMM	Digitalization= first, -ve effect then +ve effect on GDP
32	Xiaoli Hao et al (2023)	China	2013-2019	SEEA	Digitalization= +ve effect on GDP

Source- Author's own review of literature

Hence, we can say that earlier literatures give us mostly positive but mixed effects of education and foreign investment; definite effect of enrolment in education, negative effect of unemployment & corruption on a nation's growth.

Model Specification

For our study, we are going to use ARDL model approach, after application of different pre- requisite tests. The model can be developed as:

$$gdp = f\,(gfcf, erd, gee, pui, unp, cc, set) \quad (1)$$

$$lgdp_{jt} = \eta_0 + \eta_1 gfcfp_{jt} + \eta_2 erd_{jt} + \eta_3 gee_{jt} + \eta_4 pui_{jt}$$

$$+\eta_5 unp_{jt} + \eta_6 cc_{jt} + \eta_7 set_{jt}\, \omega_{it} \quad (2)$$

Herein, η_1, η_2, η_3, η_4, η_5, η_6 and η_7 are the coefficient long run parameters, of developing countries, to be estimated. lgdp is log of GDP per capita (current US $), gfcfp is the gross formation capital flow (% of GDP), erd is the expenditure on research and development (% of GDP), gee is the government expenditure on education (% of GDP), pui is the population using the internet (% from the total population), unp is unemployment as percent, cc is the control over corruption (percentile) and set is the enrolment in tertiary courses (%). Lastly, ω_{it} is the stochastic term or the error term.

The ARDL model can be specified by using ECM version of the model. It is illustrated as follows:

$$l\Delta gdp_{jt} = \alpha_0 + \sum_{p=1}^{p+1} \phi_j l\Delta gfcfp_{jt-p} + \sum_{j=0}^{p+1} \varnothing_j \Delta erd_{jt-p} + \sum_{j=0}^{p+1} \omega_j \Delta gee_{jt-p} + \sum_{j=0}^{p+1} \delta_j \Delta pui_{jt-p}$$

$$+\sum_{j=0}^{p+1} \curlyvee_j \Delta unp_{jt-p} + \sum_{j=0}^{p+1} \theta_j \Delta cc_{it-p} + \sum_{j=0}^{p+1} \lambda_j \Delta set_{it-p} + \omega ECT + \omega_{it}\,. \quad (3)$$

ϕ, $\varnothing$, ω, δ, $\curlyvee$, θ and λ are short-run parameters.

$$l\Delta gdp_{jt} = \alpha_0 + \sum_{p=1}^{p+1} \phi_j l\Delta gfcfp_{jt-p} + \sum_{j=0}^{p+1} \varnothing_j \Delta erd_{jt-p} + \sum_{j=0}^{p+1} \omega_j \Delta gee_{jt-p} + \sum_{j=0}^{p+1} \delta_j \Delta pui_{jt-p}$$

$$+\sum_{j=0}^{p+1} \curlyvee_j \Delta unp_{jt-p} + \sum_{j=0}^{p+1} \theta_j \Delta cc_{it-p} + \sum_{j=0}^{p+1} \lambda_j \Delta set_{it-p} + \omega ECT+$$

$$\eta_1 \text{gfcfp}_{jt} + \eta_2 \text{erd}_{jt} + \eta_3 \text{gee}_{jt} + \eta_4 \text{pui}_{jt} + \eta_5 unp_{jt} + \eta_6 cc_{jt} +. \tag{4}$$

These are the variants of long and short runs on a time scaling of p. Here, the null hypothesis states that, all recent trends will equal zero, meaning there is no relationship and vice versa for the alternate hypothesis.

DATA ANALYSIS OF DEVELOPING ECONOMIES

Unit Root

We need to conduct the Unit Root tests to examine the stationarity of the variables, that are, expenditure on research and development (R&D)(erd), expenditure on education by the government (gee), pupils using the internet in a nation out of whole population (pui), enrolment in tertiary education (tea), unemployment out of the total labor force (unp) and enrolment in tertiary education (set). Control on corruption in an economy(cc) is used additionally, as it is observed to be a significant factor in the developing and under developed economies. Log of GDP is used as a dependent variable. It reflects the growth of an economy. The test statistics are shown below.

Table 2. Unit root test

Independent variables	**Levin, Lin & Chu t***		**Im, Pesaran and Shin W-stat**		**ADF- Fisher Chi-square**		**PP-Fisher Chi-square**	
	Level	**First Difference**	**Level**	**First Difference**	**Level**	**First Difference**	**Level**	**First difference**
Expenditure on R&D (% of GDP) (erd)	0.359	0.000	0.509	0.000	0.652	0.000	0.770	0.000
Government expenditure on education (gee)	0.488	0.000	0.158	0.000	0.200	0.000	0.045	0.000
Gross fixed capital formation (% of GDP) (gfcfp)	0.119	0.024	0.408	0.005	0.578	0.015	0.688	0.000
Population using the internet (pui)	1.00	1.000	1.000	0.014	1.000	0.002	0.635	0.000
Enrolment in tertiary education (set)	0.616	0.000	0.994	0.000	0.996	0.000	0.991	0.000

continued on following page

Table 2. Continued

Independent variables	Levin, Lin & Chu t*		Im, Pesaran and Shin W-stat		ADF- Fisher Chi-square		PP-Fisher Chi-square	
	Level	**First Difference**	**Level**	**First Difference**	**Level**	**First Difference**	**Level**	**First difference**
Unemployment(unp)	0.971	0.248	0.929	0.000	0.766	0.000	0.784	0.000
Corruption control (percentile rank) (cc)	0.002	0.000	0.008	0.000	0.016	0.000	0.069	0.000
Log10 of GDP (lgdp)	0.000	0.000	0.110	0.000	0.188	0.000	0.646	0.000

Source- Author's own Estimation

**The result of the Fisher test is calculated with the asymptotic chi-square distribution. All other tests generally assume asymptotic behaviour.

Results of Unit Root Tests

We can clearly see from the above test statistics table that cc, gee and lgdp are stationary at level as well as at first difference. erd, gfcfp, pui, set and unp are stationary at first difference. We can, therefore say, that all are integrated at order 1, i.e. I (1). We can hence use ARDL model on our dataset of developing economies.

Cross-Sectional Dependence (CSD)

CSD refers to the relationship or association between different events or time differences. CSD means that observations between variables are not independent and may influence each other. This concept is important because it affects the validity of statistical analyses and business models. Ignoring the expected correlation can lead to biased estimates, model errors and incorrect conclusions in empirical studies.

H_0 = There is no CSD between the variables.

H_1 = There is a CSD between the variables.

Table 3. Cross-sectional dependence test

	Breusch-Pagan LM		Pesaran scaled LM		Bias-Corrected Scaled LM		Pesaran CD	
	Statistics	**Prob.**	**Statistics**	**Prob.**	**Statistics**	**Prob.**	**Statistics**	**Prob.**
Expenditure on R&D (% of GDP) (erd)	123.838	0.000	15.868	0.000	15.702	0.000	-1.158	0.246
Government expenditure on education (gee)	37.0002	0.017	2.468	0.014	2.302	0.021	0.393	0.693
Gross fixed capital formation (% of GDP) (gfcfp)	93.8265	0.000	11.237	0.000	11.071	0.000	0.713	0.475
Population using the internet (pui)	314.703	0.000	45.319	0.000	45.152	0.000	17.273	0.000
Enrolment in tertiary education (set)	327.189	0.000	47.246	0.000	47.079	0.000	17.781	0.000
Unemployment(unp)	128.852	0.000	16.642	0.000	16.475	0.000	2.763	0.005
Corruption control (percentile rank) (cc)	59.9814	0.000	6.0149	0.000	5.848	0.000	0.167	0.867
Log10 of GDP (lgdp)	438.878	0.000	64.479	0.000	64.313	0.000	20.948	0.000

Source: Author's own estimation

Results of Cross-sectional dependence: For expenditure on R&D (erd) the three tests have a probability value of 0.0000 and the Pesaran CD has 0.2466, sighting that there is cross-sectional dependence in our data. This means that the error terms are not independent and therefore, basic panel data analysis techniques may not be sufficient here. For government expenditure on education (gee), the earlier three tests have a probability value of 0.0168, 0.0136 and 0.0213, while Pesaran CD has a probability of 0.6939. This means that the error terms of the dataset are not independent, so the traditional panel data analysis techniques may not be appropriate here. Similarly, for total Gross Fixed Capital Formation (gfcfp) (% of GDP), the other three tests have a recording probability of 0.0000, while Pesaran CD has a value of 0.4757. This shows that there is CSD in the data. For proportion of population using the internet (pui), all the four tests are 0.0000. This implies that there is cross-sectional difference in the data. The school enrolment in tertiary level (% gross) (set), all the four tests have a significant probability value. This shows that there is dependence in the data. Share of unemployment (% of total labor force) (unp), all the three tests have probability of 0.0000 and 0.0057 in Pesaran CD. This indicates that there is CSD in the data. Control on corruption (level percentage) (cc), the three tests have a probability value of 0.0000. This further indicates that there is cross-sectional dependence in the data. The log base 10 of Gross Domestic Product per capita (current US$) (lgdp), all the four tests have a probability value of 0.0000. Hence, this indicates that there is cross-sectional dependence all over in the data.

Cointegration

This testing is used to determine long-term relationship, if any, between variables. There are many types of tests for variables' interaction. Here we will use the Kao cointegration test. It was created by Kao in 1999. It uses the hypothesis as:

H_0 = There is no long run relationship.

H_1 = There is a long run relationship.

Below is a list of results from our data on countries selected from the list of developing countries.

Table 4. Kao-cointegration test

ADF	**t-statistics** **-2.734020**	**Prob.** **0.0031**
Residual Variance	0.001732	
HAC Variance	0.002270	

Source: Author's own estimation

The Augmented Dickey- Fuller Test equation here becomes:

D(resid)= -0.240994 resid (-1)

With Durbin Watson stat as 1.925305 and the above independent variables have probabilities of 0.0000 and 0.1200 for d (resid (-1)). the R squared stands at 0.134379 and adjusted R squared as 0.128106.

From the above table, we can see that there is a long run relationship in the model. The data is significant at 5% level with 0.0000 probability. The negative t-statistic tells us that overall effect of independent variables is negative, i.e., inverse relation but significant. Hence, the independent variables will affect the results of dependent variable.

Panel ARDL

After following all the above test statistics, we now run ARDL model. Panel ARDL (Autoregressive Distributive Lag) testifies the relation between dependent and independent variables of the model. It can be portrayed in following hypothesis statements:

H_0= there is no long run relationship between the variables.

H_1= there is a long run relationship between the variables.

We can see the ARDL test results of our model as below.

Table 5. Panel ARDL test statistics

Variables	Coefficient	Std. Error	t-statistics	Prob.*
Long Run movements				
ERD	0.287206	0.179646	1.598733	0.1149
GEE	0.119675	0.045125	2.652097	0.0101
GFCFP	0.048693	0.006285	7.747651	0.0000
PUI	0.005921	0.001235	4.792826	0.0000
UNP	-0.187523	0.27520	-6.813992	0.0000
CC	0.005844	0.001270	4.600859	0.0000
SET	0.021959	0.003107	7.067676	0.0000
Short Run movements				
D(LGDP(-1))	-0.123092	0.105704	0.105704	0.2486
	-0.338873	0.163903	0.163903	0.0428
D(LGDP(-2))	-0.151838	0.236654	0.236654	0.5235
D(LGDP(-3))	0.027118	0.095220	0.095220	0.7767
	0.042296	0.32065	0.032065	0.1919
D(ERD)	0.012330	0.014338	0.014338	0.3931
D(GEE)	0.015736	0.007946	0.007946	0.0520
D(GFCFP)	-0.040683	0.011750	0.011750	0.0010
D(PUI)	0.001601	0.001455	0.001455	0.2752
D(UNP)	0.001893	0.007730	0.00730	0.8074
D(CC)	-0.378213	0.253088	0.253088	0.1401
D(SET)				
C				

Root MSE	0.011757	Mean dependent var	0.028275
S.D. dependent var	0.040132	S.E. of regression	0.018382
Akaike info criterion	-3.905205	Sum Squared resid	0.021288
Schwarz criterion	-2.110642	Log-likelihood	391.7008
Hannan-Quinn criterion	-3.176258		

* P values and other tests are excluded from sample selection.

Source- Author's own estimation Selected Model- (4,1,1,1,1,1,1,1)

Results of Panel ARDL Tests

Here, in the long run, it is visible that variables like GEE, GFCFP, PUI, UNP, CC and SET have significant probabilities of 0.0101, 0.0000, 0.0000, 0.0000, 0.0000 and 0.0000 which are all less than 5% significance of error. We can also see that GEE has positive impact on LGDP by a multiple of 0.119675 which is the coefficient of GEE in the equation chosen. Similarly, a 0.048693-unit change in GFCFP will cause 1 unit change in LGDP. The impact caused by it will be significant and positive. PUI has a similar positive impact on the LGDP, causing 1 unit change by change of 0.005921 in PUI which will be significant and positive. UNP impacts LGDP, if -0.187523 change in UNP comes. It affects the growth in the economy negatively, means higher the unemployment, lower the growth. CC impacts by a change of 0.005844, positively, the growth of the economy (LGDP) by one unit. SET of 0.021959 unit will make a change of 1 unit in LGDP, positively. Other variable, however, ERD have no significant impact on the GDP due to 0.1149 probability. In other words, expenditure on education by the government, pupils using the internet in a nation out of whole population, enrolment in tertiary education, unemployment out of the total labor force, control on corruption in an economy and gross fixed capital formation are significant in the long run, however research expenditure is insignificant in the developing countries. These are the long-run statistics. On the short run, in Panel ARDL, it is observed that D(LGDP(-2)), D(PUI) and D(UNP) have significant impact on LGDP, i.e., the growth per capita or simply the growth of the economy. D(LGDP(-2)) have a probability of 0.0428. A -0.338873 unit of D(LGDP(-2)) will cause one unit change in LGDP. Notably, from the results, it seems that there might be a negative effect of past the past years' growth on the current year's growth. Similarly, D(PUI) has a probability of 0.0520 and hence, it will affect LGDP as one unit, when 0.015736 unit of change is brought in D(PUI). Lastly, D(UNP) has a significant probability of 0.0010, while affecting the LGDP by -0.040683, that means, other than D(LGDP(-2)), D(UNP) also impacts LGDP negatively, in the short run. The rest of the variables have insignificant impact on the growth of the developing economy in the short run.

We can say that, in the short run, lag factors of, internet users and unemployment rate and 2-year lag of growth, all play significant role of determining the current growth in a developing country. On the other hand, last years' R&D expenditures, public education expenditure, capital flows, corruption proofing and tertiary education status of a country are insignificant for current year's growth.

CONCLUSION AND POLICY IMPLICATIONS

When examining the long-term and short-term effects of various economic variables on the growth of developing countries, it is clear that some factors are interrelated. In the long run, the public expenditure on education (GEE), the fixed capital formation (GFCFP), population using the internet (PUI), the unemployment (UNP), corruption control (CC) and enrolment in higher education (SET), are found to have a significant impact on economic growth. More importantly, GEE, GFCFP, PUI, CC and SET exhibit a positive impact on growth, while unemployment has a negative relationship towards economic growth. In contrast, research and development expenditure (ERD) does not have a significant impact on growth in developing countries in the long term.

We recommend the policymakers to increase the transparency, accountability and performance of public expenditures in order to reveal its good impact on growth. Simultaneously, encouraging domestic and international investment in education and encouraging infrastructure development can also support the economic growth (as already in operation). To maximize the effectiveness of proportion of population using internet, greater investment in critical infrastructure and strong cybersecurity measures are recommended. For unemployment, employment creation, skill development programmes and market evaluation can improve the economic growth. Strengthening the fight against corruption, encouraging public participation and strengthening public morality are essential for the effective implementation of a clean government. In addition, expanding access to higher education, encouraging cooperation between education and businesses and ensuring good job security can help impact the growth via tertiary education expansion. Although, R&D spending, does not have a direct impact on growth, the importance of developing human capital, investing in training and integrating training with the needs of the business is crucial for a sustainable growth. By implementing these recommendations, developing countries can leverage the resources of major economies to foster stronger and inclusive economic growth.

Addressing the complexities of digital divide, presents significant challenges for developing economies, where tailored solutions are crucial to meet specific contexts. One major hurdle is the lack of robust infrastructure, which hampers internet accessibility and limits opportunities for digital engagement. Moreover, inadequate digital literacy among the population exacerbates usage gaps, making it difficult for individuals to leverage available technologies for personal and economic advancement. Geopolitical tensions can further complicate access to digital resources, as countries may prioritize national security over equitable technology distribution.

Digitalization is vital for economic growth, as it fosters innovation, enhances productivity and creates job opportunities. However, without inclusive digital strategies, the benefits of technology risk being concentrated in urban areas or among certain socioeconomic groups, widens the existing inequalities.

To effectively bridge the digital divide, policymakers should adopt a multifaceted approach. This could include investing in infrastructure development, prioritizing digital literacy programs and promoting public-private partnerships to drive innovation and resource sharing. Additionally, fostering international collaboration among governments, academia and tech companies can lead to the creation of sustainable digital ecosystems. By implementing these strategies, developing economies can harness the transformative power of digitalization, ensuring equitable access to technology and fostering inclusive economic growth for all.

REFERENCES

Afzal, M., Farooq, M. S., & Ahmad, H. K. (2010). Relationship between School Education and Economic Growth in Pakistan ARDL Bounds Testing Approach to Cointegration. *School Education and Economic Growth in Pakistan*, 48(1), 39–61.

Afzal, M., Shafique, M., Ahmad, N., & Qasim, H. (2016). Education, Poverty and Economic Growth in South Asia: A Panel Data Analysis. *Journal of Quality and Technology Management*, 9(1), 131–154.

Appiah, E. N. (2017). The Effect of Education Expenditure on Per Capita GDP in Developing Countries. *International Journal of Economics and Finance*, 9(10), 136–144. DOI: 10.5539/ijef.v9n10p136

Bah, I. A. (2023). The relationship between education and economic growth: A cross-country analysis. *Research. Social Development*, 12(5), 13. DOI: 10.33448/rsd-v12i5.40522

Bhattacharyya, P. (2019). Public Expenditure on Education and Economic Growth: A state-level analysis in India, Humanities & Social. *Scientific Review (Singapore)*, 7(6), 533–539. DOI: 10.18510/hssr.2019.7683

Cabauatan, R. R. (2016). Analysing the effects of selected economic indicators on education and on the causality between education and economic growth of the Philippines. *Science and Technology Development Journal*, 19(3), 57–69. DOI: 10.32508/stdj.v19i3.479

Dangal, D. N. (2022). Tertiary Education and Economic Growth of Nepal: An ARDL-ECM Analysis. *Humanity & Social Sciences Journal*, 13(2), 25. DOI: 10.3126/hssj.v13i2.49799

Dastidar, S. G., Mohan, S., & Chatterji, M. (2013). The relationship between public education expenditure and economic growth: The case of India. *Scottish Institute for Research in Economics*, 2013(07), 14.

Emeru, G. M. (2023). Effect of Public Expenditure on Economic Growth in the Case of Ethiopia, The Scientific World Journal, vol. 2023. *TheScientificWorldJournal*, 9305196, 14. DOI: 10.1155/2023/9305196

Fernando, P., & Rajapakshe, D. (2018). *Redefining FDI-Growth Relationship under Liberalized Economic Policies Empirical Evidence from Sri Lanka*. 20–39.

Foo, Y. S., Chin, L., Chen, K. S., & Allayarov, P. (2023, December 21). Digitalization, globalization and economic growth: A panel analysis using GMM. *Proceedings of the 7th International Conference on Future Networks and Distributed Systems*. Presented at the ICFNDS '23: The International Conference on Future Networks and Distributed Systems, Dubai United Arab Emirates. https://doi.org/ DOI: 10.1145/3644713.3644790

Hao, X., Li, Y., Ren, S., Wu, H., & Hao, Y. (2023). The role of digitalization on green economic growth: Does industrial structure optimization and green innovation matter? *Journal of Environmental Management, 325*(Pt A), 116504. https://doi.org/ DOI: 10.1016/j.jenvman.2022.116504

Kabuga, N. A. (2015). Government Spending on Education and Economic Growth in Nigeria: An Empirical Investigation. [KAJEST]. *Kano Journal of Educational Studies*, 4(3), 225–236.

Kumar, N., & Chaudhary, P. (2019). The Relationship between Education Expenditure and Economic Growth in India. *J. Adv. Res. Appl. Math. Stat. 2016, 1*(2), 119–123.

Maher, M. (2022). Inflation and Education Expenditure: Evidence from Egypt. *Journal of Economics and Sustainable Development*, 13(4), 71–82. DOI: 10.7176/JESD/13-4-07

Maneejuk, P., & Yamaka, W. (2021). The Impact of Higher Education on Economic Growth in ASEAN-5 Countries. *Sustainability (Basel)*, 13(2), 520. DOI: 10.3390/su13020520

Manjuk, P., & Yamaka, W. (2021). The Impact of Higher Education on Economic Growth in ASEAN-5 Countries. *Sustainability (Basel)*, 13(2), 520. DOI: 10.3390/su13020520

Mbulawa, S., & Mehta, P. (2016). The Effect of Access and Quality of Education on Economic Development in Botswana. *International Journal of Business. Economics and Management*, 3(11), 144–159. DOI: 10.18488/journal.62/2016.3.11/62.11.144.159

Mohd Hussin, M. Y., & Muhammed, F. (2012). Education Expenditure and Economic Growth: A Causal Analysis for Malaysia. *Journal of Economics and Sustainable Development*, 3(7), 71–81.

Mukhtarov, S., Mammadov, I., & Humbatova, S. (2020). The Relationship Between Government Expenditures on Education and Economic Growth: The Case of Azerbaijan. *Review of World Economics*, 11(1), 195. DOI: 10.5430/rwe.v11n1p195

Nantwi, V. O. (2015). Education Expenditures and Economic Growth: Evidence from Ghana. *Journal of Economics and Sustainable Development*, 6(16), 69–77.

Nuţă, A. C. C.. (2023). The Impact of Public Education Spending on Economic Growth in Central and Eastern Europe. An ARDL Approach with Structural Break. *Economic Research-Ekonomska Istraživanja*, 36(1), 1261–1278. DOI: 10.1080/1331677X.2022.2086147

Obi, Zita C., Ogugua, C., & Ejefobihi, U. (2020). The efficiency of Education Expenditure in Nigeria. *European Journal of Education Studies*, 7(1), 423–447. DOI: 10.5281/zenodo.3748101

Okerekeoti, C. U. (2022). Government Expenditure on Education and Economic growth in Nigeria. [IJRRCEM]. *International Journal of Recent Research in Commerce Economics and Management*, 9(2), 126–134. DOI: 10.5281/zenodo.6656411

Oloyede, A. A., Faruk, N., Noma, N., Tebepah, E., & Nwaulune, A. K. (2023). Measuring the impact of the digital economy in developing countries: A systematic review and meta- analysis. *Heliyon*, 9(7), e17654. DOI: 10.1016/j.heliyon.2023.e17654 PMID: 37501966

Pokhrel, S., & Khadka, C. B. (2019). Assessment of Long and Short Run Relationship Amongst Macroeconomic Variables and Economic Growth of Nepal. *Economic Jornal of Development Issues(2019), 27 & 28*(1). https://doi.org/DOI: 10.3126/ejdi.v28i1-2.33196

Suwandru, A., Alghamdi, T., & Nurwantu, N. (2021). Empirical Analysis on Public Expenditure for Education and Economic Growth: Evidence from Indonesia. *Economies*, 9(4), 146. DOI: 10.3390/economies9040146

Tamang, P. (2011). The Impact of Education Expenditure on India's Economic Growth. *Journal of International Academic Research*, 11(3), 14–21.

Tayo, D. Lionel, Fouda, A., & Olivier, M. (2016). Government spending in education and economic growth in Cameroon. A Vector error Correction Model approach. *Munich Personal RePEc Archive*, 16 pages.

Trabelsi, S.SALWA TRABELSI. (2018, March). Public Education Spending and Economic Growth: The Governance Threshold Effect. *Journal of Economic Development*, 43(1), 99–122. DOI: 10.35866/caujed.2018.43.1.005

Usman, F. K., & Adeyinka, O. B. (2018). Effect of Human Capital Development on Economic Growth of Ecowas Member States. *Advances in Sciences and Humanities*, 5(1), 27–42. DOI: 10.11648/j.ash.20190501.14

Ziberi, B. F., Rexha, D., Ibraimi, X., & Avdiaj, B. (2022). Empirical Analysis of the Impact of Education on Economic Growth. *Economies*, 10(4), 89. DOI: 10.3390/economies10040089

ENDNOTES

[1] UNCTAD: United Nations Conference on Trade and Development

These endnotes display abbreviations applicable everywhere in the review literature

[2] EE= expenditure on education

[3] GFCF= Gross Fixed Capital Formation

[4] +ve= positive effect

[5] -ve= negative effect

[6] Enrolment= enrolment in education

Chapter 2

Proposing a Serious Game Design Model Towards Maritime Competency Development: A Case Study

Süleyman Gürbüz
https://orcid.org/0000-0003-0670-3914
Department of Maritime Transportation Engineering, Istanbul Technical University Maritime Faculty, Istanbul, Turkey

Metin Celik
https://orcid.org/0000-0003-0107-1380
Department of Basic Science, Istanbul Technical University, Istanbul, Turkey & Industrial Data Analytics and Decision Support Systems Center, Azerbaijan State University of Economics (UNEC), Baku, Azerbaijan

ABSTRACT

In maritime domain, interactive and authentic learning environments are needed for competency development of seafarers. This study aims to propose and pilot test a serious game design model which is specific to maritime domain for enhancing the utilization of maritime serious games. In this study, Serious Game Design for Maritime (SGDM), a holistic model to support the design of maritime serious games is firstly proposed. Using the SGDM model, Maritime Leaders at Sea (ML@S), a 3D serious game to enhance the leadership and teamwork skills of young seafarers and maritime students, has been prototyped as a case study. ML@S is conceptualized

DOI: 10.4018/979-8-3693-7863-2.ch002

as a module of the created Maritime Gamentor platform. The compliance test of ML@S proves that SGDM holistic model enables the preliminary design of ML@S in compliance with the STCW requirements and industrial expectations. Further maritime studies can follow the proposed methodology to design additional serious game-based modules for mentoring on maritime skills.

INTRODUCTION

International Convention on Standards of Training, Certification and Watchkeeping (STCW) (referred as STCW in this study), which has been issued by International Maritime Organization (IMO), defines the training and competency standards of the seafarers. It has been argued that there is an important gap between required on-board competency levels of seafarers and their actual levels of competency (ICS, 2020).

Despite the regulatory and technological advancements in shipping, human error is still the main reason in 80% of shipping accidents (Akyuz and Celik, 2018). For maritime safety, security and environmental protection, the STCW-compliant MET is of vital importance. It is critical that MET provides young seafarers with technical skills as well as soft skills such as maintaining situational awareness, risk management, problem solving, leadership and teamwork (Basak, 2017).

Ship operations currently require high amounts of human work. Well-educated and competent crew is needed for safe and efficient operation of ships (Lewin, 2015). Considering the technological developments and the lack of practical education and training in the maritime industry, experience sharing and mentorship are even becoming more important for competency development.

The administration of several MET institutions focuses on increasing opportunities for practical training sessions at maritime campuses. Maritime simulators as great infrastructures, have the capability of providing practical training. However, the program limitations might not allow to use of required quota for maritime students in practical sessions. Additionally, the practical onboard training is a critical milestone for maritime students. Nevertheless, the lack of the consistent procedures on cadetship training onboard ships might restrain development of the targeted competencies. In addition, it is difficult to provide maritime students with detailed and personalized onboard trainings due to the high costs and risks associated with using an active ship for training purposes (Mazhari, 2018).

In order to provide enhanced practical training to maritime students and thus remedying the potential gap between the necessary and acquired practical competencies of the seafarers, the maritime industry needs to find cheaper, easier and more flexible ways of training. Game-based learning, as a technology-enabled instructional method, offers a great potential for the maritime domain (Nikitakos et al., 2017).

Serious games can be used to enhance the effectiveness of education and training in MET institutions by providing active learning environments for acquiring practical competencies that maritime students need, anytime and regardless of their physical location (Bruzzone et al., 2013).

In this regard, this study aims to utilize serious gaming approach for providing maritime students with a mentoring platform in order to fulfill the need for practical training and enhancing their competency development. For this purpose, a model entitled Serious Game Design for Maritime (SGDM) is firstly proposed for designing thematic maritime serious games. Using SGDM model, the preliminary design of the Maritime Leaders at Sea (ML@S) serious game is accomplished as a case study. ML@S is conceptualized as a module on the Maritime Gamentor platform. After that, the preliminary design of the game has been prototyped on Unity 3D® and a compliance test of ML@S has been conducted by surveying some maritime experts.

LITERATURE REVIEW

Serious Games

The term "Serious Game" was first used in 1968 when Clark Abt called his book by this name (Abt, 1970). He examined war-games and simulations, which are designed for the training of administrators, students, and instructors. He defined these games and simulations as "having an explicit and carefully thought-out educational purpose and not intended to be played primarily for amusement. This does not mean that serious games are not or should not be entertaining." (Abt, 1970, p.9). Similarly, Djaouti et al. (2011) define serious games as games which are developed for educational purposes and engage players in significant learning experience.

Serious games, utilizing game elements, increase the learning efficiency in various aspects. To start with, Bai et al. (2020) tell that game elements such as points, badges, challenges, and game-like goals increase participation in learning and enhance the learning outcomes. In addition, Gray et al. (2019) and Zainuddin et al. (2020) explain that gaming features increase engagement and motivation and thus promote higher-order learning. Serious games are also reported to be useful for attitude change (Chow et al., 2020; Kolic-Vehovec et al., 2020), developing understanding and retention (Wang & Abbas, 2018), empowering critical thinking (Turner at al., 2018) and fostering goal setting (Yıldırım & Şen, 2019). Serious games also enable players to experience authentic learning experience which would be difficult or impossible in real life because of high cost or risk associated (Kapralos et al., 2015). Taking into account development in information Technologies and their positive impacts on learning, it is not surprising to see their increasing utilization in different domains.

Education and healthcare are among the domains in which serious games are most commonly utilized. To start with, Koupritzioti and Xinogalos (2020) provided a serious game application for learning programming concepts. In addition, Lee (2020) created an Augmented Reality (AR)-based mobile serious game for foreign language learning. Moreover, serious gaming perspective is utilized for enhancing cyber security (Khan et al., 2022) and engineering (Rodriguez; 2022) education. Fokides (2018) also used a serious game for teaching Math to primary school students. In these studies, it is found out that the students who played the serious game mostly outperformed the ones who did not play it, indicating more effective learning experiences with serious gaming. Moreover, serious games provide realistic training opportunities for healthcare personnel and students with no risk of harm to anyone (Haruna et al., 2019; Evans et al., 2015; Gleason, 2015; Sardi et al., 2017; Teschner, 2016). As healthcare domain requires high amount of practical skills in risky conditions, serious games are commonly utilized to provide authentic learning experiences which would not be possible or common in real life conditions. Business (Fotiadis & Sigala, 2015; Fu et al., 2016; Loon et al., 2015), language learning (Alyaz et al., 2017; Berns at al., 2011; Garrido-Inigo & Rodríguez-Moreno, 2015; Gonzalez- Pardo et al., 2014), sports (Hamari & Sjöblom, 2017), and music (Margoudi et al., 2016) are among other fields where serious games are used.

Artificial Intelligence (AI) practices play a major role on future direction of serious gaming research. Player Experience Modelling (PEM), Natural Language Processing (NLP), and advanced Non-Playing Character modelling (NPC) are among applications of AI in serious games (Westera et. al, 2020). AI practices such as machine learning algorithms (Alonso-Fernández et al, 2019; Gomez et al, 2022) and Bayesian networks (Levy, 2019) are used in serious games for enhanced validation of the games (Udeozor et al., 2022), and evaluate recruitment processes (Landers and Sanchez, 2022). AI, through analysis of gameplay data, is also used to adapt the game's difficulty in real-time (Hendrix et. al, 2018) to improve players game experience. Löytömäki et. al (2024) applied facial emotion recognition in serious gaming to improve social–emotional skills of children with neurodevelopmental disorders. In their systematic review on NPC modelling in serious games, Armanto and Rosyid (2024) stated that NPCs can provide advanced hints, feedback, or challenges tailored to player's learning curve, facilitating a more engaging learning experience.

Integration of immersive technologies such as Augmented Reality (AR) and Virtual Reality (VR) with gamification and serious games also enhances the effectiveness of game-based learning in different ways. To start with, AR and VR technologies enables interactive and realistic learning experiences (Pellas et al, 2019). AR and VR technologies also supports the 3D visualization of abstract concepts such as solar systems which are difficult or impossible to observe using traditional educational methods (Yeh and Tseng, 2020). Akçayır and Akçayır (2017) also concluded that AR approach might improve learning motivation and foster collaboration and interaction among students. In this regard, utilization of AR/VR-based serious games are commonly utilized for foreign language learning (Lee, 2022; Lee and Park, 2020), computing education (Petri and von Wangenheim, 2017), healthcare education and training (Chang et al, 2022; Mohamad et al., 2021; Plotzky et al, 2021) military and sports training (Ahir et al, 2020), as well as maritime education and training (Chae et al, 2021; Michailidis et al, 2020; Weng and Li, 2019; Bandara et al, 2020).

Serious games have been validated using different approaches. To start with, effectiveness of serious games is traditionally assessed using paired questionaries method. In this method, questionaries are applied before and after the game, the results of which are then compared to evaluate the game (Calderón & Ruiz, 2015). Similarly, pre-test and post-test experimental research design is also utilized for validation of serious games, which can also be applied together with paired questionaries method (Bai et al., 2020; Fiellin et al., 2017; Haruna et al., 2019).

Evidence-based approaches have lately been applied more commonly for validation of serious games. In this regard, learning analytics approach, defined as measurement, collection, and analysis of educational data for the purpose of understanding and enhancing the learning experience (Long et al., 2011), is commonly preferred. For instance, Cano et al. (2018) also utilized learning analytics approach for validating a serious game in transportation domain. Udeozor et al. (2022) also applied learning analytics approach for serious game evaluation and enhancing. Alonso-Fernández et al. (2023) combined traditional pre-post experiments method, Game Learning Analytics approach, and data mining method for evidence-based serious games evaluation.

Looking at the utilization of serious games in maritime domain, Bruzzone et al. (2013) designed a serious game for familiarizing the crew to operating procedures before conducting real tests at sea. In addition, Philbin-Briscoe et al. (2017) introduced a serious game for teaching the history of seafaring in the Mediterranean Sea. Similarly, Poullis et al. (2019) proposed a serious game about seaborne trade in the Mediterranean Sea in the classical period. Although these studies utilize serious gaming approach in maritime domain, it is believed that a comprehensive methodology about design and development of serious game-based trainings for enhancing maritime soft skills and hard skills is still needed.

In addition, online maritime training companies commercially provide serious games for the seafarers onboard ships and maritime students in the maritime institutions. An analysis of these serious games reveals that they can benefit from increased real life applicability, authenticity in visualization, higher utilization of gamification features, and scenario-based design. It is also explained that more serious games are needed in MET for the soft skills training and assessment (Sellberg et al., 2019). An analysis (conducted for the purpose of this study) of some of the commercial maritime serious games also reveals that they mostly focus on the technical skills rather than the soft skills.

In spite of their common utilization, the literature still needs specific approaches which are proven to enhance the instructional aspects of serious games (Silva, 2020). Similarly, additional studies which explore effects of game elements on serious game design are needed for more effective serious games (Johnson et al., 2017). It has also been explained that serious game studies mostly focus on what is being taught (Laporte & Zaman, 2018) and pay less attention to design and development efforts (Korhonen et al., 2017). Moreover, Chan and Zary (2019) put forward that allocating limited resources for design and development of serious games is among the main difficulties in their utilization in the educational domain. These studies clearly illustrate that more studies which focus on the design and development of serious games are needed.

Serious Game Design and Development

Healthcare and education are among two domains where serious game design and development frameworks/models are most common (Gurbuz & Celik, 2022). For instance, Katsantonis et al. (2019) created Conceptual Framework for E-leaning and Training (COFELET) for designing serious game-based cyber security education. COFELET consists of select the mission, realizing game conditions, creating a scenario execution flow, presenting new knowledge, performing task and presenting hint, performing assessment, and providing feedback and reward steps. Carvalho et al. (2015) offer Activity Theory Model of Serious Games (ATMSG). This model summarizes design and development process as identfying activities, representing game sequence, identifying actions, tools and objectives as well as describing implementation. Moreover, Carrion-Toro et al. (2020) propose iPlus Methodology for serious game development on engineering and social sciences education. This methodology includes identification, pedagogical objectives, ludic game script, gameplay and refining steps for the development process. In terms of healthcare education, Torrente et al. (2014) propose Educational Game Development Approach (EDGA) for serious game design. This approach suggests analysis, design, implementation and quality assurance as main steps for serious game development. Moreover, Ihsan et al. (2020) apply Serious Game Design Assessment (SGDA) Framework, a framework originally developed by Mitgutsch and Alvarado (2012), for healthcare education. This framework proposes purpose, content, fiction, mechanic, aesthetic, framing and game system as necessary steps for serious game design. De Freitas and Jarvis (2009) also suggested a serious game design framework for healthcare domain, namely Four Dimensional Framework (4DF). 4DF includes learner specifics, pedagogy, representation, and context for designing educational serious games. Before mentioned serious game design frameworks/models are summarized in Table 1.

Table 1. Summary of before mentioned serious game design frameworks/models (Adapted from Gurbuz and Celik (2022))

Name of the Framework/ Model	**Proposed Steps for SG Design/ Development**	**Strengths and Weaknesses**
Conceptual Framework for E-leaning and Training (COFELET) (Katsantonis et al., 2019)	-Select the Mission -Realize Game Conditions -Create a Scenario Execution Flow -Present new Knowledge, Skill, and Ability Related Content -Perform Task and Present Hint -Perform Assessment -Provide Feedback and Rewards	S: Provides adaptability features, and applies efficient assessment and reward schemes. W: Fails to provide concrete guidance which is strong enough to facilitate serious game design/development.
Activity Theory Model of Serious Games (ATMSG) (Carvalho et al., 2015)	-Identify Activities -Represent Game Sequence -Identify Actions, Tools and Objects -Describe Implementations	S: Explains how game elements come together for facilitating the desired learning goal. W: Fails to provide concrete guidance which is strong enough to facilitate serious game design/development.
iPlus (Carrion-Toro et al., 2020)	-Identification -Pedagogical Objectives -Ludic Game Script -Gameplay -Refine	S: Employs a flexible, and user centered approach. W: Fails to provide concrete guidance which is strong enough to facilitate serious game design/development.
Educational Game Development Approach (EDGA) (Torrente et al., 2014)	-Analysis -Design -Implementation -Quality Assurance	S: Focuses on cost efficiency, student acceptance, and learning effectiveness. W: Fails to provide concrete guidance which is strong enough to facilitate serious game design/development.

Name of the Framework/ Model	Proposed Steps for SG Design/ Development	Strengths and Weaknesses
Serious Game Design Assessment (SGDA) (Mitgutsch and Alvarado, 2012)	-Purpose -Content -Fiction -Mechanic -Aesthetic -Framing -Game System	S: Deals with assessment, evaluation, criticism and prototyping with a constructive perspective. W: Fails to provide concrete guidance which is strong enough to facilitate serious game design/development.
Four Dimensional Framework (4DF) (De Freitas and Jarvis, 2009)	-Learner Specifics -Pedagogy -Representation -Context	S: Includes context, representation, pedagogy, and learner in the design process. W: Fails to provide concrete guidance which is strong enough to facilitate serious game design/development.

In their systematic literature review, Krath et al. (2021) explained that 118 different theories have been applied by researchers in serious game design to reach the intended outcomes among which self-determination theory (Ryan & Deci, 2017), flow theory (Csikszentmihalyi, 1975), experiential learning theory (Kolb, 1984), and constructivist learning theory (Jonassen, 1999) are most popular. Krath et al. (2021) also suggested that researchers should decide which theories to use based on the intended outcome of the specific serious game. Besides, Mora et al. (2017) explained that most gamification design framework studies focus on their ad hoc experiences instead of the formal design process and thus fail to provide practical guidance for other researchers or educators.

In sum, looking critically at the serious game design and development literature, it is concluded that there are 2 important research gaps. Firstly, a serious game design model which is specific to the maritime domain does not exist. Secondly, as stated in Table-1 as the weakness of the models, there is a need for studies which provide specific guidance which is strong enough to facilitate serious game design/ development. Most of the reviewed studies theoretically explain serious game design/ development and fail to practically guide future design and development efforts. It is believed that providing more concrete and specific guidance for serious game design is the main strength of SGDM model. This study aims to contribute in closing these two research gaps for the maritime domain by proposing and applying the SGDM model.

Maritime Serious Games

Different maritime competencies and skills become required as shipping operations continue to evolve with the emerging technology. It is predicted that required maritime skills will be even more complicated as different types of ships such as manned, unmanned, shore-side control, semi-autonomous, fully autonomous etc.

sail together at sea. This being the case, MET needs continual development and updating so that it can provide these changing skills that are highly technology and technically oriented. In this regard, different maritime actors such as maritime faculties, training centers, simulator and technology providers, and shipping companies need to work together in development and utilization of enhanced MET practices (Sharma et al, 2021).

Most undergraduate students in maritime institutions do not have enough opportunity of practical training. To start with, although maritime simulators have the capability of providing practical training, their availability to undergraduate students are generally limited. Additionally, practical onboard trainings that undergraduate students have throughout their education and training in MET institutions might be incapable of developing all the competencies required for on-board duties. Due to the high costs and risks associated with using an active ship for training purpose, these trainings are not always as detailed and personalized as intended. Lack of standardization in their application can be considered as another risk in their targeted success (Mazhari, 2018).

For providing enhanced practical training to undergraduate students and thus remedying the potential gap between necessary and acquired practical competencies of seafarers, maritime industry needs to find cheaper, easier and more flexible ways of training. In this regard, game-based learning, as a technology-enabled instructional method, offers a great potential for the maritime domain. Serious games can enhance MET practices in maritime institutions by providing active learning environments for practical competency development, anytime and regardless of the physical location of the students (Nikitakos et al., 2017).

Serious gaming has been gaining popularity in maritime literature in the last decade. Researchers proposed serious games for education and training of seafarers as well as maritime students on STCW-based competencies. To start with, Nikitakos et al. (2017) proposed alpha version of the "Trader of the World" game for navigational safety training of seafarers and maritime students and reported receiving satisfactory feedback from undergraduate students about the game.

With regard to STCW-based competencies, Bruzzone et al. (2013) also created a serious game for familiarization of the crew to operating procedures onboard ships. In addition, Sartini (2020) used serious gaming approach for improving maritime english speaking skills of cadets and put forward that the game in fact enhanced their skills. Lastly, Türkistanlı and Kuleyin (2022) designed and applied a serious game for enhancing decision-making skills of maritime students in collusion prevention situations. They concluded that the game-based training supported students developing their decision-making skills.

The maritime literature also has serious game applications for providing knowledge outside the scope of STCW requirements. Firstly, Philbin-Briscoe et al. (2017) introduced "The Seafarers-1" serious game for teaching seaborne trade mechanisms and seafaring practices in the eastern Mediterranean during the Classical and Hellenistic periods, as a part of the European Union (EU)-funded "iMareCulture" Project. Within the scope of the same project, Poullis et al. (2019) proposed the "The Seafarers-2" game as the second prototype of the game introduced by Philbin-Briscoe et al. (2017). This game also aimed to provide engagement in learning about maritime cultural heritage, seafaring and trading in the Mediterranean Sea in the classical period.

In terms of maritime education outside the scope of STCW, Veronica and Calvano (2020) also presented a serious game for enhancing children's awareness of the ocean literacy and biodiversity as well as caring for life in the oceans. Steenbeek et al. (2020) combined ecosystem modelling and serious gaming approaches for providing perception of maritime spatial planning. Finally, Pruyn (2023) proposed a framework for analysing the use of serious games in academic maritime education and conducted two case studies for validation of the framework. The purpose of the first case study was teaching the students the link between maritime economics and technology while the second case study intended to provide insight into ship production activities.

Looking critically at the maritime serious gaming literature, it is discovered that most serious games dealing with the STCW-based competencies intent to develop hard skills. As soft skills facilitate application of hard skills in real life environment, it is critical that MET provides young seafarers with technical skills as well as soft skills such as maintaining situational awareness, risk management, problem solving, leadership and teamwork (Basak, 2017). In this regard, this study intends to facilitate design of serious games focusing on maritime soft skills, namely leadership and teamwork as it is believed that more research is needed for education and training of soft skills.

Leadership Education and Training in Maritime Domain

International Convention on Standards of Training, Certification and Watchkeeping (STCW) (referred as STCW in this study), which has been issued by International Maritime Organization (IMO), defines the training and competency standards of the seafarers. It has been argued that there is an important gap between required on-board competency levels of seafarers and their actual levels of competency (ICS, 2020). As there are many contributory factors to ship accidents such as environmental conditions, operational mistakes, judgment error, machinery failures (Weng & Li,

2019; Yu, Li, & Weng, 2022), well-educated and competent crew is needed for safe and efficient operation of ships (Lewin, 2015).

The administration of several MET institutions focuses on increasing opportunities for practical training sessions at maritime campuses. Maritime simulators as great infrastructures, have the capability of providing practical training and thus reducing the risk of accident. However, the program limitations might not allow to use of required quota for maritime students in simulator sessions. Additionally, the practical onboard training is a critical milestone for maritime students. Nevertheless, the lack of the consistent procedures on cadetship training onboard ships might restrain development of the targeted competencies. In addition, it is difficult to provide maritime students with detailed and personalized onboard trainings due to the high costs and risks associated with using an active ship for training purposes (Mazhari, 2018).

Serving onboard ships requires both soft skills and technical skills. Maritime technical skills are mostly practical in nature, which include theoretical knowledge and the competency to apply this knowledge (Mallam et al., 2019). Soft skills, which can be defined as the ability to interact successfully with the environment, facilitate the application of technical skills in the real world (Rao, 2014). In fact, competencies about soft skills need to be paid more attention in MET (Sellberg et al., 2019).

Ships have been manned with less personnel over the years, making the duties of the crew more challenging and diversified (Sharma et al., 2021). As ships and the operating procedures evolve in alignment with the technological developments, maritime soft and hard skills need continuous development to meet the demands of the maritime operations (Mallam et al., 2019). In order to teach those skills to maritime students, MET needs to provide active learning environments which can teach students not only new knowledge but also the competency to apply them in realistic conditions (Manuel, 2017).

Crew onboard ships need to function together as a team for most of the operations such as safe navigation, cargo handling, repairing and maintenance, maintaining physical security etc. In order to conduct these complicated operations, crew organization on merchant ships involves a strong hierarchy. This being the case, leaders onboard ships (masters, chief officers, chief engineers and others) need to have enhanced leadership and teamwork skills to manage the crew in the hierarchical organization (Kim & Mallam, 2020).

Leadership skills, which are among the most important soft skills, are particularly vital for the officers for safety and security of shipping (Água et al., 2020). In addition, leadership behaviors of officers onboard ships have an impact on safety participation of their subordinates and thus importantly affect the overall safety culture of the ship (Kim & Gausdal, 2020; Mallam et al., 2019). However, Fjeld et al. (2018) conclude in their systematic literature review that there are limited efforts to promote the leadership skills of bridge officers in the maritime industry. They further state that a comprehensive taxonomy of non-technical skills of the bridge officers which can facilitate standardized training and assessment is not available in the literature.

Although leadership and teamwork skills are among mandatory competencies at all levels based on STCW, the lack of leadership and teamwork skills is among the primary cause of maritime accidents (Barnett et al., 2006; Kim et al., 2016). It can be assumed that main reason for possible lack of leadership and teamwork competency of seafarers is the incapability of the maritime domain in training of this competency rather than the failure of seafarers. Moreover, Kitada et al. (2018), taking into account increased automatization, explain that personnel organization and management will be considerably different than today onboard ships. They also state that the maritime domain needs to use technology more effectively for soft skills training of personnel. Similarly, Sharma et al. (2021) say that maritime domain needs enhanced methods of leadership education and training as current practices might become obsolete with the advance of emerging technologies.

In sum, the literature review revealed that in spite of the potential serious games offer for enhanced practical maritime education and training, a foundational serious game design model which is specific to maritime domain does not exist. Besides, it is also found that the maritime domain needs advanced education and training methods for the development of leadership and teamwork skills of seafarers, as well as other soft skills.

Research Objective and Contribution of the Study

This study aims to contribute in closing the before mentioned research gaps by proposing a maritime serious game design model, namely SGDM model. To the extent of our knowledge, SGDM is the first serious game design model which is specific to maritime domain. By means of a case study, this study also intends to provide a holistic and applicable methodology for design and development of maritime serious games. It is believed that such as methodology will be useful for closing the before mentioned research gaps in the maritime domain.

Constructivist learning theory (Jonassen, 1999), experiential learning theory (Kolb, 1984) and situated learning theory (Brown et al., 1989) are integrated in the SGDM model for accomplishing the learning (cognitive) outcomes of maritime serious games. These theories are used in the model to meet the specific needs of the maritime domain. The proposed SGDM model is believed to be holistic and adaptable to different serious game ideas because it can be used no matter the topic of the game, the platform on which it will be used or software/tool by which it will be developed. We would like to further emphasize that the research objective is closely rooted in the literature review of serious games and the industrial survey of serious gaming in the maritime domain. For this reason, it is believed that this study offers a theoretical contribution to the literature as well as a practical contribution to the maritime domain.

METHODOLOGY

In this study, we used a design-based research method. Design-based research method aims to improve educational practices through analysis, design, development, and implementation. This method also seeks for experience-based suggestions to solve domain specific problems in practice (Wang & Hannafin, 2005), which makes it a suitable approach for this study. The methodology of this study is summarized in Figure-1 and thoroughly explained below.

Figure 1. Methodology of the study

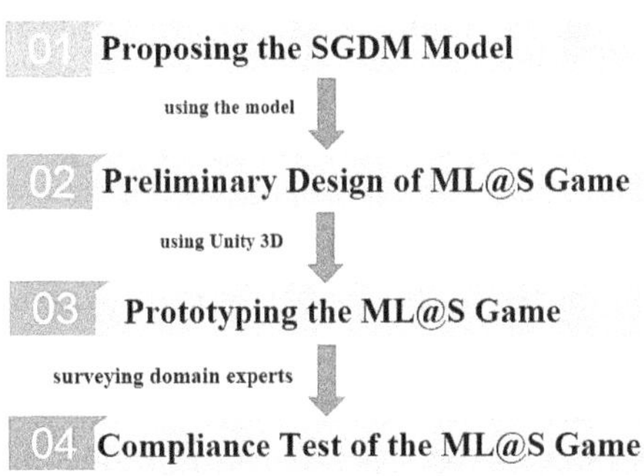

SGDM Model

The SGDM model, firstly proposed by Gurbuz (2021) is depicted in Figure-2. SGDM includes 8 consecutive steps for designing a maritime serious game from scratch. The SGDM model intends to practically guide the designer from the beginning of the design process to the end of it. More specifically, the input of the SGDM model is a maritime serious game idea and the output is a serious game design which is ready to be developed.

Figure 2. SGDM model

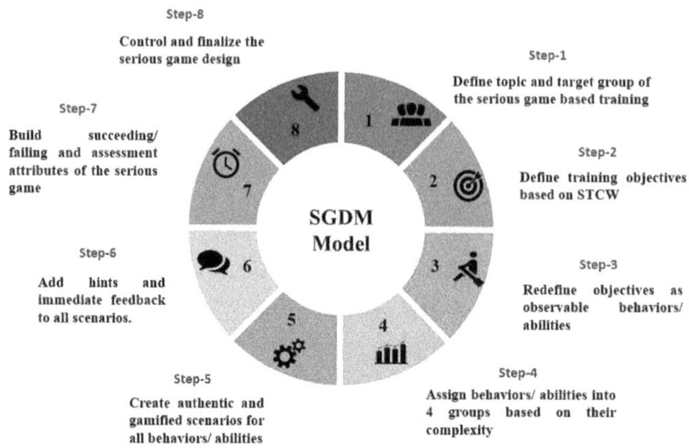

In Step-1 of the SGDM, the topic and target group of the training are defined. After that, objectives of the training should be defined based on the Knowledge, Understanding, and Proficiency column of STCW as per Step-2. If the training is not a STCW-based training, training objectives should be defined by the designer according to other maritime conventions and legislations as well as customized training requirements. In Step-3, these objectives are defined as observable behaviors/ abilities. One objective can be explained as one or multiple target behaviors/abilities. If objectives are already in forms of observable behaviors/abilities, this step is not required. Covering the training objectives in terms of observable behaviors conforms well to the constructivist (Jonassen, 1999) and experiential learning theories (Kolb, 1984) as these theories support experience-based training. In Step-4, behaviors/ abilities should be grouped into 4 quadrants of the Rigor& Relevance Educational Alignment Framework (Daggett & Jones, 2010) based on their intricacy level. For assigning each target behavior/ability to the correct quadrant of the framework, the cognitive competency level and application level of each behavior/ability should be defined separately as high or low. The quadrant of each behavior/ability will be defined based on the combination of these two levels.

In Step-5, realistic scenarios are created starting from the Quadrant A behaviors/ abilities and continue with the Quadrant B, C, and D. Scenarios should consist of realistic situations including onboard challenges. One or more scenarios can be created for each of the target behaviors/abilities provided that all behaviors/abilities are covered in the scenarios. Different levels of the game will consist of scenarios which are created for different quadrants of behaviors. This means, scenarios for the Quadrant A and Quadrant D behaviors will be in the first and last levels of the game for ensuring the increasing difficulty of the game levels. Involving the learners in realistic scenarios is in alignment with the constructivist and experiential learning theories because these theories state that effective learning takes place through realistic personal experiences rather than instruction. Besides, players have the chance to link their previous knowledge to realistic scenarios, which can enhance learning according to situated learning theory (Brown et al., 1989).

In Step-6, hints and feedback are added to the game. More comprehensive and corrective feedbacks should be provided after wrong answers/reactions of trainees so that they can learn from their mistakes. Hints should fade out as the player moves forward in the game. Additional hints can also be added to the scenarios, which the player can choose to see in exchange for punishment score points. Since hints and immediate feedbacks are closely related with the player interactions, they can be important for promoting the learning with an experiential learning perspective. As per Step-7, succeeding/failing and assessment attributes are created. For the succeeding/failing attributes, how many points the player wins for the correct answers (or lose for the incorrect answers) should be defined based on the relative difficulty of the questions and their importance to real life competencies. Similarly, the minimum score the player needs to get to win the game should be decided. In this step, final verbal assessment about future training needs of the player should also be created based on the final score in the game. Finally in Step-8, the serious game design is reviewed and finalized by making the required improvements.

CASE STUDY: MARITIME LEADERS AT SEA (ML@S)

Preliminary Design of ML@S

During the preliminary design process, each step of the SGDM model was consecutively applied. Achievements after each step of the SGDM model are summarized in Figure-3. As a result of 5 months of hard work, the researchers of this study, using their maritime and instructional experiences, accomplished the preliminary design of ML@S serious game.

Figure 3. Achievements after each step of SGDM model

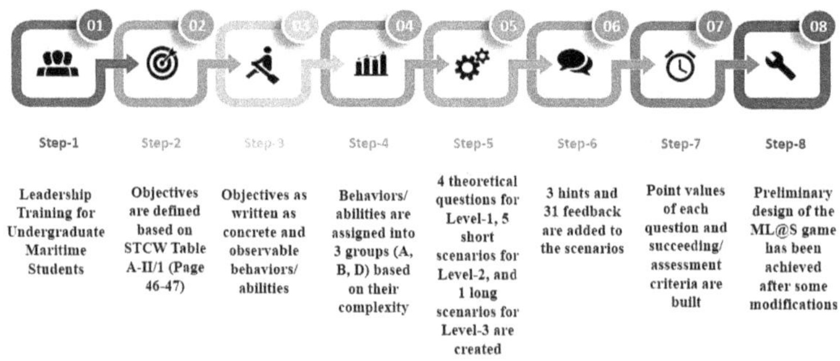

Two important points about the design process should be highlighted. Firstly, the order of design steps can be modified by the designer during the design process. For instance, the designer can create succeeding/failing and assessment attributes (Step-7) and the scenarios (Step-5) simultaneously and add hints and feedback (Step-6) afterwards. In addition, the design of the game should be prototyped in a simple but representative format so that everyone who is involved in the development process can easily understand the serious game design. In this regard, the preliminary design of ML@S was depicted as a sketch diagram (not included in this study), which enabled an easier development by providing a clear explanation of the design.

For the application of Steps 1-4 of the SGDM model; the target group was defined first. Because the scenario of the game was brainstormed as taking place on the bridge of a ship, the target group of the training was decided to be deck students in MET institutions, who already had theoretical bridge resource management and leadership training. It is believed that the game can be more useful and effective if the player already has theoretical information on the topic. It is also perceived that the ML@S, in addition to leadership and teamwork skills enhancement, can also be utilized in preparation for bridge simulator training and for assessment of deck students after completing their cadetship programs onboard.

After defining the target group, objectives of the game were defined based on STCW. After that, these objectives were written as observable abilities/behaviors. Then, these abilities/behaviors were assigned into groups based on their complexity. There were 3 (A, B, D) groups of abilities. Each group of ability was covered in a different level of the game. As per Step-5, the scenarios for each of these 3 levels were created. Brief information about the scenarios of each level is given below.

Level-0: "Understanding the Key Terminology"

The player is the master of a merchant ship M/V MARITIME LEADERS-1. The master is on the bridge, where a navigational watch is kept. On the navigational watch, 3rd Officer, who has just one year of seagoing experience is serving as officer of the watch. The lookout and the helmsman are also on the watch. The duty of lookout is maintaining a continuous state of alert by sight and hearing against dangers to navigation. Also, the helmsman is responsible for timely and correct application of rudder orders that the officer in charge or the captain gives. Additionally, it is assumed throughout the game that there is not any malfunction or failure in any system onboard the ship.

Level-1: "Answers First!"

Since this level covers objectives which require only theoretical knowledge, the player is asked four theoretical questions about leadership and teamwork skills. Each question follows one another and explanatory feedback shows up after each answer.

Level-2: "Rise with Your Team!"

This level involves objectives of high application and low cognitive complexity. In this level, the player, as the master, is involved in five short scenarios of a navigational watch on the bridge. The reactions of the player to his/her teammates will affect their physical and/or mental conditions and thus their behaviors in Level-3.

Level-3: "Save Your Ship!"

In this level, the player is trained about objectives with high application and high cognitive complexity. For this reason, this is the main and most difficult level of the game. In this level, the player is on a navigational watch sailing in Marmara Sea towards the entrance of Istanbul Strait from South. There is dense fog, which limits the visibility. Throughout the level, the player, as the master, will be involved in some cases where s/he needs to use leadership skills. Later in the level, M/V MARITIME LEADERS-1 will be involved in a risky situation with another ship in which the player needs to avoid collision to win the game.

After creating the scenarios of the game, hints and feedback were added to the scenarios as suggested by Step-6 of the SGDM model. Feedback was used after all answers for improving the instructional aspect of the game. More comprehensive and knowledge-building feedback was presented after wrong answers (compared to correct answers) so that the player can develop the necessary skills by learning from his/her mistakes. Then, as per Step-7 of the SGDM model, succeeding/failing and assessment attributes of the game were created. In this regard, the player starts the game with 100 points and loses points for each incorrect answer/reaction, which costs 1 point in Level-1, 2 points in Level-2, and 5 points in Level-3. Moreover, the player has 2 minutes for answering each theoretical question in Level-1 and 45 seconds for his/her reactions in Level-2 and Level-3. If not provided within these time limits, answers/reactions are assumed incorrect. The player needs to both avoid collision and score higher than 70 points to be successful in the game. The player will fail in case of a collision regardless of the score. The game also provides an assessment about the training need of the player. The succeeding/failing criteria and assessment of the game are depicted in Table 2.

Table 2. Succeeding/failing criteria and associated assessment of the game

Possible Outcome and Points	Result	Assessment
Collision (Regardless of Score)	Fail	The player needs comprehensive and informative training on leadership and teamwork skills urgently.
Collision avoided with 0-59 Points	Fail	The player needs comprehensive and informative training on leadership and teamwork skills urgently.
Collision avoided with 60-69 Points	Fail	The player needs comprehensive and informative training on leadership and teamwork skills. But the training need is not very urgent.
Collision avoided with 70-89 Points	Pass	The player needs short training on the competencies which he/she made mistakes.
Collision avoided with 90-100 Points	Pass	The player already has required leadership and teamwork competencies. Future training should be conservational.

Prototyping ML@S

After the preliminary design, ML@S was ready to be prototyped. Deciding the game engine to be used was the first step of prototyping.

A game engine can be defined as the main software constituent of game development which is used for rendering, visualization, physics, and interaction design in games (Bergeron, 2005). For making this decision, compatibility with the target platform(s), the programming language to be used in the game engine, capability of asset import from other sources, user-friendly interface, graphical and visualization capabilities, and animation editing are among the important criteria to take into account (Wu & Kaushik, 2015).

After considering all these criteria, Unity3D® (Version: 2019.4.12f1) was selected for prototyping the ML@S game for Windows® and Mac® platforms. Unity3D is a multi-platform game engine created by Unity Technologies. Unity3D includes 3D graphics, graphical user interface, audio, physics engine, networking components and graphics rendering and scripting features for software development. It supports scripting on JavaScript, C# and Boo programming languages with quick iteration time (Unity, 2020). User-friendly real time navigation in the game and easy object manipulation features are also among the advantages of Unity3D® (Stojanovic et al., 2013). Whether they are games or not, Unity3D is also used for developing virtual reality and augmented reality applications (Jiang, 2017). Unity3D was successfully used in this study. Especially thanks to compatibility with different platforms, ready-to-use assets, as well as easy scripting features with C# programming language, it is believed that Unity3D can be further used for development of maritime 3D serious games.

Moreover, Blender® modelling platform is another tool which has been used for the development process. Blender® is a free and open source modeling platform which is compatible with Linux, Windows and Mac systems. Blender can be used for 3D mesh models, animation control, 2D/3D texture mapping, internal rendering, supporting external rendering, lighting control, 3D sculpting, video editing and node editing. Different file formats such as blend, OBJ, JPEG, PNG, GIF, FITS, AVI, MPEG, MOV can be imported to and exported from the Blender environment (Blender, 2021). In our study, some of the 3D objects and animations were firstly developed on Blender and then transferred to the Unity3D environment.

For prototyping the ML@S game, the researchers of this study firstly worked for about 4 months to increase their competency on Unity 3D® game engine. After this period, the prototyping lasted about another 5 months. It should be stated that following a multidisciplinary game development approach (with game developers, 3D artists etc.) might decrease development time and enhance authenticity, engagement of players and thus effectiveness of the game.

Although there is considerable amount of work in the literature on different structures of game elements, there is not an agreed upon taxonomy (Dicheva et al., 2015). For example, Hunter and Werbach (2012) offered 3 groups of game elements which are game dynamics, game mechanics, and game components. Similarly, Bedwell et al. (2012) also proposed a taxonomy of game elements to be used with educational purpose. In this regard, we created a framework of the game elements sheds insight on serious game prototyping/development in the maritime domain.

During the prototyping process, we assigned elements of the ML@S game into 3 groups, which create the game when they get together. The main purpose of this assignment is providing a more straightforward understanding of the game elements and how they can be developed on Unity3D. These groups are Game Assets, Game Rules as well as Game Events and Interactions. These groups and elements under each group are depicted in Figure-4.

Figure 4. Elements of a 3D maritime serious game

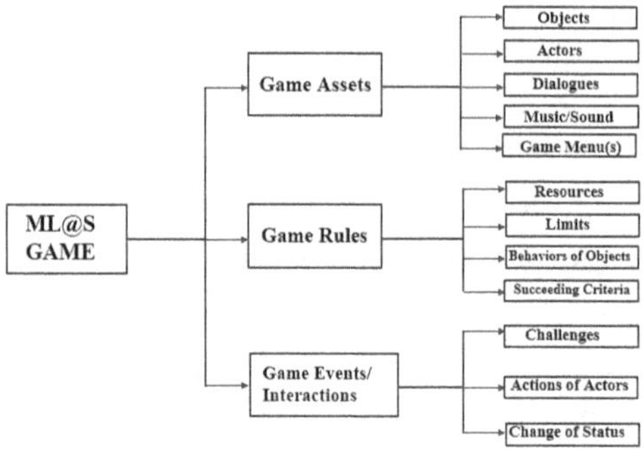

Out of these elements, game assets were developed first. For creating game objects and actors, readily available Unity3D assets were used. Additionally, dialogues in the game were created by scripting. For adding music and sound effects, the Audio Source object of Unity3D was utilized and timed by scripting. Moreover, Canvas elements of Unity3D were utilized for screen rendering, which enabled us to create game menus. M/V MARITIME LEADERS-1 ship and the bridge of the ship where the game takes place are depicted in Figures 5 and 6 respectively.

Figure 5. Maritime leaders-1 ship

Figure 6. The bridge of maritime leaders-1 ship

After the game assets, game rules were developed. For this purpose, Class and Methods features of Unity3D have been used. Classes have been defined for each element of rules and the rules are created as methods under these classes by scripting. For example, for depicting points of the player in the game, showing the time left in the scenario and assigning behaviors to objects (like helmsman and 3rd Officer), classes of points, time, helmsman, and 3rd Officer were added. After defining their classes, their changes and behaviors are represented by Methods. Figure 7 shows the officer of the watch (3rd Officer) and the helmsman during a navigational watch on the bridge with points and time properties added to the game. Moreover, Figure 8 depicts the lookout during a navigational watch.

Figure 7. Officer of the watch and helmsman during a navigational watch

Figure 8. Lookout during a navigational watch

Finally, game events and interactions were added to the game. For doing this, challenges and actions of actors were created as Methods by scripting. Then, the challenges and associated actions of actors which are based on the decision of the player were called up using the various Trigger functions in Unity3D. This way, the branching in the game was achieved, allowing the game scenario to continue according to the changes in the status of the game. Figure 9 shows the presentation of a challenge in the scenario. For instance, future behaviors of the helmsman will change according to the reaction of the master to him in this challenge. Figure 10 depicts the feedback of the wrong answer for the challenge in Figure 9.

Figure 9. Example of a challenge in the scenario

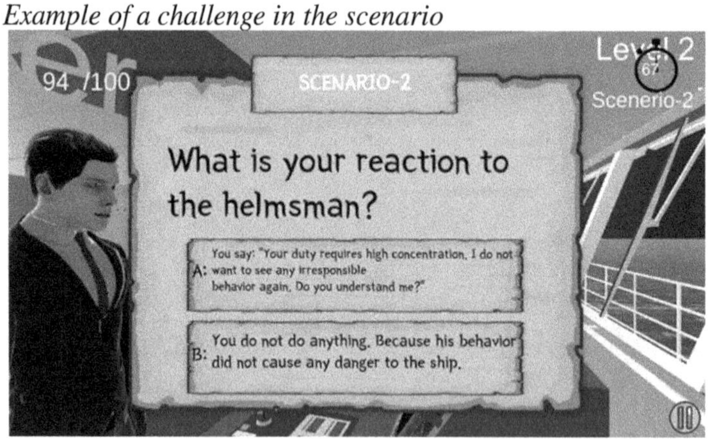

Figure 10. Feedback for the challenge

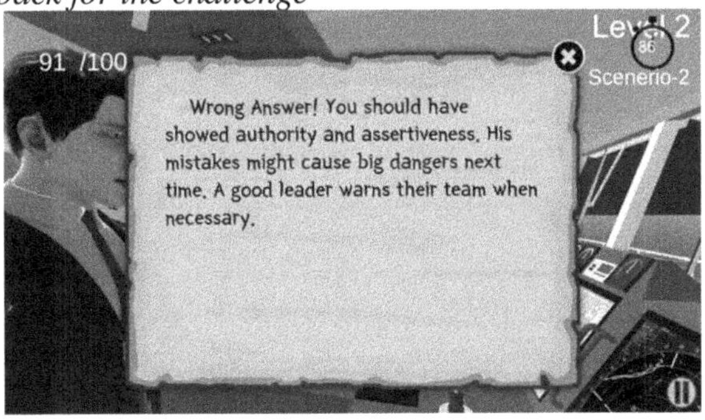

RESULTS AND DISCUSSION

Results

A survey was conducted for pilot testing the compliance of the ML@S game prototype with the STCW requirements, MET programs, and industrial expectations. The survey included 17 statements which were available for open and close-ended remarks. The compliance of ML@S with the STCW requirements, MET programs, and industrial expectations are investigated with 5, 7, and 5 statements respectively. A five-point Likert scale (strongly disagree, disagree, neutral, agree, and strongly agree) was used for close-ended remarks. Before being applied, the statements were agreed by 3 colleagues from various disciplines for ensuring the content and construct validity.

Six maritime experts participated in the survey. 3 (%50) of them (Experts #1, #2, and #3) are maritime academicians and 3 (%50) of them (Experts #4, #5, and #6) are training managers in maritime companies. All of these experts have between 10 and 20 years of experience in their fields and their ages range from 35 to 48. Five (%83) of these experts are male and 1 (%17) of them is female. Two online meetings had been conducted before they took the survey. In these meetings, we explained the SGDM model and the ML@S game to the experts. Although all experts had background information about serious gaming concepts, they declared that they have not played a serious game before. After the meetings, they played the game individually and took the survey in written format.

Table-3 summarizes the responses of 6 experts to the statements in the survey. None of the experts reported their disagreement with the compliance of the ML@S game prototype with the STCW requirements, MET programs, and industry expectations. However, some experts explained their criticism and suggestions concerning some statements as open-ended answers as provided below.

Table 3. Expert responses to the statements in the survey (N=6)

Statements	Expert Responses n (%)				
	Strongly Disagree	Disagree	Neutral	Agree	Strongly Agree
Compliance with the STCW Requirements					
The game objectives are in alignment with STCW	0(0)	0(0)	0(0)	2(33)	4(67)
The scenarios are in alignment with STCW	0(0)	0(0)	1(17)	1(17)	4(66)
The questions measure leadership competency required by STCW	0(0)	0(0)	1(17)	2(33)	3(50)
The feedbacks provide the leadership knowledge required by STCW	0(0)	0(0)	0(0)	3(50)	3(50)
Considering all, the game meets the STCW Requirements	0(0)	0(0)	0(0)	3(50)	3(50)
Compliance with the MET Programs					
The game objectives are in alignment with MET Program	0(0)	0(0)	0(0)	4(67)	2(33)
The scenarios successfully simulate the leadership education in MET	0(0)	0(0)	2(33)	1(17)	3(50)
The questions are challenging enough for MET	0(0)	0(0)	0(0)	5(83)	1(17)
The feedback provides useful leadership knowledge covered in MET	0(0)	0(0)	1(17)	2(33)	3(50)
The game can be more useful if used as a mentoring platform in MET (compared to the students play it by themselves)	0(0)	0(0)	1(17)	1(17)	4(66)
Considering all, the game can be used for education in MET	0(0)	0(0)	0(0)	1(17)	5(83)
Considering all, the game can be used for assessment in MET (for grading the students)	0(0)	0(0)	2(33)	1(17)	3(50)
Compliance with the Industry Expectations					
The game objectives are in alignment with Industry expectations	0(0)	0(0)	0(0)	2(33)	4(67)
The scenarios successfully simulate onboard situations	0(0)	0(0)	1(17)	1(17)	4(66)
The questions are challenging enough for onboard duties	0(0)	0(0)	1(17)	1(17)	4(66)
The feedbacks provide useful knowledge for onboard duties	0(0)	0(0)	0(0)	4(67)	2(33)
Considering all, the game provides practical leadership competency that the students will need for onboard duties	0(0)	0(0)	0(0)	3(50)	3(50)

DISCUSSION

Serious games, as a technology-enabled method of learning, can provide maritime students in MET institutions with authentic interactive learning environments, which can also lead to enhanced competency development. They also cause less risk and cost compared to onboard trainings. In addition, compared to simulators, they are cheaper, easier to maintain and more accessible. Considering the significant potential serious games offer, facilitating their effective utilization in maritime domain was the ultimate purpose of the study. For this purpose, SGDM model, which is the first serious game design model that is specific to maritime domain is firstly proposed.

Using SGDM model instead of other models can enable the design of more effective maritime serious games, since it is created in alignment with the needs of the maritime domain. As another important advantage of the SGDM model over the majority of serious game design models (namely EDGA (Torrente et al., 2014), SDGA (Mitgutsch & Alvarado, 2012), ATMSG (Carvalho et al., 2015), iPlus (Carrión-Toro et al., 2020), COFELET (Katsantonis et al., 2019), 4DF (De Freitas & Jarvis, 2009) etc.) SGDM is believed to provide more practical and step-by-step guidance which is also applicable to other serious game design efforts. Besides, thanks to the holistic nature of the model, it can facilitate the design of all kinds of maritime occupational modules for ports, shipping and offshore.

For reaching the ultimate purpose, a holistic and applicable methodology for design and development of maritime serious games is also needed. For achieving such a methodology, ML@S game has been preliminarily designed and prototyped as a case study. This case study also depicts the application of the proposed SGDM model.

To prove the efficiency of ML@S game and the SGDM model, the prototype of ML@S has been qualitatively tested with 6 maritime experts. All the experts explained positive feedbacks about the compliance of the game with the STCW requirements, MET outputs and industry expectations. For this reason, we conclude that the SGDM has the potential to be used in the design of effective maritime serious games. However, since it is a new model, it needs to be utilized in other studies to prove its efficiency. It should be emphasized that quantitative pre-test/post-test experiments with students are necessary for proving the efficiency of the ML@S game and thus the SGDM model. But these experiments are beyond the scope of this study and will be conducted after the final version of the game is achieved.

This study, as it proposes the SGDM model, is the fundamental basis for our further development plan. Achieving the final version of the ML@S game by improving the prototype according to the feedbacks of this study is the first step of our plan. In this regard, enhancing the graphics, modification of some scenarios in a way to make the questions more tangible, and adding more fun features are among the planned improvements. Then the efficiency of the final version of the game will be analyzed with pre-test/post-test experiments. Additional improvements to the final version of the ML@S game can also be made according to the feedbacks from the students. Using the SGDM model, more maritime serious games will be designed and added to the Maritime Gamentor platform. Enhancing the SGDM model (if necessary) based on our experiences is the next step of our further development plan. In this regard, we should state that creating the scenarios (Step-5) was the most challenging step of the preliminary design process. Based on our future experiences, we will consider modifying the model so that it can provide the users with more guidance on this step.

At the beginning of the study, some of the commercial maritime serious games have been investigated and analyzed based on the upon coordination. This investigation enabled us to gain valuable insight into the needs for improvements about those serious games are. The preliminary design and development of ML@S were difficult because of the limited availability of the resources. It is regarded that involvement and coordination of different actors such as domain experts, pedagogy experts, game designers, 3D artists and game developers can increase the effectiveness of the serious games. Although we believe that the authenticity of the game is satisfactory, functions of using a ship are limitedly available to the player. A stronger cooperation between the industry and MET institutions might facilitate a multidisciplinary design and development approach and thus enable development of more effective serious games. To strengthen this coordination and cooperation, scientific studies must be able to provide practical guidance in maritime serious game design and development efforts so that the industry can benefit from them.

CONCLUSION

This study offers SGDM maritime serious game design model. As a case study, the preliminary design of ML@S game is firstly conducted, which is then prototyped using Unity3D® game engine. After that, the prototype is pilot tested by surveying 6 domain experts. For this purpose, we firstly explained our methodology and introduced the ML@S game to the experts, who are MET academicians and training managers of maritime companies. After that, they individually played the game and we collected their opinion with both open and close-ended questions. Based on their answers, we conclude that the SGDM model has the potential to facilitate a maritime serious game design which is following the STCW requirements, MET program outputs, and industry expectations. We also noted the feedback which has been provided by the experts and all of the feedbacks will be considered in our future works while developing the final version of the game.

It is believed that this study has both practical and theoretical contributions to the literature as well as different actors in the maritime domain. To start with, the proposed SGDM model can be utilized for designing maritime serious games. To the extent of our knowledge, SGDM is the first serious game design model which is specific to the maritime domain. Secondly, preliminary version of the ML@S game has been accomplished. The expert opinions have shown that even the preliminary version of the game has a significant potential to be used for leadership and teamwork skill enhancement of maritime students as a training and mentoring/tutoring platform in maritime faculties. In fact, it is also believed that ML@S can be used by maritime companies as a part of the cadetship training programs of young seafarers for competency development. Additionally, our methodology can be utilized for design and development of similar maritime serious games. In this regard, MET institutions, shipping companies, online maritime training companies as well as maritime start-ups can significantly benefit from this study. Besides, the functions of the Maritime Gamentor platform can be further extended by creating similar serious games-based modules for crew familiarization training, bridge resource management training, accident investigations, emergency management, etc.

In spite of the novel approach and significant potential of the study, it is worth mentioning some limitations, which are intended to be covered as future work. To start with, since it is a new approach, we need to utilize the SGDM model for the design of more maritime serious games to prove its validity, efficiency and applicability. Moreover, the effectiveness of the ML@S game has only been evaluated qualitatively with expert opinions. For a more accurate evaluation of the game, quantitative pre-test/ post-test experiments will be conducted with the final version. In addition, we plan to establish Maritime Gamentor as an open platform on which the ML@S game and other games can be used for training and mentoring/tutoring of maritime students. We also plan to add user (student, seafarers, course attendees etc.) and mentor (master, chief engineer, senior pilots etc.) roles in our future maritime serious games for enhancing their instructional capability.

As future work, cooperation with other researchers is also planned so that they design maritime serious games using the SGDM model and share their feedback. Further utilization of the model will serve the purposes of validating and improving it. In fact, improving Step-5 of the model (creating gamified scenarios for all target behaviors) in a way that it can guide users more specifically on creating the scenarios has priority in the future study plans.

As another limitation to work on in future studies, the players have limited control on the functions of equipments, systems, and instruments in the games prototype. Game graphics also limit the authenticity at some parts of the game.

Besides, as serious games are games in nature, it is believed that more fun features need to be added in the final version of the game. In addition, the game prototype currently offer the same experience regardless of the position and background of the players. For enhanced instructional capability, it is believed that they need to provide the players with more personalized education and training. For eliminating this limitation, user role selection such as student, seafarer etc. including deck and engineering option, which will create different scenarios, questions and feedback in the game. For increased personalization, the existing branching in the game can also be enhanced creating more varied game scenarios and flow based on the players' game interactions.

List of Abbreviations

AR: Augmented Reality
IMO: International Maritime Organization
MET: Maritime Education and Training
ML@S: Maritime Leaders at Sea
SGDM: Serious Game Design for Maritime
STCW: Standards of Training, Certification and Watchkeeping

Authorship

All authors have made substantial contributions in all parts of this research including drafting and revising the manuscript and have given their approval for the submission of this manuscript.

Declaration of Ethical Standards

All procedures performed in this study are in accordance with the ethical standards of the institutional and national research committee and with the 1964 Helsinki Declaration and its later amendments or comparable ethical standards.

Declaration of Informed Consent

All participants have been fully informed about the study and written informed consent has been obtained from all individual participants involved in the study.

REFERENCES

Abt, C. C. (1970). *Serious games*. Viking Press.

Ahir, K., Govani, K., Gajera, R., & Shah, M. (2020). Application on virtual reality for enhanced education learning, military training and sports. *Augmented Human Research*, *5*(1), 1–9. DOI: 10.1007/s41133-019-0025-2

Akçayır, M., & Akçayır, G. (2017). Advantages and challenges associated with augmented reality for education: A systematic review of the literature. *Educational Research Review*, *20*, 1–11. DOI: 10.1016/j.edurev.2016.11.002

Akyuz, E., & Celik, E. (2018). The role of human factor in maritime environment risk assessment: A practical application on Ballast Water Treatment (BWT) system in ship. *Human and Ecological Risk Assessment*, *24*(3), 653–666. DOI: 10.1080/10807039.2017.1396184

Alonso-Fernández, C., Calvo-Morata, A., Freire, M., Martínez-Ortiz, I., & Fernández-Manjón, B. (2019). Applications of data science to game learning analytics data: A systematic literature review. *Computers & Education*, *141*, 103612. DOI: 10.1016/j.compedu.2019.103612

Alonso-Fernández, C., Calvo-Morata, A., Freire, M., Martínez-Ortiz, I., & Fernández-Manjón, B. (2023). Evidence-based evaluation of a serious game to increase bullying awareness. *Interactive Learning Environments*, *31*(2), 644–654. DOI: 10.1080/10494820.2020.1799031

Alyaz, Y., Spaniel-Weise, D., & Gursoy, E. (2017). A study on using serious games in teaching German as a foreign language. *Journal of Education and Learning*, *6*(3), 250–264. https://eric.ed.gov/?id=EJ1141668. DOI: 10.5539/jel.v6n3p250

Bai, S., Hew, K. F., & Huang, B. (2020). Does gamification improve student learning outcome? Evidence from a meta-analysis and synthesis of qualitative data in educational contexts. *Educational Research Review*, *30*, 100322. DOI: 10.1016/j.edurev.2020.100322

Bandara, D., Woodward, M., Chin, C., & Jiang, D. (2020). Augmented reality lights for compromised visibility navigation. *Journal of Marine Science and Engineering*, *8*(12), 1014. DOI: 10.3390/jmse8121014

Barnett, M., Gatfield, D., & Pekcan, C. (2006, March). Non-technical skills: the vital ingredient in world maritime technology. In *Proceedings of the International Conference on world maritime technology*. Institute of Marine Engineering, Science and Technology, London, UK, pp. 1–11.

Basak, S. K. (2017). A framework on the factors affecting to implement maritime education and training system in educational institutions: A review of the literature. *Procedia Engineering, 194*, 345–350. DOI: 10.1016/j.proeng.2017.08.155

Bedwell, W. L., Pavlas, D., Heyne, K., Lazzara, E. H., & Salas, E. (2012). Toward a taxonomy linking game attributes to learning: An empirical study. *Simulation & Gaming, 43*(6), 729–760. DOI: 10.1177/1046878112439444

Bergeron, B. (2005). *Developing serious games (game development series)*. Charles River Media, Inc.

Berns, A., Gonzàlez-Pardo, A., & Camacho, D. (2011). Implementing the use of virtual worlds in the teaching of foreign languages (level A1). *Proceedings of Learning a Language in Virtual Worlds: A Review of Innovation and ICT in Language Teaching Methodology. 2011. Warsaw*, 33-40.

Blender. (2021). *Blender 2.93 Reference Manual*. Blender Documentation. Retrieved March 13, 2021, from https://docs.blender.org/manual/en/latest/

Brown, J. S., Collins, A., & Duguid, P. (1989). Situated cognition and the culture of learning. *Educational Researcher, 18*(1), 32–42. DOI: 10.3102/0013189X018001032

Bruzzone, A. G., Massei, M., Solis, A. O., Poggi, S., Bartolucci, C., & Capponi, L. D. A. (2013, July). Serious games as enablers for training and education on operations on ships and off-shore platforms. In *Proceedings of the 2013 summer computer simulation conference* (pp. 1-8).

Calderón, A., & Ruiz, M. (2015). A systematic literature review on serious games evaluation: An application to software project management. *Computers & Education, 87*, 396–422. DOI: 10.1016/j.compedu.2015.07.011

Cano, A. R., Fernández-Manjón, B., & García-Tejedor, Á. J. (2018). Using game learning analytics for validating the design of a learning game for adults with intellectual disabilities. *British Journal of Educational Technology, 49*(4), 659–672. DOI: 10.1111/bjet.12632

Carrión-Toro, M., Santorum, M., Acosta-Vargas, P., Aguilar, J., & Pérez, M. (2020). iPlus a user-centered methodology for serious games design. *Applied Sciences (Basel, Switzerland), 10*(24), 9007. DOI: 10.3390/app10249007

Carvalho, M. B., Bellotti, F., Berta, R., De Gloria, A., Sedano, C. I., Hauge, J. B., Hu, J., & Rauterberg, M. (2015). An activity theory-based model for serious games analysis and conceptual design. *Computers & Education, 87*, 166–181. DOI: 10.1016/j.compedu.2015.03.023

Chae, C. J., Kim, D., & Lee, H. T. (2021). A study on the analysis of the effects of passenger ship abandonment training using VR. *Applied Sciences (Basel, Switzerland), 11*(13), 5919. DOI: 10.3390/app11135919

Chan, K., & Zary, N. (2019). Knowledge, use and barriers to Serious Games in undergraduate medical education. OSF Preprints. Retrieved October 9, 2022 from https://osf.io/2f7rw/download DOI: 10.31219/osf.io/2f7rw

Chang, A. H., Lin, P. C., Lin, P. C., Lin, Y. C., Kabasawa, Y., Lin, C. Y., & Huang, H. L. (2022). Effectiveness of virtual reality-based training on oral healthcare for disabled elderly persons: A randomized controlled trial. *Journal of Personalized Medicine, 12*(2), 218. DOI: 10.3390/jpm12020218 PMID: 35207706

Chow, C. Y., Riantiningtyas, R. R., Kanstrup, M. B., Papavasileiou, M., Liem, G. D., & Olsen, A. (2020). Can games change children's eating behaviour? A review of gamification and serious games. *Food Quality and Preference, 80*, 103823. DOI: 10.1016/j.foodqual.2019.103823

Csikszentmihalyi, M. (1975). *Beyond boredom and anxiety: Experiencing flow in work and play*. Jossey-Bass, https://psycnet.apa.org/record/2000-12701-000

Daggett, W. R., & Jones, R. D. (2010). *The Process of Change: Why Change, What to Do, and How to Do It.* International Center for Leadership in Education. Retrieved January 11 2021 from http://www.daggett.com/pdf/Process_of_Change_2014.pdf

de Água, P. M. G. B., da Silva Frias, A. D., Carrasqueira, M. D. J., & Daniel, J. M. M. (2020). Future of maritime education and training: Blending hard and soft skills. *Pomorstvo, 34*(2), 345–353. DOI: 10.31217/p.34.2.15

de Freitas, S., & Jarvis, S. (2009). Towards a development approach to serious games. *Games-based learning advancements for multi-sensory human computer interfaces: Techniques and effective practices*, 215-231.

Dicheva, D., Dichev, C., Agre, G., & Angelova, G. (2015). Gamification in education: A systematic mapping study. *Journal of Educational Technology & Society, 18*(3), 75–88. https://www.jstor.org/stable/jeductechsoci.18.3.75

Djaouti, D., Alvarez, J., & Jessel, J. P. (2011). Classifying serious games: the G/P/S model. In *Handbook of research on improving learning and motivation through educational games: Multidisciplinary approaches* (pp. 118–136). IGI global., DOI: 10.4018/978-1-60960-495-0.ch006

Emad, E. G. (2011). *Rethinking adult and vocational education: hauling in from maritime domain*. PhD Thesis, University of Victoria. http://hdl.handle.net/1828/3285

Evans, K. H., Daines, W., Tsui, J., Strehlow, M., Maggio, P., & Shieh, L. (2015). Septris: A novel, mobile, online, simulation game that improves sepsis recognition and management. *Academic Medicine, 90*(2), 180–184. DOI: 10.1097/ACM.0000000000000611 PMID: 25517703

Fiellin, L. E., Hieftje, K. D., Pendergrass, T. M., Kyriakides, T. C., Duncan, L. R., Dziura, J. D., Sawyer, B. G., Mayes, L., Crusto, C. A., Forsyth, B. W. C., & Fiellin, D. A. (2017). Video game intervention for sexual risk reduction in minority adolescents: Randomized controlled trial. *Journal of Medical Internet Research, 19*(9), e314. DOI: 10.2196/jmir.8148 PMID: 28923788

Fjeld, G. P., Tvedt, S. D., & Oltedal, H. (2018). Bridge officers' non-technical skills: A literature review. *WMU Journal of Maritime Affairs, 17*(4), 475–495. DOI: 10.1007/s13437-018-0158-z

Fokides, E. (2018). Digital educational games and mathematics. Results of a case study in primary school settings. *Education and Information Technologies, 23*(2), 851–867. DOI: 10.1007/s10639-017-9639-5

Fotiadis, A. K., & Sigala, M. (2015). Developing a framework for designing an Events Management Training Simulation (EMTS). *Journal of Hospitality, Leisure, Sport and Tourism Education, 16*, 59–71. DOI: 10.1016/j.jhlste.2015.03.001

Fu, K., Hainey, T., & Baxter, G. (2016, October). A systematic literature review to identify empirical evidence on the use of computer games in business education and training. In *European Conference on Games Based Learning* (p. 232). Academic Conferences International Limited.

Garrido-Iñigo, P., & Rodríguez-Moreno, F. (2015). The reality of virtual worlds: Pros and cons of their application to foreign language teaching. *Interactive Learning Environments, 23*(4), 453–470. DOI: 10.1080/10494820.2013.788034

Gleason, A. W. (2015). RELM: Developing a serious game to teach evidence-based medicine in an academic health sciences setting. *Medical Reference Services Quarterly, 34*(1), 17–28. DOI: 10.1080/02763869.2015.986709 PMID: 25611438

Gomez, M. J., Ruipérez-Valiente, J. A., & Clemente, F. J. G. (2022). A systematic literature review of game-based assessment studies: Trends and challenges. *IEEE Transactions on Learning Technologies, 16*(4), 500–515. DOI: 10.1109/TLT.2022.3226661

Gonzalez-Pardo, A., Rosa, A., & Camacho, D. (2014). Behaviour-based identification of student communities in virtual worlds. *Computer Science and Information Systems, 11*(1), 195–213. DOI: 10.2298/CSIS130214003G

Gray, S. I., Robertson, J., Manches, A., & Rajendran, G. (2019). BrainQuest: The use of motivational design theories to create a cognitive training game supporting hot executive function. *International Journal of Human-Computer Studies*, *127*, 124–149. DOI: 10.1016/j.ijhcs.2018.08.004

Gurbuz, S. C. (2021). A conceptual approach for design and development of serious game in maritime domain [Unpublished Doctoral Dissertation Progress Report-1].Istanbul Technical University, İstanbul, Turkiye.

Gurbuz, S. C., & Celik, M. (2022). Serious games in future skills development: A systematic review of the design approaches. *Computer Applications in Engineering Education*, *30*(5), 1591–1612. DOI: 10.1002/cae.22557

Hamari, J., & Sjöblom, M. (2017). What is eSports and why do people watch it? *Internet Research*, *27*(2), 211–232. DOI: 10.1108/IntR-04-2016-0085

Haruna, H., Zainuddin, Z., Mellecker, R. R., Chu, S. K., & Hu, X. (2019). An iterative process for developing digital gamified sexual health education for adolescent students in low-tech settings. *Information and Learning Science*, *120*(11), 723–742. Advance online publication. DOI: 10.1108/ILS-07-2019-0066

Hendrix, M., Bellamy-Wood, T., McKay, S., Bloom, V., & Dunwell, I. (2018). Implementing adaptive game difficulty balancing in serious games. *IEEE Transactions on Games*, *11*(4), 320–327. DOI: 10.1109/TG.2018.2791019

Hunter, D., & Werbach, K. (2012). *For the win* (Vol. 2). Philadelphia, PA, USA: Wharton digital press.

ICS (International Chamber of Shipping). (2020). *Annual Review 2020.* International Chamber of Shipping. Retrieved April 18 2021, from https://www.ics-shipping.org/wp-content/uploads/2020/11/annual-review-2020-final-compressed.pdf

Ihsan, S. N., Kadir, T. A. A., Benedict, R., & Abdullah, A. R. (2020, February). Preventive Self-Care Serious Games for Diabetes: A Game Design. In *IOP Conference Series: Materials Science and Engineering* (Vol. 769, No. 1, p. 012058). IOP Publishing. https://iopscience.iop.org/article/10.1088/1757-899X/769/1/012058/meta

Jiang, J. (2017). *A Surface-based Volume Haptics Approach and Applications in Surgical Simulation.* Doctoral dissertation, University of Illinois at Chicago. Published by ProQuest LLC. https://0-www-proquest-com.divit.library.itu.edu.tr/pqdtglobal/docview/2026669493/C1DC4247FD6D4386PQ/12?accountid=11638

Johnson, D., Horton, E., Mulcahy, R., & Foth, M. (2017). Gamification and serious games within the domain of domestic energy consumption: A systematic review. *Renewable & Sustainable Energy Reviews*, *73*, 249–264. DOI: 10.1016/j.rser.2017.01.134

Jonassen, D. (1999). Designing constructivist learning environments. In Reigeluth, C. (Ed.), *Instructional-design theories and models: A new paradigm of instructional theory* (pp. 215–239). Pennsylvania State University., https://scirp.org/reference/referencespapers.aspx?referenceid=800372

Kapralos, B., Fisher, S., Clarkson, J., & van Oostveen, R. (2015). A course on serious game design and development using an online problem-based learning approach. *Interactive Technology and Smart Education*, *12*(2), 116–136. DOI: 10.1108/ITSE-10-2014-0033

Katsantonis, N. M., Kotini, I., Fouliras, P., & Mavridis, I. (2019, April). Conceptual framework for developing cyber security serious games. In *2019 IEEE Global Engineering Education Conference (EDUCON)* (pp. 872-881). IEEE. DOI: 10.1109/EDUCON.2019.8725061

Khan, M. A., Merabet, A., Alkaabi, S., & Sayed, H. E. (2022). Game-based learning platform to enhance cybersecurity education. *Education and Information Technologies*, *27*(4), 1–25. DOI: 10.1007/s10639-021-10807-6

Kim, T. E., & Gausdal, A. H. (2020). Leaders' influence tactics for safety: An exploratory study in the maritime context. *Safety (Basel, Switzerland)*, *6*(1), 8. DOI: 10.3390/safety6010008

Kim, T. E., & Mallam, S. (2020). A Delphi-AHP study on STCW leadership competence in the age of autonomous maritime operations. *WMU Journal of Maritime Affairs*, *19*(2), 163–181. DOI: 10.1007/s13437-020-00203-1

Kim, T. E., Nazir, S., & Øvergård, K. I. (2016). A STAMP-based causal analysis of the Korean Sewol ferry accident. *Safety Science*, *83*, 93–101. DOI: 10.1016/j.ssci.2015.11.014

Kitada, M., Baldauf, M., Mannov, A., Svendsen, P. A., Baumler, R., Schröder-Hinrichs, J. U., & Lagdami, K. (2018, July). Command of vessels in the era of digitalization. In *International Conference on Applied Human Factors and Ergonomics* (pp. 339-350). Springer, Cham.

Kolb, D. A. (1984). *Experience as the source of learning and development. Upper Sadle River*. Prentice Hall., DOI: 10.1016/B978-0-7506-7223-8.50017-4

Kolić-Vehovec, S., Smojver-Ažić, S., Martinac Dorčić, T., & Rončević Zubković, B. (2020). Evaluation of serious game for changing students' behaviour in bullying situation. *Journal of Computer Assisted Learning*, *36*(3), 323–334. DOI: 10.1111/jcal.12402

Korhonen, T., Halonen, R., Ravelin, T., Kemppainen, J., & Koskela, K. (2017, September). A Multidisciplinary Approach To Serious Game Development In The Health Sector. In *MCIS* (p. 30).

Koupritzioti, D., & Xinogalos, S. (2020). PyDiophantus maze game: Play it to learn mathematics or implement it to learn game programming in Python. *Education and Information Technologies*, *25*(4), 2747–2764. DOI: 10.1007/s10639-019-10087-1

Krath, J., Schürmann, L., & Von Korflesch, H. F. (2021). Revealing the theoretical basis of gamification: A systematic review and analysis of theory in research on gamification, serious games and game-based learning. *Computers in Human Behavior*, *125*, 106963. DOI: 10.1016/j.chb.2021.106963

Landers, R. N., & Sanchez, D. R. (2022). Game-based, gamified, and gamefully designed assessments for employee selection: Definitions, distinctions, design, and validation. *International Journal of Selection and Assessment*, *30*(1), 1–13. DOI: 10.1111/ijsa.12376

Laporte, L., & Zaman, B. (2018). A comparative analysis of programming games, looking through the lens of an instructional design model and a game attributes taxonomy. *Entertainment Computing*, *25*, 48–61. DOI: 10.1016/j.entcom.2017.12.005

Lee, J. (2020). Problem-based gaming via an augmented reality mobile game and a printed game in foreign language education. *Education and Information Technologies*, •••, 1–29.

Lee, S. M., & Park, M. (2020). Reconceptualization of the context in language learning with a location-based AR app. *Computer Assisted Language Learning*, *33*(8), 936–959. DOI: 10.1080/09588221.2019.1602545

Levy, R. (2019). Dynamic Bayesian network modeling of game-based diagnostic assessments. *Multivariate Behavioral Research*, *54*(6), 771–794. DOI: 10.1080/00273171.2019.1590794 PMID: 30942094

Lewin, P. M. E. (2015). *Training effectiveness in maritime transport*. Master's thesis, Buskerud and Vestfold University College. https://openarchive.usn.no/usn-xmlui/handle/11250/1558681

Long, P. D., Siemens, G., Conole, G., & Gašević, D. 2011. International Conference Proceeding Series (ICPS). Proc. 1st International Conference on Learning Analytics and Knowledge (LAK'11), NY, USA: ACM.

Loon, M., Evans, J., & Kerridge, C. (2015). Learning with a strategic management simulation game: A case study. *International Journal of Management Education, 13*(3), 227–236. DOI: 10.1016/j.ijme.2015.06.002

Löytömäki, J., Ohtonen, P., & Huttunen, K. (2024). Serious game the Emotion Detectives helps to improve social–emotional skills of children with neurodevelopmental disorders. *British Journal of Educational Technology*, *55*(3), 1126–1144. DOI: 10.1111/bjet.13420

Mallam, S. C., Nazir, S., & Renganayagalu, S. K. (2019). Rethinking maritime education, training, and operations in the digital era: Applications for emerging immersive technologies. *Journal of Marine Science and Engineering*, *7*(12), 428. DOI: 10.3390/jmse7120428

Manuel, M. E. (2017). Vocational and academic approaches to maritime education and training (MET): Trends, challenges and opportunities. *WMU Journal of Maritime Affairs*, *16*(3), 473–483. DOI: 10.1007/s13437-017-0130-3

Margoudi, M., Oliveira, M., & Waddell, G. (2016, October). Game-based learning of musical instruments: A review and recommendations. In *European Conference on Games Based Learning* (p. 426). Academic Conferences International Limited.

Mazhari, S. (2018). *Competency of Merchant Ship Officers in the Global Shipping Labour Market: A Study of the 'Knowing-Doing' Gap*. Doctoral dissertation, Cardiff University. Cardiff University Dissertation Archieve https://orca.cardiff.ac.uk/109737/2/Shahriar%20Mazhari%20Final%20PhD%20Thesis.pdf

Michailidis, T., Meadow, G., Barlow, C., & Rajabally, E. (2020, September). Implementing remote audio as a diagnostics tool for maritime autonomous surface ships. In *2020 27th Conference of Open Innovations Association (FRUCT)* (pp. 157-163). IEEE. DOI: 10.23919/FRUCT49677.2020.9211029

Mitgutsch, K., & Alvarado, N. (2012, May). Purposeful by design? A serious game design assessment framework. In *Proceedings of the International Conference on the foundations of digital games* (pp. 121-128). DOI: 10.1145/2282338.2282364

Mohamad, U. H., Ahmad, M. N., Benferdia, Y., Shapi'i, A., & Bajuri, M. Y. (2021). An overview of ontologies in virtual reality-based training for healthcare domain. *Frontiers in Medicine*, *8*, 698855. DOI: 10.3389/fmed.2021.698855 PMID: 34307424

Mora, A., Riera, D., González, C., & Arnedo-Moreno, J. (2017). Gamification: A systematic review of design frameworks. *Journal of Computing in Higher Education*, *29*(3), 516–548. DOI: 10.1007/s12528-017-9150-4

Nikitakos, N., Sirris, I., Dalaklis, D., Papachristos, D., & Tsoukalas, V. D. (2017). Game-based learning for maritime education and training: The case of Trader of the World. *WMU Journal of Maritime Affairs*, *16*(2), 265–291. DOI: 10.1007/s13437-016-0119-3

Pellas, N., Fotaris, P., Kazanidis, I., & Wells, D. (2019). Augmenting the learning experience in primary and secondary school education: A systematic review of recent trends in augmented reality game-based learning. *Virtual Reality (Waltham Cross)*, *23*(4), 329–346. DOI: 10.1007/s10055-018-0347-2

Petri, G., & von Wangenheim, C. G. (2017). How games for computing education are evaluated? A systematic literature review. *Computers & Education*, *107*, 68–90. DOI: 10.1016/j.compedu.2017.01.004

Philbin-Briscoe, O., Simon, B., Mudur, S., Poullis, C., Rizvic, S., Boskovic, D., . . . Skarlatos, D. (2017, September). A serious game for understanding ancient seafaring in the Mediterranean sea. In *2017 9th international conference on virtual worlds and games for serious applications (VS-games)* (pp. 1-5). IEEE. DOI: 10.1109/VS-GAMES.2017.8055804

Plotzky, C., Lindwedel, U., Bejan, A., König, P., & Kunze, C. (2021). Virtual reality in healthcare skills training: The effects of presence on acceptance and increase of knowledge. *I-Com*, *20*(1), 73–83. DOI: 10.1515/icom-2021-0008

Poullis, C., Kersten-Oertel, M., Benjamin, J. P., Philbin-Briscoe, O., Simon, B., Perissiou, D., Demesticha, S., Markou, E., Frentzos, E., Kyriakidis, P., Skarlatos, D., & Rizvic, S. (2019). Evaluation of "The Seafarers": A serious game on seaborne trade in the Mediterranean sea during the Classical period. *Digital Applications in Archaeology and Cultural Heritage*, *12*, e00090. DOI: 10.1016/j.daach.2019.e00090

Pruyn, J. (2023). The use of digital games in academic maritime education: A theoretical framework and practical applications. *Maritime Policy & Management*, •••, 1–14.

Rao, M. S. (2014). Enhancing employability in engineering and management students through soft skills. *Industrial and Commercial Training*, *46*(1), 42–48. DOI: 10.1108/ICT-04-2013-0023

Romero Rodríguez, L. (2022). Engaging future engineers: The case study of a serious game implementation. *Education and Information Technologies*, •••, 1–31.

Ryan, R. M., & Deci, E. L. (2017). *Self-determination theory: Basic psychological needs in motivation, development, and wellness*. Guilford Publications., DOI: 10.1521/978.14625/28806

Sardi, L., Idri, A., & Fernández-Alemán, J. L. (2017). A systematic review of gamification in e-Health. *Journal of Biomedical Informatics*, *71*, 31–48. DOI: 10.1016/j.jbi.2017.05.011 PMID: 28536062

Sartini, S. (2020). Kahoot in Maritime English Teaching: Its Impact on Nautical Science Cadet's Oral Reproduction and Vocabulary. *English Language Teaching Educational Journal*, *3*(1), 41–51. DOI: 10.12928/eltej.v3i1.1667

Sellberg, C., Lindmark, O., & Lundin, M. (2019). Certifying navigational skills: A video-based study on assessments in simulated environments. *TransNav: International Journal on Marine Navigation and Safety of Sea Transportation*, *13*(4), 881–886. DOI: 10.12716/1001.13.04.23

Sharma, A., Kim, T. E., & Nazir, S. (2021). Implications of Automation and Digitalization for Maritime Education and Training. In *Sustainability in the Maritime Domain* (pp. 223–233). Springer., DOI: 10.1007/978-3-030-69325-1_11

Silva, F. G. (2020). Practical methodology for the design of educational serious games. *Information (Basel)*, *11*(1), 1–13. DOI: 10.3390/info11010014

Steenbeek, J., Romagnoni, G., Bentley, J., Heymans, J. J., Serpetti, N., Gonçalves, M., Santos, C., Warmelink, H., Mayer, I., Keijser, X., Fairgrieve, R., & Abspoel, L. (2020). Combining ecosystem modeling with serious gaming in support of transboundary maritime spatial planning. *Ecology and Society*, *25*(2), art21. DOI: 10.5751/ES-11580-250221

Stojanovic, V., Falconer, R., Isaacs, J., Gilmour, D., & Blackwood, D. (2013). Interactive visualisation to support sustainability assessment in land use scenario planning. Proceedings of the 29th Annual ARCOM Conference (S. D. Smith and D. D. Ahiaga-Dagbui eds.), Association of Researchers in Construction Management, Reading, UK, 2- 4 September 2013, pp. 1373-1382.

Teschner, J. (2016). *Serious Games in Medical Education: As Learning Tools*. Master's Thesis, University of Twente, Netherlands. https://purl.utwente.nl/essays/69684

Torrente, J., Borro-Escribano, B., Freire, M., del Blanco, Á., Marchiori, E. J., Martínez-Ortiz, I., Moreno-Ger, P., & Fernández-Manjón, B. (2013). Development of game-like simulations for procedural knowledge in healthcare education. *IEEE Transactions on Learning Technologies*, *7*(1), 69–82. DOI: 10.1109/TLT.2013.35

Türkistanli, T. T., & Kuleyin, B. (2022). Game-based learning for better decision-making: A collision prevention training for maritime transportation engineering students. *Computer Applications in Engineering Education*, *30*(3), 917–933. DOI: 10.1002/cae.22494

Turner, P. E., Johnston, E., Kebritchi, M., Evans, S., & Heflich, D. A. (2018). Influence of online computer games on the academic achievement of non-traditional undergraduate students. *Cogent Education*, *5*(1), 1437671. DOI: 10.1080/2331186X.2018.1437671

Udeozor, C., Russo Abegão, F., & Glassey, J. (2022). An evaluation of the relationship between perceptions and performance of students in a serious game. *Journal of Educational Computing Research*, *60*(2), 322–351. DOI: 10.1177/07356331211036989

Unity Technologies. (2020). *Unity User Manual 2020.3 (LTS).* Unity 3D Documentation. Retrieved February 23, 2021, from https://docs.unity3d.com/Manual/index.html

Veronica, R., & Calvano, G. (2020). Promoting sustainable behavior using serious games: Seadventure for ocean literacy. *IEEE Access : Practical Innovations, Open Solutions*, *8*, 196931–196939. DOI: 10.1109/ACCESS.2020.3034438

Wang, F., & Hannafin, M. J. (2005). Design-based research and technology-enhanced learning environments. *Educational Technology Research and Development*, *53*(4), 5–23. DOI: 10.1007/BF02504682

Wang, Q., & Abbas, M. (2018). Designing web-games for transportation engineering education. *Computer Applications in Engineering Education*, *26*(5), 1699–1710. DOI: 10.1002/cae.22031

Weng, J., & Li, G. (2019). Exploring shipping accident contributory factors using association rules. *Journal of Transportation Safety & Security*, *11*(1), 36–57. DOI: 10.1080/19439962.2017.1341440

Westera, W., Prada, R., Mascarenhas, S., Santos, P. A., Dias, J., Guimarães, M., Georgiadis, K., Nyamsuren, E., Bahreini, K., Yumak, Z., Christyowidiasmoro, C., Dascalu, M., Gutu-Robu, G., & Ruseti, S. (2020). Artificial intelligence moving serious gaming: Presenting reusable game AI components. *Education and Information Technologies*, *25*(1), 351–380. DOI: 10.1007/s10639-019-09968-2

Wu, W., & Kaushik, I. (2015, June). Design for aging with BIM and game engine integration. In *2015 ASEE Annual Conference & Exposition* (pp. 26-461). DOI: 10.18260/p.23799

Yeh, H. C., & Tseng, S. S. (2020). Enhancing multimodal literacy using augmented reality.

Yıldırım, İ., & Şen, S. (2021). The effects of gamification on students' academic achievement: A meta-analysis study. *Interactive Learning Environments*, *29*(8), 1301–1318. DOI: 10.1080/10494820.2019.1636089

Yu, Y., Li, G., & Weng, J. (2022). A three-step methodology to complement under-reporting maritime accident records. *Journal of Transportation Safety & Security*, *14*(9), 1451–1469. DOI: 10.1080/19439962.2021.1928353

Zainuddin, Z., Shujahat, M., Haruna, H., & Chu, S. K. W. (2020). The role of gamified e-quizzes on student learning and engagement: An interactive gamification solution for a formative assessment system. *Computers & Education*, *145*, 103729. DOI: 10.1016/j.compedu.2019.103729

KEY TERMS AND DEFINITIONS

Constructivist Learning Theory: The theory that explains that learning is an active process and effective learning takes place through actively constructing the knowledge instead of theoretically communicating it.

Experiential Learning Theory: The theory that put forwards that knowledge is learned as a result of personal experiences and interactions with the environment, instead of the instruction itself.

Gamification: Adding game features to a non-game content.

Game-Based Learning: The methodology in which serious games are used for a clear learning outcome that is effective in real life.

Serious Game: Games with educational purpose and not intended to be played primarily for amusement.

Serious Game Design: The process that includes an initial game idea, the steps of defining constraints and rules for the game, adding suitable game mechanics as well as serious which means educational content.

Serious Game Design Model: A systematic approach that is used to design a serious game.

Serious Game Development: Adding the game environment, entertainment feautures, game graphics and other visual aspects as well as audio of the game.

STCW: (International Convention on Standards of Training, Certification and Watchkeeping). The primary convention that defines the standards for training, certification and watchkeeping in the maritime domain.

Chapter 3
Understanding Student Perceptions in Digital Education Through Deep Learning Stacking Approach

Usharani Bhimavarapu
https://orcid.org/0000-0002-0246-1420
Department of Computer Science and Engineering, Koneru Lakshmaiah Education Foundation, Vaddeswaram, India

ABSTRACT

Digital education has transformed the landscape of modern learning, offering unprecedented access to resources, flexibility, and personalized learning experiences. As universities embrace digital platforms for education delivery, it becomes crucial to understand student perceptions and feedback to enhance the overall educational experience. This study aims to analyze student feedback collected from a prominent northern Indian university, focusing on six critical aspects: teaching quality, course content, lab experiences, library facilities, and the environment of the institute. Using Natural Language Processing (NLP) techniques for data preprocessing, we performed aspect extraction and sentiment classification, employing Bi-Stacked Artificial Neural Networks (ANN) to categorize sentiments as positive, negative, or neutral. The results provide a comprehensive evaluation of the student experience, offering valuable insights into the strengths and areas for improvement within the institution.

DOI: 10.4018/979-8-3693-7863-2.ch003

INTRODUCTION

Digital education refers to the integration of digital tools, resources, and technologies into the learning process to enhance the educational experience. It encompasses a wide range of approaches, from online learning platforms and virtual classrooms to the use of digital devices and multimedia content in traditional teaching settings. Digital education has gained significant prominence in recent years, driven by advancements in technology, the increasing availability of high-speed internet, and the need for more flexible and accessible learning environments. It has revolutionized how education is delivered, making it possible for students to access learning materials, participate in discussions, and collaborate with peers from virtually anywhere in the world.

One of the most significant benefits of digital education is its ability to offer personalized learning experiences. Through adaptive learning technologies, students can progress at their own pace, receiving tailored content and resources suited to their individual needs and learning styles. Moreover, digital education breaks down geographical and temporal barriers, allowing learners to access educational opportunities from anywhere and at any time, making learning more flexible. This is particularly beneficial for students in remote or underserved areas, who may not have access to traditional educational infrastructure. Additionally, digital education often incorporates interactive elements such as multimedia, gamification, and real-time assessments, which can enhance student engagement and motivation.

Despite its many advantages, digital education also presents several challenges. A significant issue is the digital divide, where unequal access to technology and the internet creates disparities in educational opportunities. Students from lower-income households or rural areas may not have the necessary devices or reliable internet connections to fully participate in digital learning. Furthermore, the shift to online education requires both teachers and students to develop digital literacy skills, which can be a barrier for those unfamiliar with technology. In the future, digital education is expected to continue evolving with advancements such as artificial intelligence, virtual reality, and more sophisticated learning management systems, which will further transform the way education is delivered and experienced. However, addressing the challenges of equity and access will be critical to ensuring that digital education benefits all learners.

In digital education, learning strategies are key to ensuring that students can effectively engage with online content and develop the necessary skills to thrive in a virtual learning environment. One primary strategy is blended learning, which combines face-to-face instruction with online elements. This approach allows for a more flexible learning experience, where students can benefit from the structure of traditional classroom settings while also having access to online resources that enable self-paced learning. Another strategy is flipped learning, where students first engage with content outside of class, often through videos or reading materials, and then use class time for interactive discussions, problem-solving, or collaborative projects. This model shifts the focus from passive consumption of information to active participation in the learning process.

Personalized learning is a central strategy in digital education that tailors the learning experience to each student's individual needs, interests, and learning pace. Digital tools such as learning management systems (LMS) and adaptive learning platforms allow instructors to create customized pathways for students, adjusting content based on assessments or learning progress. This approach fosters a more student-centered environment, where learners can take ownership of their education. For instance, students who grasp concepts quickly can move ahead, while those who need additional support can access supplementary materials or receive personalized feedback. Personalized learning also encourages deeper engagement, as students are more likely to remain motivated when the content is relevant and suited to their learning preferences.

Collaboration and interaction are critical components of successful digital education strategies. Project-based learning (PBL) is one such strategy that emphasizes teamwork, problem-solving, and real-world application. In digital education, this often involves students working together in virtual teams to solve complex problems or create digital products. Platforms such as discussion forums, video conferencing, and collaborative tools like Google Docs enable students to interact with peers and instructors in meaningful ways, despite physical distances. Additionally, gamification is increasingly being used to enhance student engagement and motivation. By incorporating elements such as badges, points, and leaderboards, gamified learning can make the educational experience more enjoyable while promoting healthy competition and reinforcing key concepts. These strategies encourage active participation, improve communication skills, and help foster a sense of community in online learning environments.

Kolb et al. (1984) proposed the Experiential Learning Theory, which emphasizes learning through experience. However, the model's limitation lies in its lack of clarity regarding how different learning styles can be effectively addressed across diverse educational settings, as it predominantly focuses on the individual learner's internal cognitive processes.

Honey et al. (2000) developed a Honey and Mumford's Learning Styles based on Kolb's framework, focusing on four key styles: activist, reflector, theorist, and pragmatist. However, one limitation is its over-simplification of learning styles, not accounting for learners who might exhibit more complex combinations of these styles. Fleming (2001) introduced the VARK Model (Visual, Auditory, Reading/Writing, Kinesthetic), categorizing learners based on their sensory preferences. A key limitation of this model is its assumption that individuals primarily use only one style, which overlooks the possibility that learners may engage multiple sensory channels simultaneously. Gardner et al. (1983) proposed that in Gardner's Theory of Multiple Intelligences, learners possess different types of intelligences, such as linguistic, logical-mathematical, spatial, musical, bodily-kinesthetic, interpersonal, intrapersonal, and naturalistic. However, the model's limitation is the lack of empirical evidence supporting the existence of distinct intelligences that are independent of each other. Felder et al. (1988) created a Felder-Silverman Model that emphasizes the importance of matching teaching strategies with students' learning preferences. The limitation of this model lies in the complexity of its application, as teachers often struggle to integrate it effectively into traditional classrooms without significant resources or training.

McCarthy (1987) developed the 4MAT system, which categorizes learning into four stages: why, what, how, and what if. Its limitation is that it assumes a fixed sequence of learning stages, which may not be applicable to all learners or subject matter areas, limiting its flexibility. Biggs (1993) introduced the Biggs 3P Model of Learning, which focuses on presage (learner characteristics), process (learning activities), and product (outcomes). The limitation of this model is its generality, as it does not delve deeply into how specific environmental factors, such as cultural context, influence learning outcomes. Dunn et al. (1978) developed the Learning Style Inventory, which identifies preferences for various elements like environmental stimuli and emotional response to learning. The model's limitation lies in its lack of clear practical application, as it is difficult to incorporate all aspects of the inventory in real-world classroom settings. Fleming et al. (1992) emphasized the Visual, Aural, Kinesthetic, and Read/Write (VARK) Learning Styles model as a method to tailor learning experiences based on sensory preferences. Its limitation is that the model may reinforce a narrow view of learning and fails to consider the dynamic, multi-modal nature of learning processes in complex environments.

Curry (1983) developed a Curry's Three-Stage Model that categorizes learning styles into three levels: cognitive, environmental, and personality-based. Its limitation is that it does not adequately account for individual differences, which makes it difficult to apply effectively in highly diverse educational settings.

Pask (1975) introduced Pask's Conversation Theory, which asserts that learning is a dynamic, interactive process. However, the limitation of this model is its complexity and lack of concrete methods for practical implementation in traditional classroom settings. Reid (1987) identified Reid's Perceptual Preferences Model as an essential element in learning, emphasizing the role of sensory input in learning processes. The limitation of Reid's model is its tendency to overemphasize one modality at a time, which does not fully reflect how learners often use a combination of sensory channels in real-life situations. Myers et al. (1995) proposed the The Myers-Briggs

Type Indicator (MBTI), which categorizes individuals into 16 personality types based on preferences in areas such as thinking and feeling. The model's limitation is that it oversimplifies personality traits and does not consider the fluidity of an individual's behavior across different contexts.

Riding et al. (1998) developed a Cognitive Style Model focusing on the cognitive styles of individuals, classifying them into categories like analytic and global. A limitation of this model is that it does not address how cognitive styles interact with emotional and motivational factors that also influence learning. Bandura (1977) proposed Social Learning Theory, emphasizing the role of observational learning, imitation, and modeling. The limitation of this model is that it does not fully address how internal cognitive processes contribute to learning, as it focuses primarily on external social factors. Bloom (1956) developed a Bloom's Taxonomy classification system for learning objectives, dividing them into six cognitive levels: knowledge, comprehension, application, analysis, synthesis, and evaluation. The model's limitation is that it lacks a clear method for addressing the varying levels of readiness among learners.

Piaget et al. (1976) and Vygotsky (1978) developed a Constructivist Learning Theory emphasized that learners construct knowledge through interactions with their environment and social context. A limitation of the constructivist approach is that it may place too much emphasis on the learner's autonomy, which may not be feasible in all educational settings. Biggs et al. (1982) proposed the SOLO taxonomy (Structure of Observed Learning Outcomes) to categorize learning outcomes in stages of increasing complexity. Its limitation is that it does not adequately address the nonlinear nature of the learning process, where learners may exhibit various levels of understanding simultaneously.

Wood et al. (1976) introduced the concept of scaffolding in Constructivism, suggesting that learners require support from instructors to progress in their learning. The limitation of this model is that it relies heavily on the instructor's ability to gauge the right level of support for each student, which can be challenging in large classrooms. Sweller (1988) developed Cognitive Load Theory, emphasizing the limitations of working memory in learning. The model's limitation is that it may lad to an overemphasis on reducing cognitive load, neglecting the importance of deep, meaningful learning strategies that involve complex cognitive processes. Knowles (1980) proposed Theory of Andragogy as the art and science of adult learning, which emphasizes self-directed learning. A limitation of this model is that it assumes all adults are inherently self-directed learners, which may not be true for every individual. Schneider et al. (1989) developed the Integrated Cognitive Model to explain how cognitive development occurs in stages. The model's limitation is that it tends to overgeneralize cognitive development stages and does not fully address individual variability in learning paths. Arbaugh et al. (2002) explored data-driven learning management systems, which track learner behaviors and outcomes to enhance learning experiences. The limitation of LMS-based models is the potential for over-reliance on technology, which may overlook the personalized aspects of learning that cannot be captured through data alone. Zull (2002) focused on integrating neuroscience with learning theory to explain how the brain processes learning. The limitation of this model is its complexity and the challenge of translating neuroscience findings into practical applications in classroom settings.

Dix et al. (2004) explored how human-computer interaction (HCI) influences learning outcomes, focusing on user interface design and usability. The limitation of HCI-based learning models is their reliance on technology, which may not be accessible or effective for all learners, particularly those in under-resourced environments.

Principal Component Analysis (PCA) and Bi-stacked Artificial Neural Networks (Bi-stacked ANN) provide significant advantages that help overcome some of the limitations seen in existing models for learning style identification and sentiment classification.

Many traditional models, such as Kolb's Learning Styles or Honey and Mumford's model, simplify learning styles into a limited set of categories, which often fails to account for the complexity and multi-dimensionality of learner preferences. PCA overcomes this by reducing the high-dimensional feature space into a smaller set of orthogonal components, capturing the most relevant underlying patterns in the data. This allows a more nuanced view of learning styles and can combine features from multiple existing categories, providing a richer understanding of learner behavior.

In models like VARK and Honey-Mumford, the subjective nature of categorizing learners into fixed styles can lead to inconsistencies. PCA aids in overcoming this limitation by transforming the raw data into a more objective set of features, which helps reduce subjectivity in the classification process. The transformation provided by PCA captures the essential features that distinguish different learning styles, regardless of the direct interpretation of sensory preferences.

The VARK model, for instance, tends to assume learners have a fixed sensory preference, but learners are often multi-modal, utilizing multiple senses during learning. Bi-stacked ANN addresses this by using a deep neural network with two stacked layers that can learn complex, non-linear patterns in the data. This flexibility allows Bi-stacked ANN to account for learners who use multiple sensory modes simultaneously, overcoming the one-dimensional approach of traditional models like VARK.

Traditional models, such as the Felder-Silverman model or Reid's Perceptual Preferences model, can struggle with the high-dimensionality of data when various learner characteristics (cognitive, emotional, environmental, etc.) are considered. PCA helps reduce dimensionality by transforming the data into fewer, more informative features. This process not only enhances the efficiency of subsequent models but also improves classification performance by focusing on the most critical aspects of the data.

One limitation of models such as Gardner's Multiple Intelligences or Pask's Conversation Theory is that they may not scale effectively with large datasets or adapt well to varying learning environments. PCA, by condensing data into principal components, enables models like Bi-stacked ANN to process larger datasets more efficiently while still maintaining accuracy. The deep layers in Bi-stacked ANN further enhance its ability to adapt to various learning contexts, capturing intricate patterns in a scalable manner.

The 4MAT system and Bloom's Taxonomy both propose fixed sequences or stages of learning, which may not apply to all learners. Bi-stacked ANN, with its deep layers, can adapt to the varying needs of individual learners by learning from their input data without strictly following predefined stages. This flexibility allows it to identify personalized learning pathways based on the learner's progression, which is a limitation of more traditional models.

Traditional models for sentiment classification, including simple machine learning classifiers, often struggle to capture the complex sentiment expressed in student feedback data due to limited feature extraction techniques. Bi-stacked ANN, leveraging the deep neural architecture, can handle multi-dimensional sentiment data and classify feedback with greater accuracy. By integrating PCA for dimensionality reduction, the model also improves its efficiency, handling large datasets of student feedback without compromising on accuracy.

In summary, PCA and Bi-stacked ANN overcome several limitations of traditional models by improving data processing efficiency, capturing complex patterns, offering greater flexibility, and allowing for more nuanced and scalable learning style and sentiment classifications. These advancements enable better personalization and more accurate predictions in digital education systems.

MATERIALS AND METHODOLOGY

The methodology involves collecting student feedback data from a prominent northern Indian university, focusing on six key aspects: teaching quality, course content, lab experiences, library facilities, and the overall environment. The data is preprocessed using NLP techniques such as tokenization, stopword removal, and lemmatization to clean and structure the text. Aspect extraction is performed using PCA for dimensionality reduction. A Bi-Stacked Artificial Neural Network (ANN) is employed for sentiment classification, labeling feedback as positive, neutral, or negative. The model is trained on the preprocessed data, capturing bidirectional context for enhanced sentiment analysis. Finally, insights from the sentiment analysis are used to evaluate and improve the university's educational offerings.

Material

We collected the dataset from a prominent northern Indian university, which serves as the foundation for generating the institutional report based on student feedback. The dataset encompasses six essential categories: teaching quality, course content, lab experiences, library facilities, and the overall environment of the institute. Each category is represented by two columns, allowing sentiment labels—0 (neutral), 1 (positive), and -1 (negative)—to be assigned. This dataset offers a comprehensive view of student opinions, making it a valuable resource for evaluating various aspects of the university experience.

Preprocessing

Preprocessing a dataset for sentiment analysis using natural language processing (NLP) techniques involves several essential steps to ensure the data is clean, structured, and ready for analysis. The first step is text cleaning, where irrelevant characters such as special symbols, punctuation marks, and numbers are removed. This also includes eliminating any HTML tags or extra whitespace that could interfere with analysis.

Next, tokenization is performed, which breaks the text into smaller units, such as words or phrases, known as tokens. Following tokenization, stopwords removal is applied to eliminate common words like "and", "the", or "is" that do not carry significant meaning for sentiment analysis. This step helps reduce noise in the data, focusing on more meaningful words.

Another crucial technique is stemming or lemmatization, where words are reduced to their root forms. For instance, words like "running" or "ran" would be transformed into "run." Stemming is generally faster but may lead to less accurate results, while lemmatization is more computationally intensive but preserves proper word forms, making it preferable for sentiment analysis tasks.

After these steps, the text is typically converted into a numerical representation through methods like Bag of Words (BoW) or TF-IDF (Term Frequency-Inverse Document Frequency). These techniques convert the cleaned and tokenized text into a vector form that machine learning models can process.

Finally, feature engineering enhance the dataset, such as by adding additional features, like sentiment scores, length of text, or word frequency, to help improve the performance of sentiment classifiers.

Through these preprocessing steps, the data is transformed into a format that allows for more accurate sentiment classification, ensuring that machine learning models can effectively evaluate the opinions expressed in the student feedback data.

Aspect Extraction and Mapping

Aspect extraction and mapping using Principal Component Analysis (PCA) is a powerful technique for reducing the dimensionality of text data while preserving the most significant features. The process begins with the extraction of aspects or key features from the dataset. In the context of student feedback, aspects may include categories like teaching quality, course content, and lab experiences. These aspects are initially represented as individual features in the dataset, where each student's feedback corresponds to a set of numerical values for these aspects.

To extract the most relevant aspects, a text vectorization method such as TF-IDF or Word2Vec is applied to convert the textual feedback into a numerical form. This results in a high-dimensional feature space, where each feedback entry is a vector representing the importance of various terms or topics. Once the data is vectorized, PCA is employed to reduce the dimensionality of this space. PCA works by identifying the directions (principal components) in the feature space that explain the maximum variance in the data. These components represent the most influential aspects, allowing for a clearer understanding of the data.

The PCA algorithm projects the original high-dimensional data into a smaller number of principal components, making it easier to identify and map the most significant aspects from the feedback. This reduction not only helps in visualizing the data but also enables more efficient processing and analysis. By mapping the student feedback onto these principal components, it becomes possible to gain insights into the underlying structure of student opinions and evaluate which aspects of the university experience are most impactful. Ultimately, PCA helps in reducing noise and focusing on the key factors that influence student sentiment, thereby aiding in more effective decision-making and reporting.

LEARNING STYLE IDENTIFICATION

Learning style identification using Fuzzy C-Means (FCM) is an effective technique for classifying students based on their unique learning preferences, allowing for a more personalized educational experience. FCM is a clustering algorithm that assigns data points to multiple clusters with varying degrees of membership, making it well-suited for identifying learning styles, as students may exhibit characteristics of more than one style. In this approach, student data, such as survey responses or behavioral data, is collected and represented as multidimensional vectors. The FCM algorithm then processes this data, grouping students into clusters that represent different learning styles, such as visual, auditory, kinesthetic, or a combination of these. The fuzzy nature of the algorithm allows for flexible membership, enabling a student to belong to more than one cluster with different degrees of belonging, reflecting the complexity of individual learning preferences. By analyzing these clusters, educators can tailor teaching methods and content delivery to accommodate the diverse learning needs of their students, ultimately enhancing learning outcomes and engagement.

Sentiment Classification

Sentiment classification using a Bi-Stacked Artificial Neural Network (Bi-Stacked ANN) is an advanced approach to analyze and predict the sentiment of textual data, such as student feedback. This method leverages the power of deep learning, particularly stacked architectures, to capture complex patterns and relationships within the text.

In a Bi-Stacked ANN, the model consists of multiple layers of neural networks, where each layer processes the data and passes it onto the next. The term "bi" in Bi-Stacked ANN refers to the use of two networks: one for processing the input data from a forward direction and another for processing the same data in a backward direction. This bidirectional structure allows the model to capture context from both past and future information in the text, which is especially important for understanding sentiment, as the meaning of a word or phrase can depend on the surrounding context.

The process begins with preprocessing the text data, including steps like tokenization, stopword removal, and lemmatization. Once the data is cleaned and vectorized (using methods like TF-IDF or Word2Vec), it is fed into the Bi-Stacked ANN. The first network processes the input text in a forward direction, while the second network processes the input in reverse, allowing the model to learn from both directions. These networks are then stacked, meaning their outputs are combined and passed through additional layers of neural networks for further processing.

The stacked architecture helps the model to better capture higher-level abstractions of the data, leading to more accurate sentiment classification. The final output is a sentiment label (positive, negative, or neutral) based on the learned patterns from the bidirectional processing. This approach is particularly effective for sentiment analysis tasks, as it can consider both local and global context within the feedback, providing a comprehensive understanding of the sentiment expressed in the text.

EXPERIMENTAL RESULTS

The experimental results of this study demonstrate the effectiveness of using Bi-Stacked Artificial Neural Networks (ANN) for sentiment classification of student feedback in digital education. After preprocessing the data using NLP techniques, including tokenization, stopword removal, and lemmatization, the dataset was fed into the Bi-Stacked ANN model, which was trained to classify feedback into positive, neutral, and negative sentiment categories. The model successfully captured key aspects of the student experience, such as teaching quality, course content, and lab facilities, and produced reliable sentiment predictions. The accuracy, precision, recall, and F1 scores were computed to evaluate the model's performance, providing a comprehensive understanding of how well the model identifies and categorizes student opinions.

Table 1 presents the cluster performance results for student data analysis, detailing various metrics across four clusters. Cluster 1 comprises 150 students with a Silhouette Score of 0.75, achieving an accuracy of 85%, and having a centroid of [0.3, 0.4, 0.2], along with a Fuzzy Partition Coefficient (FPC) of 0.87. Cluster 2, which includes 120 students, has a slightly lower Silhouette Score of 0.68 and an accuracy of 82%, with a centroid of [0.5, 0.3, 0.1] and an FPC of 0.82. Cluster 3, the largest with 180 students, attains the highest Silhouette Score of 0.80, an accuracy of 88%, a centroid of [0.4, 0.2, 0.3], and the highest FPC of 0.90. Cluster 4, comprising 100 students, has a Silhouette Score of 0.72, an accuracy of 80%, a centroid of [0.2, 0.5, 0.3], and an FPC of 0.85. Overall, the analysis spans 550 students, yielding an average Silhouette Score of 0.75, an overall accuracy of 83.75%, and an average FPC of 0.86. These results demonstrate effective clustering performance, with Cluster 3 showing the most robust results.

Table 1. Cluster performance

Cluster No.	Number of Students	Silhouette Score	Accuracy (%)	Cluster Centroid	Fuzzy Partition Coefficient (FPC)
1	150	0.75	85	[0.3, 0.4, 0.2]	0.87
2	120	0.68	82	[0.5, 0.3, 0.1]	0.82
3	180	0.80	88	[0.4, 0.2, 0.3]	0.90
4	100	0.72	80	[0.2, 0.5, 0.3]	0.85
Overall	**550**	**0.75**	**83.75**	-	**0.86**

Table 2 provides a comparative analysis of cluster performance across ten models, evaluating key metrics such as accuracy, Silhouette Score, Fuzzy Partition Coefficient (FPC), cluster consistency, and execution time. The Fuzzy C-Means

(FCM) model achieves an accuracy of 85.3%, a Silhouette Score of 0.75, and an FPC of 0.87, indicating high cluster consistency with an execution time of 12.3 seconds. Neural Networks outperformed all models with the highest accuracy of 86.2% and a Silhouette Score of 0.76, but it required the longest execution time at 30.3 seconds. Self-Organizing Maps (SOM) delivered a strong performance with 84% accuracy and a Silhouette Score of 0.73, exhibiting high consistency but at a slower execution time of 25.1 seconds.

K-Means and Gaussian Mixture Models (GMM) provided moderate results, with accuracies of 82.1% and 83.5%, respectively, and Silhouette Scores of 0.68 and 0.71. Both lacked FPC measurements and exhibited medium cluster consistency, with execution times of 8.4 and 15.2 seconds. Hierarchical and Agglomerative Clustering delivered lower accuracies of 80.2% and 81.0%, respectively, with low-to-medium consistency and relatively high execution times of 20.5 and 17.4 seconds. DBSCAN, while the least accurate at 79.8%, also had the lowest Silhouette Score of 0.65 and low cluster consistency, taking 18.7 seconds to execute.

The FCM model strikes a balance between performance and execution time with high cluster consistency, making it an efficient choice. However, Neural Networks deliver the highest accuracy and Silhouette Score, albeit with longer execution times, while other models show varying trade-offs between accuracy, consistency, and computational efficiency.

Table 2. Cluster performance comparison with existing models

Model	Accuracy (%)	Silhouette Score	Fuzzy Partition Coefficient (FPC)	Cluster Consistency	Execution Time (s)
Fuzzy C-Means (FCM)	85.3	0.75	0.87	High	12.3
K-Means	82.1	0.68	N/A	Medium	8.4
Gaussian Mixture Model (GMM)	83.5	0.71	N/A	Medium	15.2
Hierarchical Clustering	80.2	0.69	N/A	Low	20.5
DBSCAN	79.8	0.65	N/A	Low	18.7
Agglomerative Clustering	81.0	0.67	N/A	Medium	17.4
Self-Organizing Map (SOM)	84.0	0.73	N/A	High	25.1
Decision Trees (C4.5)	78.9	0.64	N/A	Medium	10.2
Random Forest	82.5	0.70	N/A	Medium	14.9
Neural Networks	86.2	0.76	N/A	High	30.3

Table 3 summarizes the results of learning style identification based on various metrics, including the number of students, accuracy, Silhouette Score, Fuzzy Partition Coefficient (FPC), and execution time. The Visual learning style, comprising 120 students, achieves an accuracy of 85.6%, a Silhouette Score of 0.75, and an FPC of 0.89, with an execution time of 12.5 seconds. The Auditory learning style, involving 100 students, shows an accuracy of 82.4%, a Silhouette Score of 0.71, and an FPC of 0.87, with the shortest execution time of 10.2 seconds.

The Kinesthetic learning style, represented by 80 students, attains an accuracy of 84.2%, a Silhouette Score of 0.73, and an FPC of 0.88, requiring 11.4 seconds for execution. The Mixed (Multi-modal) learning style, which is the largest group with 150 students, demonstrates the highest accuracy of 86.3%, a Silhouette Score of 0.76, and an FPC of 0.91, with an execution time of 14.1 seconds.

Across all learning styles with a total of 450 students, the method achieves an average accuracy of 84.6%, an average Silhouette Score of 0.74, and an FPC of 0.89, with a cumulative execution time of 48.2 seconds. These results highlight the strong performance of the Mixed learning style in terms of accuracy and cluster quality, while also reflecting consistent results across all learning styles with minimal variation in execution times.

Table 3. Learning identification

Learning Style	Number of Students	Accuracy (%)	Silhouette Score	Fuzzy Partition Coefficient (FPC)	Execution Time (s)
Visual	120	85.6	0.75	0.89	12.5
Auditory	100	82.4	0.71	0.87	10.2
Kinesthetic	80	84.2	0.73	0.88	11.4
Mixed (Multi-modal)	150	86.3	0.76	0.91	14.1
Overall	450	84.6	0.74	0.89	48.2

Table 4 compares the learning style identification performance of Fuzzy C-Means (FCM) with nine other models based on metrics such as accuracy, Silhouette Score, Fuzzy Partition Coefficient (FPC), cluster consistency, and execution time. FCM delivers strong performance with an accuracy of 86.3%, a Silhouette Score of 0.76, and the highest FPC of 0.91, indicating high cluster consistency with an execution time of 12.5 seconds. Neural Networks outperform all models in terms of accuracy (87.2%) and Silhouette Score (0.78) but require the longest execution time at 30.9 seconds.

K-Means and Gaussian Mixture Models (GMM) show moderate accuracy levels of 82.1% and 84.0%, respectively, with Silhouette Scores of 0.70 and 0.72. Both lack FPC measurements and exhibit medium cluster consistency, with execution times of 8.4 seconds for K-Means and 14.7 seconds for GMM. Hierarchical Clustering and DBSCAN achieve lower accuracy levels of 80.5% and 78.9%, respectively, with Silhouette Scores of 0.68 and 0.65, and low cluster consistency, taking longer execution times of 18.3 and 16.2 seconds.

Agglomerative Clustering and Decision Trees (C4.5) deliver medium results, with accuracies of 81.4% and 79.2%, Silhouette Scores of 0.69 and 0.67, and medium cluster consistency, requiring 17.0 and 9.8 seconds, respectively. Self-Organizing Maps (SOM) achieve an accuracy of 84.6% and a Silhouette Score of 0.74, demonstrating high cluster consistency but at the cost of longer execution times (24.5 seconds). Overall, FCM and Neural Networks stand out for their superior cluster quality and consistency, while Neural Networks trade-off computational efficiency for slightly higher performance.

Table 4. Learning identification performance comparison

Model	Accuracy (%)	Silhouette Score	Fuzzy Partition Coefficient (FPC)	Cluster Consistency	Execution Time (s)
Fuzzy C-Means (FCM)	86.3	0.76	0.91	High	12.5
K-Means	82.1	0.70	N/A	Medium	8.4
Gaussian Mixture Model (GMM)	84.0	0.72	N/A	Medium	14.7
Hierarchical Clustering	80.5	0.68	N/A	Low	18.3
DBSCAN	78.9	0.65	N/A	Low	16.2
Agglomerative Clustering	81.4	0.69	N/A	Medium	17.0
Self-Organizing Map (SOM)	84.6	0.74	N/A	High	24.5
Decision Trees (C4.5)	79.2	0.67	N/A	Medium	9.8
Random Forest	82.9	0.71	N/A	Medium	13.5
Neural Networks	87.2	0.78	N/A	High	30.9

Table 5 presents a performance comparison of sentiment classification models based on metrics such as accuracy, precision, recall, F1 score, and execution time. BERT demonstrates the best overall performance with an accuracy of 94.0%, precision, recall, and F1 score all at 0.94, but it has the longest execution time of 25.5

seconds. LSTM also delivers high performance with an accuracy of 92.3%, precision of 0.93, recall of 0.92, and F1 score of 0.92, though its execution time is significant at 20.9 seconds. Bi-Stacked ANN performs competitively, achieving an accuracy of 91.5%, precision of 0.92, recall of 0.91, and F1 score of 0.91, with an execution time of 15.2 seconds, striking a balance between accuracy and computational efficiency.

XGBoost also delivers strong results, with an accuracy of 90.1%, precision of 0.91, recall of 0.90, and F1 score of 0.90, though it requires 16.7 seconds for execution. Random Forest performs slightly lower with an accuracy of 89.2%, precision of 0.90, recall of 0.89, and F1 score of 0.89, completing its task in 14.5 seconds. Support Vector Machine (SVM) achieves an accuracy of 88.4%, precision of 0.89, recall of 0.88, and F1 score of 0.88, with an execution time of 12.3 seconds.

Logistic Regression and Naive Bayes demonstrate moderate performance, with accuracies of 85.0% and 84.3%, F1 scores of 0.85 and 0.84, and execution times of 11.1 and 9.6 seconds, respectively. Decision Trees (C4.5) and K-Nearest Neighbors (KNN) have the lowest performance, with accuracies of 82.5% and 80.7%, F1 scores of 0.82 and 0.80, and execution times of 8.4 and 10.0 seconds, respectively. Overall, BERT and LSTM stand out for their superior sentiment classification accuracy, while Bi-Stacked ANN offers a practical trade-off between performance and execution time.

Table 5. Sentiment performance comparison

Model	Accuracy (%)	Precision	Recall	F1 Score	Execution Time (s)
Bi-Stacked ANN	91.5	0.92	0.91	0.91	15.2
Support Vector Machine (SVM)	88.4	0.89	0.88	0.88	12.3
Random Forest	89.2	0.90	0.89	0.89	14.5
Naive Bayes	84.3	0.85	0.83	0.84	9.6
Logistic Regression	85.0	0.86	0.84	0.85	11.1
Decision Trees (C4.5)	82.5	0.83	0.81	0.82	8.4
K-Nearest Neighbors (KNN)	80.7	0.81	0.80	0.80	10.0
XGBoost	90.1	0.91	0.90	0.90	16.7
LSTM (Long Short-Term Memory)	92.3	0.93	0.92	0.92	20.9
BERT	94.0	0.94	0.94	0.94	25.5

Specific Real-World Examples

1. **University of California, Berkeley - Real-Time Feedback Integration**

UC Berkeley has implemented an AI-powered feedback system that collects and analyzes real-time sentiment data from students. Using AI-based sentiment analysis and NLP techniques, the system processes student feedback from surveys, discussion forums, and course evaluations. The university then uses this data to make immediate adjustments in course content and teaching methods. For example, if students express frustration with the pace of a lecture or difficulty understanding certain material, the course instructor can adjust teaching strategies or offer additional resources, ensuring that student needs are addressed promptly.

- o **How This Enhances Education**: This approach helps ensure that students feel heard, fostering a dynamic and responsive learning environment. By addressing concerns in real-time, Berkeley improves engagement and reduces dropout rates.

2. **Georgia Institute of Technology - AI-Driven Teaching Assistant**

Georgia Tech has successfully integrated an AI-powered teaching assistant named Jill Watson, which helps with answering student queries and providing feedback on assignments. Jill Watson uses machine learning algorithms to analyze students' inquiries and provides personalized responses, much like a human assistant. Through the use of sentiment analysis, Jill Watson can detect frustrated or confused students and escalate their concerns to a human teaching assistant.

- o **How This Enhances Education**: By utilizing sentiment analysis to detect students' emotional cues, the AI assistant ensures timely and appropriate responses to enhance the student experience. Students receive tailored, context-aware support that complements human teaching efforts, making learning more efficient and personalized.

3. **University of Edinburgh - AI and Predictive Analytics for Student Support**

The University of Edinburgh employs AI and predictive analytics to monitor student sentiment and engagement over the course of a semester. The system tracks feedback through course evaluations, online engagement, and even social media mentions. If negative sentiment is detected regarding a particular course or instructor, predictive models can identify at-risk students who may be struggling. University staff can then intervene early, offering support such as tutoring, counseling, or alternative learning resources.

- **How This Enhances Education**: Predictive analytics allow the university to proactively address challenges, providing targeted interventions that prevent issues like academic disengagement or mental health challenges from escalating. This approach fosters a more supportive learning environment, which leads to better retention and student success.

4. **Arizona State University (ASU) - Adaptive Learning Systems**

ASU uses AI-driven adaptive learning platforms like Smart Sparrow to offer personalized learning pathways for students in large courses. By analyzing student feedback, responses to quizzes, and participation, the platform adapts course content to suit each student's learning style and pace. The sentiment analysis on student feedback helps instructors refine course materials and adjust difficulty levels, ensuring that each student receives a personalized educational experience.

- **How This Enhances Education**: Adaptive learning systems, driven by sentiment analysis, enable ASU to create a more flexible and inclusive environment. Students can progress through materials at their own pace, and faculty can use AI-driven insights to offer targeted support where necessary, enhancing the overall learning experience.

5. **Harvard University - Using AI for Faculty Development**

Harvard University has been piloting AI systems that not only analyze student sentiment but also provide insights into teaching effectiveness. By analyzing student feedback, participation, and engagement, AI tools help faculty understand areas where they might improve their teaching practices. For instance, if students consistently express confusion over a specific teaching method, faculty can adjust their approach. AI tools can also suggest teaching materials or methods based on successful outcomes in similar courses.

- **How This Enhances Education**: By providing data-driven insights into teaching effectiveness, Harvard can foster a culture of continuous improvement among its faculty. This leads to better-quality instruction and ensures that the learning experience is consistently aligned with student needs.

6. **University of Toronto - AI and Course Design Optimization**

The University of Toronto uses AI to analyze student feedback collected through various channels, such as surveys, email, and discussion boards. By combining sentiment analysis with aspect extraction, the university identifies recurring themes in student concerns, such as issues with course structure, clarity of materials, or the effectiveness of teaching methods. Faculty members are then able to redesign course structures or materials to better align with students' needs.

- **How This Enhances Education**: This data-driven approach enables instructors to refine course delivery and content continuously. By responding directly to student feedback, the university improves the overall learning experience, making it more engaging and effective.

How Colleges and Universities Can Use Results to Enhance Education

1. **Early Identification of At-Risk Students**

Using sentiment analysis, universities can identify students who are likely to struggle academically or emotionally. For example, if a student expresses frustration or disengagement, they can be flagged for early intervention. This could involve providing additional academic support, counseling, or connecting them with peer mentors. Early identification leads to timely interventions, which can significantly improve retention rates and overall student success.

2. **Course Content Customization**

Sentiment analysis can highlight areas where students feel content is too challenging or unclear. This feedback enables educators to modify or supplement course materials, making them more accessible. Personalized learning paths can be created, allowing students to focus on areas where they need the most support, enhancing their learning experience.

3. **Real-Time Course Adjustment**

Real-time feedback allows instructors to adjust their teaching methods and content on the fly. If students express difficulty in understanding a particular concept or if engagement drops during a specific lecture, teachers can make immediate changes. This adaptability not only helps students but also increases their trust in the educational process, knowing that their feedback is valued and acted upon.

4. **Improvement in Faculty Training and Development**

By utilizing sentiment data to assess teaching effectiveness, universities can identify opportunities for faculty development. Faculty members who receive consistent negative feedback can be provided with training resources or mentoring to improve their instructional methods. This ongoing development enhances the overall quality of education at the institution.

5. **Optimized Resource Allocation**

The insights gained from sentiment analysis can also help institutions optimize resource allocation. For example, if feedback indicates a need for better lab facilities or more interactive materials, universities can prioritize funding for these areas, ensuring that resources are used effectively to improve the educational experience.

By leveraging AI and sentiment analysis, colleges and universities can create a more responsive, supportive, and personalized learning environment, ultimately enhancing the quality of education and student satisfaction.

CONCLUSION

In conclusion, this study demonstrates the effectiveness of leveraging digital tools and advanced NLP techniques to analyze student feedback and derive meaningful insights into their academic experiences. By applying Bi-Stacked ANN for sentiment classification, we successfully identified key areas where the university excels and where improvements are needed, particularly in teaching quality, course content, and lab facilities. The use of aspect extraction and PCA for dimensionality reduction further enhanced our ability to focus on the most relevant factors influencing student sentiment. Ultimately, this research underscores the potential of digital education platforms to incorporate real-time student feedback and make data-driven decisions that can significantly improve the quality of education. Further research could explore the integration of additional machine learning models or multi-modal data sources to refine sentiment analysis and broaden the scope of educational assessments.

Future Scope

Building on the insights gained from this study, the future of leveraging AI and digital tools in education is vast and promising. Several potential avenues for further research and development can enhance the accuracy, scope, and impact of sentiment analysis in educational settings.

1. **Integration of Multi-Modal Data Source**

Future research could explore the inclusion of multi-modal data sources such as audio, video, and facial recognition to assess student emotions and engagement more effectively. For instance, integrating video data from online classes with sentiment analysis could provide deeper insights into student reactions during lectures or discussions.

2. **Refinement with Advanced Machine Learning Models**

While Bi-Stacked ANN has shown promise for sentiment classification, future studies could investigate the integration of more advanced deep learning models such as **Transformer-based models (e.g., BERT or GPT)** for improved text analysis and context comprehension. These models could potentially capture more subtle sentiments and nuances in student feedback.

3. **Real-Time Feedback and Adaptive Learning Systems**

Expanding the scope of this research to real-time sentiment analysis could enable adaptive learning platforms that continuously adjust teaching methods, content delivery, and student support based on feedback. This approach would help personalize the learning experience and ensure timely interventions when students express dissatisfaction or struggle with course material.

4. **Predictive Analytics for Educational Outcomes**

Leveraging AI for predictive analytics could allow institutions to identify at-risk students based on sentiment trends over time. By correlating sentiment data with academic performance and engagement, institutions could better predict outcomes and tailor interventions accordingly to enhance student success.

5. **Cross-Institutional and Global Comparisons**

Extending the research to include cross-institutional data could help identify universal educational challenges and best practices. It would be valuable to compare sentiment analysis across different universities, countries, and educational systems to assess how global trends in student feedback align and what can be learned from different educational environments.

6. **Ethical Considerations and Data Privacy**

As sentiment analysis and AI-based assessments become more integrated into educational settings, ethical considerations regarding student privacy and consent must be addressed. Future research should prioritize the development of transparent, secure systems that respect student anonymity while ensuring the responsible use of their data.

7. **Enhanced Instructor Feedback and Development**

Using sentiment analysis not just for student feedback, but also to provide instructors with personalized insights on their teaching styles, can foster continuous professional development. Teachers could gain real-time feedback on their performance and modify their approaches to meet student needs more effectively.

Ultimately, the future of AI-driven education lies in creating more responsive, personalized, and data-informed learning environments. With continuous advancements in technology, there is great potential to revolutionize the way educational institutions adapt to and support their students, ensuring a more effective and enriching learning experience.

REFERENCES

Arbaugh, J. B., & Duray, R. (2002). Technology and the transformation of higher education: A comparative study of online and traditional courses. *Journal of Education for Business*, 77(6), 335–342.

Bandura, A. (1977). *Social learning theory*. Prentice-Hall.

Biggs, J. (1993). From theory to practice: A cognitive systems approach. *Higher Education Research & Development*, 12(1), 73–85. DOI: 10.1080/0729436930120107

Biggs, J., & Collis, K. F. (1982). *Evaluating the quality of learning: The SOLO taxonomy*. Academic Press.

Bloom, B. S. (1956). *Taxonomy of educational objectives: The classification of educational goals*. David McKay Company, Inc.

Curry, L. (1983). An organisation of learning styles theory and its applications in the classroom. In Keefe, J. W. (Ed.), *Student learning styles and their implications for teaching* (pp. 49–59). National Association of Secondary School Principals.

Dix, A., Finlay, J., Abowd, G., & Beale, R. (2004). *Human-computer interaction* (3rd ed.). Pearson.

Dunn, R., & Dunn, K. (1978). *Teaching students through their individual learning styles: A practical approach*. Allyn& Bacon.

Felder, R. M., & Silverman, L. K. (1988). Learning and teaching styles in engineering education. *Engineering Education*, 78(7), 674–681.

Fleming, N. D. (2001). Teaching and learning styles: VARK strategies. *The International Journal of Innovation in Education*, 1(1), 1–6.

Fleming, N. D., & Mills, C. (1992). Not another inventory, rather a catalyst for reflection. *To Improve the Academy*, 11(1), 137–155. DOI: 10.1002/j.2334-4822.1992.tb00213.x

Gardner, H. (1983). *Frames of mind: The theory of multiple intelligences*. Basic Books.

Honey, P., & Mumford, A. (2000). *The learning styles helper's guide*. Peter Honey Publications.

Knowles, M. S. (1980). *The modern practice of adult education: From pedagogy to andragogy*. Cambridge Adult Education.

Kolb, D. A. (1984). *Experiential learning: Experience as the source of learning and development*. Prentice Hall.

McCarthy, B. (1987). *The 4MAT system: Teaching to learning styles with right/left mode techniques*. Exposition Press.

Myers, I. B., & Myers, P. B. (1995). *Gifts differing: Understanding personality type*. Consulting Psychologists Press.

Pask, G. (1975). *Conversation theory: Applications in education and epistemology*. Elsevier.

Piaget, J. (1976). Piaget's theory. In Greenfield, P. M., & Cocking, R. R. (Eds.), *Cross-cultural roots of minority child development* (pp. 24–43). Academic Press.

Reid, J. M. (1987). The learning style preferences of ESL students. *TESOL Quarterly*, 21(1), 87–111. DOI: 10.2307/3586356

Riding, R., & Rayner, S. (1998). *Cognitive styles and learning strategies: Understanding style differences in learning and behaviour*. David Fulton Publishers.

Schneider, W., & Pressley, M. (1989). *Memory development between two and twenty*. Springer-Verlag. DOI: 10.1007/978-1-4613-9717-5

Sweller, J. (1988). Cognitive load during problem solving: Effects on learning. *Cognitive Science*, 12(2), 257–285. DOI: 10.1207/s15516709cog1202_4

Vygotsky, L. S. (1978). *Mind in society: The development of higher psychological processes*. Harvard University Press.

Wood, D., Bruner, J. S., & Ross, G. (1976). The role of tutoring in problem solving. *Journal of Child Psychology and Psychiatry, and Allied Disciplines*, 17(2), 89–100. DOI: 10.1111/j.1469-7610.1976.tb00381.x PMID: 932126

Zull, J. E. (2002). *The art of changing the brain: Enriching the practice of teaching by exploring the biology of learning*. Stylus Publishing.

Chapter 4
AI-Driven Research Methodologies:
Revolutionizing Data-Driven Discoveries in Engineering and Physical Sciences

Muhammad Usman Tariq
https://orcid.org/0000-0002-7605-3040
Abu Dhabi University, UAE & University College Cork, Ireland

ABSTRACT

This chapter examines how artificial intelligence (AI) is changing how engineering and physical science researchers do their work. It demonstrates how artificial intelligence (AI)-driven technologies—like machine learning deep learning and predictive analytics—are transforming conventional approaches by making it possible to process and analyse enormous datasets at previously unheard-of speeds and precision. In fields where sophisticated simulations and data patterns have produced ground-breaking discoveries such as materials science renewable energy aerospace engineering and manufacturing the chapter explores the integration of AI in these fields. It also discusses how AI can stimulate interdisciplinary collaboration increase predictive power and improve research efficiency. The chapter also covers obstacles such as the requirement for transparent algorithms ethical issues and data biases. The usefulness of these developments is demonstrated through case studies of effective AI applications in scientific research.

DOI: 10.4018/979-8-3693-7863-2.ch004

INTRODUCTION

AI is extending the set ways that studies are conducted in a variety of fields starting with engineering along with physical sciences. Engineering advances in Artificial Intelligence research are helping scientists and engineers study phenomena, process large data sets and find solutions to problems in ways that were unimaginable before. Due to recent improvements in computational power and availability to big data sets, AI has become one of the modern tools that offers innovative approaches to modelling, simulating, and experimenting with scientific data. Poring on the subject of how AI has transformed these research paradigms, this chapter examines how it assists scholars in these disciplines to achieve paradigmatic breakthroughs through\ data mining methodologies (Khurana, 2024). AI is useful when it comes to decentralizing research tasks, analyzing huge datasets, ad producing new insights that are hard to obtain using traditional means. For instance, in engineering, applications of artificial intelligence are in identifying better ways of designing and developing materials from cardinal data deduced from experiments and simulations. In field of physical sciences, AI enables the physicists to model and predict the physical worlds at quantum level based on data generated by particle accelerators or astronomical surveys. The application of machine learning algorithms, neural networks, AI techniques are becoming prevalent in these areas, and research is becoming more effective and identification of things that human perhaps would not be able to identify (Klami et al., 2024).

However, one major strength of employing AI in the research is the capability of analyzing large data in lesser time. Indeed, due to the current nature of information production especially in engineering and physical sciences, conventional techniques of analysis are time-consuming or unsuitable. With the help of particularly machine learning and deep learning AI algorithms can both the process and the interpretation of this data occur in real time, empowering the researchers with the ability to make decisions and predictions based on the data. For example, in material science, AI can look at over millions of compounds and predict the characteristics of each to look for new materials that possess unique properties like heat or electrical conductivity. Similarly, the use of AI models in areas like climatic change whereby large volumes of meteorological data is available to improve the climate change models (Sasmal, 2023). Application of quantitative methods are especially more common in engineering and physical sciences since it enables the investigators to estimate instead of assuming. These models can be used to estimate the behaviour of various processes, for example, the efficiency of a new plane model's construction, or the chemical reaction process. Whenever AI is employed to analyse certain results obtained through a particular experiment, the involved theoretical models can be improved on and made more precise. Such a shift from theoretical to data-based approaches is making research in many disciplines more methodologically empirical (Khurana, 2024). Secondly, AI also improves efficiency in data analysis where it gathers more accurate data that help to support research. In traditional approaches for data analysis, metrics of variation are used, and these metrics are based on statistical assumptions regarding the level of noise. These methods have proved useful but fail to identify slight patterns or correlations that AI algorithms can do. For instance, in fluid dynamics the AI can locate slight changes in the patterns of the flow that may mean turbulence or other complex phenomena. The best thing about AI is that it is capable of finding intricate patterns that no human can discover, which makes it a useful tool for researchers wishing to study and identify sluggish systems.

The modus operandi of this chapter is to therefore describe the extent to which Artificial Intelligence is transforming approaches to research in engineering and the physical sciences. Responding to the mentioned objectives, the chapter will consider major AI technologies, including and then describe how specific technologies like machine learning, deep learning, neural networks are applied to address practical challenges in these fields. We will also cover topics such as Data Driven Analytics and how AI allows researchers to find things that have never been seen before. In this chapter, we thus set out to present an overview of factual AI research methodologies across various domains of engineering and physical sciences, using existing case studies to achieve this objective and to showcase promising future applicative opportunities (Khurana, 2024). Explaining the interdisciplinarity of AI-driven research is one of the goals of this chapter. Contrary to the fact that the most direct application of AI is in computer science, the usage of AI is being incorporated more and more into engineering, physics, chemistry, and other disciplines. For example, in civil engineering, the practical application of AI is incorporated into designing and developing structures by looking at data on material and construction, and various conditions. Physicists are using artificial intelligence to investigate the basic forces of the cosmos in particle and cosmological physics experiments. The integration of interests in AI is bringing about interdisciplinary research and allowing investigators to confront issues that need knowledge from two or more fields (Klami et al., 2024).

The second purpose of this chapter is to show how limitations of mainstream research paradigms might be mitigated by AI. Conventional research entails collection of data in person or via paper-based questionnaires which may prove tiresome and inaccurate. AI makes a process of these things; thus, researchers can spend more time analyzing data instead of collecting and sorting them. Not only does it take less time to conduct research based on this automation but also there are decreased chances of errors in comparison to manual efforts. For example, in bioengineering, AI algorithms can help to identify potential targets for drug development when analyzing genetics data, which cuts the time and costs for the development of drugs (Sasmal, 2023). Precisely, AI is revolutionizing the process of experiments in engineering, physical sciences and others. Normally, experiments are conducted in accordance with hypotheses, which is observed and analysed. AI, however, is capable of establishing causal models that give hypotheses which can be deduced from patterns within the datasets. They can then be verified experimentally in case of generating the feedback loop between the models made by artificial intelligence and real-life observations. This approach is especially useful in disciplines such as materials science whereby using various indices AI is capable of estimating properties that a new material will possess before it is made in a laboratory. Likewise in astrophysics, machine models can predict how celestial bodies will act given data from telescopes and hence help astronomers schedule the next observations (Majeed & Hwang, 2021).

This chapter will also discuss the social and practical implications of AI approaches in study and research conceptualisation and procedures, as well as doubts regarding the openness of scientific results, their replicability, and that they are not distorted by the use of AI. They work very similar to what is referred to as a "black box", meaning their decision-making process is not easily understandable. This lack of interpretability makes it hard for the researcher to follow the steps that led to the AI's decision—especially when the decision is of critical importance, as in healthcare or climate modelling research studies. The chapter will go further to outline how these challenges may be addressed to ensure that AI-based research is both transparent and ethical, as well as capable of being reproduced (Sasmal, 2023).

BACKGROUND

The theoretical foundations of rural social entrepreneurship highlight the relationship between economic activity and social effect. Fundamentally, social entrepreneurship is starting companies that put social change ahead of financial viability and concentrate on developing creative, market-driven solutions to address societal issues. In rural areas, these issues frequently include poverty, lack of access to education and healthcare, and environmental deterioration. Knowledge rural social entrepreneurship requires an understanding of "embeddedness," as these businesses are firmly established in the communities in which they operate, utilizing local networks, resources, and customs to provide sustainable and timely solutions. The term Digital Renaissance in research specifically capture the changes in research due to the use of advanced digital technologies, including but not limited to AI, big data, and ML. This new era is characterized by the advancement of the rate, scale and efficiency of producing such scientific knowledge. The application of these technologies helps the researcher to analyse large data sets, discover various patterns, and draw new conclusions, which can hardly be obtained from conventional research techniques. In today's world, researchers have wide matrices at their disposal in terms of computing and algorithms which are redesigning the ways to produce knowledge in different fields. Which appears in every business, every branch of knowledge, from medicine and engineering to physics and social sciences, the Digital Renaissance offers a new way of solving tasks and developing unprecedented solutions (Adams & Hall, 2022). In essence, the Digital Renaissance means a new awakening in science, just for revived awareness of the scientific method in the frame 14th–17th centuries renaissance as a search of new knowledge and reforms in art, science, and philosophy. Today, the same is taking place through digital technologies opening new frontiers, extending the frontiers of what is known, and going where no man has gone before. Due to the use of AI and machine learning the research methodologies have transitioned into data-based approaches which are more effective, faster, and can even cover larger territory (Prince et al., 2024).

The blending of AI in research methodologies did not begin recently; it is an incremental process based on the developments in the application of computational technologies hand the progress in the research methods. Digital research techniques began with the introduction of computers in the middle of the twentieth century and the first creation of algorithms. These computers basically served in procedural arithmetic and data management functions nevertheless acquired multifaceted functions over time (Mendhe et al., 2024). In the late 20th century, the internet brought the idea of sharing data and collaborative production into a new era. The changes made it possible for the researchers to gain and process big data across different regions of the world which promoted more complex analytical methods. For instance, the use of computers concerns, for instance, the large datasets generated in genomic study, where computations became instrumental in gene sequencing analysis. This formed the basis of AI in the field of life sciences where AI algorithms are employed to discover patterns within human genetics that are indicative of the potential to develop any illness or in guiding the formation of new drugs (Adams & Hall, 2022). Of the many artificial intelligence forms, machine learning was a popular tool in early 21st-century research in diverse disciplines. Machine learning makes use and applies models, which can learn from data and make predictions. This was a marked departure from conventional research approaches where the strategies utilized were largely conjunctive hypotheses. Machine learning entails that an analyst can allow the system to abstract knowledge from vast pools of data to display conclusions that would be hard for teachers to discover. For instance, in climate science the application of machine learning models would be in preparing more accurate climate patterns from the recorded past climatic status (Kasowaki & Deniz, 2024). Now AI is used in almost all fields of study that are present today, such as engineering, physics and medical. Constant updates of the learning (machine learning) models, as well as progression of computer processing technologies help the researchers get better results much faster. This is evident in the Digital Renaissance in research where constantly advancing artificial intelligence-generated method logics are expanding scientific possibilities (Prince et al., 2024).

The use of computers and especially Artificial Intelligence has brought significant changes in conventional approaches to research. Previously, since the data gathering and analysis and sometimes even the experiments were done manually, research was time-consuming. Although these methods yielded quite meaningful developments, these methods remained constrained due to the capability of humans in terms of data handling and analysis. Modern technologies have resolved most of these issues by virtue of featuring large, automated portions of the data fulfilling research goals, and allowing researchers to deal with much larger amounts of data and experiments (Adams & Hall, 2022). Collection and analysis of large datasets is arguably the most obvious way in which digital technologies have shaped research methodologies. In contexts such as physics, biology, and engineering, scholars obtain more data than they can analyse with their eyes and hands. Such data can be analysed by the AI algorithms much faster than research would be done by an actual researcher if the researcher were to go through thousands of pages to look for patterns that would otherwise go unnoticed. For example, in astronomy, telescopes produce terabytes data daily collected from the universe. Techniques of advanced AI Computations are now being applied for go through this data to detect objects like galaxies or black holes which may have been previously left unnoticed by traditional analytical procedures (Prince et al., 2024).

There is yet another area of the digital sciences that are rapidly changing the nature of work in the field, namely simulation and modelling. Conventional research methodologies in the sciences employed analytical mathematical models to make forecasts of numerous phenomena including weather and chemistry. But these models were constrained by the data or information available at that time as well as the computers of that period. Nowadays, such models can include substantially more data and perform effective simulations with reliably high accuracy. For instance, in the materials science, the application of AI can help researchers estimate the properties of new materials before they are developed in the lab thus helping develop advanced materials cheaper and faster (Kasowaki & Deniz, 2024). Some of the impacts of digital technologies on experiments are also noted as follows. What was done in traditional research method, various forms of experiments were conducted with respect to hypothesis that were formulated in advance and data was collected in order to validate them.AI has provided the possibility of data-oriented research which is the new standard. This in contrast to hypothesis driven research where the researcher formulates a hypothesis and tests for it, the researcher can collate data, and the AI system can analyse the data and suggest potential hypothesis that arose from analyzing the data. This method is especially practical in such disciplines as genomics or neuroscience because the data obtained there are intricate and hardly allow making clear hypotheses in advance (Mendhe et al., 2024).

For instance, in neuroscience, AI is being employed to interpret the data from specially developed electrodes used to record brain activity in order to establish the pattern of interaction between various areas of the brain. While other researchers conduct analysis with focus on mere regions of interest, AI enables an analysis of the whole human brain. This has given additional understanding on how the brain works and how it reacts and has given new directions to study diseases like Alzheimer's (Patel et al., 2024). In addition, virtuality is now also helping researchers to perform more collaborative and interdisciplinary investigations. Nowadays, it is less easy because, in the past, scientists were limited by their disciplines because the sharing of data and cooperation with other disciplines was challenging. In the present time, with the help of internet and cloud computing the researchers can share data and work with other researchers of the world sitting in same or different time zone. Machine learning is capable of studying information obtained from various disciplines and discern relationships which might have not been observed by experts operating in different fields. For instance, there is an application of AI in comparing chemical, biological, and medical data for finding new treatments of diseases (Patel et al., 2024). Nevertheless, the very possibilities that digital technologies have opened in research come with new difficulties. It is good to know that AI algorithms are ''Black box'' models in most of the cases and users cannot see the working behind it. This can complicate replication of one's work by other researchers or, in fact, hamper the ability of the latter to comprehend why a given conclusion was arrived at in the first place. The need to continue making the outcomes of AI-based research transparent and reproducible increases the scientific agenda as the Digital Renaissance progresses (Mendhe et al., 2024). In aggregate, the Digital Renaissance in research is a new paradigm of the development of science based on AI and other modern digital technologies. These tools are revolutionizing standard research approaches by including higher speeds into data analysis, simulations, and interdisciplinary collaboration. Techniques such as machine learning have been in existence over the years, the application of artificial intelligence in their research has enabled researchers to venture further afield. The Effect of such technologies on research shall continue to increase as research advances to more developed digital age; hence transforming the process of research across all disciplines.

AI and Machine Learning Fundamentals

AI and ML are the core of present-day evolution and lie at the foundations of the current technological advancements covering the aspects of information processing and decision-making processes. In its basic sense AI describes the ability of machines to perform tasks by emulating human behaviour, while ML is a subcategory of AI that concerns the use of algorithms which allow machines to learn on their own. AI is very applicable in many sectors, that is research, business, healthcare and engineering and so on cause most of complicated functions like problem solving, data analysis, and pattern recognition which are hard for humans are easily done by the machines (Papadimitriou et al., 2024). Machine learning, for example, has completely changed the approach to work with big data. In traditional programming there are defined certain set of rules and instructions that a machine has to follow to act in a certain way. On the other hand, machine learning is a process that lets a machine learn from example or experience (data) and improve, over time. Contrary to supervised learning, this approach is appropriate for cases when it is impossible or too challenging to define heuristics, for example, image or time series data analyses (Agrawal & Nargund, 2024). Artificial intelligence and machine learning are revolutionizing the study and understanding of data within the researcher and society in general thus creating a breakthrough of several fields. Here are some notable examples.

Healthcare

AI is presently being employed in the diagnosis of medical records, patient's gene information, scan images, and many others. For instance, using machine learning algorithms one is capable of identifying the probability by which an individual will develop a particular illness given his/her genotype and lifestyle. Medical imaging is also being processed, for instance, X-ray, MRI to distinguish initial stages of symptoms of even cancer or Alzheimer's. Through the help of such technologies, more accurate diagnosis of ailments and proper plan of management can easily be implemented by allowing machines to handle such tasks (Milson & Levent, 2024; Tariq, 2024).

Environmental Science

AI is becoming very effective in environmental research technology, where it helps in examination of information from satellite imagery, climate instruments and other resources. For instance, AI techniques can analyse images taken by satellites to examine the loss of forest, changes in location of glaciers and effects of climate change on the biosphere. This way, based on big amount of environmental data, more effective conclusions can be derived for chosen further environmental protection strategies and policies (Ahmad et al., 2023).

Physics and Engineering

For example, in physics and engineering AI is applied in modelling of complicated structures as well as interpretation of experimental results. For instance, the use of AI is applied in the analysis of data from experiments carried out on particle accelerators where researchers focus on basic particle and force. In engineering, AI is employed for fine-tuning, designing of structures for instance aircrafts and bridges (Ohalete et al., 2023).

Social Sciences

It is also expected to create an impact on the research in the social sciences. Predictive analytics now find application in mining data gathered from social networks, questionnaires, and other sources in search of patterns in peoples' behaviour, interactions and attitudes. For instance, AI in the interpretation of tweets to monitor citizens' opinion on or to gauge when a society is likely to revolt (Nursalim et al., 2022).

AI-Driven Data Collection and Analysis

Artificial intelligence has assumed critical importance in research, particularly in Engineering and Physical Sciences, as a tool for data aggregation and analysis. Currently, researchers are dealing with large data, which are relatively inconvenient to process using classical approaches. AI provide methodological approaches that help in the optimization of data gathering procedures. Of the main applications of AI in data acquisition, the most common is the use of automated systems to pull information in real time from sensors, online databases, and social media feeds. For instance, in environmental engineering, there are AI-powered drones that take data from areas that cannot be accessed, and the sensors measures alterations in the quality of water, quality of air or the quality of the soil. This feature ensures quicker and more accurate data gathering by minimizing the need for human interaction in hazardous or difficult-to-reach areas (Ninduwezuor-Ehiobu et al., 2023).

Making sense of the massive quantity of data collected by AI systems depends on machine learning techniques. To extract significant patterns and insights, data must frequently be processed, cleansed, and analysed after it has been gathered. Data-driven judgments, result prediction, and hidden pattern detection are all accomplished by machine learning approaches. AI-powered advanced analytics in engineering and physical sciences aid in design optimization, material behaviour prediction, and simulation of a range of physical phenomena. For example, machine learning models are used in mechanical engineering to forecast component failure in machines by using past performance data. With the use of these forecasts, engineers may save costs and enhance safety by preventing system failures through prompt repair.AI-powered data analysis is revolutionizing a number of industries. In one civil engineering case study, data from sensors installed in a bridge was analysed using artificial intelligence to track the structural integrity of the structure. The AI system gathered vibration, temperature, and stress level data continually. The technology was able to identify minute structural alterations in the bridge that would have indicated future fractures or collapses through the use of machine learning methods. This predictive ability increased the bridge's longevity and safety by enabling engineers to do maintenance before any significant damage happened (Ahmadi & RabieNezhad Ganji, 2023; Tariq, 2025).

AI-driven data analysis has been effectively used in the physical sciences, including astrophysics. For instance, in order to find exoplanets, enormous volumes of data gathered from observatories have been analysed using AI systems. Planets circling far-off stars can be found by looking for patterns in light data that machine learning algorithms are taught to recognize. Several new exoplanets that would have gone unnoticed by conventional analytical methods have already been found thanks to this methodology (Agrawal & Nargund, 2024). Without a question, the use of AI in data collecting and analysis has transformed research approaches. It makes it possible for scientists to gather data more effectively, analyse it more precisely, and derive previously unreachable conclusions. AI will play a bigger part in research as it develops, opening up new avenues for discoveries and inventions in everything from engineering to the physical sciences. Artificial intelligence (AI) accelerates development at a never-before-seen rate by automating the most laborious parts of data processing, freeing up academics to concentrate on interpretation and original problem-solving.

Optimizing Research Techniques with AI

Research technique optimization has increasingly dependent on the integration of AI into processes, particularly in domains handling vast and complex data sets. Researchers may concentrate on more important parts of the study process by using AI to automate repetitive processes like data collecting, processing, and analysis. Using machine learning algorithms, which can be trained to recognize patterns and make predictions based on historical data, is one method of integrating AI into processes. AI may expedite the discovery process in materials research, for instance, by predicting the characteristics of novel materials through analysis of current data. Similar to this, AI models may mimic studies and assist researchers in determining the most promising directions for next study, saving time and money as compared to manually testing hypotheses. While there are several advantages to employing

AI in research, efficiency and accuracy rank highest. Large volumes of data may be processed far faster by AI systems than by any human. Artificial intelligence (AI) also ensures data consistency and accuracy by removing the possibility of human mistake in repeated operations like data input or preliminary analysis. For example, AI-powered image recognition systems in medical research may analyse medical scans to more accurately diagnose illnesses like cancer than traditional approaches (Ninduwezuor-Ehiobu et al., 2023).

As a result, patients not only receive better care but also receive faster diagnoses and more timely choices from medical professionals. The ability of AI to optimize research methodologies has already been shown in a number of research initiatives. One noteworthy instance is the application of AI in drug development, where it is being used to uncover possible drug candidates by analyzing large chemical databases (Tariq, 2024). Typically, years of trial and error are required to find new medications. AI, on the other hand, can quickly sort through data and identify which drugs have the best chance of succeeding in clinical trials. This strategy has already shown promise, with AI assisting in the much faster discovery of novel medications than traditional approaches for conditions like cancer and Alzheimer's (Ahmadi & RabieNezhad Ganji, 2023). AI has been included into engineering design processes to maximize product development. Automotive engineers, for instance, might revise ideas before creating actual prototypes by using AI to predict how car components would operate in various scenarios. This lowers expenses, expedites development, and yields more dependable goods. In a different instance, AI was used to aerospace engineering to enhance aircraft wing design, resulting in more fuel-efficient aircraft (Ning, 2021). Artificial Intelligence has made a wide range of areas' outputs quicker, more precise, and more efficient by refining research processes. AI will change research methods even more as it develops, giving engineers and scientists more freedom to push the envelope of what is conceivable. When AI is used as a research partner, innovation may occur considerably more quickly, leading to previously unattainable new discoveries (Akhmedov et al., 2024).

TAILORED EDUCATIONAL OPPORTUNITIES THROUGH AI

By providing customized learning experiences for students, artificial intelligence (AI) is revolutionizing education and enabling each person to study at their own speed and in accordance with their own needs. Education has traditionally aimed for personalized learning, yet traditional classroom environments sometimes find it difficult to provide each student specific attention. By evaluating students' progress, determining areas in which they require further help, and modifying teachings appropriately, AI fills this vacuum in education. AI-driven services, such as Khan

Academy and Duolingo, employ machine learning algorithms to monitor user performance and provide tailored information according to their areas of strength and weakness (Altan & Milson, 2024). When a student does well in one topic but finds it difficult in another, the AI system can help them advance in the subjects they have mastered by suggesting further practice in the difficult areas. As a result, kids learn more effectively because they get assistance when they need it most. Beyond only tailoring material, artificial intelligence (AI) also contributes to the development of dynamic, adaptable learning environments. Artificial intelligence (AI) systems are able to rapidly adapt to the changing needs of pupils by making recommendations, responding to inquiries, and giving feedback. A teacher might not always be able to answer all of the students' questions right away in a regular classroom. On the other hand, students may participate in interactive learning experiences at any time with AI-powered tools. Certain AI tutoring systems, for example, mimic one-on-one education by assisting students with challenging tasks and providing tips or answers when they run into difficulties. Students may explore, make errors, and learn at their own speed without feeling rushed to catch up with the rest of the class thanks to this interactive learning approach (Altan & Milson, 2024). Numerous case studies illustrate how AI-powered learning tools may improve student results. DreamBox, an AI-powered math tool for primary and middle school pupils, is one such example. DreamBox tracks students' arithmetic problem-solving processes using data analytics to find trends in their comprehension and errors. The system modifies the issue level based on this data, providing tailored workouts to reinforce the student's weak areas (Thomson & Anderson, 2021).

AI is being utilized to create whole new educational platforms that address the many demands of students in addition to standardized testing. Advanced algorithms are used by Squirrel AI, an AI-based tutoring system in China, to generate individualized lesson plans for pupils based on their academic background, preferred methods of learning, and learning styles. The platform lets students advance at their own speed by offering interactive courses, tests, and simulations that are catered to their individual needs. Students have found Squirrel AI to be very helpful in test preparation; many have improved their grades as a result of utilizing the platform (Brunton et al., 2021). AI has enormous potential to improve education even more as it develops. Artificial Intelligence (AI) is revolutionizing education by facilitating tailored learning experiences, fostering adaptable settings, and delivering immediate feedback to students across all age groups. Artificial Intelligence (AI) is transforming education by creating more interesting, inclusive, and productive learning environments through personalized online courses, interactive tutoring, and math exercises. The possibilities for tailored and adaptable learning will increase in the future as AI develops more, providing even more chances for individual academic achievement (Mulukuntla & Gaddam, 2021).

BEST PRACTICES AND CASE STUDIES

Here we take an overview of how artificial intelligence (AI) is being employed in research and education where new possibilities of rationalization, accuracy, and creativity are emerging. However, for these technologies to meet these expectations, best practices need to be adopted in AI integration. Accordingly, offering guidelines for applying AI in research and education, it is mentioned that one of the essential approaches is to begin with goals. The purpose can be to work on big data, create graphics, perform virtual experiments, or develop individualized learning paths, but that purpose must be clear. This enables the right choice of AI tools to use, and it has a checks and balance mechanism to determine whether the AI technology being used is relevant to the project. For instance, in a Learning Environment like Google Classroom, AI can be applied to carry out tasks such as grading, writing feedback, etc, but such must fulfil the purpose within the learning environment (Di Stefano et al., 2023). The second is the use of quality data as a fundamental principle when attempting to utilize the specialties of artificial intelligence in teaching and learning research. The major characteristic of an AI system is that it is data driven; the data on which it is trained, with which it makes predictions or comes up with insights, are of the utmost importance. Due to this, if the data collected is substandard, the results and AI implements that are inferred from it are bound to be equally substandard. Before feeding the data to AI systems, researchers and educators must ensure that the data is cleansed, pre-processed and validated. AI requires relevant reliable raw data and the correct handling of data to make sure that the results produced by the model are valid in scientific research for instance (Zaid & Milson, 2024).

Another practice that has been identified is that of combining professionals in artificial intelligence with professionals in a specific domain. Thus, the application of AI brings tremendous opportunities, but, at the same time, it implies that the input needs to be prepared by individuals familiar with the various field in which the AI technology will be used. This relationship between domain knowledge and accuracy across industries like healthcare, engineering and education is that domain specialists can offer important information when creating or utilizing AI models to ensure it fits the tasks required (Brunton et al., 2021). For instance, in conducting a medical study, the AI creators, engage with physicians and health researchers to build models that can analyse images, or identify the potential epidemics. This synergistic relationship try to fill the gap between theory and practice in either field of study (Majeed & Hwang, 2021). There are several instances that would prove the effectiveness of using AI research approach in various disciplines. For example, within the practice of engineering AI has been applied in finding ways to improve the design and testing of complicated structures. With reference to a particular application of AI in engineering, aerospace engineers applied AI in the design of components of aero planes. In the customary approach, construction of actual models and carrying out many examinations would be also possible which would take a lot of time and money. However, thanks to the advances in artificial intelligence; engineers could feed it with different designs and concerning program can predict the general performance to come up with efficient and reliable designs since the engineering physical testing phases were avoided. It not only brought faster pace in designing, but also resulted in lesser expenditure than before (Di Stefano et al., 2023).

In particular AI has transformed the research techniques in the healthcare sector through advancing the speed and precision of medical data analysis. Over the past few years, the greatest focus of AI in medicine has been in the identification of new drugs. In a study that has included research on cancer treatment, the big data of chemical substances and their effects on cancer cells were discussed as the case where AI was helpful. While using older approaches, new drugs could take years to try various compounds, while, at this time, AI assisted staff defined the list of potential drugs to work with. This resulted in the creation of new cancer treatments much more rapidly than could have been accomplished with normal procedural techniques. AI system capability to process and analyse data quickly boosted the research on treatment and helped them in generating greater output in lesser time and reduced efforts. With the help of AI integration, the field of education has also grown tremendously (Moinuddin et al., 2024). A good example is the adoption of an adaptive learning systems in the online math classes in Arizona State University (ASU). The application called ALEKS relied on machine learning to evaluate the students' knowledge about the subject matter and then offer teaching content suited to each learner's abilities. In a similar manner, the AI observed the activities of the students as well as their progress in real time and tweaked the content to give increased focus to areas which caused most difficulties among the students. Therefore, students who were under the AI-engineered system witnessed improved performance compared to those under lecture-based courses. ALEKS success at ASU proves the applicability of AI solution that can provide learning opportunities tailored to individual learning styles for learners (Zaid & Milson, 2024).

Analyzing these cases, it is possible to state that several useful lessons can be derived for integrating AI in research and education. Another important point is flexibility and consistent practice: all processes must be optimized daily. AI systems presented in the literature are fallible and very often require retraining or improvement once new data has been delivered or when goals change. In research for instance, machine learning models would have to re-adjust for a number of reasons such as new findings in the scientific community or newly developed experimentations. In education, the AI driven platforms are needed to be updated frequently in order to bring them into line with the current curriculum and educational practices (Mohammad & Mahjabeen, 2023). The second lesson is about ethic analysis. The authors assert that information technology continuing its way into the process of research and education, there must be measures put in place to avoid adverse effect of AI. In research it becomes important to pay certain amount of attention to ethical use or management of data especially when dealing with sensitive data such as the medical records. Likewise, in education established AI systems should be sensitive enough not to influence stereotyping or favour or disfavour given groups of students (Zaid & Milson, 2024). The role of the researcher and educator is to understand the AI outputs, decide upon those results, and bring creativity and critical thinking which AI cannot offer. For example, although patterns of research data can be detected by an AI system, human researchers are required to make intelligent conclusions and to develop new ideas (Mitchell & Murphy, 2022).

ETHICAL AND RESPONSIBLE USE OF AI IN RESEARCH

As about the AI development in research and education experiences, here is what these educators and scholars have to say: AI offers great opportunities for innovations, but there are also major ethical concerns. When AI systems work their way more into different aspects of research, the use of these technologies must be done responsibly. Professionals in every form of AI, especially where data use, pitfalls, and subsequent action can significantly affect individuals or society, consider the industry's ethical perspectives. For example, the AI algorithms employed in the research may be applied to patients' data which should not violate the patients' rights to privacy. As with all AI utilized in an educational environment, the tools themselves should not introduce or promote biases which could harm the student or their potential (Zhao et al., 2024). A primary problem in AI-related research is the problem of bias. Allowing bias to creep into training data is a major problem with AI systems, and that is because AI systems are designed to act based on data. This may cause bias with regards to what is discovered rolls down to policy making or even treatment methodologies in areas of social sciences or health sciences respectively. For instance, an AI system designed to predict diseases could be based on data that doesn't fully represent some demographics, and so doesn't accurately predict health risks for those populations – therefore, unequal responses in healthcare. The bias problem, therefore, means that when using AI, the researchers have to make sure that the model they develop has been trained on a diverse and balanced data set. Furthermore, to avoid accumulating bias in the system, it is recommended that such AI systems used should be audited periodically in order to correct captured bias (Mitchell & Murphy, 2022).

Another relevant ethical concern ownership of data and protection for artificial intelligence research includes. Many AI systems need lots of data to operate smoothly, and this data may include personal data. For instance, in medicine or psychology, the AI use ranges from patient record analysis to genetic and, or behavioural data analysis. This information could be accessed by unauthorized personnel, therefore, results to infringement of patients' privacy. That is why researchers need to follow certain requirements to minimize the likelihood of similar occurrences. Some of what is needed is to encrypt data, restrict it for only appropriate personnel to view, and other methods such as anonymizing the data to cover up identities. For instance, in and involving patients, their details could be stripped off identity and fed to the AI-driven analysis to produce useful research outcomes, while preserving the privacy of the patient (Zhao et al., 2024).

When an AI system is enabled to make decisions in a scientific investigation, other practitioners and investors must be able to learn about the reasoning behind those decisions. For instance, in an environmental study, if AI is applied to climate change trends, the algorithms applied, datasets used besides the assumptions made must be made available to allow for further examination of their authenticity. Reporting guarantees that the results of the AI-based research are accurate and can be easily checked by the researchers of the relevant academic fields (Moinuddin et al., 2024). That's why one of the most effective approaches to enhancing the ethical usage of AI is producing the rules and standards that have to be obeyed by the researchers. Such guidelines should respond to problems such as bias, data privacies, and the 'explainability' of AI systems, or the way that these algorithms work. As the utilization of AI rises, numerous organizations and institutions are now creating AI ethical principles whereby the researchers performing AI adheres to ethical protocols. For instance, the European Union has come up with the guidelines in regard to the trustworthy artificial intelligence that focuses on the principles such as fairness, accountability and transparency. These frameworks offer the researchers a point of reference that they can use to enhance their AI usage to fit wider ethical norms (Zhao et al., 2024).

The third meaningful area of concern with accountabilities of AI application in research is human supervision. Hence, when it comes to issues of understanding and decision making, human researchers cannot afford to be sidelined by AI. For example, in a legal research, project where the AI suggests for legal positions based on analysis of case laws there is usually still a human lawyer who reviews and considers the appropriateness and ethicality of recommendations made by the AI. This kind of system made sure that AI algorithms act under consideration with human intervention to avoid offending ethical factors (Moinuddin et al., 2024).

Another function of the proposed measures regarding ethical AI use is to popularize information on threats and opportunities to researchers and practitioners. Most of the time some of the users of AI may not even develop a deep understanding of the technology and the various questions of ethics surrounding it. Organizing awareness creation and training of those who work on AI and related projects on matters of ethical considerations is beneficial since it exposes the researcher to information on areas containing possible ethical issues with an aim of imparting the knowledge on how to handle such issues. For instance, a social science scholar may discover that, and AI algorithm is capable of reinforcing bias of in the development of algorithm, if not well thought and trailed, thus prepare themselves for any relapse when designing AI-driven methods for their research.

In the IT area, one of the important examples of the ethical employment of AI in studies is the creation of AI algorithms for the diagnosis of diseases. These models can possibly help prevent deaths in cases where large amounts of medical information have to be scrutinized to find a sign of a certain disease. However, the correct application of these models raises concerns regarding the patients themselves such as consent and also information privacy. For example, the use of artificial intelligence in diagnostics should strictly be allowed to work with only collected patient data with the patient's consent means that the patient has full knowledge of how the data will be used. Also, there has to be high-level encryption, and security against such data being exploited for the wrong reasons (Milson & Levent, 2024). Another example relates to application of the AI in education: collecting and analyzing the students' information to deliver individual learning. Despite the fact that such technologies can greatly improve education performance, they also precipitate some important ethical concerns with reference to students' confidentiality. For instance, AI-enabled learning solutions generate data on habits learners develop in their learning process, their performance, and behaviour.

If it is not processed rightfully, it may be misused and that may put undermine students for any opportunities they want to pursue in the future including education or actual job. To this, institutions implementing the courses for the AI tools must have concrete data protection policies to safeguard student information such that the information is collected and used only in learning activities and to inform the students and their families how the data will be utilized (Moinuddin et al., 2024).

FUTURE DIRECTIONS, SCOPE, AND INNOVATIONS

Consequently, with evolution of the artificial intelligence (AI), it is revolutionizing the future approaches to carrying out research. Trends indicate that advances in AI will lead to significant improvements in discovery across various disciplines with large complex data sets particularly in engineering and the physical sciences where data forms the basis of knowledge discovery. The application of AI in understanding, evaluating and even in producing data allows this kind of sector to have a face lift. On the bright side, a fantastic wave of unique opportunities is in store for those who will enter the new school year. Knowledge of these trends and future developments in AI for research purposes assists research and corporate organizations in making a better future preparation of the next phase of development (Mohammad & Mahjabeen, 2023). Among the fresh directions to develop AI technologies the most likely are the integration with other Innovative technologies like quantum computing and IoT. Quantum computing is a relatively fresh field, but it also demands vast improvements in the computational capabilities available in present-day research. Quantum computing and AI could therefore bring together big data that was hitherto unmanageable. For example, computer programs that harness artificial intelligence would be deployed to quantum computers in order to predict and design new formative materials for electronic devices or constructions for energy storage devices. In the same way the integration of AI with IoT could improve studies in the smart city, environmental, and infrastructure fields. Real-time data from a broad network of connected devices can be processed by AI algorithms in those fields to make faster and more precise decisions.

The third emerging trend in the world of AI for future research methodologies is the application of AI in automating processes of experimentation and discovery. Earlier, it was seen that investigators employed much of their effort into developing hypothesis, experiment plan and carrying out tests. However, with the advancement in technology today, AI can help in analyzing this process, and hence showing a quicker and more efficient way of analyzing them and at the same time provide an opportunity for posing more intricate queries. For instance, drawing from current advances, AI algorithms are already in use for screening chemical molecules, as well as in determining the potential of the molecules in treating disease and the likely impact of the drug discovery process on diseases. Lastly, in the field of engineering, AI can turn a manufacturing aspect, like aerodynamic studies in automobile or aerospace engineering, into a more efficient prospect that is challenging for human input alone to accomplish at the level of optimization that AI can bring about (Mohammad & Mahjabeen, 2023). In the future the use of AI is prophesized to increasingly becoming integrated into every step of the research process. For instance, with unstructured data that include image, video, voice using natural language processing AI is set to revolutionize industries. At present, data in disciplines such as physics and engineering are mainly generated in form of raw experimental data, which may take a lot of effort to analyse.

If AI can interpret and analyse such a type of data, more time will be saved, and researchers will spend their time on interpretation of results and theory crafting. For example, in astrophysics AI could be used to process large amounts of information from telescopes as to find relationships and trends that could lead to a discovery of some new phenomenon in the universe. Likewise, in advanced problems that drive fluid dynamics, AI might assist in decoding intricate flow fields of liquids and gasses in real-time, inspiring development in application areas such as meteorology or climatology (Mitchell & Murphy, 2022). However, when AI is employed in the core of research, new issues will arise. Another important problem is to manage the interpretability of such systems, so that an AI system is Open — in the sense of the Open AI charter. As of now, and especially in the case of deep learning systems, AI models are often described as ''black box'' which, though efficient in outcome production, offer little to no explanation of how to get there. Whereas validation and reproducibility reign supreme in research, this kind of approach is not an ideal one. It will be crucial for the researchers and developers to align towards the development of more robust models with high output and decision making capabilities alongside transparency and accountability in their decision making. This will be particularly essential in areas such as engineering, especially in safety related areas, and the physical sciences wherein the basis for the subject area knowledge is critical in progress. Yet another area that the research community will have to think about is the way AI will be employed for scientific research. As artificial intelligent systems advance, the generation of AI capabilities will be able to make decision with profound effect to both science and applicability to the social setting. For instance, Artificial Intelligence systems implemented in climate change prediction models may impact world energy consumption policies and Conservation regimes. Likewise, are the opportunities of discovering new treatment or even improvement of human biology by means of newly developed using the help of Artificial Intelligence (Mitchell & Murphy, 2022). They all bring up significant ethical issues as to who owns AI and what it will be utilized for as well as what part of the advantages reaped from this creation will go to whom. Improving people's understanding of how AI can be utilised in a manner that would be most helpful and less harmful for everyone will require the cooperation of the researchers, the policymakers and the entire society.

Nonetheless, the benefits associated with AI driven research methodologies are enormous. Of all the opportunities, there is one which I believe will lead to the greatest impact; this is the democratization of research. Successful AI tools, many of which have an open-source architecture or are hosted on the Cloud, enable various academics, including those in the developing world, to actively contribute to pioneering investigations. For instance, when in a cloud, AI data analysis tools can be employed by rese archers who may not afford to possibly purchase lab equipment or potentially have access to compute intensive resources. This can further increase fairness so that a range of diverse ideas can be put forward in the scientific process. Therefore, at the same time, AI's fast training capabilities on large datasets enables the researchers to tap on the existing knowledge base much more effectively making the process of research more efficient (Mitchell & Murphy, 2022). AI will also help to collaborate between sub-disciplines in the engineering and the physical sciences. Many of the issues of modern world, including climate change, sustainable energy, and advanced manufacturing, call for an interdisciplinary approach. AI can do this by connecting up information and processes from the multiple fields of knowledge and practice, opening up fresh avenues of research. For instance, it can replicate the dynamics between biological parts and physical setting and given outputs that as may help in bioengineering or environmental science among other related fields. In the realm of energy, AI can optimize systems that combine renewable energy sources with traditional power grids, helping to solve one of the greatest challenges of our time: used for the development of renewable energy systems (Thomson & Anderson, 2021).

CONCLUSION

This chapter examines the effects of artificial intelligence on the processes of research and specifically engineering and physical sciences stream have been discussed. To understand how AI is transforming research, this chapter has taken a close look at how AI is being incorporated into research. The examples and case studies described further explain how the data processing capability of AI to process large data sets with speed and accuracy is transforming science and technology ranging from materials science to climate science to engineering design. These developments prove that in order to remain relevant to science, number of pertinent procedures should embrace AI solutions. In the future, there is no denying AI's revolutionary potential for research approaches. The examples covered in this chapter are only the tip of the enormous potential for AI to propel discovery in novel and fascinating ways. When AI converges with other cutting-edge technologies like IoT and quantum computing, it will further enhance researchers' capacities and lead to the discovery of whole new areas of knowledge. But for this promise to be realized, governments, educators, and researchers must work together. In order to incorporate AI into their operations, researchers need to keep pushing the envelope on application of the technology. In order to equip the upcoming generation of scientists and engineers to work with these potent tools, educators must modify their curricula. On the other side, in order to guarantee that AI is utilized morally and responsibly, policymakers must make sure that rules keep up with technical progress.

Given these conversations, there is an obvious need for action. In an increasingly data-rich world, researchers—especially those in engineering and the physical sciences—must adopt AI-driven methodologies to be creative and competitive. AI has too much promise to be ignored when it comes to improving the scope, precision, and efficiency of research. Simultaneously, instructors are vital in providing future researchers with the tools necessary to properly use AI. This entails introducing AI instruction into academic curricula, promoting multidisciplinary cooperation, and stimulating original thought about the use of AI to complicated problem-solving. Finally, in order to create ethical frameworks and rules that support accountability, justice, and openness in AI-driven research, policymakers must collaborate closely with the research community.

Hence, AI is transforming research practices in engineering and physical sciences through efficient analysis and automation of data collection, process as well as more precise results. The role of AI in these fields continues to surge as more scholars apply AI methods and approaches to address some of the world's hardest challenges in scientific and engineering arenas. In this chapter, the author's objective is to present an overview of the use of AI in today's research and discuss how it is revolutionizing research. Due to the way that these two tools are being piloted to transform the research paradigms, the researchers can tap into these innovations to facilitate promising development of paradigms in the respective fields.

REFERENCES

Adams, H., & Hall, D. (2022). Innovations in artificial intelligence research fueled by big data analytics. *European Journal of Business and Innovation Research*, 10(2), 96–104.

Agrawal, K., & Nargund, N. (2024, January). Deep learning in Industry 4.0: Transforming manufacturing through data-driven innovation. In *International Conference on Distributed Computing and Intelligent Technology* (pp. 222-236). Cham: Springer Nature Switzerland. DOI: 10.1007/978-3-031-50583-6_15

Ahmad, K., Iqbal, W., El-Hassan, A., Qadir, J., Benhaddou, D., Ayyash, M., & Al-Fuqaha, A. (2023). Data-driven artificial intelligence in education: A comprehensive review. *IEEE Transactions on Learning Technologies*.

Ahmadi, A., & RabieNezhad Ganji, N. (2023). AI-driven medical innovations: Transforming healthcare through data intelligence. [IJBLS]. *International Journal of BioLife Sciences*, 2(2), 132–142.

Akhmedov, J., Jurayev, U., Kosimova, S., Rakhimova, G., Tursunov, Q., & Kosimov, L. (2024, May). The significant technical mantle of AI in the field of secular engineering: An innovative design. In *2024 4th International Conference on Advance Computing and Innovative Technologies in Engineering (ICACITE)* (pp. 601-606). IEEE.

Altan, B., & Milson, S. (2024). *AI-powered data revolution: Navigating the big data landscape (No. 11898)*. EasyChair.

Bappy, M. A., Ahmed, M., & Rauf, M. A. (2024). Exploring the integration of informed machine learning in engineering applications: A comprehensive review. *Manam and Rauf, Md Abdur, Exploring the Integration of Informed Machine Learning in Engineering Applications: A Comprehensive Review* (February 19, 2024).

Brunton, S. L., Nathan Kutz, J., Manohar, K., Aravkin, A. Y., Morgansen, K., Klemisch, J., & McDonald, D. (2021). Data-driven aerospace engineering: Reframing the industry with machine learning. *AIAA Journal*, 59(8), 2820–2847. DOI: 10.2514/1.J060131

Di Stefano, A. G., Ruta, M., & Masera, G. (2023). Advanced digital tools for data-informed and performance-driven design: A review of building energy consumption forecasting models based on machine learning. *Applied Sciences (Basel, Switzerland)*, 13(24), 12981. DOI: 10.3390/app132412981

Kasowaki, L., & Deniz, B. (2024). *Revolutionizing big data: AI algorithms and predictive analytics (No. 11685)*. EasyChair.

Khurana, V. (2024). Accelerating pace of scientific discovery and innovation through big data-enabled artificial intelligence and deep learning. *Emerging Trends in Machine Intelligence and Big Data*, 16(1), 38–53.

Klami, A., Damoulas, T., Engkvist, O., Rinke, P., & Kaski, S. (2024). Virtual laboratories: Transforming research with AI. *Data-Centric Engineering*, 5, e19. DOI: 10.1017/dce.2024.15

Majeed, A., & Hwang, S. O. (2021). Data-driven analytics leveraging artificial intelligence in the era of COVID-19: An insightful review of recent developments. *Symmetry*, 14(1), 16. DOI: 10.3390/sym14010016

Majid, A., & Hwang, S. O. (2021). Data-driven analytics leveraging artificial intelligence in the era of COVID-19: An insightful review of recent developments. *Symmetry*, 14(1), 16. DOI: 10.3390/sym14010016

Mendhe, D., Dogra, A., Nair, P. S., Punitha, S., Preetha, K. S., & Babu, S. B. T. (2024, April). AI-enabled data-driven approaches for personalized medicine and healthcare analytics. In *2024 Ninth International Conference on Science Technology Engineering and Mathematics (ICONSTEM)* (pp. 1-5). IEEE. DOI: 10.1109/ICONSTEM60960.2024.10568722

Milson, S., & Levent, K. (2024). Deep learning applications in big data: Expanding horizons with AI-driven solutions.

Mitchell, A., & Murphy, S. (2022). Unleashing the power of big data: A catalyst for advancements in artificial intelligence. *European Journal of Mechanical Engineering Research*, 9(1), 56–65.

Mohammad, A., & Mahjabeen, F. (2023). Revolutionizing solar energy with AI-driven enhancements in photovoltaic technology. *BULLET: Jurnal Multidisiplin Ilmu*, 2(4), 1174–1187.

Moinuddin, M., Usman, M., & Khan, R. (2024). Strategic insights in a data-driven era: Maximizing business potential with analytics and AI. *Revista Española de Documentación Cientifica*, 18(02), 125–149.

Mulukuntla, S., & Gaddam, M. (2021). Data-driven healthcare: Trends in machine learning and AI for disease prediction and prevention. *ESP Journal of Engineering & Technology Advancements*, 1(1), 25–33.

Ninduwezuor-Ehiobu, N., Tula, O. A., Daraojimba, C., Ofonagoro, K. A., Ogunjobi, O. A., Gidiagba, J. O., & Banso, A. A. (2023). Tracing the evolution of AI and machine learning applications in advancing materials discovery and production processes. *Engineering Science & Technology Journal*, 4(3), 66–83. DOI: 10.51594/estj.v4i3.552

Ning, K. (2021). Data driven artificial intelligence techniques in renewable energy system (Doctoral dissertation, Massachusetts Institute of Technology).

Nursalim, A., Judijanto, L., & Asfahani, A. (2022). Educational revolution through the application of AI in the digital era. *Journal of Artificial Intelligence and Development*, 1(1), 31–40.

Ohalete, N. C., Aderibigbe, A. O., Ani, E. C., Ohenhen, P. E., & Akinoso, A. E. (2023). Data science in energy consumption analysis: A review of AI techniques in identifying patterns and efficiency opportunities. *Engineering Science & Technology Journal*, 4(6), 357–380. DOI: 10.51594/estj.v4i6.637

Papadimitriou, I., Gialampoukidis, I., Vrochidis, S., & Kompatsiaris, I. (2024). AI methods in materials design, discovery and manufacturing: A review. *Computational Materials Science*, 235, 112793. DOI: 10.1016/j.commatsci.2024.112793

Patel, K., Beeram, D., Ramamurthy, P., Garg, P., & Kumar, S. (2024). AI-enhanced design: Revolutionizing methodologies and workflows. [IJAIRD]. *International Journal of Artificial Intelligence Research and Development*, 2(1), 135–157.

Prince, N. U., Faheem, M. A., Khan, O. U., Hossain, K., Alkhayyat, A., Hamdache, A., & Elmouki, I. (2024). AI-powered data-driven cybersecurity techniques: Boosting threat identification and reaction. *Nanotechnology Perceptions*, •••, 332–353.

Sasmal, S. (2023). Next-gen data engineering: The AI revolution.

Tariq, M. U. (2024). Generative AI in Curriculum Development in Higher Education. In Fields, Z. (Ed.), *Impacts of Generative AI on Creativity in Higher Education* (pp. 227–258). IGI Global., DOI: 10.4018/979-8-3693-2418-9.ch009

Tariq, M. U. (2024). Harnessing Persuasive Technologies for Enhanced Learner Engagement and Motivation. In M. Sanmugam, D. Lim, N. Mohd Barkhaya, W. Wan Yahaya, & Z. Khlaif (Eds.), *Power of Persuasive Educational Technologies in Enhancing Learning* (pp. 30-62). IGI Global. https://doi.org/DOI: 10.4018/979-8-3693-6397-3.ch002

Tariq, M. U. (2024). Navigating the Personalization Pathway: Implementing Adaptive Learning Technologies in Higher Education. In Minh Tung, T. (Ed.), *Adaptive Learning Technologies for Higher Education* (pp. 265–291). IGI Global., DOI: 10.4018/979-8-3693-3641-0.ch012

Tariq, M. U. (2025). *AI-Driven Learning and Engagement in Higher Education.* IGI Global., DOI: 10.4018/979-8-3693-4074-5

Tariq, M. U. (2025). The Belmont Report: Guiding Ethical Principles in Human Research. In Throne, R. (Ed.), *IRB, Human Research Protections, and Data Ethics for Researchers* (pp. 245–268). IGI Global Scientific Publishing., DOI: 10.4018/979-8-3693-3848-3.ch010

Tariq, M. U., & Sergio, R. P. (2025). Nurturing Digital Citizenship in Society 5.0 Through AI and Computational Intelligence Education. In Pandey, R., Srivastava, N., Prasad, R., Prasad, J., & Garcia, M. (Eds.), *Open AI and Computational Intelligence for Society 5.0* (pp. 59–84). IGI Global Scientific Publishing., DOI: 10.4018/979-8-3693-4326-5.ch003

Thomson, R., & Anderson, J. (2021). Bridging the gap: Big data's influence on AI algorithms and models. *EPH-International Journal of Science and Engineering*, 7(4), 52–56.

Zaid, A., & Milson, S. (2024). *Precision analytics: AI-driven solutions for big data challenges (No. 11895)*. EasyChair.

Zhao, T., Wang, S., Ouyang, C., Chen, M., Liu, C., Zhang, J., & Wang, L. (2024). Artificial intelligence for geoscience: Progress, challenges and perspectives. *Innovation (Cambridge (Mass.))*, 5(5), 100691. DOI: 10.1016/j.xinn.2024.100691 PMID: 39285902

KEY TERMS AND DEFINITIONS

Artificial Intelligence (AI): A branch of computer science focused on creating systems capable of performing tasks that require human intelligence, such as problem-solving, pattern recognition, and decision-making.

Machine Learning (ML): A subset of AI that involves training algorithms on large datasets to identify patterns, make predictions, and improve performance over time without explicit programming.

Predictive Analytics: The use of statistical algorithms and machine learning techniques to analyse historical data and make predictions about future outcomes.

Data-Driven Methodologies: Research approaches that rely on data analysis and interpretation to draw conclusions, inform decisions, and develop new theories or innovations.

Interdisciplinary Collaboration: The integration of AI across multiple fields of study to enhance research outcomes, foster innovation, and address complex scientific challenges.

Chapter 5

Optimizing Research Techniques and Learning Strategies With Digital Technologies:

The Digital Renaissance at the Workplace

Deepa Sharma
https://orcid.org/0000-0003-4374-917X
Maharishi Markandeshwar University, India

ABSTRACT

In today's era, the digital revolution is really about rebirth and reimagination. It's about using the enormous potential of digital technology to innovate, create, and solve problems that were not possible before. The Digital renaissance of work examines how digital technologies are transforming our lives and our jobs more often than we realize. In this study examined how businesses can generate significant value from their digital workplaces and found that others are lagging behind rapidly. Work is changing due to the flexibility and creativity that digital technologies provide. The digital ethic of "work as freedom" is replacing the old ethic of work as agony. Managing the digital workplace is a new position. It involves more than just technology; it also involves understanding employee demands and business constraints in order to correctly create a variety of new digital solutions that will address issues and deliver value to the company.

DOI: 10.4018/979-8-3693-7863-2.ch005

INTRODUCTION

Businesses that use digital technologies have a clear competitive edge in the Internet age. Among these tools is digital resilience, which includes cyber security, online literacy, and all the various ways businesses may employ digital systems to swiftly recover and adapt to uncertainty. The corporate climate of today demands digital transformation. Businesses should give digital resilience a priority given how quickly things are changing in order to better position themselves to succeed in the market (Al-Omoush et. al, 2023). A digital workplace is a virtualized version of the conventional, physical office setting where a variety of technological tools, including cloud computing and digital applications, are used to facilitate productivity and teamwork (Hooi et. al, 2023). By enabling workers to connect, collaborate, and communicate from any location at any time using any device, digital workplace solutions boost worker satisfaction and increase productivity and utilization. Employees should be able to communicate synchronously, or in real time, with one another in a digital workplace, regardless of where they are or what technology they may be using. When teams aren't in the same physical workplace and can't meet in person every day, it might facilitate knowledge transfer. The workplace of the future is intelligent, automated, and employee-focused it concentrates on the moments that count(Anderson et. al, 2013). The digital workplace is essentially a human-technology hybrid that produces a vibrant environment where workers are empowered, ideas grow, and creativity has no bounds. The implementation of a digital workplace has the potential to reduce noise pollution and optimize workflow, leading to increased productivity levels for the entire company. As a result, workers may do more tasks in less time. Digital skills not only increase efficiency but also encourage creativity in the workplace. Employees that keep up with the newest digital tools and techniques may solve issues in novel and creative ways, produce new goods and services, and come up with innovative ways to connect with clients. Workplace ethos Digital workplaces encourage a culture of adaptability, self-governance, and lifelong learning. They prioritize results above procedures, promoting creativity and adaptability. The foundation of this culture is a trust-based strategy that gives employees the freedom to handle their work on their own, frequently asynchronously (Barnosky et. al, 2016). The quality of an employee's interaction with the technology they use for work is known as the digital employee experience. We include specific aspects of the digital employee experience such as employee communications, social engagement, content sharing and document management systems, employee learning, mobile apps, *etc.*, all considered part of the digital workplace. While you may choose to use any of these digital workplace technologies separately, depending on your business's needs, budget, and size, *etc.* Organizations have quickly increased their productivity and efficiency via the use of technology in the workplace. Digital tools, programs, and systems enable the speedy and effective completion of tasks that were before laborious and manual. Email, texting, instant messaging, social networking, video conferencing, and more are all included. In the office, using digital communication tools may boost output, foster better teamwork, and promote customer satisfaction. Additionally, these technologies facilitate information organization and retention. We can discuss work projects, plan out-of-office notices, and manage timetables with these technologies. This makes it easier for us to collaborate across large distances. Our productivity increases when we collaborate better, which enables us to do more tasks within regular business hours. The digital renaissance concept as applied to the workplace includes key elements:

(a) **Remote Work:** The basis for effective, efficient remote work is a digital workplace. By combining cutting-edge technology, cloud-based solutions, and collaborative platforms, digital workplaces enable workers to work remotely from any location in a borderless environment. By utilizing cyber security, they also assist in protecting confidential data, resolving issues with data security. The goal is to not only facilitate remote work but also to improve it in the contemporary workplace by encouraging adaptability, teamwork, and productivity.

(b) **Collaboration and Communication**: Digital workplaces are made to make these two things easier. Digital workplaces are cloud-based systems that function as shared digital spaces with access to social networking, video conferencing, and instant messaging, going beyond traditional email. Team members may edit and access documents and projects in real-time, independent of their physical location, allowing them to collaborate smoothly and building a feeling of unity and shared purpose even when they are in various time zones and geographical locations.

(c) **Automation:** Automation is a crucial feature that involves using software to manage workflows and schedule meetings, among other regular activities. By decreasing the workload associated with administrative duties and improving job efficiency, automation solutions free up employee's time to concentrate on more strategic and creative work (Gull et. al, 2024).

(d) **Flexibility:** Desk less workers who work at the forefront of your company have demands that digital workplaces meet. An excellent example would be field personnel installing, maintaining, and upgrading equipment at a client location. These employees may execute work orders, search up pertinent information, connect with the front office, and update the status of works as they are finished by using a laptop, tablet, phone, or other mobile device equipped with a digital workplace. The digital renaissance of work focuses on how digital technologies are transforming our personal lives and our jobs at work, and how businesses can unlock significant value by harnessing the potential of their digital workplaces

(Barnosky et. al, 2016). Due to the impact of digital, every industrialist is feeling the need for digitalization in the workplace due to which everyone interprets their work in new ways. An employee prefers to work differently, given the expectations, beliefs, convictions and dynamics. Digital communication often provides a better return on investment, enabling businesses to reach a larger audience with less resource. Real-time interaction: Businesses and consumers may instantly communicate with one other through social media and other digital channels. A digital workplace includes the following technology tools as shown in Figure 1:

Figure 1. Technology tools (Author)

1. Communicate with employees through i.e. messaging, chat, e-mails, *etc.*
2. Social commitment through social feeds, rewards, recognition, reactions, comments, *etc.*
3. Employee learning process through LMS, training courses, on boarding, *etc.*

Employees in a digital workplace use various digital technologies like instant messaging, business social media, video communication, knowledge sharing, automated processes, and more to do their task. Communication tools of the past didn't always accommodate the organizational need for immediate and real-time contact. Modern connectivity tools have not only allowed for the diffusion of information and discussion faster than ever, but they have also enabled organizational agility. Before the innovative services and products emerging from digital transformation, organizational tools and capabilities have always been limited and inefficient. The introduction of automated platforms and computation has radicalized and reinvented time-consuming processes within every major sector (Brunetti et. al, 2020). In addition, modern digital tools all have the potential to improve process efficiency. In addition to facilitating the faster-than-ever spread of knowledge and debate, modern connection tools have also made organizational agility possible. Modern digital tools enable organizations to function, interact, and communicate instantly, with no communication barrier restricting the speed at which progress may be done. Accounting, financial, and monetary software are further advantages of digital tools and resources; these technologies have made it simpler and more secure to allocate, distribute, and transfer money. Being digitally resilient is a process that takes constant work and adjustment. You may handle the challenges of an increasingly online world with poise and confidence by developing your cyber security awareness, managing your digital well-being, setting boundaries, and mastering digital literacy. Using technology to improve rather than diminish our lives is the aim, not running away from it. Being proactive in your interactions with technology is a key component of adopting digital resilience. Instead of allowing you to get carried away by the digital wave, it's about making deliberate decisions that are in line with your objectives and beliefs. By using this approach, you may protect your physical and emotional well-being while still maximizing the opportunities presented by the digital world.

Background

In the wake of the Covid-19 outbreak, digital resilience became a new and important notion in society. The capacity of our society to employ digital technology to avert and respond to crises such as pandemics, natural catastrophes, cyber attacks, and hybrid warfare while maintaining our financial and security assets is known as digital resilience. The public and private IT sectors must work closely together in order for digital resilience to succeed. Although the latter controls the institutional decision-making process for the greater good, the majority of modern technological innovation and the digital infrastructure needed to quickly confront and recover from any significant disruption are mostly the property of the private sector. Businesses are seeing growth and possibilities never seen before in the era of digital transformation. Similar to the Renaissance in history, the Digital Renaissance of today is based on a number of fundamental ideas that serve as the cornerstone of contemporary corporate strategy:

1. **Originality**: The foundation of any transformation is creativity. Businesses are reinventing their brand presentation, audience engagement, and product or service delivery in the Digital Renaissance. Simply being online is no longer sufficient for businesses; they also need to differentiate themselves from the competition by producing unique and captivating experiences.
2. **Technology**: Although technology facilitates change, it should never be employed only to be new. Technology's strength is in its capacity to increase productivity, optimize workflows, and spread a company's message. In the Digital Renaissance, companies utilize technology to improve their strategy rather than as a crutch. Examples of this include data-driven insights, immersive virtual experiences, and AI-driven customer service.
3. **Design**: Strategy and execution combine in design. Functionality, user experience, identity, and telling a brand's narrative are all important aspects of successful design in the Digital Age. By fusing the traditional rules of visual harmony with the requirements of the modern, digital-first world, it bridges the gap between the old and the new.

4. **Approach:** Businesses who understand the need for timeless tactics are the ones that are prospering in the Digital Renaissance. The fundamentals of business knowing your audience, providing value, and adhering to your mission remain constant even while tools and strategies may change. Technology utilization is guided by strategy, which also makes sure that companies don't prioritize short-term trends above long-term goals.

The digital world has leveled the playing field for everyone, from start-ups to large multinational organizations, by providing access to larger audiences and cutting-edge technologies that simplify operations. But these developments also bring with them new difficulties. Because of the instability brought forth by cyber attacks, technical upheavals, and quick changes in customer behavior, having a digital presence alone is no longer sufficient. Resilience is required. As the digital era progresses, firms' capacity to adjust, bounce back, and prosper in the face of these obstacles becomes critical. In addition to receiving training to carry out their jobs, staff members are also prepared (Hamka et. al, 2022) to handle any digital disturbances, such as serious cyber attacks or software bugs. Having well defined procedures that can adjust to changing circumstances is what is meant by digital resilience.

1. **Foundation of Digital Resistance Concept:** Fundamentally, digital resilience refers to an organization's capacity to uphold its integrity and primary goals in the face of digital disruptions. It's about making sure the company can survive and even prosper in the face of difficulties by being flexible, nimble, and ready for any digital hardship. Though it's unquestionably an important part, technological safeguards against cyber attacks aren't the only aspect of digital resilience. Digital resilience encompasses several approaches:
    a) **Organization Culture:** A company that is resilient develops a culture of continuous learning and flexibility. In addition to receiving training to carry out their work, staffs members are also prepared to handle any digital disturbances, such as a serious cyber attack or software bug.
    b) **Methods and Techniques:** Having well-defined processes that can adjust to changing circumstances is what digital resilience is all about. It is about contingency plans, safety nets, and other strategies that are ready for action in case Plan A fails.
    c) **Technology:** Having appropriate technological tools and solutions is important, even though digital resilience is not just about technology. It includes not only cyber security measures, but also operational resilience and adaptability systems.

d) **Stakeholder Involvement:** A resilient company recognizes the importance of all its partners, consumers, and employees. Digital resilience is based on interacting with people, learning about their wishes and concerns, and ensuring that there is clear communication in times of crisis.

2. **The Adapting Digital Environment:** The digital world changes every day over time, and the platforms, tools, and technologies used contribute to significant developments and trends in the digital sphere:

   a) **New Technologies Emerge:** New technologies emerge every year and change the way firms run. These technological advancements, which range from augmented reality to quantum computing, provide both benefits and difficulties. Digital resilience is demonstrated by keeping up with changes and incorporating new technologies while maintaining functionality and security.

   b) **An Increase in Cyber Threats:** The frequency and complexity of cyber attacks have increased dramatically. Businesses are increasingly susceptible as they grow more digitally linked. There are several hazards that firms have to deal with, some of which include ransom ware attacks, data breaches, *etc.*

   c) **Dispersed Workforce:** The trend of remote work has intensified due to recent world events. Although this gives flexibility, it also presents issues with operational continuity, data security, and teamwork. It's critical to adjust to this new standard while maintaining efficiency.

   d) **Consumer Expectations and Behavior:** The modern customer is technologically aware and demands flawless internet interactions. Trust can be lost as a result of any error, omission, or violation. Companies need to make sure that their digital products constantly live up to these high expectations (He et. al, 2023).

   e) **Modifications to Regulation and Compliance:** Regulations pertaining to cyber security, data protection, and digital operations are getting stricter as the globe gets more linked. Static methods and stiff infrastructures are surefire ways to become obsolete in this ever changing market. Understanding these changes, foreseeing possible obstacles, and building a resilient infrastructure and culture are essential to success. Digital resilience is the ability to use these developments to your advantage in order to grow and succeed going forward (Ko et. al, 2022).

3. **Digital Resilience in Action Mode:** When digital resilience is considered from the perspective of practical applications, theoretical ideas become much more tangible. We can understand how important resilience is for modern operations by looking at examples of firms that have had to deal directly with digital disruptions.

a) **Quick Reaction of a Major Retailer to a Data Breach:** A major data breach that affected millions of consumers at a well-known international business might have been disastrous. However, the business was able to quickly notify the parties affected, contain the breach, and win back customer trust because of their strong incident response plan and open communication approach. The incident turned into a case study on the value of cyber security as well as the necessity of having a strong strategy in place for dealing with future cyber crises.

b) **Overcoming Infrastructure Failure with Streaming Services:** When a major streaming service's primary server failed amid a well-publicized event, serious difficulties resulted. However, by utilizing a blend of cloud-based backups, agile technical teams, and flexible resource distribution, they were able to promptly restore services, guaranteeing little disturbance for their extensive user community.

c) **Changes in Manufacturing Firms During the Pandemic:** After the COVID-19 epidemic disrupted global supply chains, a top manufacturing company demonstrated digital resilience by quickly shifting their business model. While many of their rivals suffered, they successfully adjusted their production lines, kept staff members informed and motivated, and met changing client expectations by utilizing digital twin technology and remote collaboration tools.

4. **The Advantages of Digital Resilience for Companies**: Businesses that embrace and exemplify digital resilience stand out not just as survivors but also as leaders in their respective sectors in an era where change is the only constant. Let's examine more closely at the particular benefits that a resilient attitude provides:

a) **Gaining a Competitive Edge in a Changing Market:** The capacity to swiftly adjust and react to disruptions might be the differentiator that sets industry leaders apart in the high-stakes game of modern business. Businesses that put a high priority on digital resilience are better able to handle unforeseen obstacles, whether they come from market dynamics, global events, or technical faults. These businesses' adaptability not only guarantees business continuity but also gives them an advantage over rivals who could be facing similar difficulties.

b) **Increased Client Loyalty and Trust:** Customers of today are fully aware of the numerous risks and interruptions that companies must deal with. A corporation conveys a strong message of dependability and dedication when it shows that it can handle and overcome these obstacles with ease. Customers see that the company is ready to produce regularly, even under difficult circumstances, and this builds strong confidence. Customers become brand ambassadors as a result of this trust, which eventually (Liu et.al, 2024) converts into steadfast devotion.

c) **Long-Term Cost Savings and Increased Efficiency:** Whether it's in technology, training, or strategy, investing in digital resilience may have some upfront costs, but the long-term benefits are significant. During interruptions, a robust structure minimizes downtime and related revenue losses. Additionally, businesses can increase operational efficiency by rationalizing procedures and incorporating redundancies. The cumulative savings from preventing possible emergencies and improving operational effectiveness over time can greatly increase a business's profitability. To put it simply, there are a lot of advantages to digital resilience. They have an impact on an organization's many levels, from its brand image to its financial stability. Resilience is not just a benefit in a dynamic and linked digital world, but it is also a prerequisite for long-term success and growth.

5. **Constructing a Digitally Robust Enterprise:** Resilience becomes an essential attribute that firms must have in the face of a quickly changing digital ecosystem. Understanding the business's core is a critical first step in developing digital resilience. Resilience is a comprehensive business strategy that goes beyond a technical activity when it is understood in the context of business operations, goals, and needs from the digital capabilities.

a) **Focus on the Business Core**: Gain a deeper grasp of your company's goals, values, and digital requirements before implementing any new technology or procedures. Setting resilience measures in order of importance is aided by understanding what is necessary for the company to operate and prosper.

b) **Basic Evaluation:** Examine your present digital infrastructure, procedures, and tactics with a clear grasp of the business requirements. Determine your strengths and weaknesses and make sure that the technology in place is in perfect harmony with the goals of the company.

c) **Invest in Sturdy Infrastructure and Technology:** Adapt your technology infrastructure to the particular requirements and subtleties of your company. This entails implementing dependable cloud backups, redundant systems, safe communication channels, and adaptable software that not only mitigates risks but also fosters company expansion.

d) **Establish a Culture of Lifelong Learning:** Even while technology is essential, the real change is made by the people who create it. Encourage a culture where understanding the always changing demands of the business is intertwined with remaining up to speed with the newest developments in digital trends.

e) **Take a Proactive Approach to Risk Management:** Change the perspective to one of proactive risk management rather than just reactive risk management. Keep an eye out for any dangers on a regular basis, considering the specific effects they might have on your company's operations.
f) **Make Sure You Are Adaptable and Flexible:** In the dynamic realm of digitalization, companies need to be adaptable. This might entail changing business models, implementing new technology, or adjusting tactics while maintaining constant attention to the primary goals and requirements of the company.
g) **Involvement and Education of Stakeholders:** Encourage comprehension of and support for digital resilience among all relevant parties. They may better understand potential effects of digital disruptions on the company and how to react by receiving regular training.
h) **Continue to Engage with the Ecosystem:** Businesses may learn about new dangers and best practices by interacting with groups and peers in the industry. They should constantly keep an eye out for how these developments can be implemented in their own particular company environment. To sum up, digital resilience is a potent combination of strategy, technology, and culture that is based on a thorough understanding of the needs and essence of a firm. It gives organizations the ability to not only survive digital upheavals but also to grow and adjust to new circumstances (Anderson et. al, 2013).

6. **The Human Aspect Of Digital Hardiness:** Despite being fundamentally technological, the field of digital resilience is highly human-centered. Even while a robust system can withstand a cyber attack, the system's resilience is ultimately shaped by the individuals who operate within it their actions, mentality, and training, for example. Let's explore in more detail how important human interaction is to building a technologically resilient company.
   a) **The Function of Leadership in Promoting Resilience:** The culture of a company is shaped by its leadership, and this is particularly true when it comes to digital resilience. It is imperative that leaders stress its significance, allot the required funds, and advance the idea of a resilient company. They are in charge of establishing an atmosphere in which resilience is viewed as a business necessity rather than merely a technological fix. Their proactive participation shows dedication and motivates everyone in the organization to do the same.
   b) **The First Line of Defense is Training**: The ever-changing digital environment demands ongoing education. Workers at all levels should be able to identify such dangers, report them, and take appropriate action. Staff may

be kept one step ahead of issues via regular training sessions, workshops, and drills.

c) **Engagement and Ownership of Workers**: Beyond required training, encouraging a sense of responsibility among staff members may have a big impact. Individuals are more likely to be watchful, proactive, and involved when they understand how important it is for them to maintain the organization's digital resilience. Further strengthening defenses can be achieved by having open lines of communication where staff members can report weaknesses or provide enhancement suggestions.

d) **Developing a Mentality of Resilience**: Resilience is essentially a state of mind. It's important to be prepared for obstacles and understand that failures are inevitable on any trip. Promote an environment in which errors are viewed as teaching moments. A culture that prioritizes flexibility, ongoing development, and group accountability may greatly increase an organization's resilience.

e) **Increasing Decision-Making Capability at Several Levels:** While centralized resilience techniques are necessary, it may be extremely beneficial to provide workers at different levels the ability to make wise decisions when things go tough. Decentralized decision-making may result in quicker, more effective responses to risks when it is supported by training and a clear grasp of the company's digital objectives.

f) **The Power of Teamwork**: The pursuit of digital resilience is not isolated. Through fostering teamwork, information sharing, and brainstorming sessions, companies may access collective expertise. Digital defenses may be greatly strengthened by a unified front in which departments cooperate with one another, acknowledging and respecting one another's functions. Essentially, the human factor is what gives digital resilience life even as technologies, protocols, and systems serve as its skeleton. When people are knowledgeable, involved, and empowered, companies can move confidently and nimbly through the complex digital maze. Those who are willing to change and adapt will, in the end, be the ones shaping the future.

LITERATURE REVIEW

Recent reviews have emphasized the significance of work-design elements and job roles in digitalizing workplaces (Chen et. al, 2022). In the midst of technological transition discovered a connection between people's views of job security and well-being. However, environmental and personal factors including formal training, the nature of the work department, professional categories, and the kind of technology employed all had an impact on how dangerous people felt about their job security. There is a dearth of research on attitudes around digital transformation. However, Chen (2022) discovered that higher support for digital transformation was associated with employees' expectations of autonomy, competence, and connection in the digital workplace. This was observed in research of work design features.

The goal of the paper to identify various stages of digital transformation, along with essential strategies and prerequisites to support transformation (Barnosky et al., 2016), and to integrate studies on digital transformation from various disciplines, contexts, and research streams (Chaiyakun et al, 2024). While some have concentrated on human resource factors, such as the role of Human resource development professionals in facilitating skills development due to technological change, others have focused on digital work design and leadership. Research on technology adoption in the workplace has shown that factors such as technology's nature such as whether it's required or optional matters (Hamka et al, 2022). Subjective standards are more noticeable under required systems, as shown by the groundbreaking research of Tim and Leidner (2023). Adoption intentions and subsequent technology use in voluntary contexts are influenced by subjective norms and opinions about the technology. Though adoption of technology happens in required contexts regardless, these views will influence attitudes toward technology and might have more significant effects on the business as a whole. More specifically, adoption rates rise when staff members believe the technology will improve their performance, be helpful in their job, and be simple to understand and use. Notably, there is a proven correlation between user happiness and IT adoption in the workplace as well, which is consistent with research done in other contexts on the perceived utility and usability of technology (Raimo et al, 2022). These results suggest that, whether or not they are required, new technologies and systems should ideally be practical and simple for the workforce to use.

The alignment of technology with activities performed by employees is another important factor to consider, as it affects their attitudes and adoption of new technology (Anderson et al, 2013). Barnosky et al. (2016) discovered that employees were more likely to use and keep learning after adopting new enterprise system software if they anticipated it would improve their performance at work and lead to better job opportunities or job security. Furthermore, adopters' favorable perceptions of the system were positively impacted by their perceptions of organizational support, whereas non-adopters (Hooi et al, 2023) utilization of the system decreased. Put differently, companies need to be cautious while implementing new technology to ensure that they gain the support of adopters while avoiding alienating non-adopters. According to Tim (2020) discovered in a research of blue collar workers that increased adoption of technology was influenced by organizational and personal resources, such as information and training opportunities and resilience. The findings highlight the need of giving all staff members access to information and training programs to support the digital transition without detracting from their level of enthusiasm (Cichosz et al., 2020).

New technologies are being introduced in today's environment of digital transformation in even shorter cycles, frequently concurrently. This calls for a reevaluation of the adoption of technology. An individual's comfort level with change and inventiveness, as well as other supportive workplace and technological conditions (Ekman et al, 2020). New technologies are being introduced into the workplace more and more, and their effective acceptance depends on the employees' collective adoption of the collaborative and social networking features (such as virtual discussion rooms, forums, and chat services). Peer social networks, such as coworkers and management, have the power to shape attitudes about innovations and, eventually, their uptake, as demonstrated by Kumar et al, 2023. These studies emphasize how crucial it is to establish constructive social norms surrounding technology use in order to promote technology adoption, as well as how difficult this may be. Research on employees' attitudes and views of technology change and digital disruption in general is expanding, in addition to studies on technology adoption. (Fischer et al., 2020) this is an important consideration since opinions about specific technologies can be influenced by opinions about more general technological changes in society and how they affect employment. Within the industrial and automotive industries, which were among the first to automate, employee views and attitudes regarding technological change are still being investigated (Isensee et. al, 2023).

However, a wide range of industries, including health care (Kraft et. al, 2022) wholesale and service sectors, banking and financial services, and education are being disrupted by recent advances in new technologies like artificial intelligence (AI), robotics, and cloud computing. Higher perceptions of job insecurity brought on by new technologies are generally linked to higher levels of cynicism, depression, and intentions to leave an organization negatively and to higher levels of career satisfaction and organizational commitment positively (Kruyen et. al, 2020). These results, however, vary depending on organizational contexts, employment positions, and other contextual elements including age, gender, and type of technology. Crucially, research has indicated that workers who participated in decision-making on the technological modifications responded more favorably to those changes than did those with lesser degrees of involvement (Li et al., 2020). According to Massaro (2022) the paper investigates the use of workplace digitalization as a mediator to study employee engagement. An integrated paradigm has been established in the context of workplace digitalization that introduces transformational leadership and creative culture as antecedents of employee engagement. And it is found that workplace digitalization has direct and indirect effects on employee engagement due to transformational leadership and innovative cultures and it also confirms the idea that workplace digitalization has a beneficial effect on employee engagement. Employee engagement is directly affected by innovative culture and to some extent indirectly through workplace digitalization. In the service industry shows that workers are typically driven to embrace new technology, such self-service technologies. Employees felt that self-service technologies increased their scope of work (hours, increased sales/clients, and client satisfaction), improved the quality of their work (more satisfying, enhanced, and faster transactions), and increased their productivity at work, according to a qualitative study by discovered, however, that the kind of employment and the type of automation influence views about self-service technology. A few centuries later, governments and organizations are being urged to take immediate action due to global concerns brought about by socioeconomic, environmental, and health related issues. To meet the immense difficulties they confront, businesses and ecosystems must reconsider and rebuild their competitiveness (Rausch et al, 2023). A "new renaissance" of the European system must make use of digital technology to augment human ability and organizational capacities and to create a synergistic "Human plus Machine" interaction, notwithstanding the Renaissance's emphasis on the grandeur of human potential (Murawski et al, 2017). Research on the relationship between digital technology and human capacities to revitalize ecosystems and organizations' competitiveness is currently lacking. The relationship between technological innovation and environmental sustainability is given particular attention in such a situation (Sousa-Zomer et. al, 2020) doing business through the sustainability lens empowered by digitalization will enable companies to create value for the business, society, and planet. According to Tim (2023) the purpose of this study was to examine and evaluate the theoretical link between organizational resilience (OR) and digital transformation, as well as the effects of organizational resilience on individuals and organizations during times of turbulence. The findings suggest that during uncertain times, such as the coronavirus disease 2019, service organizations had strong, adaptive effects in their responses and that it helps firms maintain systematic control and sustain operations in crises. Intensive change management gives a company a transformational vision. According to Tim (2020) the focus was on the need for critical knowledge of digital resilience in the context of small and medium-sized firms and family businesses. The findings show that depending on the digital maturity of the family business, young entrepreneurs have undergone digital transformations involving production, logistics, sales and human resource management. In the context of the family businesses under observation, this has provided various benefits in terms of competitiveness, decision-making effectiveness, visibility and communication, and new opportunities for value creation. According to Gull (2024) through the fundamental process of digital transformation, the influence of adaptive culture on organizational resilience was investigated. The results indicate a strong positive correlation between the components of the research. Digital transformation acted as a partial mediating factor in the relationship between organizational resilience and adaptive culture. The results provide important perspectives for scholars, politicians, and higher education institutions in building resilient cultures to achieve organizational resilience, primarily through digital transformation.

The Importance of Digital Transformation in the Workplace

The process of utilizing technology to alter a company's operations is known as digital transformation. It may significantly affect the workplace in a number of ways, such as:

1. **Enhanced Productivity:** Tasks may be made more efficient and less stressful with the aid of digital transformation.
2. **Better Customer Experience:** Companies may offer more individualized and effective services by implementing digital transformation.
3. **Increased Employee Engagement:** A more engaged workforce may be achieved through digital transformation.
4. **Improved Teamwork:** Digital transformation may facilitate more precise and effortless teamwork.
5. **Enhanced Agility:** Businesses can react swiftly to changes in the internal and external environment by implementing digital transformation.
6. **Better Brand Reputation:** Organizations may enhance their brand's reputation by implementing digital transformation.
7. **Cost Reduction:** Businesses may save expenses like store leases and the requirement for physical assets by implementing digital transformation.
8. **Generate Revenue:** By helping organizations make their daily chores more efficient, digital transformation may result in higher revenue.

How Digital Resilience Works

Digital resilience in the next ten years with a new era of technological development rapidly approaching, the complexity of the digital world is only expected to increase. In view of the growing interconnectedness, the advent of new technologies and the rapid rate of innovation, a proactive approach to digital resilience are imperative for the future. Digital resilience is essentially a comprehensive strategy for handling the digital environment. It's about anticipating difficulties and being prepared, but it's also about reacting quickly and efficiently to unexpected setbacks. As the digital landscape advances, resilience is no longer just a desirable trait, but a vital one for businesses (Rausch et al, 2023). In today's time, every person, whether an employee or a successful businessman wants to achieve success and according to the demand of time, in the digital age, everyone prefers to work in a digital environment. In many organizations, developing a digital environment is difficult but not impossible (Anderson et al, 2013). To transform a chaotic situation into a well-organized and efficient digital workplace, gradual steps must be taken, starting immediately. A resilient infrastructure uses decentralized and open-source tools to give organizations ownership and control over data. A resilient infrastructure is one that provides resources that can be used in a variety of circumstances, by personnel with different degrees of experience, and with limited Internet connections. The infrastructure itself will not be robust if a culture that supports privacy does not exist in both institutional and personnel behavior. Companies that use open-source software and other tools that reflect their principles are the first to adopt this culture. Some participants mentioned that switching to open-source technologies was not as easy as clicking a button. Employees should be periodically reminded of the reasons behind this change; this can be done through ongoing awareness campaigns, feedback gathering, and iterative training. Documenting cyber attacks and disseminating countermeasures should be part of this ongoing internal knowledge-sharing process with employees. This is especially important for companies supporting digital forensics. Building a good infrastructure requires policies and institutional behavior. The aim of these rules is to ensure that no mishaps occur but they also plan for the worst so that they can respond to digital threats more effectively. Members discussed the creation of disaster recovery plans, security frameworks, standards, and guidelines for the idea that sensitive data should be collected and stored with as little data loss as possible. Below we have discussed some more steps that can help anyone start the digital renaissance of work within your organization.

1. **Get familiar with the concept of the digital workplace:** The phrase “digital workplace” is becoming increasingly popular among businesses. It resonates with audiences in both IT and business, and it shifts the focus away from specific technologies like intranets. Does your organization understand the term? Is there interest in discussing the digital workplace? If yes, why not start a digital workplace community using your collaboration platform? You can start with some great concepts and materials to begin a conversation about the digital workplace using the most effective methods for your company. Making your digital workplace future-ready requires a significant shift, which is not an easy task. The first step to starting a discussion about the digital workplace is to get people talking about it, and this article explains how to do that. The digital workplace has evolved haphazardly for many firms, creating an environment that is hard to use and lacks cohesion. We need to take small steps toward the goal of creating a unified, productive digital workplace from this chaotic state.

Get started right away. Then how do you implement the digital renaissance of work in your company? It seems as though a business can reap benefits from using specific technologies like intranets.

2. **Identify the need for a digital workplace**: Every company has an online workplace because of how the company feels about the digital workplace now, given the competition. You can identify areas of strength and weakness in the digital workplace today and pinpoint opportunities for progress by first assessing your maturity and then using an in-depth benchmark. Additionally, you can measure the success of the business by measuring how much progress the business has made due to digital. Every company has an online workplace. How does your company feel about the digital workplace now? If it's like many organizations, it may be experiencing disorganization, annoyance, and reduced productivity. You can identify opportunities for growth and identify areas of strength and weakness in your current digital workplace by first assessing your maturity and then using an in-depth benchmark. Additionally, this will provide an important level set that you can use to measure your success as you implement your digital workplace program.
3. **Clearly communicate company goals for the digital workplace to employees:** Create goals for digital impact and connect features and functionality to your organization's strategic objectives, and discuss strategic alignment with respect to the intranet and initiatives for the digital workplace. Also, instead of assuming that everyone will get (Rausch et al, 2023) it explain the idea in a unique way. The digital workplace can improve employee working conditions. You need to know about how the digital workplace will benefit your company. Create goals for impact and connect features and functionality to your organization's strategic objectives before obsessing over them.
4. **Prioritize people in the digital workplace**: While the digital workplace is crucial to achieving company goals, it's also important to keep employees informed about the actual ways they work. The recent rise of digital workplace initiatives also ensures that this starts with making employees' daily tasks easier and more efficient. Get out there and learn what problems individuals face and what can help. And keep in mind that, as a researcher, you need to have a broad perspective to see how individuals approach their work - reality can be very different from expectations. See for yourself, and keep an eye out for workarounds created by individuals to avoid technical limitations or these can have a serious negative impact on your company's profits and employee engagement. Although your vision for the digital workplace is aligned with strategic goals, what about the actual ways people work? Digital workplace initiatives will grow tremendously, but we need to make sure it starts with making daily tasks easier and more efficient for individuals.

5. **Equal involvement of employees:** If you want to truly implement the digital renaissance in your company, you need to have a good relationship between stakeholders i.e. your company's employees and management to support this vision. Senior managers should keep informing employees about digital workplace services in a timely manner and employees should also keep asking without any hesitation. If you want to truly implement the digital renaissance Tim, Yenni (2020) in your company, you will need a wide range of stakeholders to support the vision. Lead with a senior sponsor who you think will encourage action.

Figure 2. What do we mean when talk workplace (https://www.linkedin.com/pulse/what-do-we-mean-when-talk-workplace-digitalliteracy-elizabeth-marsh)

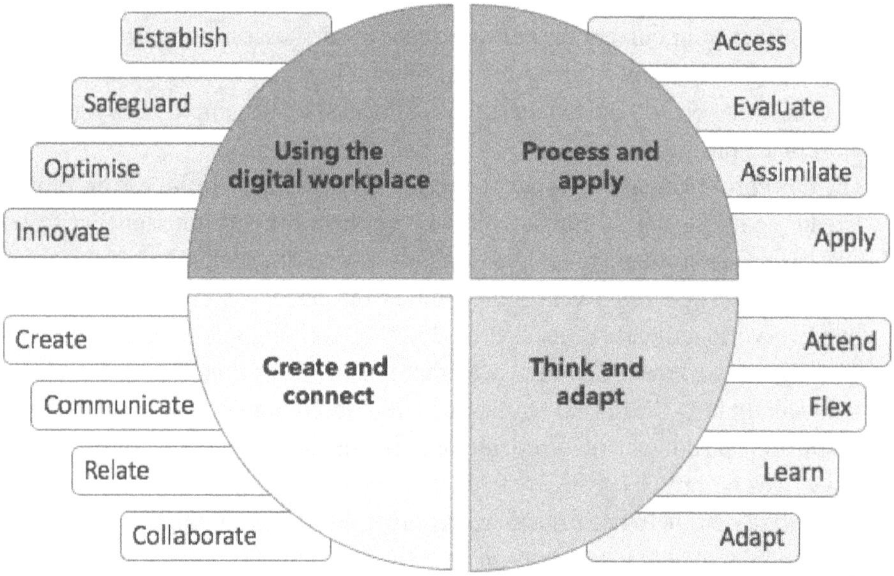

CHALLENGES FACE BY ORGANIZATION DUE TO DIGITAL RESILIENCE

When our digital goods and services break down or are not accessible to those who need them, unintended consequences arise. How to implement digital resilience within a company and what difficulties are faced.

a. **Source:** Companies can face difficulties if they lack the money, infrastructure, technology and other resources needed to transform sustainably in the digital age.
b. **Capacity:** When management and organized teams in a company are overworked and do not have enough manpower to implement effective processes, it will be difficult to maintain this change over time.
c. **Knowledge:** In a constantly changing technological world, it is difficult for teams to stay up to date with frequently changing with best practices. These difficulties manifest in their organizations in many ways. They may be unable to handle their website, communications or marketing on a day-to-day basis. Meanwhile, in the long term, there are more issues associated with it:
d. **Security Risks:** Outdated digital goods and services increase the risk of security lapses, such as website hacks, which compromise sensitive stakeholder data.
e. **Information Access:** Teams that struggle to maintain their digital goods or services do not place much value on user experience, accessibility, uptime, or other tactics that provide quick access to critical data.
f. **Technical Debt:** As a product accumulates technical debt, it becomes less responsive and unpredictable, making it harder for consumers to complete tasks. **Tim, Yenni (2020)** when major business processes are disrupted digitally resilient firms can withstand the changes and even prosper. These kinds of companies are able to foresee future difficulties and seize the chance to advance. When a company considers long-term digital resilience, it can better manage growth objectives and security requirements in an environment prone to disruptions. Furthermore, digital resilience enables companies to:
    - Adjust to shifting market conditions and a dynamic competitive environment.
    - Apply data and digital governance practices throughout the whole organization to respond to disturbances.
    - Boost capacity for innovation.
    - Quickly adapt to changing customer needs.

The following are the steps enterprises must take to enhance and strengthen digital resilience:

- Digital resilience is also an ongoing effort. To enhance and strengthen digital resilience enterprises must take into account key decision-makers, particularly: recognize the difference between cyber and digital resilience.
- Assess the extent to which the company relies on digital technologies.
- Recognize the range of threats and possibilities that exist in the digital world.

Furthermore, resilience should be considered an organizational-wide issue rather than a subset of IT or cyber security specific problems. To enhance resilience across the organization, the board must evaluate risks and the company's ability to innovate. The organization's executive team should be able to periodically review its risk management initiatives and assess whether the current state of digital resilience is still appropriate given the broader risk environment. They must ensure that the business has the capability to identify and address threats in the digital realm. In fact, this requires assessing the organization's digital infrastructure and determining how it impacts the resilience of the business as a whole. The business operations of a company increasingly include new digital breakthroughs and technology. The challenges of modern digital technologies are used to enhance and facilitate corporate operations while boosting productivity and effectiveness. A company's digital transformation is permeating every aspect of its operations and growing quickly in the market. The emergence of new digital technologies has led to the development of new business models that improve market positioning and offer new company directions, methodologies, and strategies.

Challenges Faced by Organizations in Implementing Digital Strategies

When putting digital strategy into practice, organizations encounter several obstacles, such as:

1. **Resistance to Change:** Workers who are accustomed to their present routines or who fear losing their jobs or becoming incompetent may oppose change.
2. **Absence of Strategy:** Digital projects may fall short of their objectives in the absence of a defined vision and plan.
3. **Insufficient Experience:** Insufficient experience in spearheading digital projects might impede advancement.
4. **Absence of Governance:** In the absence of governance, it may be challenging to keep processes under control, which may result in time and resource waste.
5. **Lack of Technological Resources:** Companies may experience issues with the IT hardware and equipment supply chain or shortages of microchips.
6. **Poor Customer Data Utilization:** Data is essential to digital transformation and may be used to map a client's relationship with a company.
7. **Budgetary Restrictions:** When putting digital initiatives into practice, businesses may run across financial restrictions.
8. **Organizational Structure Changes:** Organizational structure changes may present difficulties for businesses.

ETHICAL ISSUES IN ARTIFICIAL INTELLIGENCE IMPLICATIONS

Every company is becoming more productive with the help of artificial intelligence. This is increasing output along with saving money. Making AI ethics a top priority can help ensure that your company maintains its excellent position in terms of operations, regulation, and reputation. Below we describe the ethical concerns related to AI:

1. **Job Loss:** One issue commonly raised in conversations about AI is job displacement. There is concern that automation may replace some or all job functions, leading to an increase in unemployment rates in some industries. Employees are either extremely or moderately concerned about the effects of automated technology on the workforce.
2. **Privacy:** AI model training requires huge amounts of data, some of which contains PII. Concerns about who can access your data and how they might use it arise from the lack of information now available about how data is being collected, processed, and kept. The use of AI in surveillance raises additional privacy issues. AI is used by law enforcement to track and monitor the activities of suspects. Although this is extremely helpful, many are concerned that those capabilities could be misused in public settings, violating people's right to privacy.
3. **Bias:** AI bias raises further ethical questions. Even if AI is not intrinsically biased, the system is educated using deep learning and human data, which can cause bias to spread throughout the technology. For example, if the data set used to train the algorithm had bias toward a particular group, an AI hiring tool could exclude certain demographics. If this results in discriminatory behavior, there could potentially be legal repercussions.
4. **Security:** When it comes to AI, security is still of the utmost importance. The effects of inadequate security can be widespread. For example, AI is vulnerable to malicious attacks that can jeopardize results. Documented cases of autonomous car misbehavior and attacks resulting from object hiding in security camera footage have been cited by the Cyber security Infrastructure and Security Agency (CISA). More security measures are being demanded by experts and government organizations to limit any potentially harmful repercussions.
5. **Interpretability:** It is not enough to simply deploy AI techniques and watch them work. With certain AI applications, understanding the decision-making process can be very important. Sometimes it can be challenging to understand the reasoning behind the conclusions drawn by specific AI systems. This can have significant consequences, especially in areas such as law enforcement or

healthcare where real human lives are at stake and influencing factors must be taken into account.

6. **Responsibility:** We use AI tools on a regular basis to make decisions as AI is becoming more and more prevalent across all industries. When those choices result in adverse outcomes, assigning blame for the results can be challenging. Are businesses responsible for verifying the algorithms in the tools they purchase? Or do you turn to the person who developed the AI tool? Holding individuals and businesses accountable can be challenging as the search for accountability can be a complex maze.
7. **Deepfakes:** The use of deepfakes raises ethical questions. Voice and facial recognition can now be evaded by deepfakes, allowing them to bypass security protections. According to one study, easily created deepfakes were used to fool Microsoft APIs more than 75% of the time. Additional ethical issues arise when it comes to impersonation. The use of deepfakes to influence public opinion in political contests could have widespread implications. If a CEO is found to be making decisions or acting in a way that is considered questionable, there is also concern that deepfakes could be used to manipulate the stock market. Misuse of deepfakes poses a serious security risk as there are no controls in place and the software is easily accessible.
8. **Misinformation:** Harmful to companies and others, misinformation has the potential to increase social divisions and spread false beliefs. Misinformation can affect public perception and seriously damage someone's reputation, a problem that has come under greater scrutiny in the wake of recent political upheaval. Once misinformation is widely spread on social media, it is difficult to trace its source.
9. **Misuse of Intellectual Property:** The problem of AI exploitation of intellectual property is highlighted in a recent lawsuit filed against ChatGPT. Favorite authors Jodi Picoult and John Grisham were among those who recently sued OpenAI for copyright infringement, because the company used their work to train its algorithms. The lawsuit also claims that such exploitation will jeopardize the ability of authors to earn a living from their writing. Intellectual property owners are concerned about how AI will continue to affect their livelihoods as a result of such exploitation.
10. **Loss of Social Connection:** There is concern that artificial intelligence (AI) may result in a lack of social connection, empathy towards others, and general well-being, even though it has the potential to provide hyper-personalized experiences by tailoring search engine content to your preferences and improving customer service through chat bots. If you only see viewpoints that support your own ideas on social media, you won't be able to develop a mindset that enables you to empathize with others and take action for social good.

11. **Trade-Off Between Competition and Ethics:** Since there is never-ending competition for growth, new technologies present a unique challenge for businesses, both startups and large giants. Success is often based on a company's ability to deploy a specific technology or application first. When it comes to AI systems, businesses often don't make an effort to ensure that their technology is built ethically or has robust safety features.

ASPECTS OF A SUCCESSFUL DIGITAL RENAISSANCE AT WORKPLACE

Every change begins with a step forward, so that every company and individual focused on the digital customer experience is usually making immediate efforts to learn, try new things, and overcome obstacles to customer retention. The extent to which markets are changing is allowing innovation, leading to the normalization of new goods, services, and business practices. Digital technology and collaboration tools are being integrated to create the digital workplace, which is revolutionizing modern business. Improved productivity and cooperation are two advantages of its adoption, particularly when considering the trends of remote work. This change is being fueled by the demand for operational agility as well as cutting-edge technology like artificial intelligence and cloud computing. Notwithstanding its benefits, issues including employee resistance and cyber security dangers require consideration. Looking ahead, more innovation with augmented reality and advanced analytics is necessary for the digital workplace of the future. In conclusion, it is an essential component of contemporary corporate strategy, improving connectedness and efficiency while necessitating strategic adjustment to labor demands. Below we discussed the lead factors to successful of digital renaissance at workplace:

1. **Orientation:** Every company must adopt a new approach to promote significant change as time goes by. The main motive of every internal process and operation in the company should be to give priority to the needs, wants and preferences of the customers.
2. **People:** Identify the beliefs, expectations and habits of the customers if you want to succeed. To align the entire company with digital goals and plans, there must be buy-in for digital transformation at all levels, including leadership and employees.
3. **Processes:** Evaluate the process infrastructure in use and keep updating techniques, processes and guidelines to accommodate modifications. Establish collaborative and good relationships with employees and customers.

4. **Goals:** Set the goal of digital transformation and bring shareholders and other stakeholders together behind the new plan and vision. Set objectives for your digital transformation. Specifically, what areas do you want to do better with digital? What kind of results do you want? You can ensure you have achieved your goals for digital transformation by setting measurable Key Performance Indicators (KPIs).
5. **Organization:** Create a dedicated employee focused on the digital experience, with clearly defined roles, duties, goals, and responsibilities. To maintain focus, make sure everyone on the team is aware of the goals and processes.
6. **Understanding and goals:** Gather information and use it to create a plan that will guide the advancement of digital technology. Whatever the customer journey, data can help you optimize it regardless of their engagement with your company. Data can also help you assess the results of your digital transformation, including increased revenue and brand relevance.
7. **Technology:** Reevaluate front and back-end systems for seamless, natural, and integrated customer and ultimately employee experiences. Use technology to meet ever-increasing consumer demands and boost reliability. Make sure your communications and content are platform-proof so that customer experiences are not negatively impacted by algorithm changes.
8. **Implement:** Implement, learn, and adapt to guide continued work on customer experience and digital transformation. Regularly assess your transformation progress so you can adapt as needed.

Strong Pillars of Digital Resilience

Every business has taken considerable interest in digital transformation, which has emerged as a vital avenue for businesses to strengthen organizational resilience. It's also to know how does not examine how an enterprise's digital transformation affects organizational resilience. Fundamentally, digital resilience refers to an organization's capacity to uphold its integrity and primary goals in the face of digital disruptions. It's about making sure the company can survive and even prosper in the face of difficulties by being flexible, nimble, and ready for any digital hardship. Digital transformation increases organizational resilience by strengthening internal controls, facilitating financial constraints, and improving innovative capabilities. Both exploitative and exploratory innovation benefit from it and exploratory innovation benefits organizational resilience. Digital transformation also strengthens a company's security against external threats and improves its ability to quickly adapt to changing external conditions. In terms of resilience, state-owned businesses, manufacturing companies, and businesses in the East often benefit more from digital transformation. In addition, building organizational resilience is influenced by digital maturity characteristics such as change management intensity and strategic technology investments. All things considered, especially in these unpredictable and turbulent times digital transformation is essential for organizations to improve their resilience and achieve sustainable growth.

Digital systems that are resilient were previously primarily linked to cyber security. But given the speed at which innovation is developing and the fact that many businesses are gradually moving to a virtual environment, resilience is no more only an organizational strategy. Risk may arise both physically and online, and since so many assets are becoming digital, new kinds of backup plans are required. Businesses must learn to adapt swiftly to new technology solutions in a constantly changing cyber environment. They also need to learn how to rapidly bounce back and go on in the event that something goes wrong. Therefore, all internal team members at all levels should see digital resilience as a critical long-term asset as it is now an integral component of every modern business. Building and sustaining organizational digital resilience has emerged as a critical task for organizations as they continue to thrive in an uncertain and constantly changing environment. However, what does "resilient" really mean, and how companies can become resilient. The four interrelated pillars of data privacy, compliance, cyber security, and enterprise risk management can be used as a framework for thinking about resilience. When combined, these pillars strengthen organizational resilience, helping businesses recover from small and large-scale setbacks.

Figure 3. Key pillars of digital resilience (Author)

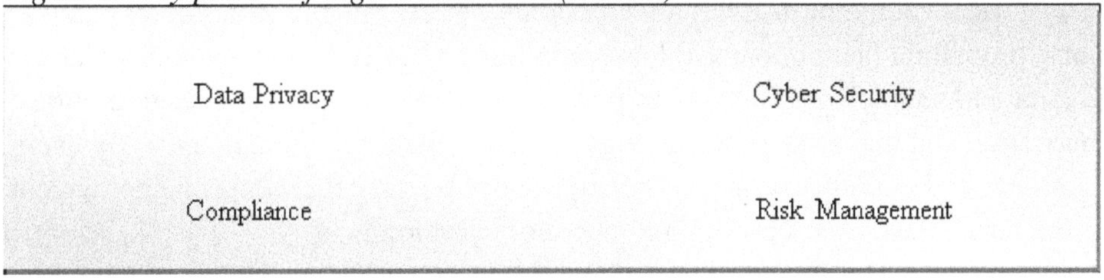

a) **Data Privacy:** Protecting sensitive information is more important than ever in today's data-driven environment. Ensuring the security and privacy of consumer and employee data is of utmost importance.
b) **Compliance:** Compliance means complying with the laws and guidelines that govern your field. Public corporations, healthcare institutions, and other private corporations, *etc.* must follow the government guidelines to avoid costly fines and penalties.

c) **Cyber Security:** In today's digital world, cyber attacks are a constant concern. Protecting your company from these threats, whether they come in the form of phishing scams, ransom ware, or other criminal activity, is the responsibility of cyber security. This includes using multi-factor authentication and strong passwords, performing frequent security audits, and updating hardware and software. Cyber security firms must provide detailed descriptions of their own guiding concepts, processes, and technical concerns. After all, all users want this information so they can choose a security provider that best meets their needs. Customers have a right to know how a cyber security provider works as well as what services it offers. Openness fosters trust. A transparent information policy is a key component of long-term trust. Also, transparency and frequent information sharing contribute to enhanced cyber security.

d) **Risk Management:** Last but not least, enterprise risk management involves detecting and mitigating potential risks in every department of the company. This includes everything from natural disasters and reputational damage to financial risks and supply chain disruptions. Organizations that implement a thorough risk management plan are better equipped to anticipate and deal with unforeseen circumstances.

Digital Renaissance Lead the Company's Growth

The 21st century has seen an accelerated digital renaissance spurred by fast technical innovation. This renaissance is happening over years, not centuries, unlike its historical counterpart. It has a revolutionary effect on companies and organizations, propelling them into unexplored frontiers propelled by exponential advances in data and technology. Businesses now have more options than ever to embrace innovation and make use of technology thanks to the digital renaissance. By using data, artificial intelligence, and automation and redefining the nature of employment in the future, businesses may attain incredible development.

1. **Effective Role of AI in World:** In the digital sphere, Artificial Intelligence (AI) is a major factor that offers both great promise and difficult obstacles. The promise of AI is demonstrated by recent investments in AI firms like Mistral.ai and Inflection.ai, whose applications across a wide range of industries are revolutionizing scientific methods and corporate processes. But the disruptive force of AI necessitates a calculated approach, especially when it comes to the erosion of trust caused by deep fakes and disinformation spread by AI. Organizations need to be well-aware of the promise and drawbacks of artificial intelligence (AI) as we enter a time when disinformation and manipulation might be greatly amplified by AI, quantum computing, and the metaverse.

2. **Leading the Digital Revolution:** Digital transformation is now a must, not a choice. It calls for a comprehensive change in business models, culture, attitude, and procedures in addition to the use of new technologies. Indeed, we live in a digital age, with technology playing a bigger and bigger role in our daily lives. Here are a few explanations for this: Digital change: Businesses in a variety of sectors are adopting digital transformation to enhance operations, expand their clientele, and develop new goods and services.
3. **Digital Transformation:** Organizations in a range of sectors are adopting this strategy to enhance their business processes, expand their clientele, and develop new goods and services. The use of cutting-edge technology like machine learning, artificial intelligence, and the Internet of Things (IoT) is what's driving this transition.
4. **Enhanced Connectivity:** As more and more systems and gadgets are connected to one another via the internet, the globe is getting more and more interconnected. Due to increased connectedness, individuals are able to work and communicate more effectively than in the past and are opening up new possibilities for cooperation, creativity, and communication.
5. **Changing Customer Behavior:** To study goods and services, make purchases, and communicate with companies, consumers are increasingly using digital platforms. Businesses are being forced by this change in consumer behavior to modify their marketing and sales tactics in order to satisfy their tech-savvy clientele.
6. **New Business Models are Emerging:** The sharing economy and the subscription economy are two examples of how new business models are emerging thanks to digital technology. Traditional sectors are being upended by these models, which also open up new doors for development and innovation.
7. **The Expanding Significance of Data:** With its ability to provide information about consumer behavior, industry trends, and operational efficiency, data is turning becoming one of business's most important assets. In many businesses, the capacity to gather, evaluate, and act upon data is increasingly becoming a critical differentiator. The Digital Renaissance restores the once-lost balance between nature and culture, as well as the sense of community and mutuality in urban areas. It also remains how people should perceive themselves in mixed reality and reestablishes boundaries for safety when using new technologies.

FINDINGS

Trends in lifestyle and communication technologies indicate that the workforce of the future will be more competent and productive than in the past. Workers dissatisfaction with workplace skills is growing as productivity and communications technologies progress. Workers are ready for a workplace that can adapt to their changing lives because they believe their current one is not sophisticated enough. The adoption of smart workplace technology has skyrocketed in the last several years. Deployments of digital workplaces and smart offices are gathering steam as more people become interested in taking use of them. However, enterprises are just beginning to scratch the surface when it comes to the potential uses of smart workplace technology due to the poor adoption rate and when correctly implemented, digital workspaces may yield significant commercial advantages. Digital technologies are incorporated into every aspect of a company in a way that provides value to its customers. Using digital technology in a way that actually transforms your daily company operations enhances customer satisfaction and increases return on investment, *etc*. Adopting new technology Digital transformation is a mindset change that also values creativity and adaptability.

Recommendations

The digital workplace has evolved haphazardly for many firms, resulting in an environment that is hard to use and lacks cohesion. Moving from this chaotic state to an integrated, productive digital workplace requires taking it one step at a time. Start today. So, how does your company implement the digital renaissance of work? The following five steps will help you get started:

1. The phrase digital workplace is becoming increasingly popular in businesses. Both business and IT audiences find it appealing, and it helps shift the discussion away from focusing on specific solutions like intranets. Does your organization understand the term? Is there interest in discussing the digital workplace? If so, why not use your collaboration platform to launch a virtual workplace community? Use the methods that are most effective for your company to talk to people about the digital workplace.
2. There is a digital workplace in every company. How does the digital workplace now feel at your company? This might lead to disarray, annoyance, and decreased productivity if it's like many other firms. You may identify your present digital workplace's strengths and weaknesses and pinpoint opportunities for growth by first evaluating your own maturity and then using a more thorough benchmark.

Additionally, this will give you a crucial level set to gauge your success as you start your digital workplace initiative.

3. Clearly state your goals for the digital workplace. You need to communicate from the start the benefits that the digital workplace will bring to your company. Don't focus too much on features and functionality unless you can demonstrate their value and link them to your company's strategic goals. Also, don't assume everyone will understand it; instead, use creativity to convey the idea. For example, use stories from employees' daily lives to demonstrate how the digital workplace can change their work habits.
4. Make people the center of the digital workplace. It is important to not only consider whether your vision for the digital workplace is in line with strategic goals, but also to examine the actual ways of operating. Integration is key in the digital workplace. While digital workplace initiatives have grown significantly, we must ensure that it plays a vital role in making daily tasks easier and more efficient. Neglecting digitalization can have a significant negative impact on company profits and employee engagement.

CONCLUSION

Companies operating in the market face both new possibilities and problems as a result of globalization and internationalization. Globalization is causing us to see new developments and emerging technologies that have a significant impact on and alter how businesses function in terms of digitalization and transformation. Business digital transformation is unavoidable and essential to an organization's continued growth in the contemporary market and environment. Without new digital technologies that set up prerequisites for establishing long-term competitiveness, it is now impossible to be competitive or to achieve it. Digital resilience is an inevitable part of modern life, whether businesses are dealing with small-scale or large-scale cyber attacks. However, a company can protect itself from potential threats by anticipating disruptions in time and position itself to take advantage of the many opportunities presented by the digital realm by incorporating resilience into the core of its digital strategy. However, digital resilience plans need to be adapted according to the digital environment. Businesses can achieve extraordinary heights by turning digital difficulties into stepping stones through proactive, educated, and flexible management. The call to action for firms navigating the digital age is very clear. Make resilience a top priority. Invest in it, nurture it, and promote it throughout the organization. Resilience is the thread that promises long-term success and progress in the large tapestry of the digital age. Programs, websites, apps, and other computerized and internet-based resources that support, improve, and implement digital processes and general digitization initiatives are known as digital tools. A collection of online resources that facilitate organizational effectiveness in navigating the ever-changing digital world through the use of modern technology and accompanying digital methods can be further defined as digital tools. Information and communication technology is always evolving. The digital world is always evolving due to the introduction of new and inventive goods and services, which also change the way society interacts with technology. As expected, digital tools need to change quickly to keep pace with the rapid advancement of new technologies.

Future Research Implications

The topic of digital renaissance in the workplace is becoming more and more popular among CEOs, engineers and HR managers. In the future, digital awareness has become a necessity rather than a luxury. For businesses to survive they will have to make not just consumers but everyone involved in the business such as employees, investors and owners become knowledgeable about digital technologies. This will require a new approach to developing technologies, encouraging creativity and embracing the digital transition responsibly.

REFERENCES

Al-Omoush, K., & McDowell, W. C. (2023). The impact of digital corporate social responsibility on social entrepreneurship and organizational resilience. *Management Decision*. Advance online publication. DOI: 10.1108/MD-11-2022-1613

Anderson, T. (2013). Digital Resilience in Higher Education, *European Journal of Open, Distance and E-Learning*, 16(1), pp. 53-66. https://eric.ed.gov/?id=EJ1017457

Barnosky, Anthony (2016). Toward a digital resilience. *Elementa: Science of the Anthropogenic*. . DOI: 10.12952/journal.elementa.000082

Brunetti, F., & Orzes, G. (2020). Digital transformation challenges: Strategies emerging from a multi-stakeholder approach. *The TQM Journal*, 32(4), 697–724. DOI: 10.1108/TQM-12-2019-0309

Chaiyakun, S., & Yang, J. W. L. (2024). Digital Renaissance: A comprehensive exploration of education transformation - hotspots, models, and strategic approaches. *International Journal of Current Educational Practice*, 12(2), 86–95. DOI: 10.5281/zenodo.10954537

Chen, K. and Xue, F. (2022). The renaissance of augmented reality in construction: history, present status and future directions, *Smart and Sustainable Built Environment*, 11 (3), pp. 575 592. .DOI: 10.1108/SASBE-08-2020-0124

Cichosz, M., & Knemeyer, A. M. (2020). Digital transformation at logistics service providers: Barriers, success factors and leading practices. *International Journal of Logistics Management*, 31(2), 209–238. DOI: 10.1108/IJLM-08-2019-0229

Del Vecchio, P., & Garzoni, A. (2024). Digital transformation and resilience in family business: An exploratory study of generational dynamics. *European Journal of Innovation Management*. Advance online publication. DOI: 10.1108/EJIM-02-2024-0137

Ekman, P., & Whitaker, J. (2020). Digital transformation of global business processes: The role of dual embeddedness. *Business Process Management Journal*, 26(2), 570–592. DOI: 10.1108/BPMJ-02-2019-0080

Fischer, G., & Lindberg, J. O. (2020). Rethinking and reinventing learning, education and collaboration in the digital age-from creating technologies to transforming cultures. *International Journal of Information and Learning Technology*, 37(5), 241–252. DOI: 10.1108/IJILT-04-2020-0051

Gull, M., & Sridadi, A. R. (2024). Resilient higher educational institutions in a world of digital transformation. *Foresight*, 26(5), 755–774. DOI: 10.1108/FS-12-2022-0186

Hamka, M. (2022). Digital resilience: Opportunities and threats for adolescents in a virtual world [AIM]. *Acta Informatica Malaysia*, 6(2), 67–71. DOI: 10.26480/aim.02.2022.67.71

He, Z., & Bilgihan, A. (2023). Building organizational resilience with digital transformation. *Journal of Service Management*, 34(1), 147–171. DOI: 10.1108/JOSM-06-2021-0216

Hooi, L. W., & Chan, A. J. (2023). Does workplace digitalization matter in linking transformational leadership and innovative culture to employee engagement? *Journal of Organizational Change Management*, 36(2), 197–216. DOI: 10.1108/JOCM-06-2022-0184

Isensee, C., & Griese, K. M. (2023). Success factors of organizational resilience: A qualitative investigation of four types of sustainable digital entrepreneurs. *Management Decision*, 61(5), 1244–1273. DOI: 10.1108/MD-03-2022-0326

Ko, A., & Szabó, Z. (2022). Influencing factors of digital transformation: Management or IT is the driving force? *International Journal of Innovation Science*, 14(1), 1–20. DOI: 10.1108/IJIS-01-2021-0007

Kraft, C., & Peter, M. K. (2022). The digital transformation of Swiss small and medium-sized enterprises: Insights from digital tool adoption. *Journal of Strategy and Management*, 15(3), 468–494. DOI: 10.1108/JSMA-02-2021-0063

Kruyen, P. M., & Helderman, J.-K. (2020). Searching for the renaissance bureaucrat: A longitudinal computer-assisted study of personality traits in government vacancies. *International Journal of Public Sector Management*, 33(1), 22–44. DOI: 10.1108/IJPSM-07-2019-0195

Kumar, V., & Pereira, V. (2023). Modelling and analysing the enablers of digital resilience for small and medium enterprises. *Journal of Enterprise Information Management*. Advance online publication. DOI: 10.1108/JEIM-01-2023-0002

Li, F. (2020). Leading digital transformation: Three emerging approaches for managing the transition. *International Journal of Operations & Production Management*, 40(6), 809–817. DOI: 10.1108/IJOPM-04-2020-0202

Liu, Y., Guo, M., & Wang, T. (2024). Effects of digital orientation on organizational resilience: A dynamic capabilities perspective. *Journal of Manufacturing Technology Management*, 35(2), 268–290. DOI: 10.1108/JMTM-06-2023-0224

Massaro, M. (2020). The challenges of digital transformation in healthcare: Aninter disciplinary literature review, framework, and future research agenda, volume 123. https://www.sciencedirect.com/science/article/abs/pii/S0166497223000275

Murawski, M., & Bick, M. (2017). Digital competences of the workforce - a research topic? *Business Process Management Journal*, 23(3), 721–734. DOI: 10.1108/BPMJ-06-2016-0126

Raimo, N., De Turi, I., Ricciardelli, A., & Vitolla, F. (2022). Digitalization in the cultural industry: Evidence from Italian museums. *International Journal of Entrepreneurial Behaviour & Research*, 28(8), 1962–1974. DOI: 10.1108/IJEBR-01-2021-0082

Rausch, A. (2023). Informal learning from dealing with software-related problems in the digital workplace. *Journal of Workplace Learning*, 35(9), 291–310. DOI: 10.1108/JWL-03-2023-0042

Rossini, M., Cifone, F. D., Kassem, B., Costa, F., & Portioli-Staudacher, A. (2021). Being lean: How to shape digital transformation in the manufacturing sector. *Journal of Manufacturing Technology Management*, 32(9), 239–259. DOI: 10.1108/JMTM-12-2020-0467

Sousa-Zomer, T. T., & Martinez, V. (2020). Digital transforming capability and performance: A micro foundational perspective. *International Journal of Operations & Production Management*, 40(7/8), 1095–1128. DOI: 10.1108/IJOPM-06-2019-0444

Tim, Y., Cui, L., & Sheng, Z. (2020). Digital resilience: How rural communities leapfrogged into sustainable development. *Information Systems Journal*, 31(2), 323–345. DOI: 10.1111/isj.12312

Tim, Y., & Leidner, D. E. (2023). Digital Resilience: A Conceptual Framework for Information Systems Research. *Journal of the Association for Information Systems*, 24(5), 1184–1198. DOI: 10.17705/1jais.00842

Chapter 6
Optimizing Research Techniques and Learning Strategies With Digital Technologies:
Exploring the Benefits of Online English Language Programs in Higher Education

Zainab Salim Al Ajmi
Military Technological College, Oman

ABSTRACT

Face-to-face strategies have been the primary method for language learning over the past decades, particularly for teaching English. However, online platforms were less utilized in educational institutions until the rapid shift caused by the COVID-19 pandemic. This shift highlighted the potential of virtual programs in language education, leading scholars to recognize their benefits. This study explores the importance of online English platforms in addressing literacy challenges and improving proficiency in Higher Educational Institutions (HEIs). Through surveys of Foundation Programme Department (FPD) students and instructors, the research will analyze platforms like Microsoft Teams and Zoom, assessing their effectiveness in English language learning.

DOI: 10.4018/979-8-3693-7863-2.ch006

INTRODUCTION

The COVID-19 pandemic brought unprecedented disruptions to the educational sector worldwide, forcing institutions to rapidly adapt to new methods of teaching and learning. As a precautionary measure to curb the spread of the virus, face-to-face interactions, including lab sessions, workshops, and other practical learning activities, were halted. In response, providers of higher education quickly implemented social distancing strategies, which necessitated a swift and widespread transition to online teaching environments. This shift was not merely a temporary solution but rather a complete overhaul of the traditional educational model, where curricula had to be redesigned to suit the dynamics of virtual classrooms (Mohmmed, Khidhir, Nazeer, & Vijayan, 2020). The pandemic accelerated the need for innovative solutions, pushing educational institutions to adopt advanced technological tools to ensure continuity in learning. With students unable to physically attend classes due to lockdowns and travel restrictions, online modes of learning became essential, allowing them to adhere to safety guidelines while continuing their education (Zoom, San Jose, California).

The abrupt transition to online learning environments posed significant challenges but also presented opportunities for the integration of digital technologies that could potentially enhance the learning experience. Various platforms have emerged as essential tools during this period, with technologies like Microsoft Teams, Slack, and Kaizala playing pivotal roles in facilitating virtual education (Slack Technologies, San Francisco, CA). Microsoft Teams, in particular, was adopted widely due to its user-friendly interface, robust communication features, and seamless integration with other Microsoft Office applications. It provided a comprehensive suite of tools that made it easier for educators to deliver lessons, share resources, and engage with students effectively. Platforms like Zoom became synonymous with virtual classrooms, enabling synchronous learning and live interaction, which helped bridge the gap created by the absence of physical classrooms. Slack, a platform initially designed for workplace communication, also found its way into educational institutions, serving as a tool for project collaboration, group discussions, and instant messaging.

At the Military Technological College, Microsoft Teams was chosen as the primary platform for online learning, considering its versatile features and secure, integrated cloud system. This platform allowed educators and students to conduct lectures, share PowerPoint presentations, and distribute essential documents seamlessly (Almarzooq, Lopes, & Kochar, 2020). The ability to store files on a secure intranet, combined with tools for real-time communication, made Microsoft Teams an ideal solution for the college's academic and administrative needs. Additionally, it provided a centralized platform for departmental meetings, enabling faculty members to collaborate, share ideas, and communicate with their teams without the need for physical presence. The flexibility offered by these platforms meant that students could engage in learning activities from any location, breaking down geographical barriers and providing more inclusive access to education (San Jose, California)

This research paper delves into an important aspect of modern education—the use of online learning platforms in improving English language skills among students at the Military Technological College. English proficiency is crucial for students' academic and professional success, and traditional face-to-face language classes have always been the primary method of instruction.

The integration of online platforms into the educational system has raised several critical questions that this research aims to address, including:

1. What is meant by online learning platforms?
2. What are the functions of online learning programs?
3. What is the students' perception of online learning platforms?

LITERATURE REVIEW

1. Overview of Online English Language Programs

1.1. Defining Online English Language Learning and Teaching

Online teaching and learning can be simply described as education conducted via the Internet. Online learning is often considered a form of distance education, sometimes referred to as web-based or digital learning (Matthew, Philip, & Sarhan, 2018). It also involves the use of various devices, including iPads, smartphones, and laptops, along with Internet access, in either synchronous or asynchronous settings (Pham & Vo, 2021). With the advancement of the Internet, online courses have now become a crucial aspect of higher education (Kebritchi, Lipschuetz, & Santiague, 2017; Luyt, 2013).

1.2. Historical Context of E-Learning

E-learning, considered a method of computer-assisted learning, has been around since the 1960s, but its wide usage and dissemination started mainly after the popularization of the Internet and the Web. From its appearance up to today, e-learning has undergone fast changes as far as the technology and methodology/tools used for e-learning are concerned. E-learning, having in mind that it has many benefits-on one side for the teacher/instructors and on the other side for the learners-found its application in education, business, and the military, or wherever needed. E-learning concept has been here for over two decades. What once was just a radical idea now evolved into mainstream phenomenon. The way the e-learning methodology evolved can be approached as a chain process. When the Internet started to change, people using the Internet started to change and just importantly e-learning pedagogy techniques originated to evolve. It has been said that recent modern e-learning tendencies must be "learner-oriented design". Students will be able not only to control the appearance of virtual elements but also fully control the whole learning process (Downes, 2005).

1.3. Emergence of English Language Programmes Online

Over the past few years, higher educational institutions have faced a drastic transformation as they were forced to shift to online learning due to the pandemic of Covid-19 using various platforms to ensure that learning and teaching practices continue. In response to the COVID-19 pandemic, governments enforced lockdowns, including the closure of public spaces and schools, to safeguard public health and reduce the spread of infection. Consequently, the pandemic compelled governments to adopt and implement Virtual Learning Environments (VLEs), with their associated benefits and drawbacks, as billions of students worldwide faced an abrupt and unplanned transition from traditional classrooms to home-based education, supported by various concerned organizations (Li C, Lalani F, 2020; Reimers F, Schleicher A, Saavedra J, Tuominen S, 2020).

Artificial intelligence (AI) has proven to be a transformative technology in many fields, one of which is education. AI technologies have been growingly applied to the academic setting, assuring enhanced learning and performance. The prevalence in research and development over the last ten years has led schools, both nationally and globally, to increasingly adopt AI.

The adaptations need to be tailored, taking into consideration both the requirements of facilitating digital natives and ensuring that deep learning is not compromised. In a nutshell, the advent of technology has created an entire generation of digital natives who consume information differently and therefore have different learning requirements (Machmud, 2018). To better reach this group of digital natives, educators need to adapt their pedagogy and resources to align with how this generation prefers to learn. This includes implementing technology-enabled teaching and learning, utilizing online platforms for outcome-based education, and providing interactive multimedia content. Such efforts would allow educators to create digital learning spaces tailored to the needs of digital natives and enhance their academic success (Nurgiansah, 2022). Digital natives can move their interactions and activities from a face-to-face environment to the digital world with ease using online learning platforms. Moreover, these platforms offer a myriad of features and advantages that enrich learning for digital natives. One key aspect is that this generation can easily access a range of educational resources like e-books, videos, and interactive simulations, catering to their diverse learning styles and preferences (Nur, 2019).

1.4. Types of Online Learning Programs

The incorporation of GenAI technology has significantly benefited students' writing development. Notably, the personalized feedback provided promptly by GenAI has led to noticeable improvements in students' writing proficiency following its use (Marzuki, Rusdin,and Indrawati 2023; Rad, Alipour, and Jafarpour 2023). GenAI technology has the potential to alleviate negative emotions, such as anxiety, that are commonly experienced during the process of learning to write (Guo et al. 2024). Primarily, the use of GenAI can impact multiple aspects of self-regulated writing learning, encompassing emotional, cognitive, behavioral, and metacognitive dimensions (Zhang, Zou, and Cheng 2023). In a study involving 30 L2 English writers at a university in Hong Kong (Zhang, Zou, and Cheng, 2023) found that GenAI technology supports the planning phase of writing by providing recommendations and guidance for writing tasks. Additionally, it fosters self-evaluation by addressing students' learning progress.

Due to the outbreak of Covid-19, the institutions have shifted from traditional to online teaching and there are various types of platforms offered online teaching and learning programs to ensure that learning and teaching practices are ongoing. (Allen & Seaman, 2007) categorized courses into four types: traditional courses, web-facilitated courses, blended or hybrid courses, and online courses. Their classification was based on the proportion of content delivered online as shown in the table below:

Table 1. Types of courses

Proportion of Content Delivered Online	Type of Course	Typical Description
0%	Traditional	Course with no online description used-Content delivered in writing or orally.
1 to 29%	Web Facilitated	Course that uses web-based technology to facilitate what is essentially a face-to-face course. Uses a course management system (CMS) or web pages to post the syllabus and assignments, for example.
30 to 79%	Blended/ Hybrid	Course that blends online and face-to-face delivery. Substantial proportion of the content is delivered online, typically uses online discussions, and typically has some face-to-face meetings.
80+%	Online	A course where most or all the content is delivered online. Typically has no face-to-face meetings.

(Allen & Seaman, 2007)

Online learning has been defined in multiple ways. Specifically, it can be seen as the teaching and learning interaction between instructors and students through digital platforms like Zoom, Microsoft Teams, and Google Classroom (Zulaikha, Azlin, Khairul, & Bity, 2021) As (Allen & Seaman, 2007) pointed out, educational institutions can implement online learning differently depending on their circumstances.

2. KEY BENEFITS OF ONLINE ENGLISH LANGUAGE PROGRAMS

2.1. Flexibility and Accessibility

There is an abundance of research on the potential advantages for teachers and students in online teaching. These areas can involve things like the development of pedagogy, ways to instruct students, and training for faculty in curriculum design or language learning (Wang & Vasquez, 2012). Online learning can be convenient for both instructors and students, while classroom engagement, communication skills, and self-confidence (Halim & Hashim, 2019) also facilitate through online environments. In addition, student motivation can also be increased through fun and engaging online learning activities (Morat et al., 2016). It may help create an online learning experience by enabling the utilization of authentic learning resources such as videos, television clips, and other media readily available from websites that provide commercial multimedia (Pazilah et al., 2019).

One, online ELT learning has been labelled with 'online characteristic' characteristics (Ally, 2008; Harmer, 2007; Long, 2004; Moore, 2009) and doing so allowed students to develop in ambient care conditions propounded by the nature of internet education as a flexible access. The learning process can be flexible and easy to access because students could learn or re-learn the material using online form schools whenever, wherever they wanted (Budiarta & Santosa, 2020). Dieterich & Hamsher (2020) also agreed, arguing that the organic flexibility and accessibility for learning online ELT programs and courses may be an advantage to students. The way online assessment is done also gives a sense of ease, flexibility, and adequacy (Laily et al., 2023)

There was a study conducted by researchers in Shanghai University of Finance and Economics ensured that online learning programmes provided a lot of flexibility and convenience in the education system allowing some immunity to physical segregations as well (Zhao, 2023)Apart from this move to online education, COVID-19 has also spurred other new practices in Chinese higher ed. Universities have tried to adapt by forming hybrid educational experiences which encompass both online and digital components (Tenhunen M.-L, Towey D., 2022; Pike M, Stecuła, 2021; K., Wolniak, R, 2022). Moreover, institutions have invested significantly in the development of a strong digital infrastructure and training faculty to employ technology effectively for teaching (Tenhunen M.-L, Towey D., Pike M, Stecuła, K., 2022).

2.2. Challenges in Online English Language Programs

Despite the advantages of online teaching and learning, there are still some drawbacks to consider. First, not all students are prepared to participate in online courses (Hung et al., 2010; Luu, 2022; Pham et al., 2022), which can negatively affect their final performance. Therefore, it is crucial for online instructors to find ways to encourage student engagement in online learning (Kebritchi et al., 2017). Instructors must focus on five key areas to support these students: self-directed learning, learner control, computer and Internet self-efficacy, motivation for learning, and online communication self-efficacy (Hung et al., 2010).

Second, to engage students in online lectures, instructors should diversify their teaching methods and materials. However, this can pose a challenge for lecturers due to the increased time demands and workload (Hartman et al., 2000; Cavanaugh, 2005; Li & Irby, 2008; Kebritchi et al., 2017).

Third, lecturers often lack adequate training and support for teaching online (Kyei & Keengwe, 2011). To enhance the effectiveness of online instruction, it is recommended that lecturers incorporate dynamic presentations, simulations, conceptual discussions, and foster interaction and collaboration with students (Juan et al., 2011).

Lastly, students can be easily distracted by other online content, which may lead to a lack of active participation in class activities (Daniel & Andrea, 2020; Pham et al., 2022). To address this issue, instructors need to be trained in effective virtual classroom management skills (Tran & Pham, 2021).

3. THE FRAMEWORK OF E-LEARNING AND ITS INFLUENCE ON STUDENTS

The Virtual Learning Environment, or VLE, is an institutionally managed platform that supports teaching and learning through digital technologies. It therefore provides different online tools related to interacting with others and communicating among users to make them feel more connected and collaborative. HEIs increasingly consider the VLE as a strategic institutional support to complement programs and collaborative learning activities (Al Hajri, 2020). HEIs are expected to adopt recent technological changes as well as use the same for upgrading and refining the VLE. HEIs in the Sultanate of Oman are also trying to keep pace with the global developments regarding the adoption of VLE tools that integrate latest developments such as cloud computing. Gradual evolution of smartphones and greater accessibility to broadband Internet is shaping the mode of delivery of educational services. According to (Titcomb, 2016) "websites are more and more visited through smartphones rather than desktops. Thus, collaborative VLEs will become more developed and efficient nosily. However, risk management, security, and governance problems obstruct the full implementation of cloud computing for HEIs. These issues are due to a number of reasons; most of them are technical. Therefore, application of various aspects—technical variable, organizational variables, and environmental ones—may be critical in promoting and streamlining the services of the institution accordingly. The Virtual Learning Environment has had a relative impact on the students at MTC in terms of their performance, with many of them showing tremendous understanding of the course work. Despite the challenges faced by the MTC students regarding online learning—such as limited infrastructure and sometimes access to a laptop that most students passed the course. This is great, considering the average marks attained by these students reflected that they could adapt to recent changes at MTC. It may mean that VLE can be used as an alternative whenever there is a need for immediate change in the future. Jadara University started using Microsoft Teams at the beginning of the COVID-19 pandemic in the latter part of 2019. "More recently, in an ongoing quest to improve ICT literacy, Jadara University has implemented several initiatives. Several classrooms have also been digitized and used for synchronous learning and could be available asynchronously for future cohorts" (Rababah, 2020). Rababah's study provided a general overview of the adaptation of Jadara University to the pandemic and the Virtual Learning Environment using Microsoft Teams, where the focus served primarily for attitude assessment towards the platform by students. Kaizala, being quite a new application, has very few studies conducted on it. However, it "Kaizala goes beyond mere communication to enhance collaboration and organizational productivity." Some of the key unique features that Kaizala possesses are its very ability to connect with an unlimited number of users, systematically sending and retrieving information through action cards, and integrated analytics that draw valuable insight from data (Yani, 2019). Further study of this platform will be required in the immediate future for greater understanding of its functionalities.

3.1. The Importance of E-Learning Platforms to Grow Language Learning

This reflects that smartphones have become an important part of daily digital life, as they are widely used by higher education students all over the world. In addition to this, unlimited data packages make it easy for students to connect to the internet through reasonable access to Wi-Fi at home and on campus. These days, especially with the evolution of operating systems like Symbian, iOS, Windows Mobile, and Android, this is increasing a lot. With this, they have a reason to be attracted, especially Android has a wide variety of applications. In the words of Jadhav, Bhutkar, and Mehta "the easy availability of the internet on Smartphones enables students to access different apps, some of which include WhatsApp, Facebook, Skype, GO SMS Pro among others" (Alqahtani, Bhaskar, Vadakalur Elumalai, Abumelha, 2018). In contrast to these, the virtual learning packages have a combination of the following functions:

3.2. Provides Personalized Learning Opportunities for All English Language Learners

Advanced technology engages students on more than one level, and it is well understood that a student of any age sometimes has motivational problems. It allows learners to find their own way to learn using all types of apps and multimedia technologies. By providing them with different kinds of tools and resources via networks, students are much more likely to be motivated and interested in learning (Alsaboosi, n.d.). Through the integration of technology into language programs, learners feel naturally guided to develop their speaking, listening, writing, and reading skills—all-round development that will eventually build proficiency and confidence in the English language.

3.2.1. ELT Students Would Develop More Robust Foundational Skills

Technology can, in today's modern world, enhance many basic future skills more effectively. It enhances critical thinking, enhances leadership ability, and also enhances communication skills, a most definitely wide avenue for growth. Learners who use technology to enhance their English skills have yet another advantage applying their new knowledge of digital technology in many areas. By mastering various online tools, it would add an advantage to their competitive edge in the job market and skill set as well. Besides, there are various advantages to the educators and other ELT professionals by taking into consideration digital technology integration into their English language programs.

3.2.2. Digital Technologies Can Enhance the Relationship Between Teachers and Students

Providing learning resources and tools online can also help educators refine their teaching methods. Additionally, it can keep students engaged, allowing teachers to dedicate more time to those who need extra support (Alsaboosi, n.d.). Effective learning applications are increasingly used to support student learning and manage classroom dynamics. These platforms enable educators to track student progress more easily and provide substantial support for classroom management. They also make it easier for the teacher to keep track of the pupils' performances and make early detections on the areas the students need to improve, rather than at the end of the course.

4. DEVELOPING A STRONG ONLINE PRESENCE TO COMPLEMENT THE TRADITIONAL CLASSROOM ELT MODEL

Creates new opportunities for businesses targeting ELT students. This includes reaching younger audiences and those with limited time but significant financial resources to invest in their education (Alsaboosi, n.d.).

4.1. Microsoft Teams: Advantages and Disadvantages

4.1.1. Advantages of Microsoft Teams

Microsoft Teams increases productivity while reducing distances. Sometimes, all the collaboration options available in Microsoft 365 may overwhelm the end-user. But Teams streamlines your workforce operations by packing all collaboration aspects—conversations, messages, online meetings, shared documents, and tasks—into one application with an integrated interface. In addition to the usual suite of Microsoft applications, Teams incorporates hundreds of third-party apps, which enables users to complete their tasks without having to leave the Teams environment. Since Microsoft Teams was built from scratch by Microsoft, it is immediately ready, out of the box, for rich communication features like likes, GIFs, emojis, live link previews, and more that drive engagement and improvement. Teams helps you stay focused more on work-related matters and better prioritize your time. Instead of trying to create order from the inbox full of messages about everything from everybody, Teams categorizes information into channels, which keeps your data in a structured environment. Each channel contains discussions, meetings, and files associated with a particular subject or topic. In that way, you won't be distracted by random emails or fight with your inbox; instead, you can put your focus on what does matter and invest your limited time in the channels where your actual work takes place.

4.1.2. Enhanced Focus with Teams

Teams helps you streamline your focus on work-related matters and manage your time better. Instead of investing time wading through an overloaded inbox full of messages from various sources, in Teams, information is organized into channels, each one devoted to specific topics. That means you only see discussions, meetings, and documents related to the subject of the channel. This way, you will not be distracted by irrelevant emails or waste time managing your inbox, allowing you to focus on essential tasks in those channels where your work gets done.

4.1.3. Enhanced Transparency

Many companies struggle with keeping everyone in the loop and ensuring that everyone is aware of what's happening. Teams make this much easier. There's no need to worry about who to cc in an email or who to invite to a meeting. Instead, you can post your message in the relevant channel, @-mention the contacts you want to inform, and leave it for others to read if they choose. By making meetings visible to everyone on the channel, you enhance transparency and allow everyone on the channel to stay informed.

4.1.4. Seamless Transition to a Modern Work Environment

Transitioning to a cloud-based work environment offers numerous business advantages, and Teams facilitates this shift seamlessly. As a fully cloud-based solution, Teams allows you to access data from anywhere on any device, providing a significant business benefit. Additionally, with your workspace in the cloud, you can leverage advanced data processing and artificial intelligence capabilities to make smarter decisions (Stroyals, 2019, January).

4.1.5. Disadvantages of Microsoft Teams

This might ultimately lower engagement and participation in Teams because students will often opt to view the classes, reviews, and meetings later rather than in real time. This can lead to missed sessions and tasks not being completed. While instructors can gauge individual student activity through reports in the LMS, a way to ensure this further is to embed interactive questions within videos for more engaging and responsible learning. There is several tools that can provide this and one example is H5P, which is integrated into the LMS through a plugin. If however the students do not engage with the recordings, then their learning is hampered, and also not all students have technology although Teams is available on smartphones via the app and most students would probably possess a phone or tablet. One thing worth noticing is that some of the features, like editing, might be more powerful in its desktop version. Finally, recording meetings or presentations on Teams is rather cumbersome nowadays; continuous updates from Microsoft are probably going to fix that (Poston, Apostel, & Richardson, 2020).

4.2. Benefits and Drawbacks of the Kaizala Application

4.2.1. Advantages of Microsoft Kaizala

Microsoft Kaizala was specifically built to enhance efficiency in communication dissemination among large-scale organizations and those that require strong group interactions. Users can connect with frontlines, employees operating remotely, and more through a chat-like interface. You can collect information from a single user or groups of users, see details about people outside of your organization, and gather insights from digital records.

4.2.2. The Benefits of Microsoft Kaizala

Streamlined Workplace Coordination: Kaizala helps you manage your workplace better in a dynamic environment when employees are distributed remotely and on the move. Kaizala enables you to organize routine tasks much better with in-built features to manage task assignments, meeting planners, and performance tracking. Now, you can create custom 'Tasks' as per your needs using the Open API framework.

Make Data-Driven Decisions: Analytics by Microsoft Kaizala will give you better insight into future decision-making. You can set up automatic reports that will go directly to your business leaders, helping you understand how your teams are performing.

Access Control and Security: In a nutshell, the Kaizala Administration portal is holistic, because it gives the administrator complete control over his activities and data. The administrator can manage membership in groups, remove users from groups in real-time, and top it all off, he can even erase data from any of the external devices that have the data (Carter, 2019).

5. THEORETICAL PERSPECTIVES ON ONLINE PLATFORMS FOR LANGUAGE LEARNING

In addition to these established sites, newer online tools are also enhancing teaching and learning in the classroom. Numerous online resources support educators who want to use these platforms as part of teaching practices. Articles published on institutional Web sites, personal blogs, and general sites illustrate some of the advantages in employing online applications within education. With features such as groups for chatting, audio, video, and multimedia, teachers and students keep in constant communication with one another even outside the classroom, and learning has expanded outside the class. Special features of these networks allow learners to make friends and communicate in any language with anyone out there anywhere in the world. Yet to exploit these applications, users must hold a good command of English since these applications demand ‘English Proficiency’ at various points. All the above-mentioned features are proof that online platforms indeed bear huge potential in the English language learning context at a university level (Alqahtani et al., 2020).

6. IMPLEMENTATION OF KAIZALA AND MICROSOFT TEAMS AT MILITARY TECHNOLOGICAL COLLEGE

At Military Technological College (MTC), several online platforms, including Kaizala and Microsoft Teams, have been integrated to enhance English language use. These applications are valuable to MTC's academic environment, as they enable students to communicate with their advisors or lecturers in English. This has led to improved interaction and language skills among students. During the COVID-19 outbreak, MTC especially relied on Microsoft Teams to deliver course content. Although Microsoft Teams is not a new product, there is still some confusion about its capabilities and its potential to enhance workplace efficiency. Some perceive it merely as a chat application or an updated version of Skype for Business. However, Microsoft Teams is a powerful tool designed to improve collaboration and communication in modern work environments. Unlike other productivity software with legacy systems and large user bases, Microsoft Teams was built from the ground up to address the needs of the contemporary workplace. This shift represents a new approach to work that may be challenging for those accustomed to traditional email (Storyals, 2020).

Initially, there were challenges in teaching students online, especially with new students who lacked sufficient knowledge on how to access the college portal and join the lectures. However, we were able to overcome these challenges within a set period of time. Another hurdle faced during online learning was that some part-time students struggled with using computers, as they were more accustomed to relying on mobile phones for most of their educational activities.

Additionally, some students were unable to attend MTC due to inadequate infrastructure, causing them to miss several classes and eventually drop the course. Microsoft Teams served as an effective alternative for conducting online assessments during the Covid-19 era, eliminating the need for on-campus presence. We were able to evaluate student presentations, conduct online quizzes, and handle exam-related tasks such as invigilation, grading, review, and moderation. All of these processes were carried out efficiently and within a short timeframe.

7. THE DISTINCTION BETWEEN KAIZALA AND MICROSOFT TEAMS APPLICATIONS

Microsoft Kaizala is a secure messaging and communication app that enables mobile users to send texts, Kaizala Actions, and share various media, such as images, documents, videos, and audio files. It also allows for instant feedback from users on any topic of your choice. With Kaizala Actions, you can distribute polls and surveys to a large number of users, and all responses are automatically compiled and presented in an easy-to-read report, assisting in decision-making (Chuckedmonson, SuPotter, Pebaum, MaabSaleem, 2019).

Install Microsoft Kaizala on your mobile device

To get Microsoft Kaizala on your smartphone, the app is compatible with the following devices:

- Android phones running version 4.3 or higher
- iOS devices running version 9.0 or higher
- Windows phones running Windows 10, version 10240.0 or higher

An active internet connection, either via Wi-Fi or mobile data, is required to use Microsoft Kaizala. It does not support Wi-Fi-only tablets.

Verify Your Phone Number

To validate your phone number, you must be able to receive calls and text messages on the number you're trying to confirm. A Microsoft Kaizala account can only be verified with one phone number on a single device. If you attempt to use the same phone number on multiple devices, you will be logged out from all previous devices, and all Kaizala data on those devices will be erased.

Manage your profile and work account in Kaizala.

To update your profile in the Kaizala app, navigate to the Profile page. Here, you can modify information such as your photo, display name, and personal email. You can also log in with your Office 365 or school account from the Profile section. When you do this, other Kaizala users within your organization will be able to see and collaborate with you. You'll also have access to an organization page, where you can initiate chats or create groups (Chuckedmonson, SuPotter, Pebaum, MaabSaleem, 2019).

Find Contacts and Start Messaging

1. Use Kaizala to search for your phone book contacts and initiate one-on-one conversations with them.
2. Navigate to the People section.
3. Search for any contact from your phone book; if your contact is using the app:
    - Click or tap their picture to view their profile summary.
    - Click or tap their name to start a text conversation.

You can also easily send an invitation to any contact who isn't using Kaizala. Click or tap “Invite” to send an SMS inviting them to install the app.

To start a chat in the Kaizala mobile application:

- Go to Chats > + > Start a chat
- Click or tap on any contact's name to initiate a text conversation.

You can find all your recent discussions in the Chat section, where you can also start or continue conversations.

Make and Arrange Gatherings

1. Go to **Chats > + > Create a group**.
2. You may either add individuals or different gatherings to another gathering. Tap the names of contacts or a gathering and afterward choose Next to include. You'll see a spring up revealing to you that you can invite them to Kaizala at that point if they are not a person from your affiliation. Click Okay to proceed. Give your gathering a name, include an image in the event that you need, and, at that point, tap Create to wrap up.

7.1. Manage and Create Large Groups for Your Organization

The Kaizala management portal is an online platform that offers access to management, reporting, and extended features of Kaizala. With this portal, your organization can quickly onboard thousands, or even millions, of users to Kaizala, including employees, partners, vendors, or customers. All you need is their phone numbers. Learn more about the Kaizala Management Portal (Chuckedmonson, SuPotter, Pebaum, & MaabSaleem, 2019).

7.2. Using Kaizala Actions

You can send Actions with the icon on the top right corner of the chat. Enhanced Kaizala Actions allow you to make frequently employed tasks simpler for normal workflow situations. You can refer and use the Kaizala Actions from the Discover page inside the application. Following are the list of Kaizala Actions available:

- **Announcement**: This lets you make important announcements or even just share updates with your team. Announcements are a powerful way to convey messages across groups within an organization or a broadcast group. You can engage your audience by asking them to like and comment on the announcement (Chuckedmonson, Supotter, Pebaum & MaabSaleem, 2019).
- **Work**: In this feature, one is able to assign tasks with the facility to get updates regarding the status of that completion through chat messages. Both the creator of the task and the assignee can add quick comments to mark the

progress of it. The other group members can also comment on the task and the status.

Let's Meet - This feature enables sending meeting invites with just a few taps. The invitees can respond to the invite right there in the chat and confirm their availability to meet.

- **Live Location** - You can request the location of a friend or colleague. A user is allowed to share their live location with the receiving party for a certain duration, enabling real-time tracking.
- **Location Photo** - Share photos bearing GPS coordinates of exactly where the photo was taken. With just a single tap, team members can send an image with location tags attached, useful for confirming a task completed at a specific place or for location-based attendance verification.
- **Find Sharing** - You can share your location with colleagues or contacts in your phonebook using Kaizala to enhance coordination among team members.
- **Quick Poll** - You can create a poll to gather responses from either a team or a client. Responses are quick and easy to give, updating in real time in a comprehensible format. You can also create poll questions with predefined answers.
- **Request Location** - Use this feature to request the recent location of a Kaizala user. This is helpful for attendance tracking or monitoring your team's presence at any given time (Chuckedmonson, SuPotter, Pebaum, & MaabSaleem, 2019).

Submit Bill - Use this feature to quickly capture a photo of a receipt and share it along with the relevant details.

- **Survey** - Surveys and polls function similarly, but with a few key differences:
- A survey allows you to ask only one question, while a study can include multiple questions.
- In a survey, you can only set a multiple-choice format for responses, whereas a study allows various response formats, including multiple-choice, text, numbers, or even images.
- **Checklist** - Utilize this feature to share a task list with an individual or group, enabling them to complete each task individually. You can create to-do lists and track everyone's progress.

7.3. Explore More Kaizala Actions

We regularly release new Kaizala Actions, which you can find by navigating to Discover > Kaizala. You also have the option to create custom Kaizala actions. For more information, you can contact kaizalaDev@microsoft.com. Common custom Kaizala Actions include:

1) Member Feedback
2) Note to Administrator
3) Anonymous Record.

7.4. Explore and Subscribe to Broadcast Groups

Broadcast groups allow you to provide feedback or raise issues to the organizations you want to connect with. Most end users interact directly with organizations and utilize custom Actions to enhance productivity, speed, and information flow. You can discover and subscribe to broadcast groups from the Groups page under Discover > Broadcast in the Kaizala app. Simply tap on the name of a broadcast group and choose to subscribe.

Privacy

You can block someone from contacting you on Kaizala. Blocked contacts will no longer be able to send you messages. To block a contact, go to their profile in the Kaizala app, then click on the profile settings icon in the upper right corner and select Block. You can view the list of blocked contacts in the Blocked List section of the settings. Additionally, you can unblock any number from that list whenever you choose.

Microsoft Teams is a global communication and collaboration platform that combines persistent workplace chat, video conferencing, file storage (including collaborative documents), and app integration. The service is integrated with the Office 365 subscription productivity suite and offers enhancements that can connect with non-Microsoft products.

Microsoft Teams competes with services like Slack and represents the evolution and upgrade of Microsoft's previous platform, Skype (Microsoft Teams, 2020).

Microsoft announced Teams at an event in New York, launching the service globally on March 14, 2017. The platform was developed during an internal hackathon at the company's headquarters and is currently led by Brian MacDonald, Corporate Vice President at Microsoft.

Teams allows communities, groups, or teams to join through a specific link or invitation sent by a group leader or owner. Teams for Pedagogy enables administrators and educators to create dedicated groups for classes, professional learning communities (PLCs), staff members, and more (Microsoft Teams, 2020).

8. CASE STUDIES OF SUCCESSFUL ONLINE ENGLISH LANGUAGE PROGRAMS

8.1. Case 1: University-Level English Program

A study was carried out to see how virtual materials might influence the motivation and performance of first-year English learners at the undergraduate level. Participants in the study, who were all freshmen, were split into two groups: an experimental group and a control group. The primary focus was on the learning mechanism, treated as the independent variable.

For the experiment group, researchers integrated the theory of situated cognition into the learning approach, incorporating virtual characters from the Second Life platform into the English teaching materials. Meanwhile, the control group followed the same curriculum but without the virtual programs, relying instead on traditional lecture-based instruction. The study measured two key outcomes: language achievement and learning motivation, which served as the dependent variables.

The methodology consisted of three main tools: a Learning Motivation Scale, an English proficiency test, and a survey assessing students' attitudes towards using virtual reality as part of their studies. Over the course of a semester, both groups participated in various English activities focused on vocabulary, grammar, and reading comprehension.

While both groups used identical educational materials, the experiment group interacted with animated virtual characters, making the lessons more engaging. On the other hand, the control group received standard lecture-style teaching. The virtual characters, created using the Second Life platform, played a central role in the experimental setup.

The study delved into the potential of virtual reality as a means to improve English language learning among college students. Researchers turned to the Second Life platform to build realistic settings where English lessons were conducted. This approach introduced virtual characters, known as avatars, into the educational content, aiming to offer a more engaging and immersive learning experience.

The primary objective of the study was to examine how these digital teaching aids could influence both the learners' performance and their motivation. The findings revealed several key insights. First, the integration of avatars into lessons significantly enhanced the language skills of undergraduate English learners. The students in the virtual learning environment showed a marked improvement in vocabulary, grammar, and communication skills, suggesting that the digital approach was more effective than traditional teaching methods.

Quantitative results further underscored the benefits. There was a significant rise in language achievement scores among students who used the digital English materials with noticeable improvements compared to those who followed traditional lecture-based courses. The digital method's adaptability allowed students to interact at their own pace, ask questions freely, and learn through practical scenarios.

Overall, the study strongly indicated that using virtual characters and digital environments can make English language learning more effective, engaging, and student-centered.

The study identified a notable improvement in learning outcomes among undergraduate English students who used different types of learning materials. Specifically, when virtual materials were used, they helped create engaging interactions and realistic settings that greatly boosted student participation (Chung, L. Y, 2012).

9. FUTURE TRENDS IN ONLINE ENGLISH LANGUAGE EDUCATION

9.1. AI-Driven Personalization in Language Learning

In the changing realm of global education, the incorporation of Artificial Intelligence (AI) has led to a significant transformation, especially within higher vocational English education. This shift represents more than just a passing trend; it marks a profound evolution that reshapes teaching approaches and operational practices in educational settings (Crompton & Burke, 2023). The drive to integrate AI into higher vocational English education arises from the crucial need to cater to diverse learner profiles and improve educational outcomes in a rapidly digitalizing world. While traditional teaching methods remain fundamental (Yan, Y, 2019). Traditional teaching methods often struggle to meet the personalized needs of today's varied student population. AI's ability to customize educational experiences and deliver real-time feedback offers a unique opportunity to address these challenges. Additionally, the continued globalization of business and communication necessitates a higher level of English proficiency, which vocational schools are tasked with providing. This need drives the integration of advanced AI tools, capable of transforming passive learning settings into dynamic, interactive, and adaptive educational environments. AI is being integrated into higher vocational English education through various innovative applications. One notable example is the use of automated assessments powered by advanced algorithms, which are transforming the evaluation of students' language skills. Unlike traditional paper-based exams, these AI-driven systems offer more dynamic and interactive forms of assessment. They not only measure linguistic accuracy but also assess communicative effectiveness and fluency, providing students with comprehensive feedback to help direct their learning progress. AI-powered personalized learning systems leverage extensive data on students' performance and learning preferences to create tailored educational experiences. By adjusting the complexity and pacing of content based on each individual's learning curve, these systems enhance student engagement and improve retention. Furthermore, AI-driven language learning apps and platforms demonstrate how technology can create a more immersive and adaptive learning environment. Utilizing natural language processing, these platforms simulate real conversational scenarios, providing students with practical, real-world language practice. AI-powered interactive virtual teaching assistants highlight the seamless integration of technology and education. These assistants offer round-the-clock support, responding to student queries and enabling language practice without the typical limitations of human availability. Their capacity to provide consistent and immediate feedback helps foster a supportive and enriched learning environment, enhancing the overall educational experience for students. Looking to the future, the role of AI in higher vocational English education is set for significant expansion. With continued advancements in AI and machine learning, future developments are likely to include a more refined understanding of natural language, enabling deeper discourse analysis and culturally sensitive content that better equips students for global communication. The incorporation of augmented and virtual reality into AI-based educational systems could also lead to more engaging and experiential learning experiences.

In conclusion, as we approach this educational shift, the integration of AI in higher vocational English education is not merely enhancing traditional teaching practices; it is paving the way for a future where learning is more personalized, accessible, and in line with the global need for proficient English communicators.

10. RESEARCH PROCEDURES

10.1. How Did the Military Technological College Mitigate Online Learning Platforms Threats?

Our college implemented several solutions to address the technical challenges students faced during online learning. For instance, lecturers use the Kaizala application to monitor student progress and maintain communication. The Center for

Foundation Studies also reaches out to students via phone calls and utilizes departmental funds to provide them with credit for accessing the college website during English quizzes. Additionally, the college offers laptops to students with limited income to support their studies.

To further mitigate issues during online classes, the Foundation Programme Department has introduced measures such as extending deadlines for assignments and offering additional opportunities to make up missed quizzes for students working outside Muscat (SWOM). These initiatives aim to help MTC students achieve a strong GPA by the end of the semester.

10.2. Research Methodology

This paper presents a questionnaire designed to capture students' perspectives on online learning platforms. The survey explores students' views on online learning applications and was subject to MTC's procedural requirements. Participants needed to complete a form before the survey could be distributed to the Foundation Programme Department (FPD). The questionnaire was distributed after receiving approval from Dr. Abdullah Al Shibli, Head of the MTC Research Center.

The questionnaire consists of approximately 17 questions, and feedback was generally positive, thanks to the guidance provided by instructors. The survey reveals that most participants are IELTS students, reflecting the lower number of students in Level 3. Participants' ages range from 17 to 24, with most being 22 or older. On average, students spend between three to six hours per week using PCs for educational purposes. About 51.61% of learners can effectively access the Internet for their coursework. Most FPD students can interact well with their classmates and instructors electronically. Additionally, 41.91% of FPD students believe that possessing technical skills is beneficial for their current studies. Agree that they can manage their study time efficiently and effectively to complete assigned tasks on schedule.

10.3. Discussion

Most students prefer working in groups with their peers during their sessions. Twelve students agreed or strongly agreed that they enjoy interacting with their teacher and supporting their classmates in their studies. Many students find it beneficial to compose text on a computer in an online learning environment. Approximately 41.94% of FPD students feel comfortable communicating in English while studying online. Additionally, sixteen students strongly agreed that they can ask their teacher questions and receive prompt responses during online activities outside of campus. Most FPD students believe that personal interaction with their teacher is crucial for learning.

Half of the learners feel they can practice English grammar effectively during online sessions, while 3.33% strongly disagree. Twelve students believe that online learning outside of campus is more effective than traditional study methods, although only 16.13% strongly agree with this view. Seventeen learners agree that an entire semester could be delivered online without issues, with nine students strongly agreeing. Thirteen students strongly agreed that while online courses are feasible, learning English might be challenging, though nine students strongly supported this perspective. Finally, ten students agreed that they could complete the semester online without any instructor support, with eight students strongly agreeing.

Overall, this analysis indicates that FPD students find online study both engaging and essential for skill development. The pandemic has increased students' technological proficiency, as they adapted to using PCs more extensively and enhanced their learning during this period.

Figure 1. Student preferences and behaviors in online learning

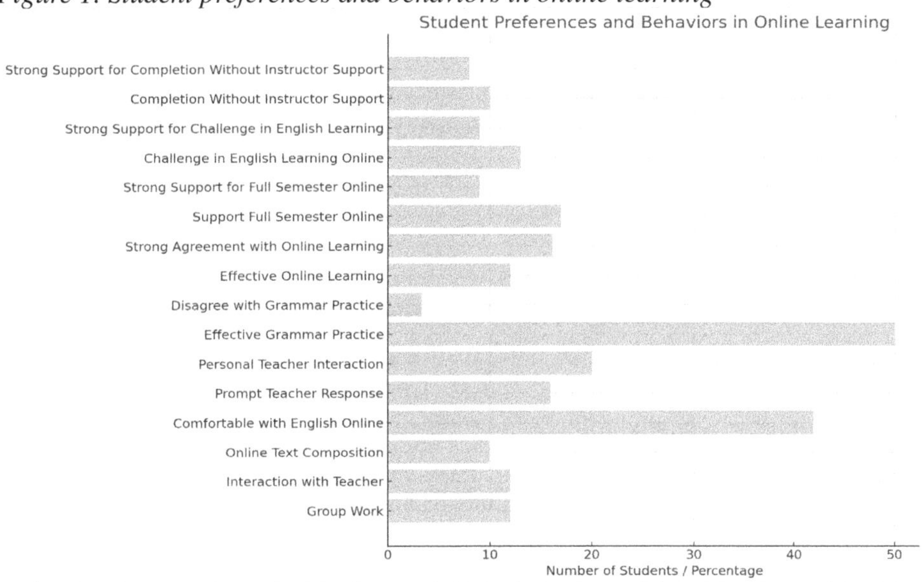

Here is the bar chart displaying student preferences and behaviors in online learning. It shows various aspects, such as group work, interaction with teachers, and comfort with English, as well as opinions on online learning effectiveness and challenges.

11. FUTURE SCOPE

The future scope of this research abstract highlights several significant avenues for further exploration and application in the domain of online English language learning. Below are key points outlining its potential impact and future development areas:

Enhancement of Virtual Language Learning Platforms

- **Improved Tools and Features**: Insights from the study can guide the development of more effective, interactive, and user-friendly virtual language learning tools tailored to English proficiency development.
- **Customization for Diverse Learners**: The research findings could help in designing platforms that cater to varying levels of language proficiency and cultural contexts in HEIs.

Integration of Emerging Technologies

- **AI and Machine Learning**: The study can lay the foundation for integrating AI-based personalized learning paths, automated feedback mechanisms, and advanced linguistic analysis tools into virtual platforms.
- **Gamification and VR/AR**: Future studies might explore how gamification and virtual/augmented reality tools can enhance engagement and interactivity in online language learning.

12. LIMITATIONS

1. Sample Size and Diversity: One of the primary limitations is the sample size and demographic diversity of participants. If the study primarily focused on a specific group of students, such as those from a particular institution or region, the findings may not be fully representative of the broader student population. Online English language programs may have varying levels of effectiveness depending on factors such as cultural background, language proficiency, and access to technology. Future studies could benefit from including a more diverse set of participants from multiple institutions and geographic regions to enhance the generalizability of the results.
2. Technology Access and Digital Literacy: The study may not have fully accounted for disparities in access to technology and digital literacy skills among students. While online programs offer flexibility and convenience, they also rely heavily on stable internet connections, suitable devices, and the ability to navigate digital platforms effectively. Students from regions with limited technological infrastructure or those lacking digital literacy skills might face significant barriers,

which can hinder their learning experience. This limitation suggests that while online programs have numerous benefits, they may not be equally accessible to all students, and future research should explore strategies to mitigate these barriers.

3. Limited Focus on Pedagogical Effectiveness: The study might have emphasized the benefits of online programs, such as flexibility and accessibility, without deeply exploring the pedagogical effectiveness of these digital learning methods compared to traditional classroom settings. For instance, while online platforms can facilitate learning through multimedia resources, they may lack the interactive, real-time feedback that in-person classes provide. Future research could compare the learning outcomes of students in online programs with those in traditional classroom environments to determine which methods lead to better language acquisition and fluency.
4. Limited Longitudinal Data: The study may have relied on short-term assessments of student performance and satisfaction, which can be limiting when evaluating the long-term benefits of online English language programs. Language learning is a gradual process, and short-term data might not accurately reflect students' language retention and proficiency over time. Future research should include longitudinal studies to assess the sustained impact of online programs on students' language skills and overall academic performance.

13. CONCLUSION AND RECOMMENDATIONS

In conclusion, this research emphasizes the pivotal role of Virtual Learning Environments (VLEs) in contemporary education, particularly in the realm of English language learning. The study's findings highlight that a significant portion of VLE users are military students, a demographic that has embraced the shift from traditional, campus-based education to online learning. This shift has been facilitated by the growing awareness and comfort with technology among students, which has made virtual platforms a viable and effective alternative to in-person classrooms. The increasing reliance on digital tools has underscored the importance of selecting the right platforms to support various aspects of learning.

Microsoft Teams and Kaizala are prime examples of such platforms, offering a suite of features that help educators and students collaborate, communicate, and manage coursework efficiently. Microsoft has further supported this transition by providing extensive online training videos and guidance materials that cater to users of all skill levels, ensuring that both novice and experienced users can navigate these platforms effectively (Microsoft, 2019a). However, to maximize the benefits of these digital tools, it is essential for educators to streamline communication and avoid redundancy by clearly designating which platform should be used for specific tasks. This will not only reduce confusion among students but also enhance the overall learning experience by ensuring that discussions, assessments, and collaborations are organized and accessible.

Moreover, the study underscores the need for educators to differentiate between the functionalities of Microsoft Teams and other popular Learning Management Systems(LMS)like Blackboard and Moodle. Each platform offers unique features, and understanding these differences is crucial for effective integration and use. For instance, while Microsoft Teams excel in real-time collaboration and communication, platforms like Blackboard and Moodle provide comprehensive course management capabilities that may better suit certain academic needs. Recent advancements, such as Microsoft's announcement of the integration of Microsoft Teams with Moodle, represent a significant step forward in enhancing collaborative learning experiences (Microsoft, 2019b).This integration allows institutions to synchronize assessments, manage tasks, and collaborate seamlessly on Moodle courses, offering higher education institutions enhanced opportunities to streamline their educational processes (Martin & Tapp, 2019).

Overall, this research has provided a comprehensive overview of the benefits and practical considerations associated with using online learning platforms for English language education. It has explored various aspects of these tools, offering insights into how platforms like Microsoft Teams and Kaizala can be utilized effectively to enhance the learning experience. The study recommends that educators continue to explore and integrate virtual learning tools, keeping in mind the importance of clarity and consistency in their application. By doing so, they can maximize the benefits of online learning, ensuring that students have access to high-quality educational resources and support, regardless of their physical location.

REFERENCES

Al Hajri, M. (2020). A cloud-based collaborative virtual learning environment for the higher education institutions in the Sultanate of Oman [Unpublished doctoral dissertation]. Bournemouth University.

Allen, I. E., & Seaman, J. (2007). *Online nation: Five years of growth in online learning*. Retrieved from ERIC.

Almarzooq, Z., Lopes, M., & Kochar, A. (2020). Virtual learning during the COVID-19 pandemic: A disruptive technology in graduate medical education. *Journal of the American College of Cardiology*, 75(20), 2635–2638. DOI: 10.1016/j.jacc.2020.04.015 PMID: 32304797

Alqahtani, S. M., Bhaskar, C. V., Vadakalur Elumalai, K., & Abumelha, M. (2018). WhatsApp: An online platform for university-level English language education. *Arab World English Journal*, 9(4), 108–121. DOI: 10.24093/awej/vol9no4.7

Carter, R. (2019, January 8). Microsoft Kaizala: App for comms & work management. *Uctoday.com*. https://www.uctoday.com/collaboration/microsoft-kaizala-review-mobile-app-for-comms-work-management

Cavanaugh, D. (2005). Teaching online – A time comparison. *Online Journal of Distance Learning Administration*, 8, 1–9.

Chuckedmonson, SuPotter, Pebaum, & MaabSaleem. (2019, May). Kaizala mobile app. *Docs.microsoft.com*. https://docs.microsoft.com/en-us/office365/kaizala/kaizala-mobile-app

Crompton, H., & Burke, D. (2023). Artificial intelligence in higher education: The state of the field. *International Journal of Educational Technology in Higher Education*, 20(1), 22–33. DOI: 10.1186/s41239-023-00392-8

Daniel, R. B., & Andrea, R. L. (2020). Learning from experience in the midst of COVID-19: Benefits, challenges, and strategies in online teaching. *Computer-Assisted Language Learning Electronic Journal*, 21(2), 176–196.

Downes, S. (2005). E-learning 2.0. *eLearn,* 4-7.

Guo, K., Li, Y., Li, Y., & Chu, S. K. W. (2024). Understanding EFL students' chatbot-assisted argumentative writing: An activity theory perspective. *Education and Information Technologies*, 29(1), 1–20. DOI: 10.1007/s10639-023-12230-5

Harmer, J. (2007). How to teach English (New ed.). Pearson Education Limited.

Kebritchi, M., Lipschuetz, A., & Santiague, L. (2017). Issues and challenges for teaching successful online courses in higher education: A literature review. *Journal of Educational Technology Systems*, 46(1), 4–29. DOI: 10.1177/0047239516661713

Laily, F. N., Suparno, S., & Ngadiso, N. (2023). Classroom-based assessment practices during the Covid-19 outbreak in Indonesia: EFL students' perceptions and challenges. *VELES: Voices of English Language Education.*

Luu, T. M. V. (2022). Readiness for online learning: Learners' comfort and self-directed learning ability. *International Journal of TESOL & Education*, 2(1), 213–224. DOI: 10.54855/ijte.222113

Machmud, K. (2018). The smartphone use in Indonesian schools: The high school students' perspectives. *Journal of Arts and Humanities*, 7(3), 33–40. DOI: 10.18533/journal.v7i3.1354

Martin, L., & Tapp, D. (2019). Teaching with Teams: An introduction to teaching an undergraduate law module using Microsoft Teams. *Innovative Practice in Higher Education*, 3(3), 58–66.

Matthew, N. O., Philip, O. A., & Sarhan, M. M. (2018). Online teaching and learning. *International Journal of Advanced Research in Computer Science and Software Engineering*, 8(2), 73–75. DOI: 10.23956/ijarcsse.v8i2.549

Microsoft Teams. (2020, August 26). In *Wikipedia.*https://en.wikipedia.org/wiki/Microsoft_Teams

Mohmmed, A. O., Khidhir, B. A., Nazeer, A., & Vijayan, V. J. (2020). Emergency remote teaching during coronavirus pandemic: The current trend and future directive at Middle East College Oman. *Innovative Infrastructure Solutions*, 5(3), 1–11. DOI: 10.1007/s41062-020-00326-7

Nugroho, A., Andriyanti, E., Widodo, P., & Mutiaraningrum, I. (2024). Students' appraisals post-ChatGPT use: Students' narrative after using ChatGPT for writing. *Innovations in Education and Teaching International*, •••, 1–13. DOI: 10.1080/14703297.2024.2319184

Nur, M. (2019). Literasi digital keagamaan aktivis organisasi keagamaan di Madrasah Aliyah Negeri (MAN) di Kota Bandung. *Jurnal SMART (Studi Masyarakat, Religi, dan Tradisi, 5*(1), 1-14. DOI: 10.1080/14703297.2024.2319184

Nurgiansah, T. H. (2022). Meningkatkan minat belajar siswa dengan media pembelajaran konvensional dalam pembelajaran pendidikan kewarganegaraan. *Jurnal Pendidikan dan Konseling (JPDK, 4*(3), 1529-1534. https://doi.org/DOI: 10.1080/14703297.2024.2319184

Pham, M. T., Luu, T. T. U., Mai, T. H. U., Thai, T. T. T., & Ngo, T. C. T. (2022). EFL students' challenges of online courses at Van Lang University during the COVID-19 pandemic. *International Journal of TESOL & Education*, 2(2), 1–26. DOI: 10.54855/ijte.22221

Pham, V. P. H., & Vo, N. D. T. (2021). CALL in Asia during COVID-19 and models of e-learning. In *Proceedings of the 17th International Conference of the Asia Association of Computer-Assisted Language Learning (AsiaCALL 2021)* (Vol. 533, pp. 1-10). https://doi.org/DOI: 10.2991/assehr.k.210226.001

Stecuła, K., & Wolniak, R. (2022). Advantages and disadvantages of e-learning innovations during COVID-19 pandemic in higher education in Poland. *Journal of Open Innovation*, 8(3), 159–180. DOI: 10.3390/joitmc8030159

Storyals. (2020, March). What is Microsoft Teams. *Storyals.*https://storyals.com/blog/what-is-microsoft-teams

Tenhunen, M.-L. (2022). Digitalisation innovation in university education. In *Proceedings of the EL 2022 Proceedings* (pp. 85-92). Lisbon, Portugal. ISBN 978-989-8704-39-9

Towey, D., & Pike, M. (2021). Not a silver bullet, but a silver lining: Metamorphic marking administration. In *2021 IEEE Global Engineering Education Conference (EDUCON)* (pp. 928-935). Vienna, Austria. https://doi.org/DOI: 10.1109/EDUCON46332.2021.9454074

Tran, T. T. O., & Pham, V. P. H. (2021). Experiences of the e-learning environment of students at the University of Danang – University of Foreign Language Studies. *The University of Danang – Journal of Science and Technology, 19*(12.2), 41-46. https://doi.org/DOI: 10.3390/joitmc8030159

Yani, B. S. H. (2019). Developing students' critical thinking through assessing evidence by utilizing Microsoft Kaizala. In *Committee of the 16th Jeta International Conference 2019 Patron.*https://www.researchgate.net/publication/335824689_Adapting_Authentic_Texts_for_Reading_Material

Zhang, D., & Zhang, L. J. (2019). Metacognition and self-regulated learning (SRL) in second/foreign language teaching. In Gao, X. (Ed.), *Second Handbook of English Language Teaching* (pp. 883–897). Springer., DOI: 10.1007/978-3-030-02899-2_47

Zhang, R., & Zou, D. (2022). Self-regulated second language learning: A review of types and benefits of strategies, modes of teacher support, and pedagogical implications. *Computer Assisted Language Learning*, 37(4), 720–765. DOI: 10.1080/09588221.2022.2055081

Zhao, X. (2023). The impact on higher education under COVID-19 pandemic prevention and control in China. *The International Conference on Interdisciplinary Humanities and Communication Studies, 7*, 226-232. https://doi.org/DOI: 10.54254/2753-7048/7/20220808

Zulaikha, M. B., Azlin, N. M., Khairul, A. J., & Bity, S. A. (2021). The effectiveness and challenges of online learning for secondary school students – A case study. *Asian Journal of University Education*, 17(3), 119–129. DOI: 10.24191/ajue.v17i3.14514

Chapter 7

Personalized Learning in the Digital Era: Unlocking Potential Through AI and Data Analytics

Usharani Bhimavarapu
https://orcid.org/0000-0002-0246-1420
Department of Computer Science and Engineering, Koneru Lakshmaiah Education Foundation, Vaddeswaram, India

ABSTRACT

Learning strategies with digital technologies have revolutionized educational practices, offering new opportunities for personalized, adaptive, and engaging learning experiences. The integration of digital tools, such as Artificial Intelligence (AI), machine learning, and digital platforms, enables educators to tailor learning strategies to individual student needs, promoting more effective and efficient learning. This study explores the potential of digital technologies in enhancing learning strategies, focusing on the role of Artificial Neural Networks (ANNs) in personalizing learning pathways for students. By leveraging data such as student performance, learning styles, and engagement, digital technologies can create adaptive learning environments that continuously evolve based on real-time feedback. The study investigates how these technologies can improve learner outcomes by providing targeted support, personalized content delivery, and dynamic feedback mechanisms.

DOI: 10.4018/979-8-3693-7863-2.ch007

INTRODUCTION

In recent years, digital technologies have significantly transformed research techniques and learning strategies across various fields. With the growing accessibility of online platforms, artificial intelligence (AI), and advanced data analytics, the way research is conducted has evolved. Researchers now have access to powerful tools that can enhance data collection, analysis, and collaboration. For example, digital tools such as data mining software and machine learning algorithms enable researchers to analyze vast datasets with increased efficiency, allowing for more accurate insights. Additionally, AI-driven platforms can automate tedious tasks, thus freeing up time for researchers to focus on higher-order analysis and creative problem-solving.

In the field of education, digital technologies are revolutionizing learning strategies by providing more personalized, interactive, and engaging experiences. Learning management systems (LMS), for instance, enable educators to track student progress, deliver content, and provide personalized feedback. Similarly, adaptive learning technologies, which adjust content to fit a student's learning pace and style, offer more tailored educational experiences. These advancements not only make learning more efficient but also help address diverse student needs, allowing educators to adopt a more student-centered approach in the classroom.

Furthermore, AI-powered tools like virtual tutors and chatbots have become increasingly integrated into the learning environment. These tools provide real-time assistance, support, and even simulate human interaction to help students grasp complex concepts. AI algorithms can track a student's learning patterns, identify weaknesses, and provide customized resources to improve understanding. This shift towards intelligent tutoring systems has the potential to complement traditional teaching methods, offering students an interactive and adaptive learning experience that can cater to their individual learning styles.

Another important aspect of digital technologies in research and education is the role of collaborative tools. Platforms such as online forums, video conferencing, and cloud-based collaboration tools enable researchers and students to connect across geographic boundaries, fostering more diverse and inclusive discussions. This collaborative environment encourages the sharing of ideas, perspectives, and resources, ultimately enhancing the quality of research and learning. Researchers can work together in real-time, share findings instantly, and receive immediate feedback, which accelerates the pace of discovery and innovation. For students, collaboration through digital tools helps develop important skills like communication, teamwork, and problem-solving.

Lastly, digital technologies have made significant strides in facilitating access to educational resources and research materials. Online databases, open-access journals, and digital libraries provide researchers and students with vast amounts of information at their fingertips. This accessibility is democratizing knowledge, enabling individuals from various backgrounds and regions to engage with academic content and contribute to research. Moreover, the use of digital platforms for learning allows students to explore subjects beyond the confines of their formal curriculum, fostering a lifelong learning mindset. As digital technologies continue to evolve, their integration into research techniques and learning strategies will likely expand, creating more opportunities for growth, discovery, and innovation in both fields.

The integration of digital technologies into research and education has significantly optimized both research techniques and learning strategies. One of the most prominent ways digital tools have enhanced research is through the ability to collect and analyze vast amounts of data at unprecedented speeds. With the help of AI-driven analytics platforms, researchers can sift through large datasets, detect patterns, and generate insights with minimal human intervention. Machine learning algorithms, for instance, can improve the accuracy of predictive models and automate data categorization, which streamlines the research process. These tools allow researchers to focus on deeper analysis, theory-building, and application, rather than spending time on repetitive tasks, thus speeding up the discovery process.

Similarly, in the realm of education, digital technologies have transformed learning strategies by offering more interactive, engaging, and personalized learning experiences. Learning Management Systems (LMS) such as Moodle and Blackboard allow instructors to design custom learning experiences tailored to individual students' needs. These platforms enable real-time tracking of student progress, assessments, and the integration of multimedia resources, enhancing both the teaching and learning processes. Furthermore, adaptive learning technologies dynamically adjust to the learning pace and preferences of each student, ensuring that learners are continually challenged without being overwhelmed, promoting better retention of knowledge and skill acquisition.

Another area in which digital technologies have optimized learning and research is through AI-powered educational tools. Virtual tutors, chatbots, and automated feedback systems provide real-time, personalized support to learners, answering questions and clarifying concepts outside of class time. These AI-driven tools are increasingly sophisticated, using natural language processing to understand student queries and deliver responses that are contextually relevant. This provides an opportunity for students to learn at their own pace, while teachers can focus on more complex and nuanced teaching moments. Similarly, AI-powered research tools can help researchers identify gaps in existing literature, recommend related studies, and even assist in the drafting of research papers, allowing for more efficient and comprehensive academic work.

Collaboration in research and learning has also been significantly enhanced through the advent of digital tools. Online collaboration platforms like Google Workspace, Microsoft Teams, and Slack provide seamless environments for researchers and students to work together, regardless of their geographic locations. These platforms allow for the sharing of ideas, resources, and data, enabling real-time feedback and fostering a collaborative approach to problem-solving. For instance, researchers can co-author papers, share findings, and engage in discussions across continents, enhancing the diversity and quality of their work. In education, collaborative tools promote peer-to-peer learning, enabling students to work together on projects, share insights, and learn from each other, thus reinforcing their understanding of complex concepts.

Finally, digital technologies have democratized access to educational content and research materials. Open-access journals, online databases, and digital libraries have made it easier for researchers to find relevant literature, analyze trends, and stay up to date with the latest findings in their fields. In education, resources such as online courses, podcasts, and video lectures enable students to learn beyond the classroom, allowing them to explore topics of personal interest and gain knowledge at their own pace. By making high-quality resources more accessible, digital technologies empower both learners and researchers to continue their education and research independently, fostering a culture of lifelong learning and continuous academic growth.

In conclusion, digital technologies have optimized research techniques and learning strategies by enhancing data analysis capabilities, providing personalized learning experiences, facilitating collaboration, and improving access to resources. These innovations are not only making research and education more efficient but also more inclusive, interactive, and accessible to a wider range of individuals. As technology continues to evolve, its integration into both research and education will likely continue to expand, offering even more opportunities for optimization, creativity, and growth in these fields.

Existing models of learning strategies with digital technologies face several limitations that hinder their effectiveness in enhancing education. One major challenge is the lack of personalization and adaptability; many digital learning tools struggle to deliver customized learning experiences that address individual student needs (Ingkavara et al., 2022). Additionally, while these models can improve content delivery, they often reduce teacher-student interaction, which is crucial for promoting engagement and critical thinking (Schiff, 2022). Moreover, the misalignment between AI tools and educational goals is a concern, as many current models prioritize technical features over pedagogical frameworks, limiting their pedagogical value (Zawacki-Richter et al., 2019).

Ethical issues and bias in AI systems also pose significant challenges, with many digital learning models failing to address fairness and privacy concerns adequately (Schiff, 2023). Another significant barrier is the scalability of these models; their effectiveness diminishes when applied across large and diverse educational contexts (Palmer, 2006). Furthermore, the digital divide exacerbates access and equity issues, leaving students from underprivileged backgrounds with limited access to the necessary resources for effective digital learning (Holmes & Tuomi, 2022).

Existing models also tend to rely excessively on data-driven outcomes, neglecting important aspects of learning, such as emotional and social growth, which are essential for a holistic educational experience (Celik et al., 2022). Furthermore, many digital learning models are not designed to support informal learning environments, reducing their applicability beyond formal education settings (Ahel & Schirmer, 2023). Resistance to these tools, stemming from student anxiety or teacher preparedness gaps, also limits their widespread adoption (Hopcan et al., 2024; Coker & Mercieca, 2023).

The cost of implementing these digital tools can be prohibitive, making them inaccessible to many institutions (Darvishi et al., 2024). In terms of quality control, AI-powered learning tools often fail to meet educational standards consistently, resulting in suboptimal learning experiences (Rawas, 2023). Additionally, AI models typically over-automate learning processes, which may stifle creativity and critical thinking by making students overly reliant on technology (Guilherme, 2019). These systems are also often designed with a focus on specific learning styles, which can limit their effectiveness for diverse learners (Zhai et al., 2021).

Privacy and security risks associated with personal data collection in AI-based educational systems remain a major concern, as many models do not sufficiently address these challenges (Flores-Vivar & García-Peñalvo, 2023). Moreover, AI models are often limited in their ability to assess qualitative outcomes such as creativity and problem-solving skills, focusing more on quantitative measures (Cope et al., 2021). The resistance to technological change from both educators and students further complicates the adoption and effective use of these tools (Celik et al., 2022).

In addition, existing AI tools often fail to provide real-time feedback, which is crucial for optimizing the learning process (Acevedo-Duque et al., 2023). Many of these models are also limited in their support for cognitive and social-emotional skills, which are essential for the overall development of students (Celik et al., 2022). Finally, despite the growing use of AI in education, there is still limited understanding and awareness of the ethical implications associated with its application, such as algorithmic biases and the need for fairness (Holmes & Tuomi, 2022). These limitations highlight the need for future improvements to address issues related to personalization, equity, ethical considerations, and the holistic development of learners.

Artificial Neural Networks (ANNs) offer several advantages that can help overcome the limitations found in existing digital learning models. One key benefit is their ability to personalize learning experiences, which addresses the challenge of tailoring content to individual student needs (Acevedo-Duque et al., 2023). By using data to adapt learning paths, ANNs can provide customized feedback and recommendations, promoting a more engaging and effective learning experience. This adaptability allows for greater flexibility in meeting the diverse needs of students, overcoming the lack of personalization seen in traditional digital tools (Ingkavara et al., 2022).

In terms of enhancing teacher-student interaction, ANNs can assist in improving engagement by providing real-time, dynamic support. For instance, AI-powered tools that incorporate ANNs can offer instant feedback, helping students stay engaged and motivated throughout their learning process (Rawas, 2023). Unlike static models, ANNs can continuously learn and adapt to student behavior, fostering a more interactive and supportive environment that encourages active learning and critical thinking. This ability to simulate human-like feedback addresses the gap in teacher-student interaction that other digital tools often fail to provide (Schiff, 2022).

Another advantage of ANNs is their ability to address scalability and accessibility challenges. By processing large datasets and making sense of diverse student profiles, ANNs can scale more effectively across various educational contexts, from small classrooms to large institutions (Zawacki-Richter et al., 2019). Moreover, ANNs can optimize learning materials and resources, ensuring that they are accessible to students from different backgrounds, thus reducing the impact of the digital divide (Holmes & Tuomi, 2022). They can be integrated into existing educational frameworks, providing an equitable learning experience that other models may struggle to deliver.

ANNs also improve ethical and bias mitigation by using advanced algorithms that can detect and correct biases in learning content (Schiff, 2023). By continuously analyzing data and outcomes, these networks can minimize discrimination or unfair treatment in learning processes, addressing privacy concerns and promoting fairness in education (Flores-Vivar & García-Peñalvo, 2023). Additionally, the ability of ANNs to analyze complex, non-linear patterns enables a more nuanced understanding of student behavior and learning outcomes, which can help in reducing the over-reliance on standardized, quantitative metrics that other digital tools often depend on (Guilherme, 2019).

Finally, ANNs can significantly enhance the quality of cognitive and social-emotional learning by integrating affective computing and analyzing emotional cues in students' interactions with the system. This ability to assess and respond to emotional and cognitive states allows ANNs to support both academic and personal development, an area where many traditional digital models fall short (Celik et al., 2022). By recognizing and adapting to a student's emotional needs, ANNs provide a more holistic approach to education, fostering not just academic growth but also emotional intelligence and resilience.

ANNs can overcome several of the limitations present in traditional digital learning models by offering personalized learning, improving teacher-student interaction, addressing scalability and accessibility, reducing bias, and supporting both cognitive and emotional development. These advancements position ANNs as a powerful tool for enhancing the effectiveness and inclusivity of digital education.

MATERIALS AND METHODOLOGY

The methodology employed in this study is qualitative and descriptive, focusing on exploring student teachers' perceptions of AI in education. Data were gathered through self-reflection tasks from 240 participants, analyzing their views on the strengths and weaknesses of using AI in teaching and learning. The collected data were transcribed, coded, and categorized using thematic analysis. A content analysis technique was applied, employing the Code-Category-Theme method for data triangulation. The study maintained high reliability, with an average reliability of 92%. Ethical considerations were followed, ensuring participant confidentiality and securing necessary permissions.

Material

The study gathered data through self-reflection tasks completed by 240 student teachers from various educational departments who participated in a seminar on the use of AI in education. The self-reflection tasks aimed to assess the participants' perceptions of AI in teaching and learning, highlighting both its strengths and weaknesses. The dataset was collected during the fall semester of 2023, and the participants were informed that their responses would remain confidential to ensure the reliability of the data. The collected dataset was analyzed using a content analysis technique, which included a triangulation process based on the Code-Category-Theme method. The data were transcribed, coded, and categorized into meaningful sections to identify key themes related to the research questions. The reliability of the study was calculated using the formula suggested by Miles and Huberman, yielding an average reliability of 92%. Direct quotations from the participants were included in the findings to provide an authentic representation of their experiences and thoughts regarding the integration of AI in education.

Preprocessing

The preprocessing of the collected dataset involved several NLP techniques to ensure the data was clean and suitable for analysis. First, the text data from the self-reflection tasks were tokenized to break down the responses into smaller, meaningful units (tokens) such as words or phrases. Following tokenization, stopword removal was performed to eliminate common, non-informative words (such as "the," "and," "is") that do not contribute significant meaning to the analysis. Next, stemming and lemmatization techniques were applied to reduce words to their root form, ensuring consistency in the dataset (e.g., converting "running" to "run"). The text was also normalized by converting all characters to lowercase, removing any special characters, and handling punctuation, ensuring that the data was uniform and free from irrelevant symbols. Additionally, any irrelevant or noisy data, such as incomplete sentences or responses that did not address the research questions, were filtered out to maintain data quality. After these preprocessing steps, the dataset was ready for thematic analysis, enabling a clearer extraction of key themes related to the student teachers' perceptions of AI in education.

Feature Extraction

Feature extraction using Explicit Semantic Analysis (ESA) was employed to enhance the understanding of the student teachers' perceptions of AI in education. ESA is a technique that maps textual data into a high-dimensional semantic space, where words or phrases are represented by vectors derived from external knowledge sources, such as Wikipedia or other large corpora. In this study, ESA was applied to the preprocessed dataset by transforming each response into a vector representation that captures the semantic meaning of the text. This transformation involved extracting relevant concepts and topics from the self-reflection tasks, which were then linked to the nearest corresponding concepts in the external knowledge base. The vector representation allowed for a more accurate comparison of the underlying meanings within the responses, enabling the identification of patterns and thematic clusters related to the strengths and weaknesses of AI in education. Through ESA, subtle semantic nuances in the participants' reflections were captured, providing deeper insights into their experiences and perceptions of AI integration in educational practices. The extracted features were then used for further analysis, such as clustering or classification, to gain a comprehensive understanding of the student teachers' views.

Enhancing Personalized Learning

Enhancing personalized learning with Artificial Neural Networks (ANNs) offers significant potential in tailoring educational experiences to individual students' needs, preferences, and learning styles. ANNs can analyze vast amounts of student data, such as past performance, learning habits, and engagement levels, to predict the most effective learning pathways for each student. By processing this data, ANNs can identify patterns and make real-time recommendations, adjusting the learning content and pace to match the student's unique requirements. This dynamic adaptation not only helps to address knowledge gaps but also challenges students at an appropriate level, promoting deeper learning. Additionally, ANNs can support personalized feedback, guiding students toward areas needing improvement while reinforcing their strengths. The ability to continuously learn from student interactions and adapt to their evolving needs makes ANNs an invaluable tool for fostering a more individualized and efficient learning environment. By integrating ANNs into educational systems, educators can ensure that each student receives the right level of support, ultimately enhancing their learning outcomes and overall experience.

EXPERIMENTAL RESULTS

The experimental results of this study reveal valuable insights into student teachers' perceptions of using AI in education. The analysis of the self-reflection tasks demonstrated a range of views regarding the strengths and weaknesses of AI in teaching and learning. Key themes emerged, highlighting the potential of AI to enhance personalized learning, improve efficiency, and support teachers in administrative tasks. However, concerns about data privacy, the need for teacher training, and the risk of over-reliance on technology were also identified. These findings underscore the importance of balanced integration, where AI complements traditional teaching methods while addressing its challenges and limitations.

Table 1 presents the AI tools most frequently utilized by teachers, along with their respective purposes and usage frequencies. ChatGPT leads as the most commonly used tool, with 45% of teachers utilizing it primarily for lesson planning, content creation, and enhancing student engagement. Quillbot follows closely at 38%, with its main function being paraphrasing and improving students' writing skills. Kahoot!, a tool used for creating quizzes and interactive activities, is utilized by 30% of teachers, while Socratic by Google, designed to assist with answering student questions and providing explanations, is used by 25%. Grammarly, for proofreading and grammar checks, is used by 22% of educators. Pear Deck, which helps in creating interactive presentations, has a usage rate of 20%, and WriteSonic, for generating writing prompts and articles, is employed by 18%. GPT-3, mainly used for automating administrative tasks and generating reports, is utilized by 15% of teachers. Jasper, a tool for generating lesson plans and curriculum materials, is used by 12%, and DeepL Translator, which is used for translating content in multilingual classrooms, is the least used, with a frequency of 10%. These tools reflect the varied ways AI is being integrated into educational practices, assisting teachers in improving efficiency and student interaction.

Table 1. AI tools most frequently utilized by teachers

AI Tool	Purpose	Frequency of Use (%)
ChatGPT	Assisting with lesson planning, content creation, and student engagement	45%
Quillbot	Paraphrasing and improving writing skills	38%
Kahoot!	Creating quizzes and interactive activities	30%
Socratic by Google	Answering student questions, explanations	25%
Grammarly	Proofreading and grammar checks	22%
Pear Deck	Creating interactive presentations	20%
WriteSonic	Generating writing prompts and articles	18%
GPT-3 (via various platforms)	Automating administrative tasks, generating reports	15%
Jasper	Generating lesson plans and curriculum materials	12%
DeepL Translator	Translating content for multilingual classrooms	10%

Table 2 summarizes the survey responses from teachers regarding the use of generative AI tools in their teaching practices. When asked about the frequency of AI tool usage, 30% of teachers reported using these tools occasionally, while 25% used them frequently, and 20% used them rarely. Only 15% indicated they never used AI tools, and 10% used them always. The primary purpose for using generative AI tools was identified as lesson planning by 40% of teachers, followed by content creation (30%), student engagement (20%), and grading (10%). Regarding the specific AI tools used, ChatGPT was the most popular, with 45% of teachers utilizing it, followed by Quillbot (35%), Kahoot! (25%), and Grammarly (20%).

In terms of effectiveness, 50% of teachers found AI tools to be effective in enhancing their teaching, with 30% rating them as very effective. A smaller portion, 10%, felt neutral about their effectiveness, while 5% considered them ineffective. The biggest challenges faced by teachers when using AI tools included concerns about content accuracy (35%), technical issues (30%), training needs (25%), and privacy concerns (15%). Despite these challenges, 70% of teachers would recommend AI tools to other educators, with only 15% expressing uncertainty and 15% against it.

When it comes to comfort levels with integrating AI tools into their curriculum, 40% of teachers felt comfortable, and 35% felt very comfortable, while 15% remained neutral and 10% were uncomfortable. Regarding the impact on student learning outcomes, 60% of teachers believed AI tools improved outcomes, while 30% were unsure, and 10% disagreed. The tools teachers thought would benefit students the most included interactive learning tools (50%), content creation tools (30%), and assessment tools (20%). Lastly, only 25% of teachers reported receiving adequate training on AI tools, while 50% said they had not received sufficient training, and 25% received partial training.

Table 2. Survey responses from teachers

Survey Question	Response Options	Percentage of Teachers Responding
How frequently do you use generative AI tools in your teaching?	Never, Rarely, Occasionally, Frequently, Always	30% Occasionally, 25% Frequently, 20% Rarely, 15% Never, 10% Always
What is the primary purpose of using generative AI tools?	Lesson planning, Content creation, Grading, Student engagement, Other	40% Lesson planning, 30% Content creation, 20% Student engagement, 10% Grading
Which AI tools do you use most often?	ChatGPT, Quillbot, Kahoot!, Grammarly, Other	45% ChatGPT, 35% Quillbot, 25% Kahoot!, 20% Grammarly
How effective do you find AI tools in enhancing your teaching?	Very Effective, Effective, Neutral, Ineffective, Very Ineffective	50% Effective, 30% Very Effective, 10% Neutral, 5% Ineffective, 5% Very Ineffective
What are the biggest challenges you face when using AI tools?	Accuracy of content, Technical issues, Training needs, Student distraction, Privacy concerns	35% Accuracy of content, 30% Technical issues, 25% Training needs, 15% Privacy concerns
Would you recommend the use of AI tools to other educators?	Yes, No, Maybe	70% Yes, 15% Maybe, 15% No
How comfortable are you with integrating AI tools into your curriculum?	Very Comfortable, Comfortable, Neutral, Uncomfortable, Very Uncomfortable	40% Comfortable, 35% Very Comfortable, 15% Neutral, 5% Uncomfortable, 5% Very Uncomfortable
Do you feel that AI tools help improve student learning outcomes?	Yes, No, Unsure	60% Yes, 30% Unsure, 10% No
What type of AI tools do you think would benefit your students the most?	Content creation tools, Assessment tools, Communication tools, Interactive learning tools	50% Interactive learning tools, 30% Content creation tools, 20% Assessment tools
Have you received adequate training to use AI tools effectively?	Yes, No, Partially	25% Yes, 50% No, 25% Partially

Table 3 provides an overview of the integration of Artificial Intelligence (AI) with teachers in education based on survey responses. Regarding the frequency of AI tool usage in teaching, 30% of teachers reported using AI tools rarely, while 25% used them frequently, and 20% used them occasionally. Only 10% of teachers reported using AI tools always, and 15% never used them. The primary use of AI tools in teaching was for lesson planning (40%), followed by content creation (35%), grading (15%), and student feedback (10%).

In terms of effectiveness, 45% of teachers found AI tools to be effective in supporting their teaching, while 35% considered them very effective. A small portion (15%) was neutral, and 5% found them ineffective. The main challenges teachers faced when using AI tools included technical issues (30%), lack of training (25%), accuracy of AI outputs (20%), and privacy concerns (15%). When asked whether AI improves student learning outcomes, 60% of teachers affirmed that AI has a positive impact, while 30% were unsure and 10% disagreed.

Regarding the recommendation of AI tools to other educators, 70% of teachers would recommend them, 20% were unsure, and 10% would not recommend them. Teachers' comfort with using AI in their classrooms was relatively high, with 40% feeling comfortable and 35% feeling very comfortable. However, 10% reported being uncomfortable. A significant portion of teachers (55%) believed AI helps in personalizing learning for students, while 35% were unsure, and 10% did not think it was helpful. Despite these positive views, only 30% of teachers reported receiving adequate training on AI tools, with 40% stating they had not received any training, and 30% receiving partial training. Finally, the most useful AI tools identified by teachers were ChatGPT (40%), Kahoot! (30%), Quillbot (25%), and Grammarly (15%).

Table 3. Integration of Artificial Intelligence (AI) with teachers in education

Survey Question	Response Options	Percentage of Teachers Responding
How often do you use AI tools in your teaching practice?	Never, Rarely, Occasionally, Frequently, Always	20% Occasionally, 25% Frequently, 30% Rarely, 15% Never, 10% Always
What do you primarily use AI for in your teaching?	Lesson planning, Grading, Content creation, Student feedback, Other	40% Lesson planning, 35% Content creation, 15% Grading, 10% Student feedback
How effective do you find AI in supporting your teaching?	Very Effective, Effective, Neutral, Ineffective, Very Ineffective	45% Effective, 35% Very Effective, 15% Neutral, 5% Ineffective
What challenges do you face when using AI tools?	Technical issues, Accuracy of AI outputs, Lack of training, Privacy concerns, Other	30% Technical issues, 25% Lack of training, 20% Accuracy of AI outputs, 15% Privacy concerns

continued on following page

Table 3. Continued

Survey Question	Response Options	Percentage of Teachers Responding
Do you think AI improves student learning outcomes?	Yes, No, Unsure	60% Yes, 30% Unsure, 10% No
Would you recommend AI tools to other educators?	Yes, No, Maybe	70% Yes, 20% Maybe, 10% No
How comfortable are you with using AI in your classroom?	Very Comfortable, Comfortable, Neutral, Uncomfortable, Very Uncomfortable	40% Comfortable, 35% Very Comfortable, 15% Neutral, 10% Uncomfortable
Do you feel AI helps in personalizing learning for students?	Yes, No, Unsure	55% Yes, 35% Unsure, 10% No
Have you received adequate training for using AI tools?	Yes, No, Partially	30% Yes, 40% No, 30% Partially
What type of AI tools do you find most useful?	ChatGPT, Quillbot, Kahoot!, Grammarly, Other	40% ChatGPT, 30% Kahoot!, 25% Quillbot, 15% Grammarly

Table 4 provides an analysis of how students integrate Artificial Intelligence (AI) tools into their educational processes, based on survey responses. Regarding the frequency of AI tool usage, 30% of students reported using AI tools frequently, while 25% used them occasionally, 20% rarely, and 15% never. Only 10% of students used AI tools always. The primary purposes for using AI in learning were research (35%), study aid (30%), assignment help (25%), and content exploration (10%).

When it comes to specific AI tools, the most frequently used by students were ChatGPT (45%), Grammarly (30%), Duolingo (25%), and Coursera (15%). In terms of effectiveness, 50% of students found AI tools effective in enhancing their learning, while 30% found them very effective. A smaller percentage (10%) were neutral, and 10% felt they were ineffective. The main challenges students encountered when using AI tools included technical issues (40%), lack of accuracy (25%), privacy concerns (15%), and dependency on AI (10%).

Most students (60%) felt that AI tools helped personalize their learning experience, while 25% were unsure, and 15% disagreed. Regarding recommending AI tools to peers, 70% of students would recommend them, 20% were unsure, and 10% would not recommend them. The comfort level of students using AI tools was generally high, with 40% feeling comfortable and 35% feeling very comfortable. A small portion (5%) expressed discomfort. In terms of reliance on AI for completing assignments, 30% of students relied on AI occasionally, 25% rarely, 20% frequently, and 15% never, with only 10% relying on it always. Lastly, 55% of students believed AI tools improved their academic performance, while 35% were unsure, and 10% disagreed.

Table 4. Integration of Artificial Intelligence (AI) in conjunction with students in education

Survey Question	Response Options	Percentage of Students Responding
How often do you use AI tools in your learning process?	Never, Rarely, Occasionally, Frequently, Always	25% Occasionally, 30% Frequently, 20% Rarely, 15% Never, 10% Always
What is the primary purpose of using AI tools for your learning?	Research, Content exploration, Assignment help, Study aid, Other	35% Research, 30% Study aid, 25% Assignment help, 10% Content exploration
Which AI tools do you use most often for learning?	ChatGPT, Grammarly, Duolingo, Coursera, Other	45% ChatGPT, 30% Grammarly, 25% Duolingo, 15% Coursera
How effective do you find AI tools in enhancing your learning?	Very Effective, Effective, Neutral, Ineffective, Very Ineffective	50% Effective, 30% Very Effective, 10% Neutral, 5% Ineffective, 5% Very Ineffective
What challenges do you face when using AI tools?	Technical issues, Lack of accuracy, Privacy concerns, Dependency, Other	40% Technical issues, 25% Lack of accuracy, 15% Privacy concerns, 10% Dependency
Do you feel that AI tools help in personalizing your learning experience?	Yes, No, Unsure	60% Yes, 25% Unsure, 15% No
Would you recommend the use of AI tools to other students?	Yes, No, Maybe	70% Yes, 20% Maybe, 10% No
How comfortable are you with using AI tools in your learning?	Very Comfortable, Comfortable, Neutral, Uncomfortable, Very Uncomfortable	40% Comfortable, 35% Very Comfortable, 20% Neutral, 5% Uncomfortable
How often do you rely on AI for completing assignments?	Never, Rarely, Occasionally, Frequently, Always	25% Occasionally, 30% Rarely, 20% Frequently, 15% Never, 10% Always
Do you think AI tools improve your academic performance?	Yes, No, Unsure	55% Yes, 35% Unsure, 10% No

Table 5 provides an overview of how students perceive AI's role in enhancing engagement during lessons, based on survey responses. Regarding the frequency of AI's impact on engagement, 30% of students reported that AI helped them stay engaged occasionally, 25% frequently, 20% rarely, 15% never, and 10% always. The AI tools that students found most effective in maintaining engagement were gamified learning tools (40%), virtual assistants (30%), interactive simulations (25%), and other tools (15%).

When asked if AI tools provided adequate opportunities for interaction during lessons, 55% of students responded positively, while 30% were unsure and 15% disagreed. In terms of effectiveness, 40% of students found AI effective in keeping them motivated during lessons, 35% considered it very effective, and 15% felt neutral. Only a small percentage (5%) found it ineffective or very ineffective.

AI's impact on different types of engagement revealed that 45% of students felt AI most improved active participation, 35% saw benefits in visual engagement, 20% in problem-solving tasks, and 10% in collaboration. Lastly, 65% of students would recommend AI tools for improving classroom engagement, 25% were unsure, and 10% would not recommend them.

Table 5. AI in enhancing student engagement

Survey Question	Response Options	Percentage of Students Responding
How often does AI help you stay engaged during lessons?	Never, Rarely, Occasionally, Frequently, Always	30% Occasionally, 25% Frequently, 20% Rarely, 15% Never, 10% Always
Which AI tools keep you engaged during lessons?	Interactive simulations, Virtual assistants, Gamified learning tools, Other	40% Gamified learning tools, 30% Virtual assistants, 25% Interactive simulations, 15% Other
Do AI tools provide adequate opportunities for interaction during lessons?	Yes, No, Unsure	55% Yes, 30% Unsure, 15% No
How effective do you find AI in keeping you motivated during lessons?	Very Effective, Effective, Neutral, Ineffective, Very Ineffective	40% Effective, 35% Very Effective, 15% Neutral, 5% Ineffective, 5% Very Ineffective
What type of engagement does AI improve the most?	Visual engagement, Active participation, Problem-solving tasks, Collaboration	45% Active participation, 35% Visual engagement, 20% Problem-solving tasks, 10% Collaboration
Would you recommend AI tools for improving classroom engagement?	Yes, No, Maybe	65% Yes, 25% Maybe, 10% No

Table 6 presents insights into how AI impacts student motivation based on survey responses. When asked how often AI increases their motivation to learn, 35% of students reported that AI occasionally boosts their motivation, 30% frequently, 20% rarely, 10% never, and 5% always. The feature of AI that most boosts student motivation is personalized learning, with 50% of students selecting it, followed by instant feedback (30%), rewards (15%), and progress tracking (5%).

Regarding whether AI tools make learning feel more rewarding, 60% of students answered affirmatively, 25% were unsure, and 15% disagreed. In terms of assignment completion motivation, 50% of students felt more motivated due to AI tools, 40% sometimes, and 10% did not feel motivated. When facing challenges, AI tools positively impact motivation for 55% of students, with 25% reporting no impact and 20% indicating a negative effect. Lastly, 70% of students would recommend AI tools for improving student motivation, 20% were unsure, and 10% would not recommend them.

Table 6. AI's impact on student motivation

Survey Question	Response Options	Percentage of Students Responding
How often does AI increase your motivation to learn?	Never, Rarely, Occasionally, Frequently, Always	35% Occasionally, 30% Frequently, 20% Rarely, 10% Never, 5% Always
Which AI feature most boosts your motivation?	Personalized learning, Instant feedback, Progress tracking, Rewards	50% Personalized learning, 30% Instant feedback, 15% Rewards, 5% Progress tracking
Do AI tools make learning feel more rewarding?	Yes, No, Unsure	60% Yes, 25% Unsure, 15% No
Do you feel more motivated to complete assignments due to AI tools?	Yes, No, Sometimes	50% Yes, 40% Sometimes, 10% No
How do AI tools impact your motivation when facing challenges?	Positively, Negatively, No Impact	55% Positively, 25% No Impact, 20% Negatively
Would you recommend AI tools to improve student motivation?	Yes, No, Maybe	70% Yes, 20% Maybe, 10% No

A Brief Timeline of AI in Education

1. **1950s–1960s: The Foundations of AI in Education**
   - o **1956**: The term "Artificial Intelligence" was coined at the Dartmouth Conference, marking the formal beginning of AI as a field.
   - o Early efforts focused on rule-based systems and symbolic reasoning, laying the groundwork for AI applications in problem-solving and learning.
2. **1970s: Early Intelligent Tutoring Systems (ITS)**
   - o Development of the first ITS, such as **SCHOLAR**, a program designed to teach geography by answering student questions.
   - o Focus on structured knowledge representation and adapting instruction based on user queries.
3. **1980s: Expansion of ITS and Cognitive Science**
   - o Systems like **Andes** (physics tutor) and **SOPHIE** (electronics tutor) introduced more sophisticated models for understanding student behavior.
   - o Research emphasized aligning AI systems with cognitive theories of learning, paving the way for personalized learning.
4. **1990s: Multimedia and Adaptive Learning**
   - o Increased computing power enabled multimedia-rich educational content and interactive tools.

- o AI began incorporating adaptive learning, where systems like **ALEKS** (Assessment and Learning in Knowledge Spaces) tailored content to individual learner needs.

5. **2000s: Online Learning and AI Integration**
   - o Growth of online education platforms like **Khan Academy** introduced data-driven insights into student learning patterns.
   - o AI technologies, such as recommender systems and automated grading, became integrated into educational platforms.
6. **2010s: Rise of Machine Learning and AI-Powered Platforms**
   - o Introduction of platforms like **Duolingo** and **MATHia**, leveraging AI to personalize language learning and STEM education.
   - o Virtual assistants like **IBM Watson Tutor** and **Google Classroom** incorporated AI for real-time feedback and resource management.
7. **2020s: AI for Scalable and Inclusive Education**
   - o Widespread adoption of AI in response to the COVID-19 pandemic, with platforms like Oak National Academy providing personalized resources at scale.
   - o Use of Natural Language Processing (NLP) for AI-powered chatbots, plagiarism detection, and content curation.
   - o Integration of emerging technologies such as Augmented Reality (AR), Virtual Reality (VR), and AI-driven predictive analytics for immersive and data-informed learning.

CASE STUDIES

Given some examples of institutions that have successfully integrated AI-based personalized learning systems, which could serve as case studies:

1. Summit Public Schools (United States)

Summit Public Schools partnered with Facebook to develop the Summit Learning Program, a platform leveraging AI to deliver personalized learning experiences. The program uses student performance data to offer customized learning pathways, enabling students to progress at their own pace. Teachers receive real-time insights into student progress, allowing for targeted interventions. The program has been widely adopted across the U.S., enhancing student engagement and academic outcomes.

2. Minerva Schools at KGI

Minerva Schools employ an AI-powered platform called Active Learning Forum, designed to personalize and optimize the learning experience. The platform adapts content based on individual student responses and participation, fostering critical thinking and active engagement. Data collected from the platform is analyzed to continuously refine teaching methodologies, making the learning process more efficient and student-centered.

3. ALT School (United States)

ALT School, a network of micro-schools, integrates AI into its curriculum to create tailored learning experiences. The school's proprietary platform tracks individual student progress and adapts lesson plans accordingly. Teachers use AI-driven insights to provide one-on-one guidance and curate resources specific to each student's learning style and needs.

4. Oak National Academy (United Kingdom)

During the COVID-19 pandemic, the Oak National Academy leveraged AI technologies to provide personalized learning materials to students. By analyzing data from thousands of users, the platform offered tailored educational content, ensuring continuity of education despite disruptions. This large-scale implementation demonstrates the potential of AI in adapting to diverse student requirements under challenging conditions.

5. Carnegie Learning (United States)

Carnegie Learning developed MATHia, an AI-driven math tutoring platform. It adapts in real-time to student performance, identifying strengths and weaknesses and providing personalized feedback. Studies have shown significant improvements in math proficiency among students using MATHia, making it a benchmark for personalized learning in STEM education.

PRACTICAL IMPLICATIONS FOR EDUCATORS AND POLICYMAKERS

1. **Personalized Learning Pathways**
   - **For Educators**: AI allows teachers to create individualized learning plans tailored to student strengths and weaknesses. For example, plat-

forms like MATHia provide adaptive math tutoring, helping educators focus on students requiring additional support.

  - **For Policymakers**: Policies should promote the adoption of AI-based tools in schools, ensuring equitable access and training for teachers. Subsidized programs like those implemented in Estonia's digital education initiative can serve as a model.

2. **Teacher Support and Professional Development**
   - **For Educators**: AI-powered tools automate administrative tasks like grading and lesson planning, freeing up time for teachers to focus on instruction and mentorship. For instance, Turnitin employs AI for plagiarism detection, reducing workload while ensuring academic integrity.
   - **For Policymakers**: Invest in professional development programs that equip educators with the skills to effectively integrate AI into classrooms, as seen in Singapore's AI Literacy Framework.
3. **Enhanced Accessibility and Inclusion**
   - **For Educators**: AI can support diverse learners, including those with disabilities. Tools like Microsoft's Immersive Reader improve accessibility by converting text into audio, translating languages, and adapting font styles.
   - **For Policymakers**: Implement policies that mandate accessibility features in educational technologies to cater to students with special needs, inspired by frameworks like the U.S. Individuals with Disabilities Education Act (IDEA).
4. **Data-Driven Decision Making**
   - **For Educators**: AI systems provide actionable insights into student performance, helping teachers identify trends and intervene early. Platforms like Knewton analyze learning data to predict outcomes and recommend resources.
   - **For Policymakers**: Develop data privacy regulations to protect student information while enabling its ethical use for educational improvement, similar to the European Union's GDPR guidelines.
5. **Equity and Resource Allocation**
   - **For Educators**: AI can bridge resource gaps in underfunded schools by providing scalable, cost-effective solutions, such as AI-driven virtual tutors or free platforms like Khan Academy.
   - **For Policymakers**: Prioritize investments in digital infrastructure to ensure rural and economically disadvantaged areas can leverage AI technologies effectively, as demonstrated by India's PM eVIDYA initiative.
6. **Curriculum and Policy Adaptation**

- **For Educators**: Integrating AI into curriculums helps students develop 21st-century skills like computational thinking and problem-solving. Examples include programs like AI4ALL, which introduces AI concepts to K-12 students.
- **For Policymakers**: Update national education policies to include AI literacy and ethics in school curriculums, as initiated by Finland's "Elements of AI" course for students and citizens alike.

Real-World Example

- **China's Smart Education Platforms**: The Chinese government's large-scale AI integration in education uses adaptive platforms to assess and personalize learning. Schools equipped with AI-powered cameras monitor classroom engagement, and platforms like Squirrel AI offer one-on-one tutoring, demonstrating how policy and technology can scale personalized education effectively.

By addressing these practical implications and learning from real-world examples, educators and policymakers can harness AI to create more inclusive, efficient, and impactful educational systems.

CONCLUSION

In conclusion, the incorporation of digital technologies, particularly Artificial Neural Networks, into learning strategies holds immense promise for transforming educational practices. The ability to personalize learning experiences based on individual student data enhances engagement, improves learning outcomes, and supports continuous progress. By offering tailored recommendations, adaptive content, and real-time feedback, digital technologies help bridge the gap between diverse student needs and educational goals. However, the successful integration of these technologies requires careful consideration of challenges such as data privacy, system scalability, and the need for appropriate teacher training. Moving forward, the continued evolution of digital technologies will play a pivotal role in reshaping education, fostering more inclusive, effective, and personalized learning environments that cater to the unique needs of every learner.

Future Scope

The potential of digital technologies, particularly Artificial Neural Networks, in education is vast and ever-expanding. Future research and development efforts should focus on enhancing the scalability and accessibility of these technologies to ensure their benefits reach underserved communities and regions with limited resources. Advancements in AI and machine learning algorithms can further refine personalization, enabling even more accurate predictions of student needs and challenges.

Moreover, integrating emerging technologies such as augmented reality (AR), virtual reality (VR), and the Internet of Things (IoT) with neural network-driven learning systems could create immersive and interactive learning environments. Long-term studies should evaluate the impact of these systems on various educational metrics, such as student retention rates, skill acquisition, and career readiness.

Addressing ethical considerations, including bias mitigation in AI algorithms and robust frameworks for safeguarding student data, will remain critical. Collaboration among educators, policymakers, and technologists is essential to establish standards and best practices that prioritize equitable and secure implementation.

By exploring these avenues, digital technologies can continue to evolve as a cornerstone of modern education, driving innovation and fostering a generation of empowered, lifelong learners.

REFERENCES

Acevedo-Duque, Á., Jiménez-Bucarey, C., Prado-Sabido, T., Fernández-Mantilla, M. M., Merino-Flores, I., Izquierdo-Marín, S. S., & Valle-Palomino, N. (2023). Education for sustainable development: Challenges for postgraduate programmes. *International Journal of Environmental Research and Public Health*, 20(3), 1759. DOI: 10.3390/ijerph20031759 PMID: 36767126

Ahel, O., & Schirmer, M. (2023). Education for sustainable development through research-based learning in an online environment. *International Journal of Sustainability in Higher Education*, 24(1), 118–140. DOI: 10.1108/IJSHE-07-2021-0305

Alenezi, M. (2023). Digital learning and digital institution in higher education. *Education Sciences*, 13(2), 88. DOI: 10.3390/educsci13010088

Bulathwela, S., Pérez-Ortiz, M., & Sánchez, J. M. (2023). Smart learning environments in education: A systematic review and future directions. *Educational Technology Research and Development*, 71, 887–907.

Celik, I., Dindar, M., Muukkonen, H., & Järvelä, S. (2022). The promises and challenges of artificial intelligence for teachers: A systematic review of research. *TechTrends*, 66(5), 616–630. DOI: 10.1007/s11528-022-00715-y

Chatterjee, R., Bandyopadhyay, A., Chakraborty, S., & Dutta, S. (2023). Digital education: The basics with slant to digital pedagogy—An overview. In *Digital Learning Based Education: Transcending Physical Barriers* (pp. 63–80). Springer.

Coker, H., & Mercieca, D. (2023). Digital technology for inclusive education: Reflecting on the role of teachers. In *Inclusion, Equity, Diversity, and Social Justice in Education: A Critical Exploration of the Sustainable Development Goals* (pp. 233–243). Springer Nature.

Cope, B., Kalantzis, M., & Searsmith, D. (2021). Artificial intelligence for education: Knowledge and its assessment in AI-enabled learning ecologies. *Educational Philosophy and Theory*, 53(11), 1229–1245. DOI: 10.1080/00131857.2020.1728732

Darvishi, A., Khosravi, H., Sadiq, S., Gašević, D., & Siemens, G. (2024). Impact of AI assistance on student agency. *Computers & Education*, 210, 104967. DOI: 10.1016/j.compedu.2023.104967

Di Vaio, A., Hassan, R., & Alavoine, C. (2022). Data intelligence and analytics: A bibliometric analysis of human–artificial intelligence in public sector decision-making effectiveness. *Technological Forecasting and Social Change*, 174, 121201. DOI: 10.1016/j.techfore.2021.121201

Flores-Vivar, J. M., & García-Peñalvo, F. J. (2023). Reflections on the ethics, potential, and challenges of artificial intelligence in the framework of quality education (SDG4). *Comunicar*, 31(72), 37–47. DOI: 10.3916/C74-2023-03

Guilherme, A. (2019). AI and education: The importance of teacher and student relations. *AI & Society*, 34(1), 47–54. DOI: 10.1007/s00146-017-0693-8

Henderson, K., & Loreau, M. (2023). A model of Sustainable Development Goals: Challenges and opportunities in promoting human well-being and environmental sustainability. *Ecological Modelling*, 475, 110164. DOI: 10.1016/j.ecolmodel.2022.110164

Hickmann, T., Biermann, F., Spinazzola, M., Ballard, C., Bogers, M., Forestier, O., Kalfagianni, A., Kim, R. E., Montesano, F. S., Peek, T., Sénit, C.-A., van Driel, M., Vijge, M. J., & Yunita, A. (2023). Success factors of global goal-setting for sustainable development: Learning from the Millennium Development Goals. *Sustainable Development (Bradford)*, 31(6), 1214–1225. DOI: 10.1002/sd.2461

Holmes, W., & Tuomi, I. (2022). State of the art and practice in AI in education. *European Journal of Education*, 57(4), 542–570. DOI: 10.1111/ejed.12533

Hopcan, S., Türkmen, G., & Polat, E. (2024). Exploring the artificial intelligence anxiety and machine learning attitudes of teacher candidates. *Education and Information Technologies*, 29(6), 7281–7301. DOI: 10.1007/s10639-023-12086-9

Ingkavara, T., Panjaburee, P., Srisawasdi, N., & Sajjapanroj, S. (2022). The use of a personalized learning approach to implementing self-regulated online learning. *Computers & Education: Artificial Intelligence*, 3, 100086.

Legard, R., Keegan, J., & Ward, K. (2003). In-depth Interviews. In J. Richie & J. Lewis (Eds.), *Qualitative Research Practice* (pp. 139–168). Sage Publications.

Miles, M. B., & Huberman, A. M. (1994). *An Expanded Sourcebook: Qualitative Data Analysis* (2nd ed.). Sage Publications.

Ogata, H., Flanagan, B., Takami, K., Dai, Y., Nakamoto, R., Takii, K. (2024). EXAIT: Educational eXplainable Artificial Intelligent Tools for personalized learning. *Research and Practice in Technology Enhanced Learning, 19*, 019.

Palmer, M. (2006). *Data is the new oil.* ANA Marketing Maestros.

Patton, M. Q. (1990). *Qualitative Evaluation and Research Methods* (2nd ed.). Sage Publications.

Rawas, S. (2023). ChatGPT: Empowering lifelong learning in the digital age of higher education. *Education and Information Technologies*, 29(5), 6895–6908.

Schiff, D. (2022). Education for AI, not AI for education: The role of education and ethics in national AI policy strategies. *International Journal of Artificial Intelligence in Education*, 32(3), 527–563. DOI: 10.1007/s40593-021-00270-2

Schiff, D. S. (2023). Looking through a policy window with tinted glasses: Setting the agenda for US AI policy. *The Review of Policy Research*, 40(5), 729–756. DOI: 10.1111/ropr.12535

Tahiru, F. (2021). AI in education: A systematic literature review. *Journal of Cases on Information Technology*, 23(1), 1–20. DOI: 10.4018/JCIT.2021010101

Tien, J. M. (2017). Internet of things, real-time decision making, and artificial intelligence. *Annals of Data Science*, 4(2), 149–178. DOI: 10.1007/s40745-017-0112-5

Zawacki-Richter, O., Marín, V. I., Bond, M., & Gouverneur, F. (2019). Systematic review of research on artificial intelligence applications in higher education–where are the educators? *International Journal of Educational Technology in Higher Education*, 16(1), 39. DOI: 10.1186/s41239-019-0171-0

Zhai, X., Chu, X., Chai, C. S., Jong, M. S. Y., Istenic, A., Spector, M., Liu, J. B., Yuan, J., & Li, Y. (2021). A review of artificial intelligence (AI) in education from 2010 to 2020. *Complexity*, 2021(1), 8812542. DOI: 10.1155/2021/8812542

Chapter 8
Leveraging AI to Enhance Teaching and Learning in Education:
The Role of Artificial Intelligence in Modernizing Classroom Practices

Seema Yadav
https://orcid.org/0000-0002-8477-5895
Bhopal School of Social Sciences, India

ABSTRACT

The integration of Artificial Intelligence (AI), Virtual Reality (VR), and Augmented Reality (AR) in education is reshaping the learning landscape by providing immersive and personalized learning experiences. Immersive learning through VR and AR allows for practical simulations and experiential learning, bridging the gap between theoretical knowledge and real-world application. However, challenges such as ethical considerations, data privacy, and the digital divide need to be addressed to ensure inclusive and equitable access to these advanced learning tools. The chapter explores the benefits of AI-driven immersive learning, including improved student motivation, engagement, and retention, while also discussing scalability and the potential for widespread adoption across diverse educational settings. It emphasizes the importance of incorporating ethical frameworks and continuous research to align AI, VR, and AR applications with the evolving needs of modern education, ensuring that these technologies contribute positively to student outcomes and lifelong learning.

DOI: 10.4018/979-8-3693-7863-2.ch008

INTRODUCTION

The history of technological advancements in education reflects a continuous effort to enhance teaching and learning, beginning with basic tools like chalkboards and progressing through transformative innovations such as the printing press, which made textbooks widely accessible. The 20th century saw the introduction of audio-visual aids, radio, and television as educational tools, followed by the emergence of computers in the 1980s, which paved the way for digital learning and the internet revolution. The widespread use of personal computers and, later, mobile devices led to the development of e-learning platforms and online courses, making education more flexible and accessible. By addressing some of the most pressing issues facing education today, artificial intelligence (AI) has the potential to revolutionize teaching and learning methods and, eventually, hasten the achievement of SDG 4 (Miao et al., 2023). The complexity, speed, and intelligence of machines are increasing throughout time. The ability to deduce, infer, and make decisions exactly like humans is still a ways off, but recent years have seen some impressive advancements in the use of machine learning and artificial intelligence (AI) techniques (Mukhallafi, 2020). Today, the integration of AI in education marks a significant leap forward, with AI-powered tools supporting personalized learning, automating administrative tasks, and providing real-time analytics to improve teaching strategies. Intelligent tutoring systems, adaptive learning platforms, and virtual assistants are increasingly used to cater to individual student needs, while AI's data processing capabilities help educators identify patterns in student performance for more targeted interventions. In practically every aspect of our lives, artificial intelligence (AI) is being used. AI is a thriving technology that is changing how we interact with others. In education, AI will now create new teaching and learning solutions that will be tested in various scenarios. New educational technologies can better manage and achieve educational goals (Joshi et al., 2021). Despite its potential, the current state of AI in education also faces challenges such as ethical concerns, data privacy issues, and unequal access, which must be addressed to fully realize its benefits and ensure that advancements are equitably distributed across diverse educational contexts. Recent years have seen the rapid advancement of artificial intelligence (AI) technologies, which have had a significant impact on every aspect of society, including politics, business, science, and education. Teachers at all levels of education are using these tools more and more. Artificial intelligence (AI) technologies, which are becoming more and more common in education, have enormous potential to improve both teachers' teaching methods and students' learning experiences and performance (Yetişensoy & Karaduman, 2024). A multitude of new opportunities, potential, and challenges for comprehending and promoting learning have been brought about by artificial intelligence (AI) (Järvelä et al., 2023).

Artificial intelligence (AI) education is being offered at the K–12 level more frequently in response to the growing acceptance of AI use in daily life, and related projects are being started all over the world (Yue et al., 2022). The need for people who understand artificial intelligence (AI) will grow in the future due to the rapid technological advancements brought about by AI. Building the AI competencies of the future generation and teaching them how to use and collaborate with AI are essential (Su & Zhong, 2022). Education is changing quickly as a result of artificial intelligence (AI), which presents new opportunities to improve learning outcomes and advance inclusive teaching methods. Teachers are investigating creative teaching approaches that use AI to address a range of learning requirements and foster more inclusive learning environments as these technologies become more advanced and available (Olabisi Oluwakemi Adeleye et al., 2024). The science of artificial intelligence (AI) has developed, and this has affected nearly every element of human existence. The Sustainable Development Goals (SDGs) are among the developmental issues it has lately come into play for (Singh et al., 2024). In 2022, sophisticated AI-generated creative content started to gain traction in the media when user-friendly apps that produced images with remarkably realistic "humanness" started to surface (Bender, 2024). The rapid development of complex algorithms, low-cost graphic processors, and large annotated databases is responsible for the rapid rise of AI in modern culture. AI has become an essential part of healthcare education in the last several years and is being used by many medical schools throughout the world. Compared to developing nations, medical education in Western nations makes extensive use of artificial intelligence (Naqvi et al., 2024).

The world is changing dramatically as a result of artificial intelligence (AI); while some of these effects are undoubtedly positive, the technology can also have widespread and long-lasting negative effects. AI is being incorporated into many facets of human life, and the complicated ethical issues that have arisen from its development, application, and use serve as a reminder that it is time to review the lessons that professionals and upcoming developers are learning about AI (Borenstein & Howard, 2021). Within the quickly changing field of education, artificial intelligence (AI) plays a central role, and English Language Teaching (ELT) is undergoing significant change (Baskara, 2023). Unquestionably, using artificial intelligence in English language instruction can significantly aid in the development of oral communication skills. AI has made it possible for students to participate in interactive speaking practice, receive feedback, and complete customized assignments. Artificial intelligence has several benefits, one of which is its capacity to assess pupils' pronunciation and offer recommendations and guidance to improve their oral communication (Kemelbekova et al., 2024). AI reduces prejudice and effort and is useful for curriculum development, course material preparation, instructional design, and student assessment from the standpoint of the educator. AI tools provide students with individualized learning experiences, prompt feedback, and assistance with a range of academic tasks (Sağın et al., 2024). In recent years, artificial intelligence (AI) has become increasingly prevalent across multiple industries and has revolutionized task execution. Artificial Intelligence (AI) holds great promise for transforming conventional teaching and learning approaches in the realm of education, especially when it comes to ESL (English as a Second Language) classes (Sharifuddin & Hashim, 2024). AI is transforming education by giving teachers access to sophisticated tools and resources that will help them customize instruction, foster better teamwork, and increase accessibility. With the help of AI-powered tools, teachers may customize training to meet the needs of each unique student by analyzing massive volumes of data to find patterns and trends. Furthermore, immersive and interactive learning environments are being created using AI technology. Examples of these include augmented reality (AR) and virtual reality (VR) apps that engage students in novel and interesting ways (Olabisi Oluwakemi Adeleye et al., 2024).

Artificial intelligence (AI) is transforming the educational landscape by introducing innovative methods that enhance both teaching and learning experiences (Ouyang & Jiao, 2021). With AI-driven personalization, educational content can be tailored to meet the unique needs of each student, thereby fostering a more engaging and effective learning environment. Intelligent tutoring systems, automated grading, and AI-powered analytics enable educators to focus more on interactive and high-impact teaching activities, while administrative burdens are minimized (Vázquez-Cano, 2021). Additionally, AI facilitates the creation of immersive learning experiences through virtual and augmented reality, making complex concepts more accessible and understandable. As AI continues to evolve, its integration in education promises to revolutionize traditional methods, ensuring that teaching strategies are more adaptive, inclusive, and efficient. Education technology powered by artificial intelligence (AI) extends beyond the classroom and includes online platforms, virtual reality, and interactive tools. It explores the integration of AI in curriculum development, content creation, and assessment methods, providing insights into how these technologies augment the teaching and learning experience. The introduction of AI in education has ushered in a transformative era, redefining traditional methods of teaching and learning (Oyebola Olusola Ayeni et al., 2024).

There has been a lot of interest in the use of AI-based chatbots in language instruction. Chatbots like ChatGPT-4o and Claude 3 have been developed as a result of the quick growth of artificial intelligence (AI), and they are being used more and more in a variety of educational applications, including language acquisition (Xiao et al., 2024). Artificial intelligence (AI) is rapidly transforming the field of education, introducing innovative approaches that enhance both teaching and learning experiences. The evolution of AI, driven by advances in complex algorithms, affordable graphic processors, and large annotated datasets, has made it an integral part of modern society, influencing areas such as healthcare, English language teaching (ELT), and curriculum development. AI-powered tools enable educators to personalize learning by analyzing vast amounts of data to identify patterns, thus allowing for tailored instruction that meets the unique needs of each student. These tools also reduce bias, streamline administrative tasks, and enhance collaboration by providing prompt feedback, automated grading, and intelligent tutoring systems. Furthermore, immersive and interactive environments created through AI technologies, such as augmented and virtual reality, engage students in novel ways, making complex concepts more accessible. With AI's integration, education is undergoing a significant shift that promises to revolutionize traditional methods, fostering more adaptive, inclusive, and efficient teaching strategies while extending the learning experience beyond the classroom through online platforms and interactive tools. As AI continues to advance, it holds great potential to address various developmental challenges, including those related to the Sustainable Development Goals (SDGs).

AI-DRIVEN PERSONALIZATION IN LEARNING

Rapid technological development is having an impact on the planet's socioeconomic status through innovation and the development of applications that make it simpler and quicker to obtain goods and services. Education has been impacted by new technology development as well (Hasan & Wagner, 1996). Education is changing as a result of artificial intelligence (AI), which mimics human cognitive functions and increases adaptability and efficiency in a variety of fields. The effective use of musical resources is facilitated by this AI integration with music education, which incorporates a rich tapestry of history, culture, theory, and instrument tuition. The landscape of learning and music instruction is changing due to the increasing demand for AI-driven online education, especially in the field of music education where the integration of AI technology signals the arrival of cutting-edge teaching methodologies (Luo, 2024). Artificial intellect is a method that uses machines, particularly computer systems, to produce human intellect. Expert systems, natural language processing, speech recognition, and machine vision are a few specific uses of AI. Through the degree of difficulty that has been determined, AI may carry out tasks or functions that are similar to those of humans thanks to the sophisticated system (Mohamed et al., 2022).

AI is becoming a more significant part of our everyday lives, with applications ranging from economic forecasting to personalized advertising. Concerns about the transhumanist viewpoint and related conversations in relation to technology-human interaction, as well as the impact of artificial intelligence (AI) on critical pedagogy and education, are raised by these developments (SARI et al., 2024). The use of AI writing tools like ChatGPT and Claude 2.0 has resulted in a dramatic change in educational approaches in the quickly changing field of English composition instruction (Hutson et al., 2024). The rapid advancement of technology and the increasing demand for adaptability define higher education in the modern day. Enhancing the efficacy of educational initiatives in the digital age, the integration of artificial intelligence and emerging technologies in higher education provides invaluable guidance for decision-making (Moncayo Cueva et al., 2024). The expanding societal significance and pedagogical benefit of Artificial Intelligence in Education (AIED) have garnered a lot of attention in recent years (Wang & Cheng, 2021). The process and impact of teachers' instruction as well as students' learning in a classroom setting are evaluated through in-class teaching evaluation, which is becoming more and more important in monitoring and advancing the quality of education. The idea of smart education has been continuously refined and progressively incorporated into every facet of educational application due to the quick growth of artificial intelligence (AI) technology (Guo et al., 2021).

AI-driven personalization in learning is revolutionizing the educational experience by tailoring instruction to meet the unique needs and preferences of individual students. Through sophisticated algorithms and data analytics, AI systems can assess a learner's strengths, weaknesses, learning pace, and style, enabling educators to provide customized content and resources. For instance, intelligent tutoring systems adapt in real-time, offering exercises that align with a student's current understanding, thus enhancing engagement and motivation. Additionally, AI can analyze vast amounts of data to identify patterns and trends, allowing for proactive interventions when a student struggles or excels, ultimately fostering a more supportive learning environment. Personalized learning pathways can incorporate diverse multimedia resources, interactive simulations, and gamified elements, catering to various learning styles and preferences. Furthermore, AI can facilitate differentiated assessments, allowing students to demonstrate their understanding in ways that best suit their skills, which enhances inclusivity. As a result, AI-driven personalization not only improves learning outcomes but also empowers students to take ownership of their education, promoting lifelong learning habits and preparing them for future challenges in a rapidly evolving world. However, while the potential of AI in personalizing education is vast, it is essential to ensure that these technologies are implemented ethically and equitably to avoid exacerbating existing disparities in educational access and quality.

AI-driven assistive technologies have the potential to offer extra assistance and (Olabisi Oluwakemi Adeleye et al., 2024) modifications, enabling students with disabilities to engage completely in educational pursuits. For students who speak languages other than the main language of instruction or who are deaf or hard of hearing, AI-driven captioning and translation tools can increase accessibility (Olabisi Oluwakemi Adeleye et al., 2024). Artificial intelligence (AI) is increasingly becoming a significant part of daily life, influencing areas such as economic forecasting, personalized advertising, and education. The rapid advancement of technology has transformed higher education, emphasizing the need for adaptability and the integration of AI to enhance educational effectiveness. In particular, AI is revolutionizing learning experiences through personalization, where sophisticated algorithms and data analytics tailor instruction to meet individual students' needs, preferences, and learning styles. This customization allows educators to deliver content and resources that align with each learner's strengths and pace, fostering engagement and motivation. AI-driven tools, such as intelligent tutoring systems, adapt exercises in real-time and offer personalized feedback, creating supportive learning environments and promoting lifelong learning habits. Additionally, AI facilitates differentiated assessments and incorporates diverse multimedia resources, catering to various learning preferences and enhancing inclusivity. Assistive technologies powered by AI also improve accessibility for students with disabilities or those facing language barriers, enabling more equitable participation in education. While AI holds great promise in transforming educational practices and preparing learners for future challenges, it is essential to implement these technologies ethically to ensure they do not exacerbate existing inequalities in access and quality.

BENEFITS AND CHALLENGES: IMPROVED STUDENT ENGAGEMENT AND LEARNING OUTCOMES

The term artificial intelligence (AI) is being widely used. Our lives are being impacted by technology in so many ways that we are forced to face its effects. AI development and use are transforming our communities and lives in a myriad of ways (Borenstein & Howard, 2021). Artificial intelligence (AI) technologies are being integrated into schooling and other aspects of human life on a daily basis. However, teachers' awareness, preparedness, and actual use of the whole AI toolkit in their professional activities determines how much of these tools are integrated into the educational process (Sysoyev, 2023). The application of artificial intelligence (AI) in educational settings could have an impact on instructors' use of formative assessment in the classroom in both positive and negative ways (Hopfenbeck et al., 2023). Artificial intelligence (AI) is becoming more and more used in a variety of medical disciplines since it has the undeniable ability to address global issues related to healthcare provision. The application of various AI techniques in medical education has increased as a result of the growing integration of AI into medical practice, particularly in recent decades. However, there are benefits and challenges to using AI in medical education. The benefits include improved clinical simulation organization, objective student assessment, and more educational transparency. On the other hand, assessing the efficacy of these instructional strategies, scaling constraints, ethical and legal concerns, and technological challenges are the primary obstacles to AI integration in education (Zarei et al., 2024). Incorporating Artificial Intelligence (AI) technology into the language curriculum is one of the important implications of Education 4.0. AI technology offers a variety of educational resources and methods for teaching and learning languages, particularly for ESL students. Language curricula undergo a significant paradigm shift as a result of AI. Artificial Intelligence Assisted Language Learning (AI-ALL) is the term used to describe the use of AI technology in language curricula. Learning objectives including supporting different learning periods of difficulty and improving learners' accomplishments may be supported by the use of artificial intelligence (AI) technology, especially in and outside of the classroom (Moulieswaran & Kumar, 2023).

Improving student engagement significantly enhances learning retention, as students actively participate in the learning process through interactive methods such as discussions, group work, and project-based learning, fostering a deeper understanding of the material. Engaged learning also boosts intrinsic motivation, with activities like gamification and real-life problem-solving increasing enthusiasm for learning. This heightened engagement leads to better academic performance, as students grasp concepts more effectively and perform well in assessments. Moreover, engagement nurtures the development of critical thinking skills, encouraging problem-solving, inquiry-based learning, and exploration of new ideas. Additionally, group work and discussions enhance communication and collaboration skills, enabling students to learn from each other and engage in collaborative problem-solving. Personalized learning experiences, supported by technology and adaptive learning models, allow students to learn at their own pace and in line with their preferences. Ultimately, these strategies foster a love for lifelong learning, as engaged students are more likely to continue learning and applying knowledge throughout their lives. Chatbots are thought to be a technology application model that successfully fosters cross-border communication and learning; they offer a variety of information and knowledge through interactive techniques and user-friendly interfaces, and they can even be used as a tool for consulting with individuals (Hwang & Chang, 2023).

Benefits of Improving Student Engagement and Learning Outcomes

1. **Enhanced Learning Retention:**
   - o Engaged students are more likely to retain information as they actively participate in the learning process. Interactive methods such as discussions, group work, and project-based learning foster deeper understanding.
2. **Increased Motivation:**
   - o Engaging in learning activities boosts students' intrinsic motivation, leading to greater enthusiasm for learning. This can be achieved through gamification, real-life problem-solving, or active learning strategies.
3. **Better Academic Performance:**
   - o Engaged students are more likely to achieve better grades and perform well in assessments. Continuous engagement ensures that students grasp concepts effectively, leading to stronger academic outcomes.
4. **Development of Critical Thinking Skills:**
   - o Engaged learning often involves problem-solving, inquiry-based learning, and the exploration of new ideas. This promotes critical thinking and higher-order cognitive skills.
5. **Improved Communication and Collaboration:**
   - o Group work, discussions, and peer interactions help students develop strong communication and teamwork skills. This also encourages students to learn from each other, enhancing collaborative problem-solving abilities.
6. **Personalized Learning Experiences:**
   - o Technology, blended learning models, and adaptive learning systems allow educators to cater to individual learning preferences and needs. This personalized approach ensures each student engages with the content at their own pace and style.
7. **Increased Lifelong Learning:**
   - o When students are actively engaged, they develop a love for learning that goes beyond the classroom. They are more likely to continue learning and applying knowledge in various contexts throughout their lives.

Applications of artificial intelligence (AI) in education are becoming more widespread and have drawn a lot of interest in recent years. Artificial Intelligence (AI) and adaptive learning technologies are highlighted as significant advancements in educational technology (Zawacki-Richter et al., 2019). Student engagement, motivation, and academic accomplishment have all been demonstrated to benefit from adaptive learning systems. These systems have the potential to boost student engagement and motivation by enhancing learning through more relevant, meaningful, and pleasurable personalized learning experiences that are customized to each student's specifications (Olabisi Oluwakemi Adeleye et al., 2024). AI-driven assistive solutions are essential for removing obstacles to accessibility and meeting the needs of students with impairments. These devices analyze and interpret human input such as text, speech, or gestures using AI algorithms, then provide the proper replies or actions to meet the demands of the user (Olabisi Oluwakemi Adeleye et al., 2024). AI-powered assistive technology could have a big impact on making classrooms more welcoming to all students. These technologies assist in ensuring that all students have equal access to educational opportunities by helping to level the playing field by offering accommodations and support for students with impairments (Olabisi Oluwakemi Adeleye et al., 2024). Early childhood education (ECE) professionals are increasingly using artificial intelligence (AI) tools to improve young children's learning and development (Su & Yang, 2023).

AIEd, or artificial intelligence in education, is one of the newest areas of educational technology, according to numerous international reports. Although it has existed for roughly 30 years, educators are still unsure of how to use it more broadly for pedagogical purposes and how it may truly have a significant impact on teaching and learning in higher education (Zawacki-Richter et al., 2019). Improving student engagement and learning outcomes comes with several challenges, including the diverse learning styles of students, which make it difficult to design engagement strategies that cater to all preferences, as some excel in hands-on activities while others thrive in traditional lecture-based environments. Limited resources, particularly in schools with tight budgets, make it difficult to implement engagement strategies that require costly technology and innovative tools. Teachers also face the challenge of needing training in new pedagogical techniques, such as integrating technology or active learning strategies, which increases their workload and can lead to burnout. Additionally, not all students are receptive to new learning methods, with some resisting changes to their habitual learning practices. The alignment of assessments with active learning approaches is another challenge, as traditional standardized tests may not accurately reflect deeper learning or critical thinking skills. Students are more concerned about the AI approach than they are about live humans and mixed proctoring. The proctoring setting needs to take into account things like time, nervousness, and a few technical issues that may arise throughout the exam. Furthermore, the students express satisfaction with the use of both blended and live-human proctoring strategies (Mutawa & Sruthi, 2022).

Furthermore, while technology has the potential to enhance engagement, issues like technical difficulties, unequal access to devices, and lack of digital literacy can hinder its effective use. Time constraints also play a role, as active learning techniques often require more time than traditional methods, making it difficult to balance curriculum coverage with depth of engagement. Lastly, cultural and institutional barriers within some educational settings resist change, making it challenging to implement innovative engagement strategies.

Challenges to Improving Student Engagement and Learning Outcomes

1. **Diverse Learning Styles:**
    - o Students have varied learning preferences, and it can be difficult to design engagement strategies that cater to all. Some students may prefer hands-on activities, while others may excel in traditional lecture-based environments.
2. **Limited Resources:**
    - o Implementing engagement strategies, especially those involving technology or innovative teaching methods, can be costly. Schools with limited budgets may struggle to provide the necessary resources (e.g., smart classrooms, interactive tools).
3. **Teacher Training and Workload:**
    - o Teachers need to be trained in new pedagogical techniques, such as using technology effectively or applying active learning strategies. However, this requires time and effort, adding to their workload, which can result in burnout.
4. **Student Resistance:**
    - o Not all students are open to engaging learning methods, especially if they are used to traditional forms of instruction. Changing learning habits can meet resistance, and students may disengage if they find the new methods uncomfortable or difficult.
5. **Assessment Alignment:**
    - o Traditional assessments (like standardized tests) may not align with active learning or engagement-focused methods. Educators must find ways to assess student learning outcomes in ways that reflect deeper learning and problem-solving abilities.
6. **Technology Integration Issues:**
    - o While technology can enhance engagement, technical difficulties, a lack of digital literacy among students or teachers, and unequal access to devices can hinder its effectiveness in improving engagement and learning.
7. **Time Constraints:**

- o Active learning techniques often require more time than traditional methods, limiting the amount of content that can be covered. Balancing the depth of engagement with curriculum coverage is a challenge for many educators.

8. **Cultural and Institutional Barriers:**
   - o Some educational institutions may have rigid structures or traditional practices that resist change. This can create challenges in implementing new engagement strategies and innovative learning methods.

Artificial intelligence (AI) is increasingly being integrated into education and other aspects of daily life, shaping teaching approaches and influencing student engagement. The extent to which AI tools are adopted in education largely depends on teachers' awareness, preparedness, and willingness to utilize them. In the medical field, AI plays a crucial role in education, offering benefits such as better clinical simulation, objective assessments, and transparency, though challenges remain with scaling, ethical concerns, and technological limitations. AI is also enhancing student engagement by tailoring learning experiences to individual needs through adaptive learning systems, which have been shown to improve motivation, retention, and academic performance. However, increasing student engagement comes with challenges, such as diverse learning styles, limited resources, and the need for teacher training. Integrating technology in classrooms can face barriers like unequal access to devices, technical difficulties, and cultural resistance to new methods. Active learning strategies, although beneficial for critical thinking and lifelong learning, require time and may not always align with traditional assessment models. Despite these obstacles, AI-powered assistive tools are making classrooms more inclusive by providing support for students with disabilities and ensuring equitable access to educational opportunities. As AI continues to evolve, addressing these challenges will be crucial to fully realize its potential in transforming education and improving learning outcomes. The instructional potential of artificial intelligence (AI) applications in higher education (HE) has garnered increasing attention over the past ten years. The true effects of AI-driven large language models (LLMs), such OpenAI's ChatGPT, on higher education institutions and participants have not been well understood, despite the current surge in interest in their sophisticated features and methodologies (Zawacki-Richter et al., 2024).

AI FOR ENHANCING TEACHER CAPABILITIES AND CONTINUOUS PROFESSIONAL DEVELOPMENT

Artificial intelligence (AI) and other technological advancements offer educators and learners the opportunity to address problems and enhance their teaching and learning outcomes (Mohamed et al., 2022). AI plays a pivotal role in enhancing teacher capabilities and supporting continuous professional development. It personalizes learning for teachers by offering tailored resources and training based on their unique strengths and areas for growth. By automating administrative tasks such as grading, attendance, and lesson planning, AI frees up time for teachers to focus on student engagement and self-improvement (Mohamed et al., 2022). Additionally, AI provides data-driven insights into student performance, allowing teachers to identify learning gaps and adjust their teaching methods. Virtual coaching and mentorship through AI-powered platforms offer instant feedback on teaching techniques and classroom management. Moreover, AI gives teachers access to global best practices, enabling them to stay updated on the latest educational innovations and integrate them into their classrooms.

Personalized Learning for Teachers: AI can tailor professional development programs to individual teachers' needs, offering personalized resources, training, and feedback based on their specific strengths and areas for improvement.
Automated Administrative Tasks: By automating tasks such as grading, attendance, and lesson planning, AI frees up teachers' time, allowing them to focus on student engagement and their own professional growth.
Data-Driven Insights: AI provides teachers with real-time analytics on student performance, helping them identify learning gaps and adjust their teaching methods accordingly, which contributes to continuous skill development.
Virtual Coaching and Mentorship: AI-powered platforms can offer virtual coaching, allowing teachers to receive instant feedback on their teaching techniques, lesson plans, and classroom management strategies.
Access to Global Best Practices: AI can curate teaching strategies, case studies, and research from around the world, allowing teachers to stay updated on the latest educational innovations and integrate them into their classrooms.

(Olabisi Oluwakemi Adeleye et al., 2024) draw attention to the revolutionary possibilities of artificial intelligence in education and how it may support inclusive teaching methods. Teachers can ensure that every student has the chance to achieve by utilizing AI technologies to build more accessible, collaborative, and personalized learning environments. Artificial intelligence (AI) is used by adaptive learning systems to deliver individualized learning experiences that are catered to the needs, interests, and skills of each learner. These systems evaluate student data, such as exam results, interactions with course materials, and curriculum progression, using AI algorithms. To find and close learning gaps, AI algorithms in adaptive learning systems employ a range of strategies. The student data is analyzed by these algorithms to find patterns and trends, as well as misconceptions, areas of strength and weakness, and the potential need for more support (Olabisi Oluwakemi Adeleye et al., 2024). Artificial intelligence (AI) is transforming education by enhancing teacher capabilities and supporting continuous professional development. By personalizing learning for educators, AI offers tailored resources, training, and feedback based on individual strengths and areas for improvement. This customization extends to automating administrative tasks like grading, attendance, and lesson planning, which allows teachers to devote more time to student engagement and self-development. AI also provides data-driven insights into student performance, enabling educators to identify learning gaps and adjust their teaching methods accordingly. Virtual coaching through AI-powered platforms offers instant feedback on teaching techniques and classroom management, while access to global best practices helps teachers stay informed about the latest educational innovations. In addition, adaptive learning systems driven by AI deliver personalized learning experiences by analyzing student data to identify patterns, strengths, weaknesses, and misconceptions, thus providing the necessary support to close learning gaps. By leveraging AI, teachers can create more accessible, collaborative, and individualized learning environments, ensuring that all students have opportunities for success.

INNOVATIVE AI APPLICATIONS IN EDUCATION

Innovative AI applications in education are transforming the learning landscape by enhancing personalized learning experiences, automating administrative tasks, and facilitating data-driven decision-making. AI-powered tools like intelligent tutoring systems and adaptive learning platforms cater to individual students' needs by adjusting content, pace, and difficulty levels based on real-time assessments, enabling a more tailored educational journey. Moreover, AI-driven analytics help educators identify students' strengths and weaknesses, allowing for targeted interventions and improved learning outcomes. Administrative burdens such as grading and scheduling can be streamlined with AI algorithms, freeing up educators to focus on student engagement and instruction. Language processing tools, like chatbots and virtual teaching assistants, provide instant feedback, answer student queries, and support learning outside the classroom, fostering a more interactive and accessible educational environment. Additionally, AI's ability to analyze large datasets supports educational research, predicting trends, and informing policy-making.

As AI continues to evolve, its applications are expected to extend into immersive technologies, such as augmented and virtual reality, further enhancing experiential learning and making education more engaging, inclusive, and efficient. Prioritising student emotions in chatbot design and deployment is essential as the field of AI-based language instruction develops further. We can fully realise the potential of this technology to revolutionise language learning by developing chatbot experiences that are ethically sound, culturally relevant, and emotionally comforting. Future studies should concentrate on creating increasingly sophisticated affective computing methods, examining the long-term effects of chatbots on language acquisition and learner emotions, and figuring out the most effective ways to incorporate chatbots into various educational settings (Xiao et al., 2024).

AI in education has a lot of promise to enhance student learning and advance inclusion. To make sure that AI is implemented in a fair, responsible, and advantageous manner for all students, it is necessary to address the ethical issues and difficulties that surround it.

Through the implementation of techniques addressing data privacy, algorithmic bias, and equality, educators and policymakers can effectively leverage artificial intelligence (AI) to build more inclusive and effective learning environments for all students (Olabisi Oluwakemi Adeleye et al., 2024). Innovative AI applications are reshaping education by enhancing personalized learning, automating tasks, and enabling data-driven decision-making. AI-powered tools such as intelligent tutoring systems and adaptive learning platforms tailor educational experiences to individual students by adjusting content, pace, and difficulty based on real-time assessments, resulting in a more customized learning journey. These tools also provide valuable insights into students' strengths and weaknesses, allowing educators to target interventions and improve outcomes. Administrative tasks like grading and scheduling can be streamlined with AI, freeing educators to focus on instruction and student engagement. Language processing tools, including chatbots and virtual teaching assistants, offer instant feedback and support learning beyond the classroom, fostering a more interactive and accessible educational experience. Additionally, AI's capacity to analyze large datasets aids educational research, trend prediction, and policy-making. As AI evolves, its applications are expected to extend into immersive technologies like augmented and virtual reality, further enriching experiential learning and promoting a more engaging, inclusive, and efficient educational environment. To fully realize these benefits, ethical considerations such as data privacy, algorithmic bias, and equity must be addressed, to ensure AI's responsible and fair implementation in education.

VIRTUAL REALITY (VR) AND AUGMENTED REALITY (AR): IMMERSIVE LEARNING EXPERIENCES POWERED BY AI

As generative artificial intelligence (AI) technologies become more widely available, academic institutions worldwide are attempting to create rules to address what they see as an existential danger to the fundamental essence of their institutions. Academics and administrators seem overly preoccupied with risks to academic integrity, neglecting to take into account the possibility that AI could be a transformational and beneficial technology that improves student learning results (Mattalo, 2024). Artificial intelligence (AI) is one example of how technology is advancing and how it can assist instructors and students solve problems and enhance teaching and learning outcomes (Mohamed et al., 2022). AI-powered tools ought to be created with parent, teacher, and student cooperation and communication in mind. Features that support group projects, peer evaluations, and parent-teacher contact could fall under this category and improve students' education as a whole (Olabisi Oluwakemi Adeleye et al., 2024). Virtual Reality (VR) and Augmented Reality (AR), when combined with AI, are reshaping educational landscapes by providing immersive learning experiences that engage students in unprecedented ways. These technologies allow learners to interact with digital environments that replicate or augment real-world settings, making abstract concepts more tangible and accessible. VR offers a fully immersive experience where students can explore virtual worlds, conduct experiments in simulated laboratories, or travel back in time to witness historical events firsthand. AI-powered VR environments can dynamically adjust difficulty levels, provide personalized feedback, and track student progress, ensuring that each learner's experience is tailored to their individual needs and learning pace. This level of immersion not only increases student engagement but also enhances retention by allowing students to learn through "doing" rather than merely reading or listening. For instance, medical students can practice surgical procedures in a risk-free virtual environment, while language learners can engage in realistic conversations with AI-powered virtual characters. This hands-on approach supports deeper understanding and mastery of complex subjects, making learning more relevant and meaningful. AI-powered applications are used to support learners' learning activities in the modern language learning approach known as Artificial Intelligence (AI) Assisted Language Learning (AI-ALL). In relation to educational activities, numerous academics have been working with AI applications (Moulieswaran & Kumar, 2023).

AR complements these experiences by overlaying digital content in the real world, providing contextual learning that enhances students' interaction with their physical environment. AI-driven AR applications can enrich textbook lessons with interactive 3D models, real-time data, and simulations, bringing static content to life. For example, in a biology class, students can use AR to visualize the anatomy of the human body, with AI providing instant feedback and identifying areas where the student might need further practice. AR can also be used in vocational training to guide students step-by-step through technical tasks, such as repairing machinery or assembling complex devices, with AI algorithms assessing their performance and suggesting improvements. These technologies not only make learning more engaging but also bridge the gap between theoretical knowledge and practical application. As AI continues to advance, the combination of VR and AR is expected to become even more seamless, offering educators powerful tools to create adaptive, inclusive, and interactive learning experiences that cater to diverse educational needs and learning styles.

CHALLENGES AND CONSIDERATIONS FOR AI INTEGRATION IN EDUCATION

Integrating AI into education presents several challenges and considerations that need careful attention to ensure effective and ethical implementation. One major concern is data privacy and security, as AI systems often require access to sensitive student information, raising issues around consent and data protection. Additionally, the cost of AI technologies and the digital divide can exacerbate existing inequalities, limiting access to underfunded schools and students in low-income areas. The reliance on AI systems also raises concerns about bias, as algorithms can unintentionally reinforce stereotypes or inequities present in the training data, potentially leading to unfair outcomes in areas like grading and admissions. Furthermore, the role of educators may shift, requiring professional development and training to help teachers effectively incorporate AI tools while maintaining the human element essential to learning. Resistance to change and skepticism about AI's effectiveness can hinder adoption, particularly if stakeholders perceive AI as a replacement rather than a support for teachers. Additionally, ethical considerations about the extent of AI's decision-making power in educational contexts must be addressed, ensuring that AI complements rather than dictates pedagogical approaches. Hence, the integration of AI in education demands a thoughtful approach that balances technological advancements with the need for equity, privacy, and human oversight. Academic staff members are not well-versed in the ways that AI tools can be used for learning, teaching, and organization. Many educators lack a comprehensive understanding of the potential applications of artificial intelligence (AI) in education because of their fragmented expertise, which is mostly tied to their work as teachers of particular subjects. However, the majority of university instructors exhibit a neutral viewpoint or are willing to include AI tools in their lesson plans. The experience of applying AI tools in the pedagogical process is restricted to a small number of instances when particular technologies are used to teach particular subject areas (Sysoyev, 2023). Although learning tools have become more extensive and effective due to advancements in the learning sciences, educators should tailor them to each unique learning setting. The AI-generated courseware allows students to learn by doing by combining a wealth of formative practice questions with textbook content in specialised disciplines (Schroeder et al., 2022).

The possibility of collaboration between AI and healthcare practitioners is a crucial issue to emphasize. AI is best considered as an auxiliary tool, that is, as a partner that can manage complex data analysis, offer diagnostic support, and free up more time for healthcare professionals to spend directly caring for patients, rather than as a replacement for these professionals. Healthcare professionals would be able to capitalize on their special abilities—empathy, sophisticated decision-making, and direct patient communication that AI is unable to match with the successful application of AI (Bekbolatova et al., 2024). Integrating AI into education presents significant challenges and considerations that require careful management to ensure ethical and effective implementation. Data privacy and security are primary concerns, as AI systems often handle sensitive student information, raising issues about consent and protection. The cost of AI technologies and the digital divide can worsen existing inequalities, limiting access to underfunded schools and students in low-income regions. There are also concerns about algorithmic bias, as AI systems can unintentionally reinforce stereotypes or inequities present in their training data, potentially leading to unfair outcomes in grading and admissions. Additionally, the role of educators is evolving, necessitating professional development to help teachers effectively integrate AI tools while preserving the essential human aspects of learning. Resistance to change and skepticism about AI's impact can slow adoption, especially if AI is seen as a substitute rather than a complement to teachers. Ethical considerations about the extent of AI's decision-making in education must also be addressed, ensuring AI supports rather than dictates pedagogical practices. While many educators are open to incorporating AI, their experience with AI tools remains limited to specific applications within certain subjects, indicating a need for broader training. Moreover, in sectors like healthcare, AI should be viewed as an auxiliary tool that supports professionals by managing data analysis and providing diagnostic assistance, rather than replacing the unique human skills of empathy, decision-making, and patient interaction.

FUTURE DIRECTIONS AND RESEARCH OPPORTUNITIES: RECOMMENDATIONS FOR POLICYMAKERS TO SUPPORT THE EFFECTIVE AND ETHICAL INTEGRATION OF AI IN EDUCATIONAL SYSTEMS

The development of artificial intelligence in education (AIED) has the power to change the face of education and impact the roles of all parties involved. Applications of AIED have been progressively embraced in recent years to improve learning outcomes and experiences while also advancing our knowledge of students' learning (Nguyen et al., 2023). Policymakers have a critical role in supporting the effective and ethical integration of AI in educational systems by creating a framework that promotes equitable access, transparency, and responsible use of technology. To begin, they should prioritize funding and resource allocation to bridge the digital divide, ensuring that all students and schools, regardless of socioeconomic status, can benefit from AI advancements. Establishing clear guidelines on data privacy and security is essential to protect students' information while allowing data-driven innovations to flourish. Policymakers should advocate for the development of AI systems that are fair and unbiased, mandating rigorous testing and diverse datasets to prevent algorithmic discrimination. Additionally, investment in professional development is crucial; educators need ongoing training to understand AI's potential and limitations, enabling them to use AI tools effectively and ethically. Collaborations between governments, tech companies, and educational institutions can foster research into AI's long-term impacts on learning outcomes and identify best practices. Policymakers should also encourage the integration of AI ethics and digital literacy into curricula, preparing students to navigate a world increasingly influenced by AI. Finally, fostering an open dialogue with stakeholders, including teachers, parents, and students, will help shape policies that are inclusive and adaptable to the evolving educational landscape. These strategic efforts can create an educational environment where AI enhances learning while upholding principles of equity, privacy, and human-centered values. Accelerated technical advancements and an increasing demand for adaptability define higher education today. Artificial intelligence and emerging technology integration in higher education improve the efficacy of instructional practices in the digital age and provide useful information for decision-making (Moncayo Cueva et al., 2024). The approach used in the chatbot-based educational experiments was called "guided learning," which is a simple method where students are prompted to practice or look up information utilizing application applications in order to finish learning sheets or carry out teacher-requested learning activities. The basic goal of other learning strategies including inquiry-based learning, project-based learning, video sharing, synchronous sharing, issue-based learning, peer evaluation, and computers as Mindtools (like idea mapping) is to get students to connect with one another and use higher-order thinking skills (Hwang & Chang, 2023). AI has a lot of potential for innovative pedagogical applications that could open up new avenues for knowledge acquisition. Additional research is required to unlock new pedagogical practices employing AI, including theorizing about its capabilities and testing theories empirically to see if they can improve pedagogical outcomes (Mattalo, 2024). Teachers and students strongly support the positive usage of AI in the classroom. However, teachers are more used to the latest technology advancements than students are (Joshi et al., 2021).

Teachers ought to be trained in the moral use of AI in the classroom, which includes identifying and reducing bias, safeguarding student privacy, and advancing equity. Guidance on how to ethically integrate AI technologies into teaching practices should be part of the training as well (Olabisi Oluwakemi Adeleye et al., 2024). Teachers may design more interesting and productive learning environments for every student by investigating cutting-edge teaching strategies that make use of AI. By addressing learning obstacles and giving students the instruments and resources they require for success, these approaches can assist (Olabisi Oluwakemi Adeleye et al., 2024). By granting all students, regardless of their background or ability, access to excellent, individualized training, AI-driven personalized learning has the potential to boost inclusion. Artificial intelligence (AI) algorithms have the potential to meet a wide range of learning demands and guarantee that every student has the chance to succeed by evaluating student data and offering customized instruction and feedback (Olabisi Oluwakemi Adeleye et al., 2024). New methods of teaching, such as chatbots and flipped learning, have been made possible by technological advancements. By offering individualized help and chances for active learning, these technologies have the potential to improve learning outcomes and student engagement. Using chatbots in a flipped learning environment requires caution and consideration for the best interests of the students in order to address ethical and privacy issues. Chatbots ought to be designed with student privacy, data security, and anonymity in mind (Baskara, 2023). AI can assist with student correspondence. For example, AI can be used to create preliminary versions of answers to questions posed by students. With a little more work, an AI chatbot can be put on a course website to automatically respond to student inquiries about the scheduling of the exam or midterm, the assigned readings for the week, the dates of any breaks or canceled classes, answers to frequently asked questions, and much more (Mattalo, 2024).

Artificial Intelligence-driven teaching approaches will probably have a big impact on education in the future. Policymakers, educators, and researchers can collaborate to guarantee that AI integration in education is both ethical and successful by realizing the potential of these technologies to facilitate student growth, improve personalized learning, and advance inclusion (Olabisi Oluwakemi Adeleye et al., 2024). Artificial intelligence (AI) has the potential to revolutionize education through personalized learning experiences and inclusivity through innovative teaching approaches (Olabisi Oluwakemi Adeleye et al., 2024). AI-driven teaching approaches have a number of benefits, such as the capacity to accommodate a range of learning styles and skills, improved student collaboration and communication, and personalized learning experiences catered to particular student needs. It has been demonstrated that AI tools like personalized learning platforms, collaborative learning environments, and adaptive learning systems increase student motivation, engagement, and academic success (Olabisi Oluwakemi Adeleye et al., 2024). The application of generative AI to increase the efficacy and efficiency of instruction should be studied by academics (Mattalo, 2024). More creative technologies are being created to help with student monitoring. AI systems, for instance, have been developed to keep an eye on pupils during class and give teachers immediate feedback on how well their teaching strategies are working (Mattalo, 2024). Instructors are able to perform the little manual modifications needed to maintain and operate these AI-based tools. AI-based programs for English language instruction and acquisition are only feasible with help. When it comes to program modifications, the AI-based software development team can be of tremendous assistance to educators. It means that teachers are now more of a guide than a leader, and they may even teach students how to use AI-based software (Moulieswaran & Kumar, 2023).

Studying the long-term retention of language abilities learned by AI-based learning is crucial for the sustainable incorporation of AI into education. Researchers also need to investigate how AI systems might operate well with different pedagogical frameworks in Kazakhstan's higher education institutions. Future research ought to look into how AI affects intrinsic motivation, learner autonomy, and the function of teachers in AI-mediated learning settings. In order to provide individualized experiences, research should also look at how AI-driven systems may adjust to the features of learners (Kemelbekova et al., 2024). Given the ongoing use of AI tools in education, more study is needed to assess the viability and feasibility of current AI platforms in order to guide different pedagogical approaches to instruction (Ali et al., 2024). Policymakers play a crucial role in ensuring the ethical and effective integration of AI in education by developing frameworks that promote equitable access, transparency, and responsible technology use. Addressing the digital divide is essential, with funding and resources needed to ensure all students benefit from AI advancements regardless of socioeconomic background. Data privacy and security guidelines should be established to protect student information while enabling data-driven innovations. Policymakers must also advocate for fair and unbiased AI systems by mandating rigorous testing and using diverse datasets to prevent algorithmic discrimination. Investments in professional development are vital, equipping educators with the skills to ethically incorporate AI and address issues such as bias and privacy. Collaborations between governments, tech companies, and educational institutions can foster research into AI's long-term impact on learning outcomes and establish best practices. Integrating AI ethics and digital literacy into curricula will prepare students for a technology-driven world. A comprehensive and relevant set of ethical guidelines for AI in education is required due to its complexity (Nguyen et al., 2023). Engaging with stakeholders, including teachers, parents, and students, ensures that policies are inclusive and responsive to evolving educational needs. By focusing on personalized learning, adaptive instruction, and overcoming learning barriers, AI-driven approaches can enhance engagement, inclusivity, and academic achievement. Moreover, ongoing research is needed to understand AI's effects on student motivation, teacher roles, and long-term skill retention, ensuring AI-driven education remains sustainable and effective in diverse learning environments.

CONCLUSION

The integration of AI in education presents vast opportunities for transforming learning experiences, enhancing inclusivity, and addressing individual learning needs. With the potential to personalize education, streamline administrative tasks, and provide data-driven insights, AI can significantly boost student engagement, motivation, and achievement. However, its implementation also brings challenges related to data privacy, algorithmic bias, digital inequities, and the evolving role of educators. Policymakers must prioritize equitable access to AI technologies, establish robust data protection measures, and invest in teacher training to ensure AI is used ethically and effectively. Collaborations among governments, educational institutions, and technology providers can help shape AI policies that balance innovation with ethical considerations, fostering an educational environment that supports diverse learning styles while maintaining the human elements essential for meaningful education. Engaging with all stakeholders, including educators, students, and parents, will be critical in shaping a future where AI complements teaching practices rather than replacing them, ensuring a sustainable integration that supports lifelong learning and equitable outcomes. Continued research on AI's impact across different educational settings will guide its responsible adoption, ultimately leading to a more inclusive, adaptive, and effective education system that prepares learners for the demands of a rapidly changing world.

REFERENCES

Adeleye,, Olabisi Oluwakemi, Eden,, Chima Abimbola, & Adeniyi, Idowu Sulaimon (2024). Innovative teaching methodologies in the era of artificial intelligence: A review of inclusive educational practices. *World Journal of Advanced Engineering Technology and Sciences, 11*(2), 069–079. DOI: 10.5539/ijel.v10n6p40

Al Mukhallafi, T. R. (2020). Using Artificial Intelligence for Developing English Language Teaching/Learning: An Analytical Study from University Students' Perspective. *International Journal of English Linguistics*, 10(6), 40–53. DOI: 10.5539/ijel.v10n6p40

Ali, O., Murray, P. A., Momin, M., Dwivedi, Y. K., & Malik, T. (2024). The effects of artificial intelligence applications in educational settings: Challenges and strategies. *Technological Forecasting and Social Change, 199*(June 2023), 123076. DOI: 10.5539/ijel.v10n6p40

Ayeni, O. O., Al Hamad, N. M., Chisom, O. N., Osawaru, B., & Adewusi, O. E. (2024). AI in education: A review of personalized learning and educational technology. *GSC Advanced Research and Reviews*, 18(2), 261–271. DOI: 10.30574/gscarr.2024.18.2.0062

Baskara, F. R. (2023). AI-Driven Dynamics: ChatGPT Transforming ELT Teacher-Student Interactions. *Lensa: Kajian Kebahasaan, Kesusastraan. Dan Budaya*, 13(2), 261–275. DOI: 10.26714/lensa.13.2.2023.261-275

Bekbolatova, M., Mayer, J., Ong, C. W., & Toma, M. (2024). Transformative Potential of AI in Healthcare: Definitions, Applications, and Navigating the Ethical Landscape and Public Perspectives. *Healthcare (Basel)*, 12(2), 1–31. DOI: 10.3390/healthcare12020125 PMID: 38255014

Bender, S. M. (2024). Awareness of Artificial Intelligence as an Essential Digital Literacy: ChatGPT and Gen-AI in the Classroom. *Changing English*, 31(2), 161–174. DOI: 10.1080/1358684X.2024.2309995

Borenstein, J., & Howard, A. (2021). Emerging challenges in AI and the need for AI ethics education. *AI and Ethics*, 1(1), 61–65. DOI: 10.1007/s43681-020-00002-7 PMID: 38624388

Guo, J., Bai, L., Yu, Z., Zhao, Z., & Wan, B. (2021). An AI-application-oriented in-class teaching evaluation model by using statistical modeling and ensemble learning. *Sensors (Basel)*, 21(1), 241. Advance online publication. DOI: 10.3390/s21010241 PMID: 33401482

Hasan, A., & Wagner, A. (1996). The school of the future. *International Journal of Emerging Technologies in Learning*, 18(199), 6–9. DOI: 10.3991/ijet.v18i09.38133

Hopfenbeck, T. N., Zhang, Z., Sun, S. Z., Robertson, P., & McGrane, J. A. (2023). Challenges and opportunities for classroom-based formative assessment and AI: A perspective article. *Frontiers in Education*, 8, 1–9. DOI: 10.3389/feduc.2023.1270700

Hutson, J., Plate, D., & Berry, K. (2024). Embracing AI in English Composition: Insights and Innovations in Hybrid Pedagogical Practices. *International Journal of Changes in Education*, 1(1), 19–31. DOI: 10.47852/bonviewIJCE42022290

Hwang, G. J., & Chang, C. Y. (2023). A review of opportunities and challenges of chatbots in education. *Interactive Learning Environments*, 31(7), 4099–4112. DOI: 10.1080/10494820.2021.1952615

Järvelä, S., Nguyen, A., & Hadwin, A. (2023). Human and artificial intelligence collaboration for socially shared regulation in learning. *British Journal of Educational Technology*, 54(5), 1057–1076. DOI: 10.1111/bjet.13325

Joshi, S., Rambola, R. K., & Churi, P. (2021). Evaluating artificial intelligence in education for next generation. *Journal of Physics: Conference Series*, 1714(1), 012039. Advance online publication. DOI: 10.1088/1742-6596/1714/1/012039

Kemelbekova, Z., Degtyareva, X., Yessenaman, S., Ismailova, D., & Seidaliyeva, G. (2024). AI in teaching English as a foreign language: Effectiveness and prospects in Kazakh higher education. *XLinguae*, 17(1), 69–83. DOI: 10.18355/XL.2024.17.01.05

Luo, Z. (2024). The Application of Artificial Intelligence Technology in Music Education. *Lecture Notes in Education Psychology and Public Media*, 35(1), 305–310. DOI: 10.54254/2753-7048/35/20232155

Mattalo, B. (2024). Artificial Intelligence: The Future of Pedagogy. *Journal of Legal Studies Education*, 41(1), 49–71. DOI: 10.1111/jlse.12146

Miao, F., Holmes, W., Huang, R., & Zhang, H. (2023). *AI and education : Guidance for policymakers*. UNESCO. https://discovery.ucl.ac.uk/id/eprint/10130180/1/Miao and Holmes - 2021 - AI and education guidance for policy-makers.pdf

Mohamed, M. Z. (2022). Artificial intelligence in mathematics education: A systematic literature review. *International Electronic Journal of Mathematics Education*, 17(3), em0694. Advance online publication. DOI: 10.29333/iejme/12132

Moncayo Cueva, H. L., Cuesta-Chávez, G., Ramírez, A., & Zambrano Pintado, R. N. (2024). Utilizing Emerging Technology Trends and Artificial Intelligence in Higher Education. *Journal of Higher Education Theory and Practice*, 24(3). Advance online publication. DOI: 10.33423/jhetp.v24i3.6847

Moulieswaran, N., & Kumar, P. N. S. (2023). Investigating ESL Learners' Perception and Problem towards Artificial Intelligence (AI) -Assisted English Language Learning and Teaching. *World Journal of English Language*, 13(5), 290–298. DOI: 10.5430/wjel.v13n5p290

Mutawa, A. M., & Sruthi, S. (2022). Students' perspective towards online proctoring in exams during COVID-19. *Journal of Engineering Research (Kuwait)*, 10(4), 96–113. DOI: 10.36909/jer.14749

Naqvi, W. M., Sundus, H., Mishra, G., Muthukrishnan, R., & Kandakurti, P. K. (2024). AI in Medical Education Curriculum: The Future of Healthcare Learning. *European Journal of Therapeutics*, 30(2), e23–e25. DOI: 10.58600/eurjther1995

Nguyen, A., Ngo, H. N., Hong, Y., Dang, B., & Nguyen, B. P. T. (2023). Ethical principles for artificial intelligence in education. *Education and Information Technologies*, 28(4), 4221–4241. DOI: 10.1007/s10639-022-11316-w PMID: 36254344

Ouyang, F., & Jiao, P. (2021). Artificial intelligence in education: The three paradigms. *Computers and Education: Artificial Intelligence*, 2(April), 1–6. DOI: 10.1016/j.caeai.2021.100020

Sağın, F. G., Özkaya, A. B., Tengiz, F., Geyik, Ö. G., & Geyik, C. (2024). Current evaluation and recommendations for the use of artificial intelligence tools in education. *Türk Biyokimya Dergisi*, 48(6), 620–625. DOI: 10.1515/tjb-2023-0254

Sari, T., Nayír, F., & Bozkurt, A.SARI. (2024). Reimagining education: Bridging artificial intelligence, transhumanism, and critical pedagogy. *Journal of Educational Technology and Online Learning*, 7(1), 102–115. Advance online publication. DOI: 10.31681/jetol.1308022

Schroeder, K. T., Hubertz, M., Van Campenhout, R., & Johnson, B. G. (2022). Teaching and Learning with AI-Generated Courseware: Lessons from the Classroom. *Online Learning : the Official Journal of the Online Learning Consortium*, 26(3), 73–87. DOI: 10.24059/olj.v26i3.3370

Sharifuddin, N. S., & Hashim, H. (2024). Benefits and Challenges in Implementing Artificial Intelligence in Education (AIED) in ESL Classroom: A Systematic Review (2019-2022). *International Journal of Academic Research in Business & Social Sciences*, 14(1), 1–19. DOI: 10.6007/IJARBSS/v14-i1/20422

Singh, A., Kanaujia, A., Singh, V. K., & Vinuesa, R. (2024). Artificial intelligence for Sustainable Development Goals: Bibliometric patterns and concept evolution trajectories. *Sustainable Development (Bradford)*, 32(1), 1–31. DOI: 10.1002/sd.2706

Su, J., & Yang, W. (2023). A systematic review of integrating computational thinking in early childhood education. *Computers and Education Open*, 4(100122), 1–12. DOI: 10.1016/j.caeo.2023.100122

Su, J., & Zhong, Y. (2022). Artificial Intelligence (AI) in early childhood education: Curriculum design and future directions. *Computers and Education: Artificial Intelligence*, 3(100072), 1–12. DOI: 10.1016/j.caeai.2022.100072

Sysoyev, P. V. (2023). Artificial Intelligence in Education: Awareness, Readiness and Practice of Using Artificial Intelligence Technologies in Professional Activities by University Faculty. *Vysshee Obrazovanie v Rossii = Higher Education in Russia, 32*(10), 9–33. DOI: 10.31992/0869-3617-2023-32-10-9-33

Vázquez-Cano, E. (2021). Artificial intelligence and education: A pedagogical challenge for the 21st century. In *Educational Process: International Journal* (Vol. 10, Issue 3, pp. 7–12). Universitepark. DOI: 10.22521/edupij.2021.103.1

Wang, T., & Cheng, E. C. K. (2021). An investigation of barriers to Hong Kong K-12 schools incorporating Artificial Intelligence in education. *Computers and Education: Artificial Intelligence*, 2, 100031. Advance online publication. DOI: 10.1016/j.caeai.2021.100031

Xiao, Y., Zhang, T., & He, J. (2024). The promises and challenges of AI-based chatbots in language education through the lens of learner emotions. *Heliyon*, 10(18), 1–14. DOI: 10.1016/j.heliyon.2024.e37238 PMID: 39309898

Yetişensoy, O., & Karaduman, H. (2024). The effect of AI-powered chatbots in social studies education. *Education and Information Technologies*, 29(13), 17035–17069. Advance online publication. DOI: 10.1007/s10639-024-12485-6

Yue, M., Jong, M. S. Y., & Dai, Y. (2022). Pedagogical Design of K-12 Artificial Intelligence Education: A Systematic Review. In *Sustainability (Switzerland)* (Vol. 14, Issue 23, pp. 1–29). DOI: 10.3390/su142315620

Zarei, M., Eftekhari Mamaghani, H., Abbasi, A., & Hosseini, M. S. (2024). Application of artificial intelligence in medical education: A review of benefits, challenges, and solutions. *Medicina Clinica Practica*, 7(2), 7–11. DOI: 10.1016/j.mcpsp.2023.100422

Zawacki-Richter, O., Bai, J. Y. H., Lee, K., Slagter van Tryon, P. J., & Prinsloo, P. (2024). New advances in artificial intelligence applications in higher education? *International Journal of Educational Technology in Higher Education*, 21(32), 1–4. DOI: 10.1186/s41239-024-00464-3

Zawacki-Richter, O., Marín, V. I., Bond, M., & Gouverneur, F. (2019). Systematic review of research on artificial intelligence applications in higher education – where are the educators? *International Journal of Educational Technology in Higher Education*, 16(39), 1–27. DOI: 10.1186/s41239-019-0171-0

KEY TERMS AND DEFINITIONS

Immersive: Creating a highly engaging learning environment where students feel surrounded by and deeply involved in the educational content.

Personalized: Tailoring educational experiences to meet the individual needs, interests, and learning pace of each student for more effective outcomes.

Engagement: Actively involving students in the learning process to maintain their attention and foster deeper understanding.

Interactive: Enabling learners to actively participate in and influence their educational experiences, often through hands-on activities or digital interfaces.

Adaptive: Modifying content and teaching strategies in response to the real-time performance and progress of each student.

Simulation: Recreating real-world environments or scenarios in a controlled, digital setting for practical, experiential learning.

Practical: Providing skills and knowledge that can be directly applied to real-life situations, enhancing learning relevance.

Inclusion: Ensuring that educational tools and strategies are accessible and beneficial to students from diverse backgrounds and abilities.

Scalability: The ability of educational technologies or programs to expand and serve a larger number of students without sacrificing quality.

Ethics: Addressing the moral considerations involved in the use of educational technologies, such as data privacy, bias, and equitable access.

Chapter 9

Incorporating AI in Educational Leadership: Trends and Innovations

Hala Al Ruheili
Sohar University, Oman

Sheikha Ali Salim Al-Buraiki
https://orcid.org/0000-0002-9509-3822
Sohar University, Oman

ABSTRACT

This book chapter explores the integration of AI tools into higher educational institutions and uncovers the current trends in utilizing AI tools by educators and educational leaders. Via an interview, the research data was collected from six higher education leaders. Five themes emerged answering the three research questions. The themes highlighted the current practices of AI in Omani higher educational institutions, explained the perceived effects of AI tools on learning, teaching and educational leaderships, and pointed to AI-related challenges. Additionally, the interviewees proposed some strategies to overcome the challenges and recommendations for future implementations of AI. In light of the findings, it becomes clear that AI use in education is unavoidable. Thus, it is recommended that educational leaders offer on-going training to all concerned staff, encourage the participation of educators in making decisions regarding the appropriate application of AI as well as developing guidelines to address the ethical concerns.

DOI: 10.4018/979-8-3693-7863-2.ch009

1. INTRODUCTION

The term Artificial Intelligence (AI) typically refers to computing systems that emulate human capabilities (Russell & Norvig, 2020). This technology is driving significant changes, particularly in the field of education. AI encompasses a range of technologies, including machine learning, data analytics, and natural language processing. These are considered vital tools capable of revolutionizing educational leadership. These innovations not only facilitate the adoption of innovative teaching methods but also enhance decision-making processes. Indeed, the level of success in educational institutions is prominently influenced by the competency of the leaders as the head of academic administrator. Leaders in educational institutions usually have numerous responsibilities and even expanded duties to empower especially the staff working under their supervision. They act as academic facilitators between the faculty governance, the needs of staff to be appropriately equipped to work in a successful manner with numerous interests so as to promote the mission of the institution and the academic unit they are heading. These educational leaders need to effectively participate in realizing various policy and principles related to the vision and mission of integrating artificial Intelligence (AI) into higher education. Thus, it became a main interest of this study to investigate the influence of AI on educational leadership at higher education institutions in Oman.

1.2 Overview of Artificial Intelligence (AI) in Omani Higher Education System

In the context of Oman, the integration of artificial intelligence (AI) into higher education systems has emerged as a transformative force. AI can improve learning experiences and streamline administrative tasks. Leadership has a great influence on organizational effectiveness in higher education. In Oman, leadership is an organizational management issue that has gone through rapid research and development, enabling institutions to focus on developing critical thinking skills and fostering innovative curricula. The interest in the issue is not surprising as leadership practices have become ideal measures of progress and prosperity for the improvement of educational institutions.

Thus, one's ability to serve as an effective leader within an academic institution represents a great challenge in the world of higher education. Moreover, the implementation of AI within leadership frameworks can facilitate making decisions and reflect on overall educational landscapes. Studies show that educational leaders dedicate great support to their faculty members and students' learning, along with developing numerous skills. Therefore, in Oman, the entrepreneurs and policymakers are in need for adaptive strategies that align with both cultural and global educational trends (Bimani A et al., 2021). Literature shows that leaders influence the performance of faculty members and the achievements of individual students. To improve the organizational outcomes, educational leaders are drawn to AI globally. Despite these benefits, the incorporation of AI into educational leadership roles is associated with several obstacles.

However, the last few years have witnessed tremendous changes in higher education's system of operations. Recent studies indicate that leaders in higher education institutions are integrating AI to improve decision making practices and efficiency in administration (Al-Khater & Alshahrani, 2021). Oman's vision 2040 emphasizes sustainability and innovations. As Hasan and Alharthy (2022) stated, Oman endeavors to elevate its learning, teaching and decision-making frameworks. Thus, it is necessary to understand the trends to develop strategies that align with vision goals.

1.3 Statement of Problem

Researchers of higher education and university administrators are very much concerned about the integration of Artificial Intelligence (AI) within various educational institutions. Most faculty leaders have begun to take comprehensive measures to address this issue by developing student experiences, decision-making and administrative efficiency. Prominent within the approaches undertaken by the educational leaders in this case are mentoring, development and assisting, all of which are described as characteristics of effective leadership styles (Robertson, 2016). Concurrently, academic leaders oversee staff development so as to improve the micro-climates within the faculty and the daily conduct of the faculty members.

However, several institutions encounter significant obstacles in implementing AI tools effectively. The complexity of today's leadership positions and the ethical concerns about the implementation of AI such as data privacy, lack of strategic framework and insufficient awareness of AI's advantages must be taken into consideration. Therefore, the leadership practices of academic leaders are very necessary not only for the success of the whole institution, but also for the development of all the faculty members. To identify these barriers of AI integration, educational leaders ought to explore strategies to overcome these challenges. The present study seeks to investigate further how the leadership practices of academic deans influence the demand of the digital age to align with Oman's vision 2040 goals for engaging learning environment and innovations.

1.4 Research Objectives

The objectives of this study are:

i. To identify the current trends in the implementation of AI tools among educational leaders in Omani higher education institutions.
ii. To examine how AI affects decision making and organizational tasks.
iii. To identify the challenges educational leaders encounter while applying AI technologies.
iv. To assess the development strategies through moral standards that promote the ethical application of AI in education.

1.5 Research Questions

This study aims to seek answers to the following research questions:

i. Research Question 1: How has the integration of AI technologies impacted teaching and leadership practices implementation at higher educational institutions in Oman?
ii. Research Question 2: What are the perceived effects of artificial intelligence on students' learning and educational leadership?
iii. Research Question 3: What are the obstacles that educational leaders encounter while implementing AI technologies?

1.6 Significance of the Study

There has been a lack of research that investigated how the educational leaders in Oman navigate the complexity of artificial intelligence in their higher education institutions. In reality, by identifying barriers and influencing strategies for effective implementation, the research will contribute to the improvement of policies and practices that enhance innovations and educational outcomes. In addition, the findings of this study can help align higher education initiatives with Oman's Vision 2040. Thus, this study seeks to ensure stakeholders that AI technologies are manipulated to develop administrative tasks, learning experiences, and the quality of higher education in Oman.

The impact of leadership styles and engagement on overall organizational effectiveness in higher education is one of the priorities for further research. Harter et al. (2022) in their study found that the engaged staff will exhibit better working ethics and higher performance and satisfaction compared to disengaged staff. Deans who develop leadership styles can actually generate highly committed members of staff. The results of the current study may help organizational leaders and faculties to develop strategies that will enable them to determine their weaknesses and strengths within their institutions and to develop appropriate strategies to overcome any deficiencies. By doing so, the research itself becomes part of the self-evaluation and review process integral to the current Oman Academic Accreditation Authority (OAAA) standards.

In summary, this study will be of great significance in the following ways:

i. It will help reveal the adaptive AI learning systems that tailor educational experiences.
ii. It will contribute to advancing student engagement by enhancing their motivation and interaction as well as providing feedback and support.
iii. It will help faculty deans to be more aware of the factors that motivate the performance of their staff. AI can analyse data to improve curriculum design and optimize decision making.
iv. It will identify the culture of innovations by fostering collaborations and encouraging new AI ideas.
v. It will explore the alignment with global trends by investigating if AI systems in higher education institutions in Oman are in line with global educational advancements.

It is hoped that the results of the current study will be used as a resource for both leaders and staff members to enhance AI implementation, which will in turn improve teaching and learning processes. Finally, although the focus is on leaders and faculty members from various University within the Omani Ministry of Higher Education, it is also hoped that the research process, instrument, and findings may be of use to other ministries in Oman and the Gulf region.

2. LITERATURE REVIEW

2.1. The Rise of Artificial Intelligence

Artificial intelligence (AI) refers to particular behaviors and characteristics of computer software that mimic the human mind and mental capabilities and patterns of functions. The most significant characteristics include the ability of AI to learn, reason and react (Hassan, 2022). Hence, it is worth noting that AI technologies differ from other computer programs and information systems in their abilities to realize what should be done or not done and thus to make their own conclusions rather than following pre-programmed steps. However, the use of AI and other types of smart technologies is unlikely to replace human presence rather than enhance human's contributions to society.

Artificial intelligence (AI) is being divided into three broad models: narrow artificial intelligence, strong artificial intelligence and artificial super intelligence. The first model represents the simplest form of AI which responds to certain situations whereas the second model has the ability to make decisions based on gathering information. The third model of AI represents a highly intelligent generation of AI which seeks to comprehend human ideas and is able to interact with humans. It can also predict the feelings of others, confront electronic attacks and be used in wars and medicine (Timms, 2016).

Artificial intelligence continues to play a substantial role in digitizing human societies. AI technologies have revolutionized many aspects of our daily life due to their capabilities to "automate tasks, process large quantities of data, and provide predictive insights" (Cooper, 2023, p.444). Generative AI (GenAI) is the most recent technology which has the potential to evolve education (UNESCO, 2023). GenAI is transforming how high education institutions operate including how students approach learning and how leaders make decisions (Donasco & Oliveros, 2024). GenAI has become more popular in education particularly with the use of ChatGPT. According to Adiguzel et al. (2023), ChatGPT describes itself as a powerful machine software that has the potential to learn while being fed by requests. This software uses the Generative Pre-Trained Transfer (GPT) algorithm enabling it to generate human-like responses based on the given input. The wide usage of ChatGPT, which was developed by OpenAI, has given rise to both improved personalized teaching and decision making and implementation challenges and numerous ethical issues that relate to the teaching and learning processes (Donasco & Oliveros, 2024; Fullan et al., 2024).

Overall, AI powered tools have substantially transformed the ways teachers teach, students learn and educational institution's function (Kamalov et al., 2023). The impact of AI in education has inevitable implications for both teaching and leadership. Undoubtedly, AI technologies hold both potentials and challenges for integrating these technologies into existing school systems meeting the needs and interests of students, teachers and leaders (Chernov & Chernova, 2019). Thus, the question now is not whether AI tools play a role in leadership anymore (Van Quaquebeke & Gerpott, 2023), but the question is how AI redefines the new roles of educational leaders in a way that prepare students for a future in which AI is an integral and important part of their lives (Fullan et al, 2023).

2.2 The Contribution of AI in Education

Artificial intelligence powered tools are making paradigm shifts in how students approach learning and how educators teach. These technologies are playing critical roles in upgrading the quality of all aspects of education. Choi (2020) asserted that AI learning approaches are making giant leaps in elevating higher education. First, AI provides students with customized learning experiences that address their needs. Second, the inevitable presence of AI in our lives makes it imperative for educators to adjust their teaching methods in order to prepare students for future job markets. Students need to master ways of thinking critically, dealing with difficulties and other skills that will likely aid their future careers. Third, AI will help educators in fulfilling some administrative tasks, sparing more time for teaching and counseling. Fourth, AI can do other tasks like taking attendance, grading and communicating students' progress. In other words, AI powered tools are being utilized to "evaluate students' performance records, determine their strengths and weaknesses and provide them with customized learning experiences that are tailored to their individual needs" (Rahiman & Kodikal, 2024, p. 2).

AI-supported technologies such as adaptive learning systems, chatbots and virtual assistance tools provide meaningful and engaging experiences for students, allowing them to comprehend complex theories. These processes of learning are offered in an interactive learning environment (Chaudhry et al., 2023; Pradana et al., 2023).

2.3 AI-Related Challenges

GenAI can be integrated effectively into classrooms as indicated by several recent studies (Mollick & Mollick, 2022 among others). Teachers who utilize GenAI tools in their instruction should "make additional efforts to update the strategies and tools they use in their teaching programs and use their professional judgment" (Fullan et al., 2024, p. 341). More importantly, the assessment schemes may become more challenging given the wide range of GenAI products are now becoming more sophisticated and accessible (Zhang & Mao, 2023).

While AI tools offer a vast range of potentials to improve the teaching and learning process, there are limitations and changes associated with the usage of these advanced technologies. The assistance received by GenAI raises the issue of academic dishonesty particularly among higher education students. For instance, assessments like take-home assignments will be completed most probably using GenAI, Chat GPT as an example. Learners need to know that over-dependence on ChatGPT may lead to dependence and possibly underperformance or worse failure (Donasco & Oliveros, 2024; Hargreaves, 2023). AI technologies can be considered as a threat to teaching and leading (Holmes et al., 2019) if they redefine the roles of teachers and leaders as playing functional roles rather than enhancing their essential role of teaching and leading.

Cardona et al. (2023) reported that traditional homework given to the students to answer at home will be significantly impacted. Thus, a big challenge will be to embark on new approaches in education that allows to redefine the future of education. Interestingly, AI forces educators to transform education affecting all involved in the educational system including school leaders. The emerging educational paradigm forces educators and educational leaders to rethink their roles and how they work (Azorin & Fullan, 2022).

Additional disadvantages of AI in education include the probable high cost of implementing AI in education, reverse effect on the employment of teaching staff, and possible hacks and viruses attacking robots/bots. Furthermore, the learning atmosphere will be devoid of students' collaboration and real time discussions that lectures provide to the students. Engaging and interacting with a machine creates boredom and a tendency to dislike learning. Also, it may be difficult to use AI technologies without proper training (Hassan, 2022).

2.5 Artificial Intelligence and Educational Leadership

Artificial intelligence is unprecedentedly revolutionizing the job market, automating many jobs and reshaping the future of labor (Frank et al., 2019). For instance, in the USA, more than a third of the jobs favored by students are now considered at risk for the potential of automating them in the next fifteen years (Zeira, 2018). Similarly, AI is expected to automate 40% of teachers' tasks including tracking students' progress and other non-instructional tasks (Herlod, 2019). Bryant et al. (2020) reported that AI powered tools could do more of teachers' routine tasks freeing up about one-third of teachers' working hours for more human-related tasks such as inspiring students via one-to-one focused relationships and collaborating with colleagues. It is worth noting that, automating some teachers' routine tasks, with the aid of AI, would result in reducing teachers' burnout, which has been a challenging issue for school leaders for a long time.

Application of AI technology in education is inevitable. Many educational institutions are keen to benefit from AI technology to create the best educational experience for all concerned parties. When we speak about AI in educational leadership, we refer more to leadership processes rather than technically-related issues. Artificial intelligence in education is applied in several educational dimensions such as automated grading, feedback for lectures, virtual facilitation, campus conversations, personalized learning, adaptive learning, distance learning and helping students with special needs. Detailed description of the educational dimensions is provided below.

1. **Automated Grading:** In this dimension of AI in education, the AI- injected technological tools assess students' knowledge by analyzing their responses and providing appropriate feedback. Subsequently, the AI tools inform students of their grades and create personalized follow-up training plans. This method in grading is thought to be error and favoritism-free.
2. **Feedback for Lecturers:** In the realm of education, AI technologies provide tools that offer feedback about students' learning and performance. Feedback injected with AI encompasses technologies such as chatting with AI bots, electronic and machine learning, and adapting conversations according to students' responses that reflect their personality and intelligence and educational levels.
3. **Virtual Facilitations:** Some educational institutions assist students in terms of providing them with answers that they constantly need. An example of a virtual facilitator is the robot called Jill Watson from Georgia Institute of Technology supported by the system emanating from AI.
4. **Campus Conversations:** Within the application of AI, on-campus chats act as electronic dialogue sessions between the students and the robot in order to obtain assistance related to university life and study. These AI-supported robots aid students to find their lecture halls, parking lots, communicate with the faculty members, and any matter related to the educational environment.
5. **Personalized Learning:** In this dimension, AI-supported technologies provide applications that meet students' individual needs. Specifically, these technologies help in identifying learners' strengths and weaknesses within the educational curricula.
6. **Adaptive Learning:** As a useful application of AI, adaptive learning contributes to the success of the educational experience by teaching students individually. Educators are also provided with detailed reports measuring the difficulty level of the materials given to the students and thus adjusting accordingly.
7. **Distance Learning:** Remote education has proven to be a prominent form of learning. Hence, modern technological tools support the experience of distance learning including taking online examinations and utilizing proctoring systems that injected with AI features to monitor students while taking online examinations. Proctoring systems supported by AI detect any cheating and ensure the credibility and accuracy of the tests.
8. **Helping Students With Special Needs:** AI extends its applications to encompass students with special needs offering them an adaptive educational environment and learning experiences that assimilate educational materials that lead towards successful achievement. Such tools enhance students' social skills.

Some advocates of AI technology caution about the incorporation of this latest technology in education. They point out the pros and cons of its educational use (Bernacki et al., 2020). GenAI like ChatGPT impacts education positively by improving learning, teaching and pedagogy, and educational administration (Cooper, 2023). The existing research suggests that AI powered tools can benefit educational leaders performing routine, mechanical tasks, thus allowing them to focus on other more productive and creative issues that demand their human skills and their social intelligence" (Fullan et al., 2024, p. 342). In other words, AI-powered tools would remove the heavy burdens of the administrative and managerial workload currently placed on school leaders. AI supported technologies are capable of making decisions, solving problems even when fed with incomplete data and they can also deal with contradictory data (Hassan, 2022). Generally speaking, for both educators and learners, technologies powered by AI save time and effort.

Technological advancement, particularly AI technologies, will continue to mark a leap in the educational field as they will continue to improve the quality of education. AI has the potential to study the learners' behaviors and thus offer targeted support (Liu, et al., 2019). AI supports students' learning and boosts their interest in their studies particularly at higher educational institutions (Donasco & Oliveros, 2024). Learners view AI technologies as effective and useful tools that promote classroom engagement, enhance their attention (Moussa et al., 2024), improve academic achievement and elevate motivation (Xu, 2024).

It has been noted that research on the impact of AI on educational leadership is still scarce (Hejres, 2022; Papa & Moran, 2021). In educational leadership, it is fundamental to establish strong human connections that exhibit compassion for others. Therefore, GenAI may not be able to replace this function of the moral aspect of leadership. The introduction of AI in education will alter the way leadership is conceived and executed (Fullan et al., 2024). It is argued that school leaders may be more prepared to deal with the existence of AI in educational institutions since they have had the experience of shifting to leading at a distance during COVID-19 pandemic (Harris & Jones, 2022). Definitely, AI technologies offer further and new prospects for school leaders; however, they bring novel challenges related to morality, ethics and educational practices (Fullan, et al., 2024). Educational leaders should cope with the advancement of AI-related technologies via developing both technical and soft skills to effectively integrate such technologies in their leadership (Milton & Al-Busaidi, 2023).

2.5 Review of Past Studies

This section reviews the pertinent past studies that were conducted internationally and regionally. These studies primarily focused on the role of integrating AI into educational settings particularly into higher educational institutions.

Donasco and Oliveros (2024) examined how AI impacts learning and educational leadership. Seven educators from public colleges in the Philippines were interviewed and the findings revealed that AI technologies influence decision-making, teaching practices and student outcomes. Some ethically related issues were highlighted including data privacy and bias. However, there were mixed findings related to the activation of AI in learning. On one hand, AI tools “enhance students’ engagement and critical thinking” (Donasco & Oliveros, 2024, p. 228). On the other hand, there are continuous concerns about ‘over-dependence’ and there is a pressing need to cautiously incorporate AI technologies into education.

Abduljaber (2024) conducted a transcendental phenomenological study for the purpose of describing the perceived influence of AI on three dimensions of educational leadership: decision-making, teaching and learning outcomes. His study participants included fifteen educational leaders from various public secondary schools in the middle east. He drew his findings based on individual interviews, focus group interviews and a survey. Based on a descriptive analysis of the findings, four themes emerged: critical thinking, decision-making, ethical concerns and grading and feedback. Overall, the researcher concluded that “educational leaders perceived that AI would play a crucial role in the educational environment, impacting both themselves and the students”.

Xu (2024) investigated the role of AI in enhancing students’ learning experiences as well as their learning outcomes. A case study design was employed to understand how AI tools, particularly machine learning, augmented reality, virtual reality and automation, are utilized to promote learning experiences and outcomes. The findings of the study confirmed that AI powered tools resulted in positive learning outcomes in certain educational areas such as academic performance, motivation, engagement and learning progression.

Kurkan and Cetin (2024) examined the perception of educational leaders towards digital leadership within the framework of artificial intelligence. They employed semi-structured interviews with fifteen educational administrators in Turkey. The findings of the study revealed that the participants hold positive perceptions towards the use of artificial intelligence. They believed that AI was making their professional life easy, facilitating knowledge management, improving the thought systems and saving their time. However, they expressed some limitations linked to the use of AI including posing threats, the inability to meet social and psychological needs and the unlikelihood to replace human beings.

Rahiman and Kodikal (2024) conducted a research study to identify the level of awareness of faculty members in high education institutions on the adoption and application of AI. The sample of the study comprised of the faculty members from different high education institutions around Asia. The researchers also examined how AI enhanced the learning experience and the level of work engagement of lecturers in these institutions. This study utilized a quantitative research approach coupled with a structural equation model to collect data from 250 faculty members from QS ranked universities. The findings indicate that AI implementations played a significant role in revolutionizing assessment and evaluation methods which resulted in elevated faculty engagement levels.

Ghamrawi (2024) investigated the preparedness of school leaders in Qatar to lead in the era of new technologies like AI tools. The researcher also examined their perspectives towards the integration of AI technologies in educational leaderships. He conducted a qualitative study with 24 school leaders who participated in six focus group interviews. Based on these interviews, the participants measured their own understanding of AI, expressed their perceptions and pointed out the required skills to effectively maneuver through the ever-changing landscape of AI. The findings revealed the knowledge gap these school leaders exhibited in relation to the nature and application of AI. Their perceptions involved positive and negative points in relation to its wide implementations in schools.

Ayed (2022) investigated the current opportunities, situations and challenges of Artificial Intelligence (AI) in higher education institutions (HEIs) in the Sultanate of Oman. The purpose of this study was to assess the effectiveness of existing AI tools by seeking students' perceptions and analyzing the impact of AI tools on their academic endeavors. The findings pointed to the varying views on the effectiveness of AI usage, the need for on-going trainings and the resistance to change. Overall, while AI introduced promising opportunities for enhancing educational practices in Oman, addressing the barriers is vital for successful implementation.

Al Harrasi et al. (2021) explored the impact of AI on leadership roles in government organization in the Sultanate of Oman. The study was conducted in four ministries and it revealed that current leadership practices focused on strategy improvement and administrative tasks. It highlighted the areas that can enhance leadership effectiveness such as creative problem solving, trust and innovation, tech proficiency, strategic planning, holistic thinking and future anticipation. The integration of AI into educational leadership practices has a great significance in developing the innovations and performance in Oman's public sector.

Al Matari et al. (2023) investigated the current practices of AI and the future of teaching in higher educational settings, particularly in one private university in the Sultanate of Oman. The researchers conducted four interviews with whom they described as "technologically capable teachers who have been employing artificial intelligence in teaching" (p. 182). The findings of the study demonstrated that AI is being used to "personalize learning, automate grading, provide virtual assistance and analyze data" (p. 182). The findings suggested that educators should consider ethical and equitable use of AI in teaching.

It is not about how to use AI in our life, but it is about understanding how it impacts our life in general, and education in particular. It is of high necessity to assess the impact of AI technology on teaching and learning, whether positive or negative. Noted by Holmes et al. (2019), there is lack of large-scale research with robust evidence that touches upon the efficacy of AI tools in education compared to the widespread use of AI tools in schools. Research examining the ethical issues linked to these applications of AI tools in education is also lacking. Based on the above discussion, the present study aims to explore the current practices of AI, its potentials and challenges in educational leadership in high educational institutions in the Sultanate of Oman. Specifically, this research study targets the following research questions:

1. How has the integration of AI technologies impacted teaching and leadership practices implementation at higher educational institutions in Oman?
2. What are the perceived effects of artificial intelligence on students' learning and educational leadership?
3. What are the obstacles that educational leaders encounter while implementing AI technologies

3. RESEARCH METHODOLOGY

3.1 Introduction

This section provides a detailed description of how the study has been conducted. It outlines the research design and procedures used to explore the incorporation of artificial intelligence (AI) in educational leadership, focusing on trends and innovations. It attempts to describe the research framework, population, sample size, sampling procedure, instrumentation and data analysis procedure. The study aims to identify how AI technologies can enhance leadership practices in educational institutions to enlighten the findings of the study.

3.2 Research Design

The present study employs a qualitative research design that aims to understand trends and innovations from the perspectives of educational leaders. It involves the educational leaders of different universities as well as the departmental heads to explore the incorporation of AI in educational leadership. In order to explore leadership practices among the leaders in Omani higher educational institutions, educational leaders were asked to respond to interview questions uncovering their current practices, and perceptions regarding the effects and concerns related to using AI tools in higher education institutions.

This study collected data via conducting interviews as a main research instrument to gain substantive information from the respondents (Roulston, 2023). An interview is defined as a technique for qualitative data collection (Bryman, A. 2021) that yields in-depth information and draws a comprehensive picture of each educational leader's practices of AI, the impact of AI on leadership tasks, teaching and learning.

3.3 Participants

The participants of the present study are six educational leaders who work in three different high educational institutions in the Sultanate of Oman. They were all experienced educational leaders. Some of them illustrated that they do some academic duties besides their leadership tasks. The purpose of the study was communicated to them.

3.4 Data Collection

The research data was collected through structured interviews. This method will facilitate in-depth discussions about participants' experiences and perceptions regarding the integration of AI in leadership practices. Individual interviews were conducted to gain insights into specific leadership practices of incorporating AI. Each interview will be guided by a set of seven questions that include open questions related to AI applications, challenges, and perceived benefits. Each interview lasted for almost half an hour. The interview data were transcribed verbatim using a software called Inqscribe. It is a transcription software used to play video and audio files and type the written scripts in the same window. The transcripts were double-checked by the researchers of the present study. After transcribing the interviews, they were read several times by the researchers to jot down "notes, comments, observations and queries" (Merriam & Tisdell, 2026, p. 204).

3.5 Ethical Considerations

In research projects, ethical considerations relate to the privacy, confidentiality and anonymity of the participants. In the present study, an ethical approval letter was obtained from the selected higher education institutions (universities and colleges). Participants were informed about the purpose of the study, the voluntary nature of their participation, and their right to withdraw at any time. They were assured that their identity would be kept anonymous and they would be given pseudonyms to optimize the security of their personal data. Confidentiality was ensured by anonymizing and storing all data that would only be used for analysis purposes.

3.6 Data Analysis

The qualitative data were analyzed for emerging themes that represent the educational leaders' current practices, their perceptions regarding trends and challenges of using AI in their professions. Thematic analysis involves coding the data to identify the key themes and patterns related to AI integration in educational leadership.

4. FINDINGS

The respondents listed the following AI tools as the most common AI tools used in education: ChatGPT, gamma, Co-pilot, Google Bert, text and image generators, natural language processing tools like Grammarly and writeLab, smart sparrow, automated grading systems like Gradescope, Socrates, adaptive learning platforms like Carnegie learning's MATHia, Jill Watson (Georgia Tech), tools integrated into other software like Canva, Blackboard, Moodle, virtual and augmented reality as in platforms like Google Expeditions, and data analytics, prediction software, AI plagiarism detectors like Turnitin, Civitas that identifies at risk students, proofreading and translation AI tools and other tools for transcribing audios and videos, referencing and research mapping.

Thematic analysis is employed to extract emerging themes based on the interviews. Five themes emerged based on the transcribed interviews: 1. current practices of AI in higher education, 2. the perceived effects of AI on learning, teaching and educational leaderships, 3. AI-related challenges, 4. strategies to overcome challenges, 5. and recommendations for future implementations of AI in education.

1. How has the integration of AI technologies impacted teaching and leadership practices implementation at higher educational institutions in Oman?

4.1 Current Practices of AI in Higher Education

The respondents mentioned numerous ways in which AI technologies have impacted education whether the realm of teaching or leadership. For instance, Talal expressed his thoughts stating that "AI tools are shifting the dynamics of educational leadership. He listed the four dimensions AI tools have impacted education. They are: "Enhancing decision-making, streamlining administrative tasks, promoting data-driven strategies, and encouraging personalized learning". Jana, as a language lecturer, stated that AI tools "can be viewed as a great potential for learning to explore different options for teaching and learning language skills and subskills, research skills and other academic skills". Another respondent, Waed, added that AI technologies have altered how we define literacy. Thus, educators cannot ignore their existence as students will eventually use these tools. Shahad, an assistant professor, explained saying; "the use of AI tools has added a sense of creativity to my profession particularly with the use of GenAI". She added that such tools are making her professional life easier than before. They are saving her time and effort to support her to meet her job requirements.

Using AI tools can accelerate learning and save time and effort. In this regard, Jana answered the questions; "How do these tools help you as an educator/leader?" saying that; "AI tools can be very useful and practical in performing quick tasks such as preparing activities that focus on active learning, autonomous learning, project-based learning and so on". To many educators, AI tools have the potential to assist them in finding "alternatives to certain activities, images or tips on how to conduct a certain task", Jana.

Shaheen believed that AI tools can provide educational leaders with "real-time data and analytics" that can enable them to make more informed decisions based on reliable evidence. He highlighted the possibility that leaders, having "access to predictive models, pattern recognition and performance metrics" will be empowered to evaluate trends more accurately and thus adjust their strategies accordingly. Hajer, an assistant professor, voiced the role of AI technologies in facilitating administrative tasks and improving decision-making processes.

2. What are the perceived effects of artificial intelligence on learning, teaching and educational leadership?

4.2 Perceived Effects of AI on Learning, Teaching and Educational Leadership

4.2.1 Impact on Learning

AI technologies are significantly impacting learning. Waed, as an EFL lecturer, expressed her worries and concerns regarding the over-reliance on AI tools by EFL students, particularly those who are considered as beginners with low English proficiency level. She stated, "If these students depend highly on AI tools to generate their wirings, they may not receive the necessary support from their teachers".

4.2.2 Impact on Teaching

The interviewees stated various effects of the use of AI tools in their teaching professions. For instance, Waed described AI technologies as great tools "when it comes to material writing and creating interesting and personalized content for teaching". She added that some AI tools "help in marking long essays which saves time and effort". Shahad admitted that she is currently using GenAI tools like ChatGPT "to generate texts and assessment questions".

4.2.3 Impact on Leadership

The interviewees stated that AI tools support leadership roles in various facets. AI tools are capable of improving efficiency of leaders by automating routine tasks such as grading, scheduling and record-keeping. Second, AI technologies enhance human communication using tools like chatbots. Third, these technologies facilitate strategic planning and decision making by utilizing data visualization and trend analysis. Moreover, AI technologies support leaders in implementing personalized learning paths and improving learning environments. Hajer mentioned that AI tools saves her time in different areas of teaching and learning. She stated that AI powered tools helped her "personalize learning for students, provided valuable insights about students' performance, and enhanced communication with students and fellow colleagues". According to Hajer, her utilization of AI tools has made her "job more effective and engaging".

3. What are the obstacles that educational leaders encounter while implementing AI technologies?

The interviewees pointed to several challenges. In addition to that, they proposed some strategies to overcome the challenges, and also, they offered some recommendations for future implementations of AI in education. The emphasized obstacles include skills gap, cost-related concerns and ethical issues and data privacy while the proposed strategies related to developing clear visions, training and on-going development, fostering a culture of innovation.

4.3 AI-Related Challenges

The six interviewees expressed their concerns related to the use of AI tools in various educational contexts. The challenges they echoed included skills gap, cost-related concerns and ethical issues and data privacy.

4.3.1 Skills Gap

All interviewees expressed similar concerns relating to the skills gap of educators. Shaheen explained that the skills gap encompasses "AI development, implementation, and management". Talal stated that, "even though higher institutions welcome the use of AI into their educational systems, there are several challenges", He explained that such challenges include "insufficient training for staff". Jana shared the same concern stating that "lack of continuous in-service training for faculty on AI, its use, potential, challenges and solutions to challenges" as a major challenge linked to AI. She expressed her concerns regarding educators' and leaders' updates in AI technologies, and thus students may be "ahead of them in their use of AI". Similarly, Waed mentioned that the most challenging thing with AI tools related to educators and leaders "is to be up-to-date with the latest tools and know how to use them". In the same vein, Hajer said; "I struggle with lack of training on AI tools". The same notion is echoed by Shahad stating that one of the challenges associated with AI use is offering proper training and clear introduction to AI tools that enhance any professional experience.

4.3.2 Cost-Related Concerns

Additionally, Talal also raised the issue of the high cost of implementing AI tools, and the fact that many institutions are not sufficiently equipped with the necessary hardware and software". Regarding the ethical concerns associated with AI in education, Talal expressed his worries about fairness as AI tools may disseminate biases if they are not managed properly. He also stated that; "over-reliance on AI may disadvantage students and educators alike". Shahad shared the same concern stating that, "There is also the problem of high cost. Most AI tools have premium schemes that require paid subscription".

4.3.3 Ethical Issues and Data Privacy

Ethical concerns and data privacy were echoed by all the interviewees. A concern related to "students' academic misconduct as they work on their projects and home assignments" was expressed by Jana as a challenge that needs to be addressed. She added that nowadays there is a buzzing issue among educators. She explained this issue by stating "Users copy-paste whole texts/essays/projects/presentations from different AI platforms without exerting any effort on the production or the modification" is continuing to distort the teaching-learning process. Similarly, Shahad explained that "these tools are posing some new challenges related to students' completion of assignments. Students tend to rely heavily on AI tools to write their assignments". Thus, there is the challenge of copying from AI tools negatively impacting students' level of writing. Subsequently, learners' mental faculties might be deactivated holding back their mental progress, especially higher order thinking skills. Waed emphasized plagiarism and copyright issues as the most ethical issues associated with using AI tools. Furthermore, the interviewee raised the issue of stereotypes against certain ethnic and religious groups, particularly linked to image and video generated tools. Hajer highlighted the question; "who is responsible for AI decisions?" Another ethical issue is the inequal access to technology that "could widen the gaps in education" as expressed by Hajer.

4.4 Strategies to Overcome Challenges

The interviewees stressed a number of techniques that educational leaders can use to deal with the challenges. These include developing clear visions, investing in training and development, creating and fostering a culture of innovation, piloting AI, and working on data security and ethics.

4.4.1 Developing Clear Visions

Talal suggested "balancing AI support with human oversight" in order not to over-depend on artificial intelligence and decay the role of human intelligence. Jana is concerned about regulating the use of AI in educational institutions. She mentioned that "both teachers and learners should be aware of the guidelines, expectations, limitations and penalties in case of academic misconduct". Hajer explained that leaders can contribute to the implementation of AI into their institutions by "creating clear policies to protect students while encouraging a positive attitude toward technology". In the same vein, Shahad mentioned that educators should "maximize the benefits of AI to enhance their educational experience and to find solutions to leadership and educators routine tasks".

4.4.2 Training and On-Going Development

All the interviewees pointed to the urgent need to offer proper training to all concerned parties in educational institutions. Shahad emphasized the importance of being up-to-date with the emerging AI technologies. Jana highlighted educators' need for upskilling in terms of being aware of how to detect AI plagiarized texts and other forms of AI misconduct. Waed also emphasized the significance of "creating the opportunity for AI related professional development events and embracing some of these tools to be officially used by teachers and students and provide the necessary training to do so". Another point stressed by Waed was the need for educators and educational leaders "to be highly aware of the strengths of these tools and how they can benefit from them in educational contexts". What also goes under the umbrella of on-going training is developing educators "critical thinking and ethical awareness", expressed by Hajer. She also pointed to the need for educational leaders to be "AI data literate, tech-smart and being adaptable to technological changes". Shahad voiced the importance of setting up awareness raising programs that should tap on all AI-related issues including ethical considerations and data privacy.

4.4.3 Fostering a Culture of Innovation

Waed thought that leaders need "to help educators feel comfortable with these tools and not resist them". She elaborated on the role of leaders in education indicating that they should encourage teachers to use AI technologies in various educational contexts. The interviewee believed that educators and educational leaders alike need to create communities of learning in which they can help one another and share their experiences about implementation of AI tools in teaching, learning and leading.

4.5 Recommendations for Future Implementations of AI in Education

The interviewees expressed similarities in their envisions about the further development of AI in education. For example, Talal expected that AI in education will evolve significantly in ways that further support personalization of instructions that "will offer more tailored learning experiences". Interestingly, Talal expected an expansion of AI-powered learning assistants like virtual tutors and mentors and also an integration of AI into lifelong learning experiences that will ensure the provision and continuity of professional learning.

Jana tended to think that "AI is going to be more advanced in terms of humanizing the texts and being able to process advanced requests that take into account shades of mood and higher order thinking skills". It is no surprise that that, as expressed by Jana, "institutions will have to consider AI platforms as resources for learning". She further explained this notion by speculating that "AI is going to be incorporated into teaching, learning and assessment at a larger scale".

Waed strongly believed that AI tools will play a powerful role in enhancing the educational systems. She also indicated that "more courses and programs will be introduced to embrace these technological advancements". She mentioned that many higher educational institutions have already introduced degree programs in AI, a note also voiced by Shahad. Hajer listed a number of tips for educational institutions to embark upon. They are offering customized learning experiences, using highly engaging AI tools, considering ethical issues and privacy, offering proper professional training to staff, and establishing on-going communication with tech specialists." Hajer anticipated that in five years, there will be "more AI tutors, better data insights to support students making education more effective and accessible to all".

5. DISCUSSION

The field of education is witnessing rapid and transformative changes due to the profound impact of AI powered tools used by learners, teachers and educational leaders. Educators and leaders need to clearly understand this new paradigm shift influencing their professions while upholding ethical-related issues. This study investigated the trends and potential of integrating AI tools into higher educational institutions. This section discusses the main findings of the study and compares it to previous research, implications and directions for future research.

The findings of the present study revealed that educators and leaders in higher education in Oman perceived AI tools as highlight helpful technologies that streamline professional processes and enhance the teaching-learning experiences. They acknowledged their substantial role in expediting their routine tasks and easing other managerial duties, which is in line with many past studies (i.e. Arslan, 2020). Educators uncovered the immense support they are getting from AI tools and technologies. Thus, AI powered tools prove to largely benefit the profession of teaching and leadership by simplifying teachers' tasks, accelerating assessment and evaluation processes and analytically identifying areas of strengths and weaknesses based on examination results. Previous studies like Arslan (2020 and Ahlquist (2020) support these findings. While considering the paramount potential of AI in education, the data raised the flag towards associated challenges and on-going risks of misuses by learners and educators alike. Wang (2021) portrayed similar concerns.

With respect to challenges, handling concerns related to data privacy and safety is seen as a key challenge accompanying the utilization of AI powered tools. All the interviewees echoed this concern, which is in line with several previous studies (i.e.

Rahiman & Kodikal, 2024, among many other studies). It is self-evident that more students are now using AI powered learning platforms and sharing their personal data online. Thus, it becomes imperative that such data is kept safe and confidential. In order to achieve this, educational institutions should take the responsibility of establishing "clear guidelines and criteria" (Rahiman & Kodikal, 2024, p. 17) monitoring the use of AI- powered technologies and addressing the issues of data privacy, security and other ethical concerns. Of an equal importance is the role of universities to provide supportive training programs that boost the essential knowledge and skills related to the effective use of AI-powered learning systems.

6. CONCLUSION, RECOMMENDATIONS AND IMPLICATIONS

The incorporation of AI tools into education is growing, redefining the roles of educational leaders, educators, and learners. The present research study explored the integration of AI tools into higher educational institutions uncovering the current trends of their utilization, effects, and challenges. It is empirically evident that AI powered tools have the potential to enhance learning experiences and educational leadership, particularly in higher education institutions.

A number of recommendations for educators and educational leaders in higher education is made to meet the arising issues related to the utilization of AI tools. First, specialized and on-going training development programs should be offered to address the need to keep up with the new advancement in AI technologies. All concerned staff ought to undergo such training programs to upskill them and to discuss any issues related to the use of AI in teaching and learning. Second, educational leaders should encourage the participation of educators, lecturers and other staff in making shared informed decisions related to the application of AI. Eventually, this procedure is hoped to lead to more secure and effective use of AI and innovative ideas. In terms of ethics, educational leadership should develop guidelines and regulations that tap upon the ethical and data privacy issues linked to AI use in education. This is an important step to ensure the protection of students' data and to uphold ethical standards. In research-related fields, it is recommended that future research endeavors focus on how to develop applicable guidelines and frameworks to address ethical standards related to data privacy, security, and biases.

Recently, education has witnessed a growing trend toward the integration of AI in higher education around the world. Hence, numerous universities have started to incorporate AI technologies into their instructional practices including the use of intelligent tutoring systems, chatbots, and automated grading and attendance systems. The current research paper suggests employing multifaceted approaches to address the implementation of AI involving educational leaders, educators, learners, policy makers and technical supports in order to optimize the potentials of AI. Policy makers should provide the necessary financial aid to promote the development of AI supported platforms and to upgrade infrastructure support systems in higher education. Additionally, it is pivotal that educational institutions embrace a culture of innovation and collaboration through which educational leaders, educators, students, and technical support units come together to work on implementing AI tools.

In conclusion, while it is true that the implementation and utilization of AI-supported learning and leadership systems can empower educators, learners and leaders alike, there are still significant challenges that need to be tackled such as privacy, security, biases and ethical issues.

REFERENCES

Abduljaber, M. F. (2024). Perceived influence of artificial intelligence on educational leadership's decision-making, teaching, and learning outcomes: A transcendental phenomenological study. DOI: 10.30935/cedtech/13152

Adıgüzel, T., Kaya, M. H., & Cansu, F. K. (2023). Revolutionizing education with AI: Exploring the transformative potential of ChatGPT. *Contemporary Educational Technology*, 15(3), ep429. DOI: 10.30935/cedtech/13152

Ahlquist, J. (2020). *Digital leadership in higher education: Purposeful social media in a connected world*. Routledge.

Al Harrasi, N., El Din, M. S., & Al Balushi, B. (2021). Towards an artificial intelligence (AI)-driven government in the Sultanate of Oman: Transforming and augmenting leadership competencies. In *Managerial Issues in Digital Transformation of Global Modern Corporations* (p. 13). IGI Global., DOI: 10.4018/978-1-7998-2402-2.ch016

Al Matari, A. S., Mukit, A., Al Saadi, S., Balushi, W. A., & Al-Abri, J. S. Artificial intelligence and the future of teaching in higher education at A'Sharqiyah University (ASU) in Oman. DOI: 10.1007/s10833-021-09448-w PMID: 38624840

Ayed, I. A. H. (2022). *Oman higher education institutions dealing with artificial intelligence* [Doctoral dissertation, Universidade do Minho]. ProQuest Dissertations & Theses. https://doi.org/DOI: 30227343

Azorín, C., & Fullan, M. (2022). Leading new, deeper forms of collaborative cultures: Questions and pathways. *Journal of Educational Change*, 23(1), 131–143. DOI: 10.1007/s10833-021-09448-w PMID: 38624840

Bernacki, M. L., Greene, J. A., & Crompton, H. (2020). Mobile technology, learning, and achievement: Advances in understanding and measuring the role of mobile technology in education. *Contemporary Educational Psychology*, 60, 101827. DOI: 10.1016/j.cedpsych.2019.101827

Bryant, J., Heitz, C., Sanghvi, S., & Wagle, D. (2020). How artificial intelligence will impact K-12 teachers. McKinsey & Company. Retrieved September 8, 2020, from https://www.mckinsey.com/industries/social-sector/our-insights/how-artificial-intelligence-will-impact-k-12-teachers

Bryman, A. (2021). *Social research methods* (5th ed.). Oxford University Press.

Cardona, M. A., Rodríguez, R. J., & Ishmael, K. (2023). Artificial intelligence and the future of teaching and learning: Insights and recommendations. DOI: 10.1007/s10833-021-09448-w PMID: 38624840

Chaudhry, I. S., Sarwary, S. A. M., El Refae, G. A., & Chabchoub, H. (2023). Time to revisit existing student's performance evaluation approach in higher education sector in a new era of ChatGPT — A case study. *Cogent Education*, 10(1), 2210461. DOI: 10.1080/2331186X.2023.2210461

Chernov, A., & Chernova, V. (2019) Artificial intelligence in management: challenges and opportunities. In Hammes, K., Machrafi, M., & Samodol, A. (Eds.) The proceedings of the 38th international scientific conference on economic and social development (pp. 133-140). Varazdin Development and Entrepreneurship Agency.

Choi, K.-S. (2020). Opportunities for higher education of artificial intelligence in Korea. *International Journal of Engineering Research & Technology (Ahmedabad)*, 13(11), 3428–3430. DOI: 10.37624/IJERT/13.11.2020.3428-3430

Cooper, G. (2023). Examining science education in ChatGPT: An exploratory study of generative artificial intelligence. *Journal of Science Education and Technology*, 32(3), 444–452. DOI: 10.1007/s10956-023-10039-y

Cresswell, J. W. (2014). *Research design: Qualitative, quantitative, and mixed methods approaches* (4th ed.). Sage Publications.

Donasco, A., & Oliveros, S. T. R. (2024). AI's impact on educational leadership and learning. [IMJRISE]. *International Multidisciplinary Journal of Research for Innovation, Sustainability, and Excellence*, 1(8), 228–236.

Frank, M. R., Autor, D., Bessen, J. E., Brynjolfsson, E., Cebrian, M., Deming, D. J., & Wang, D. (2019). Toward understanding the impact of artificial intelligence on labor. *Proceedings of the National Academy of Sciences of the United States of America*, 116(14), 6531–6539. DOI: 10.1073/pnas.1900949116 PMID: 30910965

Fullan, M., Azorín, C., Harris, A., & Jones, M. (2024). Artificial intelligence and school leadership: Challenges, opportunities and implications. *School Leadership & Management*, 44(4), 339–346. DOI: 10.1080/13632434.2023.2246856

Ghamrawi, N. (2024). Educational Leadership in the Age of Artificial Intelligence: Are We Ready? The 8th Annual International Educational Conference: (Visions and Ideas for Hot Issues in education in the Arab Education: reality challenges and future prospects, 18-41. Hargreaves, S. (2023). "Words are flowing out like endless rain into a paper cup": ChatGPT & law school assessments. *Legal Education Review, 33*, 69.

Harris, A., & Jones, M. (2023). Compassionate leadership. *School Leadership & Management*, 43(3), 185–188. DOI: 10.1080/13632434.2023.2235540

Hassan, A. (2022). The influence of artificial intelligence on smart learning: An overview. In *Technologies, artificial intelligence and the future of learning post-COVID-19: The crucial role of international accreditation* (pp. 591-615).

Hejres, S. (2022). The impact of artificial intelligence on instructional leadership. In *Technologies, artificial intelligence and the future of learning post-COVID-19: The crucial role of international accreditation* (pp. 697–711). Springer International Publishing. DOI: 10.1007/978-3-030-93921-2_36

Holmes, W., Bialik, M., & Fadel, C. (2019). *Artificial intelligence in education: Promises and implications for teaching and learning*. Center for Curriculum Redesign.

Kamalov, F., Santandreu, C. D., & Gurrib, I. (2023). New era of artificial intelligence in education: Towards a sustainable multifaceted revolution. *Sustainability (Basel)*, 15(16), 12451. DOI: 10.3390/su151612451

Kurkan, G., & Çetin, M. (2024). The perceptions of educational administrators towards digital leadership in the age of artificial intelligence: A qualitative study. *International Journal of Contemporary Educational Research*, 11(3), 425–439. DOI: 10.52380/ijcer.2024.11.3.602

Liu, Z., Yang, C., Rüdiän, S., Liu, S., Zhao, L., & Wang, T. (2019).. . *Interactive Learning Environments*, •••, 1–30.

Merriam, S. B., & Tisdell, E. J. (2015). *Qualitative research: A guide to design and implementation*. John Wiley & Sons.

Miller, D. (2017). *Case study research: A guide for researchers and practitioners*. Cambridge University Press.

Milton, J., & Al-Busaidi, A. (2023). New role of leadership in the AI era: Educational sector. *SHS Web of Conferences*. https://doi.org/DOI: 10.1051/shsconf/202315609005

Mollick, E. R., & Mollick, L. (2022). New modes of learning enabled by AI chatbots: Three methods and assignments. Available at *SSRN* 4300783. DOI: 10.2139/ssrn.4300783

Moussa, N., Bentoumi, R., & Saali, T. (2024). Promoting student success with neutrosophic sets: Artificial intelligence and student engagement in higher education context. *International Journal of Neutrosophic Science*, 23(1), 238–38. DOI: 10.54216/IJNS.230121

Papa, R., & Jackson, K. M. (Eds.). (2021). *Artificial intelligence, human agency and the educational leader*. Springer Nature. DOI: 10.1007/978-3-030-77610-7

Pradana, M., Elisa, H. P., & Syarifuddin, S. (2023). Discussing ChatGPT in education: A literature review and bibliometric analysis. *Cogent Education*, 10(2), 2243134. DOI: 10.1080/2331186X.2023.2243134

Rahiman, H. U., & Kodikal, R. (2024). Revolutionizing education: Artificial intelligence empowered learning in higher education. *Cogent Education*, 11(1), 2293431. DOI: 10.1080/2331186X.2023.2293431

Roulston, K. (2023). *Interviews in education research.* Sage Publications.

Timms, M. J. (2016). Letting artificial intelligence in education out of the box: Educational cobots and smart classrooms. *International Journal of Artificial Intelligence in Education*, 26(2), 701–712. DOI: 10.1007/s40593-016-0095-y

UNESCO. (2023). *Global Education Monitoring Report. Technology in Education: A Tool on Whose Terms?* UNESCO.

Vaioleti, T. (2016). Talanoa: A transformative research method. *New Zealand Journal of Educational Studies*, 51(2), 191–202. DOI: 10.1007/s40841-016-0001-1

Van Quaquebeke, N., & Gerpott, F. H. (2023). The now, new, and next of digital leadership: How artificial intelligence (AI) will take over and change leadership as we know It. *Journal of Leadership & Organizational Studies*, 30(3), 265–275. DOI: 10.1177/15480518231181731

Wang, F., & Hannafin, M. (2020). Design-based implementation research: An emerging model for transforming education. *Educational Technology Research and Development*, 68(1), 1–25. DOI: 10.1007/s11423-019-09714-1

Wang, Y. (2021). When artificial intelligence meets educational leaders' data-informed decision-making: A cautionary tale. *Studies in Educational Evaluation*, 69, 100872. DOI: 10.1016/j.stueduc.2020.100872

Xu, Z. (2024). AI in education: Enhancing learning experiences and student outcomes. *Applied Computational Engineering*, 51(1), 104–111. DOI: 10.54254/2755-2721/51/20241187

Zeira, J. (2018). Workers, machines, and economic growth. *The Quarterly Journal of Economics*, 113(4), 1091–1117. DOI: 10.1162/003355398555847

Zhang, B., & Mao, J. (2023, July). On the teaching and learning in the information age of “Big Data + Internet?”—Some thoughts on the application of ChatGPT in teaching. In *2023 2nd International Conference on Educational Innovation and Multimedia Technology (EIMT 2023)* (pp. 1005-1016). Atlantis Press.

ADDITIONAL READING

Akgun, S., & Greenhow, C. (2022). Artificial intelligence in education: Addressing ethical challenges in K-12 settings. *AI and Ethics*, 2(3), 431–440. DOI: 10.1007/s43681-021-00096-7 PMID: 34790956

Alam, A. (2021, November). Possibilities and apprehensions in the landscape of artificial intelligence in education. In *2021 International Conference on Computational Intelligence and Computing Applications (ICCICA)* (pp. 1-8). IEEE. DOI: 10.1109/ICCICA52458.2021.9697272

Bates, T., Cobo, C., Mariño, O., & Wheeler, S. (2020). Can artificial intelligence transform higher education? *International Journal of Educational Technology in Higher Education*, 17(1), 1–12. DOI: 10.1186/s41239-020-00218-x

Chen, X., Zou, D., Xie, H., Cheng, G., & Liu, C. (2022). Two decades of artificial intelligence in education. *Journal of Educational Technology & Society*, 25(1), 28–47.

Huang, J., Saleh, S., & Liu, Y. (2021). A review on artificial intelligence in education. *Academic Journal of Interdisciplinary Studies, 10*(3).

Luan, H., Geczy, P., Lai, H., Gobert, J., Yang, S. J., Ogata, H., Baltes, J., Guerra, R., Li, P., & Tsai, C. C. (2020). Challenges and future directions of big data and artificial intelligence in education. *Frontiers in Psychology*, 11, 580820. DOI: 10.3389/fpsyg.2020.580820 PMID: 33192896

Nalbant, K. G. (2021). The importance of artificial intelligence in education: a short review. *Journal of Review in science and engineering, 2021*, 1-15.

Nguyen, A., Ngo, H. N., Hong, Y., Dang, B., & Nguyen, B. P. T. (2023). Ethical principles for artificial intelligence in education. *Education and Information Technologies*, 28(4), 4221–4241. DOI: 10.1007/s10639-022-11316-w PMID: 36254344

Ouyang, F., & Jiao, P. (2021). Artificial intelligence in education: The three paradigms. *Computers and Education: Artificial Intelligence*, 2, 100020. DOI: 10.1016/j.caeai.2021.100020

KEY TERMS AND DEFINITIONS

Artificial Intelligence (AI): Refers to technology that simulates how humans think and learn through machines performing tasks that typically require human cognition and smarts.

Higher Education: Refers to education beyond high school, such as universities and colleges, where people can get degrees and advance their studies.

Omani Higher Education System: Collection of colleges and universities in Oman that provide post education and offer degrees for students.

Educational Leadership: The process of guiding educational institutions to achieve their goals. It includes making decisions, mentoring, and planning.

Data Analytics: The process of examining data to draw conclusions and decision-making.

Natural Language Processing (NLP): A field of AI focused on the interaction between computers and humans through natural language.

Ethical Considerations: Issues related to the moral implications of AI, including data privacy, bias, and accountability.

Vision 2040: Oman's strategic plan for the future, aimed at fostering sustainable development and innovation in different areas, including education.

Student Engagement: The degree of how students are involved and interested in their learning.

Adaptive Learning Systems: Refer to tools that tailor learning experiences based on individual student performance and learning styles.

Challenges of AI Integration: Obstacles that institutions face when incorporating AI technologies, such as lack of resources, resistance to change, and insufficient training.

APPENDIX

The interview questions:

1. Based on your knowledge and experience, what AI tools are being used in education?
2. How are these AI trends/tools changing your profession?
3. How do these tools help you as an educator/leader?
4. What problems do educators/leaders face with AI? How can leaders fix these problems?
5. What ethical issues come up with AI?
6. What skills should educators/leaders learn to use AI?
7. What tips do you suggest for educators/leaders using AI? What do you think AI will look like in education in five years?

Chapter 10
Integration of Digital Technologies in Entrepreneurship Education in Nigeria

Fatai Kayode Wahab
https://orcid.org/0000-0002-9680-9132
Ahman Pategi University, Nigeria

Elizabeth Abidemi Akintade
https://orcid.org/0009-0006-0630-2933
Federal University of Technology, Akure, Nigeria

ABSTRACT

This chapter, titled "Integration of Digital Technologies in Entrepreneurship Education in Nigeria," explores how digital technologies can transform and enhance entrepreneurship education in Nigeria. It addresses key issues such as accessibility, content quality, the digital divide, and the need for ongoing professional development for educators. The chapter highlights the shift from traditional classroom methods to more experiential learning, driven by technological advancements. Furthermore, it discusses the benefits and challenges of digital learning, presents case studies, and provides recommendations for stakeholders to foster an innovative and inclusive entrepreneurial ecosystem in Nigeria.

DOI: 10.4018/979-8-3693-7863-2.ch010

1.0 INTRODUCTION

Nigeria, a country abundant in both human and natural resources, is currently navigating a significant digital transformation that is reshaping various sectors of its economy. One of the most critical areas experiencing this shift is entrepreneurship education. The integration of digital technologies into this field is not just an incremental improvement but a transformative necessity that holds the potential to drive economic development and foster innovation across the nation. As the world increasingly recognizes the role of digital technology in shaping the future of education, this trend takes on special significance in Nigeria. With its rapidly expanding population and the pressing need to create employment opportunities for its youthful demographic (Wahab, 2022); Nigeria stands at a pivotal point where embracing digital technologies could yield substantial benefits.

The range of digital tools available today, from basic internet access to more sophisticated technologies like artificial intelligence and virtual reality is revolutionizing the way entrepreneurship is taught and practiced. As Yamin (2019) notes, these technologies offer unprecedented opportunities to enhance the learning experience, making education more accessible, engaging, and effective. Historically, entrepreneurship education in Nigeria has been heavily reliant on conventional pedagogical methods. These methods, while foundational, have often been constrained by limited resources and outdated curricula, which fail to fully prepare students for the complexities of the modern business environment. As Wahab (2022) highlights, the introduction of digital technologies has opened up new possibilities for teaching and learning, allowing for more interactive, flexible, and contextually relevant educational experiences. These technologies are not just enhancements; they represent a fundamental shift in how education can be delivered and accessed.

One of the primary objectives of this chapter is to explore how digital technologies can improve the accessibility, quality, and relevance of entrepreneurship education in Nigeria. Accessibility is a critical concern in a country where the digital divide remains a significant barrier to equal educational opportunities. This divide, characterized by disparities in access to digital technologies between urban and rural areas, as well as among different socio-economic groups, poses a considerable challenge. As Eze et al. (2020) emphasize, it is imperative to address these disparities to ensure that all aspiring entrepreneurs, regardless of their background, have the chance to benefit from digital education. While government initiatives, private sector partnerships, and non-profit organizations have made strides in bridging this gap, more coordinated and sustained efforts are needed to achieve a substantial impact.

Furthermore, the integration of digital technologies into entrepreneurship education requires a focus on continuous professional development for educators. It is not enough to introduce new technologies into the classroom; educators must be adequately trained and supported to use these tools effectively. Grigg (2021) emphasizes the importance of professional development programs that focus on digital pedagogy. These programs are essential for empowering educators to lead the transformation in entrepreneurship education, ensuring they can facilitate learning in ways that maximize student engagement and learning outcomes. Without such training, there is a risk that digital tools may be underutilized or misapplied, diminishing their potential impact.

The potential benefits of integrating digital technologies into entrepreneurship education in Nigeria are vast, but realizing these benefits requires addressing several key challenges. The digital divide, while not insurmountable, poses a significant barrier that must be overcome through targeted interventions and sustained efforts. Ensuring that all students have access to the necessary technologies is the first step toward creating an equitable educational environment. Additionally, the relevance of educational content must be continually reassessed and updated to reflect the evolving business landscape, ensuring that students are equipped with the skills and knowledge they need to succeed.

2.0 THE DIGITAL TRANSFORMATION OF ENTREPRENEURSHIP EDUCATION

The digital transformation of entrepreneurship education is a pivotal development in the modern educational system, reshaping how entrepreneurship is taught, learned, and practiced. This transformation is characterized by the integration of digital tools and technologies into educational curricula, enabling more dynamic, accessible, and personalized learning experiences. The shift toward digital education is driven by several critical factors. Firstly, there is a growing recognition of the importance of digital literacy in the global economy, where technological proficiency is becoming a fundamental skill for entrepreneurs. Secondly, there is a pressing need for innovative teaching methods that go beyond traditional classroom settings to better prepare students for the complexities of the modern business world. Lastly, the demand for skills that align with the rapid technological advancements in the business environment underscores the necessity of this digital transformation (Othman et al., 2021).

2.1 The Role of Digital Technologies in Entrepreneurship Education

Digital technologies have become instrumental in enhancing the effectiveness and reach of entrepreneurship education, offering tools and platforms that significantly enrich the learning experience. These technologies facilitate the creation of interactive and engaging educational environments that extend beyond the limitations of traditional classroom settings, providing learners with more flexible, personalized, and impactful learning opportunities. For example, online platforms like Coursera and Udemy have revolutionized access to entrepreneurship education by offering a wide range of courses that learners can take at their own pace. These platforms connect students to a global network of peers and provide them with opportunities to learn from industry experts, making education more accessible and diverse. Kaplan and Haenlein (2020) highlight how these platforms have democratized access to high-quality entrepreneurship education, allowing learners from different parts of the world to acquire critical entrepreneurial skills without the constraints of location or time.

Furthermore, digital tools such as simulation software, virtual reality (VR), and artificial intelligence (AI) are increasingly being integrated into entrepreneurship curricula to create immersive and experiential learning experiences. Simulation software, for instance, enables students to engage in virtual business scenarios where they can experiment with various entrepreneurial strategies, make critical decisions, and observe the consequences of those decisions in a risk-free environment. This hands-on approach to learning helps students develop practical skills and a deeper understanding of the complexities of entrepreneurship. Virtual reality (VR) takes this experiential learning a step further by immersing students in simulated business environments where they can practice and refine their entrepreneurial skills. Through VR, learners can experience real-world business challenges in a controlled setting, enhancing their ability to handle similar situations in real life.

2.2 Benefits of Digital Transformation in Entrepreneurship Education

The digital transformation of entrepreneurship education brings with it a multitude of benefits that significantly enhance the learning experience and better prepare students for the realities of the modern business world. Among these benefits are increased accessibility, enhanced engagement, and the development of crucial digital competencies that are essential for today's entrepreneurs. One of the most notable advantages of digital transformation is the democratization of education. Digital platforms make entrepreneurship education accessible to a much broader audience, including individuals in remote or underserved areas. This is particularly impactful in countries like Nigeria, where disparities in access to quality education are a significant challenge.

As Eze et al. (2024) highlight, the use of digital technologies helps bridge the educational gap by providing access to quality learning resources and opportunities that would otherwise be unavailable to many. This increased accessibility ensures that aspiring entrepreneurs, regardless of their geographical location or socio-economic background, have the opportunity to acquire the skills and knowledge necessary for entrepreneurial success. Moreover, digital technologies significantly enhance student engagement by creating more interactive and immersive learning experiences. The use of multimedia content, such as videos, podcasts, and interactive quizzes, helps to maintain student interest and improve information retention. These diverse learning materials cater to different learning styles, making education more inclusive and effective. Olanrewaju et al. (2023) emphasize that this collaborative environment not only enriches the learning experience but also helps students build valuable networks that can support their entrepreneurial endeavors in the future.

Another key benefit of digital transformation in entrepreneurship education is the seamless integration of real-world experiences into the curriculum. Digital platforms can connect students with successful entrepreneurs and business leaders through webinars, virtual mentoring sessions, and online networking events. This exposure to real-world entrepreneurship provides students with practical insights and allows them to apply theoretical knowledge in real-world contexts. As Oluwakemi (2019) notes, such experiences are invaluable in helping students understand the complexities of entrepreneurship and in preparing them to navigate the challenges they will face in their own ventures.

2.3 Challenges of Digital Transformation in Entrepreneurship Education

While the digital transformation of entrepreneurship education offers numerous benefits, it also brings with it a series of significant challenges that must be addressed to fully realize it's potential. These challenges range from issues related to the digital divide and the need for continuous professional development of educators to concerns about the quality and relevance of digital content. Each of these challenges poses unique obstacles that require careful consideration and strategic solutions. One of the most pressing challenges is the digital divide, which refers to the disparity between those who have access to digital technologies and those who do not. This divide is particularly pronounced in developing countries, where limited access to the internet and digital devices can significantly hinder the widespread adoption of digital education.

Grigg (2021) highlights that in many regions, especially in rural and underserved areas; the lack of infrastructure such as reliable internet connectivity, electricity, and affordable digital devices prevents students from accessing digital educational resources. This not only limits their ability to participate in digital entrepreneurship education but also exacerbates existing inequalities in access to quality education. Bridging this digital divide is essential to ensuring that all students, regardless of their location or socio-economic status, have the opportunity to benefit from the advancements in digital education. This requires coordinated efforts from governments, private sector entities, and non-profit organizations to invest in infrastructure, provide affordable devices, and promote digital literacy on a large scale. Another significant challenge is the need for continuous professional development for educators.

Nwosu et al. (2023) argue that this continuous learning process is critical to maintaining the relevance and effectiveness of digital entrepreneurship education. Educators need ongoing training and support to develop the necessary digital literacy and pedagogical skills required to navigate the complexities of digital education. However, access to such professional development opportunities is often limited, particularly in regions where educational resources are already stretched thin. To address this challenge, it is essential to provide educators with accessible and affordable professional development programs that focus on digital pedagogy, as well as to create supportive networks that allow educators to share best practices and collaborate on innovative teaching strategies.

Moreover, the quality and relevance of digital content are crucial factors that determine the success of digital entrepreneurship education. The content used in digital platforms must be carefully designed to meet the needs of a rapidly changing business environment and should be aligned with industry standards and practices. As the business environment continues to evolve with advancements in technology, it is imperative that educational content keeps pace with these changes. This requires a collaborative effort between educators, industry professionals, and technology providers to ensure that digital content is up-to-date, culturally relevant, and pedagogically sound. The challenge lies in creating content that not only addresses the theoretical aspects of entrepreneurship but also provides practical, real-world insights that students can apply in their future endeavors.

2.4 The Future of Digital Entrepreneurship Education

The future of entrepreneurship education is intricately linked to the ongoing advancements in digital technologies, which are poised to redefine how entrepreneurship is taught, learned, and practiced. As the global economy continues to evolve, driven by technological innovation, the need for a digitally literate and technologically savvy entrepreneurial workforce becomes increasingly critical. Emerging technologies such as artificial intelligence (AI), virtual reality (VR), and augmented reality (AR) are expected to play a pivotal role in shaping the future of entrepreneurship education, offering new ways to engage students, personalize learning experiences, and prepare the next generation of entrepreneurs for the challenges and opportunities of the digital age.

Artificial intelligence is one of the most promising technologies in this space, with its potential to transform the educational landscape through AI-driven analytics, personalized learning paths, and intelligent tutoring systems. AI can provide educators with deep insights into student performance, enabling them to tailor educational content and strategies to meet the unique needs of each learner (Permatasari & Anggadwita, 2019). For instance, AI algorithms can analyze patterns in student behavior and learning outcomes to identify areas where individual students may need additional support or challenges. This level of personalization allows for a more adaptive learning experience, where students can progress at their own pace, focusing on areas that require further development while advancing in areas where they excel. By doing so, AI not only enhances the effectiveness of entrepreneurship education but also helps in cultivating a more resilient and adaptable entrepreneurial mindset.

Moreover, the integration of virtual reality (VR) and augmented reality (AR) into entrepreneurship education is set to revolutionize the way students experience and interact with business concepts. These immersive technologies offer a unique opportunity to create simulated environments that mirror real-world business scenarios, allowing students to practice and hone their entrepreneurial skills in a risk-free setting. For example, through VR, students can step into a virtual marketplace where they can launch and manage a business, make strategic decisions, and observe the consequences of those decisions in real-time. This hands-on approach to learning not only reinforces theoretical knowledge but also helps students develop critical thinking, problem-solving, and decision-making skills, key competencies for any successful entrepreneur.

The application of AR further enhances this experiential learning by overlaying digital information onto the physical world, thereby creating a blended learning environment that bridges the gap between theory and practice. For instance, AR can be used to provide real-time feedback or guidance as students work on entrepreneurial projects, such as product design or market analysis. This interactive and engaging learning experience helps students better understand complex concepts and apply them in real-world contexts, ultimately leading to a deeper and more practical understanding of entrepreneurship. As these technologies continue to advance and become more accessible, their integration into entrepreneurship education will likely become more widespread. The decreasing cost of VR and AR hardware, along with the increasing availability of AI-powered educational tools, will make it feasible for educational institutions across various regions, including those in developing countries, to adopt these innovations.

However, the successful integration of these technologies into entrepreneurship education will require more than just access to the latest tools. It will necessitate a rethinking of traditional pedagogical approaches and the development of new curricula that leverage the full potential of digital technologies. Educators will need to be equipped with the skills and resources to effectively incorporate AI, VR, and AR into their teaching practices, ensuring that these technologies are used to enhance, rather than replace, the fundamental principles of entrepreneurship education.

3.0 ACCESSIBILITY AND EQUITY IN THE INTEGRATION OF DIGITAL TECHNOLOGIES IN ENTREPRENEURSHIP EDUCATION

The integration of digital technologies into entrepreneurship education holds the promise of democratizing learning and making it more accessible to a diverse audience. This democratization is particularly significant in a global context where education has historically been unevenly distributed, favoring those in urban areas with better infrastructure over those in rural and underserved regions. Rippa and Secundo (2019) emphasize that access to technology-driven educational tools can break down barriers to entrepreneurship education, enabling a wider range of individuals to gain the skills and knowledge necessary to succeed in the modern economy.

Accessibility to digital entrepreneurship education is intrinsically linked to the availability of essential digital infrastructure such as reliable internet connectivity, electricity, and affordable digital devices. In many parts of Nigeria, these basic resources are scarce, particularly in rural and low-income areas. According to Rippa and Secundo (2019), without addressing these fundamental issues, the benefits of digital education will remain out of reach for many potential learners, perpetuating a cycle of exclusion that limits the potential for broad-based economic development. This digital divide is not merely a technological gap but a significant social and economic barrier that hinders inclusive access to educational opportunities. To address this issue, it is crucial to bridge the digital divide through targeted interventions. One approach is to expand internet connectivity, particularly in remote and underserved areas.

In addition to expanding internet connectivity, promoting digital inclusion is another key strategy. Digital inclusion goes beyond providing access to technology; it also involves equipping individuals with the necessary digital literacy skills to effectively use these technologies. For many students in Nigeria, particularly those from disadvantaged backgrounds, lack of familiarity with digital tools can be a significant barrier to participation in digital education. Rippa and Secundo (2019) argue that comprehensive digital literacy programs are essential to ensure that all students can fully engage with digital entrepreneurship education.

Fostering collaborative efforts to provide affordable access to digital technologies is also critical. This can be achieved through public-private partnerships that leverage the resources and expertise of both sectors to deliver cost-effective solutions. For instance, tech companies could collaborate with educational institutions to provide discounted devices and software, while the government could offer subsidies or tax incentives to lower the cost of digital access for students.

Another important consideration is the need for culturally relevant and context-specific content. The integration of digital technologies in entrepreneurship education should not be a one-size-fits-all approach. It is essential to develop educational content that resonates with the local context and addresses the unique challenges and opportunities faced by learners in Nigeria.

3.1 Bridging the Digital Divide

The digital divide in Nigeria is a significant issue that underscores the disparity in access to digital technologies, particularly the internet and computing devices, between urban and rural areas, as well as among different socioeconomic groups. This divide is a major barrier to equitable participation in the digital economy and highlights the broader social and economic inequalities that persist in the country. Urban areas in Nigeria generally benefit from better infrastructure, which leads to higher levels of digital accessibility. In cities, there is relatively widespread access to high-speed internet, reliable electricity, and a variety of affordable digital devices. These factors create an environment conducive to digital literacy and innovation, allowing individuals in urban centers to participate fully in the digital economy. Businesses, educational institutions, and government services in these areas are increasingly moving online, further integrating digital technologies into daily life. As a result, urban residents have more opportunities to engage in e-commerce, online education, and other digital activities that contribute to economic growth and social development.

Conversely, rural regions in Nigeria face significant challenges that exacerbate the digital divide. Poor connectivity is one of the most critical issues, with many rural areas lacking access to reliable and affordable internet services. This is often due to inadequate telecommunications infrastructure, such as limited broadband coverage and weak mobile networks. Additionally, the high cost of digital devices and internet services in these regions further restricts access for many individuals. As a result, residents of rural areas are often excluded from the benefits of digital technologies, including access to online education, digital financial services, and e-government initiatives. This exclusion not only limits their ability to improve their socio-economic status but also widens the gap between urban and rural areas in terms of economic development and quality of life (UNESCO, 2023; Research ICT Africa, 2023).

The digital divide in Nigeria also reflects broader socioeconomic disparities. Wealthier individuals and families, typically residing in urban areas, can afford the latest technologies and have greater access to digital literacy resources. In contrast, those from lower-income backgrounds, especially in rural areas, may struggle to afford basic digital devices or internet services, further entrenching social inequalities. This divide is particularly problematic for educational opportunities, as students in rural or low-income settings may lack the resources to participate in online learning, thereby falling behind their urban counterparts in acquiring essential digital skills. This lack of access perpetuates a cycle of poverty and underdevelopment, where disadvantaged groups are unable to take advantage of the opportunities provided by the digital economy.

Addressing the digital divide in Nigeria requires a multifaceted approach involving targeted interventions to improve infrastructure and accessibility. First and foremost, there needs to be significant investment in telecommunications infrastructure, particularly in rural areas. Expanding broadband coverage and enhancing mobile network quality are essential steps in ensuring that rural communities have reliable access to the internet. Government and private sector partnerships could play a pivotal role in financing and implementing these infrastructure projects, making high-speed internet more accessible and affordable for rural populations.

Moreover, enhancing digital literacy through targeted training programs is vital. These programs should be designed to cater to the specific needs of rural and low-income populations, ensuring that they have the skills required to navigate and utilize digital technologies effectively. Digital literacy initiatives could be integrated into the formal education system and community-based programs, focusing on practical skills that empower individuals to leverage technology for economic and social advancement. Inclusivity must also be a key priority in bridging the digital divide. This includes creating digital content and platforms that are accessible to people with disabilities, ensuring that all individuals, regardless of their physical abilities, can benefit from digital technologies. Universal design principles should be applied to digital platforms and services, making them usable by as many people as possible, regardless of their location, socioeconomic status, or physical abilities (UNESCO, 2023).

3.2 Promoting Digital Inclusion and Expanding Internet Connectivity

Promoting digital inclusion and expanding internet connectivity are crucial strategies for enabling equitable access to digital technologies and ensuring that all citizens can benefit from the opportunities presented by the digital age. Governments, through strategic policies and programs, play a fundamental role in addressing these issues, particularly in countries like Nigeria where disparities in digital access are pronounced. In Nigeria, various government-led initiatives have been implemented to enhance internet connectivity and digital inclusion. A notable example is the National Broadband Plan 2020-2025, which outlines a comprehensive strategy for expanding internet access across the country. This plan focuses on overcoming infrastructure challenges that have historically limited connectivity, particularly in rural and underserved areas. The initiative aims to provide affordable and reliable internet services, which are critical for fostering digital transformation in essential sectors such as education, healthcare, and agriculture (WebManager.NG, 2023).

The National Broadband Plan seeks to achieve its goals by addressing several key areas. One major focus is the expansion of broadband infrastructure to increase internet penetration in areas that have traditionally been underserved. This involves enhancing the physical infrastructure necessary for broadband connectivity, such as laying fiber-optic cables and improving mobile network coverage.

Furthermore, government initiatives also emphasize the importance of digital literacy programs to complement infrastructure improvements. Effective digital literacy programs are essential for ensuring that individuals not only have access to digital technologies but also possess the skills needed to use them effectively. In Nigeria, programs like the Digital Nigeria Program and the National Information Technology Development Agency's (NITDA) Digital Literacy and Skills Pillar play a crucial role in this regard (WebManager.NG, 2023). These programs are designed to equip marginalized groups including women, the elderly, and individuals living in remote areas with the necessary digital skills to participate fully in the digital economy.

The Digital Nigeria Program, for instance, aims to enhance digital skills across various demographics, providing training and resources to help individuals navigate digital platforms and tools. This initiative targets communities that have historically been excluded from the digital revolution, thereby promoting greater inclusivity. Similarly, the NITDA's Digital Literacy and Skills Pillar focuses on improving digital competencies among the Nigerian workforce, fostering an environment that supports digital entrepreneurship and innovation in the ICT sector.

3.3 Collaborative Efforts to Provide Affordable Access

Public-private partnerships (PPPs) are increasingly recognized as vital mechanisms for enhancing accessibility and equity in the digital domain. By leveraging the strengths and resources of government entities, private companies, and non-profit organizations, these collaborations are instrumental in bridging the digital divide and making technology more accessible to underserved communities. In Nigeria, PPPs have played a significant role in expanding internet connectivity and providing affordable digital devices. Telecom companies, in partnership with government agencies, have spearheaded initiatives to extend low-cost internet services to rural and remote areas. By promoting private sector investment in broadband infrastructure and addressing infrastructure challenges, this plan aims to make reliable and affordable internet access a reality for more Nigerians (WebManager.NG, 2023).

PPPs are essential in promoting digital literacy through community-based initiatives. Effective digital literacy programs are tailored to the specific needs of the communities they serve and draw on the diverse expertise of various stakeholders. Technology firms may provide the necessary tools and training materials, while local non-profits often manage implementation and community outreach. This collaborative approach ensures that digital literacy initiatives are relevant and resonate with the target population, thereby enhancing their impact.

These programs are often supported by partnerships between government agencies, tech companies, and non-profit organizations, which work together to deliver training and resources effectively. Public-private partnerships also contribute to global objectives, such as the United Nations' Sustainable Development Goals (SDG 4), which advocate for inclusive and equitable education and promote lifelong learning opportunities for all.

Overall, collaborative efforts between various sectors are crucial for addressing digital inequities and fostering a more inclusive digital economy. By integrating resources, expertise, and innovative solutions from multiple stakeholders, PPPs can significantly enhance digital inclusion and ensure that the benefits of digital technologies are accessible to all (Guardian Nigeria, 2024; World Economic Forum, 2023). As digital inclusion continues to evolve, these partnerships will play a key role in shaping a more equitable and connected future.

4.0 CONTENT QUALITY AND RELEVANCE IN THE INTEGRATION OF DIGITAL TECHNOLOGIES IN ENTREPRENEURSHIP EDUCATION

As digital technologies become increasingly integrated into entrepreneurship education, ensuring the quality and relevance of educational content is paramount. In the context of Nigerian entrepreneurship education, the challenge of maintaining content quality is dynamic. First, educational content must be rigorously aligned with the current realities of the business landscape. This means that curriculum developers and educators need to stay abreast of the latest industry trends, technological advancements, and entrepreneurial practices. As the business world becomes more globalized and interconnected, there is an imperative to equip students with knowledge and skills that are not only relevant locally but also applicable in a broader, international context. This dual focus ensures that graduates are prepared to operate effectively in both local and global markets (Permatasari & Anggadwita, 2019).

To address these needs, educators must design and curate digital content that reflects contemporary business practices and addresses the unique challenges faced by Nigerian entrepreneurs. At the same time, integrating global perspectives and practices helps students understand and adapt to international business norms and opportunities. This approach ensures that the educational content is not only relevant but also comprehensive, equipping students with a well-rounded understanding of entrepreneurship (Eze et al., 2020).

Another critical aspect of content quality is ensuring that it is engaging and interactive. Digital technologies offer various tools for enhancing student engagement, such as multimedia resources, interactive simulations, and online collaboration platforms. High-quality content should leverage these tools to create dynamic learning experiences that stimulate student interest and promote deeper understanding.

4.1 Ensuring Relevance to the Modern Business Environment

For digital content to be effective in entrepreneurship education, it must closely align with the dynamic needs of the contemporary business environment. This alignment is crucial for ensuring that students gain relevant knowledge and skills that are directly applicable to their entrepreneurial endeavors. In the context of Nigeria, where entrepreneurs face distinct challenges and opportunities, the content delivered through digital platforms must be carefully tailored to address these specific needs.

The modern business environment is characterized by rapid changes and technological advancements that impact how businesses operate and thrive. Therefore, entrepreneurship education must reflect current trends, challenges, and opportunities to remain relevant. For example, the curriculum should incorporate up-to-date business practices, emerging technologies, and industry-specific knowledge that students will encounter in the real world. This includes understanding the implications of digital transformation, the impact of globalization, and the integration of innovative technologies such as artificial intelligence (AI) and blockchain.

In Nigeria, where the entrepreneurial climate is shaped by unique factors such as informal markets, limited resources, and economic fluctuations, digital content must address these specific conditions (Wahab, 2019). Entrepreneurs in Nigeria often navigate informal market structures, where traditional business practices may not always apply. Therefore, educational content should include practical skills that are vital for operating successfully in these environments. Topics such as financial management, digital marketing, and e-commerce are particularly important. Financial management skills are essential for effectively handling limited resources and managing cash flow, while digital marketing and e-commerce capabilities enable entrepreneurs to reach broader markets and compete in a digital economy (Eze et al., 2024).

Furthermore, the adaptability of digital content is key to meeting the diverse needs of learners. As entrepreneurship education increasingly moves online, it is important to design content that can be customized based on individual learner goals and contexts. This adaptability ensures that students can tailor their learning experiences to their specific entrepreneurial activities or business ventures.

4.2 Developing Resources that Resonate with Nigerian Learners

Culturally sensitive content is vital for ensuring that digital educational resources are both effective and engaging for Nigerian learners. As digital technologies become increasingly integral to education, it is essential that the content delivered through these platforms resonates with the cultural, social, and economic realities of the Nigerian context. This approach not only enhances the relevance of the material but also fosters a more meaningful and impactful learning experience.

One of the primary aspects of culturally sensitive content is the inclusion of examples, case studies, and business scenarios that reflect the local environment. Digital entrepreneurship education in Nigeria should feature content that highlights local entrepreneurs, businesses, and market dynamics. For instance, incorporating case studies of successful Nigerian startups or analyzing business models that thrive in Nigerian markets can provide students with practical insights and real-world relevance. Such content demonstrates the applicability of theoretical knowledge within the Nigerian business landscape, making the learning experience more tangible and directly relevant to students' entrepreneurial endeavors (Dynamic Language, 2023).

Moreover, adapting language and communication styles to suit the preferences of Nigerian students is crucial. Nigeria is a multilingual country with a rich tapestry of local languages and dialects. While English is widely used in education and business, many students and communities use local languages in their daily lives. Therefore, providing content in local languages or dialects, where feasible, can significantly enhance comprehension and engagement. For example, educational materials that offer translations or explanations in major Nigerian languages such as Hausa, Yoruba, or Igbo can help bridge language barriers and ensure that all students can access and benefit from the content (Dynamic Language, 2023).

Furthermore, culturally sensitive content can address specific challenges faced by Nigerian entrepreneurs, such as navigating informal markets, managing local supply chains, and responding to economic fluctuations.

4.3 Facilitating Effective Learning and Promoting Active Engagement

Pedagogical soundness is essential for creating digital content that not only imparts knowledge effectively but also supports meaningful learning experiences. In the realm of digital entrepreneurship education, this involves designing content that is engaging, interactive, and conducive to active learning. Effective digital content leverages various multimedia elements, such as videos, interactive simulations, quizzes, and discussion forums, to enhance the learning experience. These tools are integral to making content more dynamic and engaging, enabling learners to apply concepts in real-time and receive immediate feedback (Clark & Mayer, 2016).

Interactive multimedia elements play a crucial role in fostering a more engaging learning environment. For instance, videos can provide visual and auditory explanations of complex entrepreneurial concepts, while interactive simulations allow learners to experiment with business strategies and scenarios in a controlled setting. Quizzes and discussion forums further enhance the learning process by offering opportunities for self-assessment and peer interaction. This approach aligns with Clark and Mayer's (2016) assertion that well-designed multimedia instruction can significantly improve learning outcomes by catering to different learning styles and preferences.

Another critical aspect of pedagogical soundness in digital content is the incorporation of principles of adult learning. Many students in entrepreneurship education are working professionals or individuals with prior business experience. Merriam and Bierema (2014) argue that adult learners benefit from having the flexibility to determine how and when learning takes place. Therefore, digital content should offer flexible learning options, such as self-paced modules and asynchronous discussions, to accommodate the diverse schedules and responsibilities of adult learners.

Incorporating adult learning principles also involves recognizing and valuing learners' existing knowledge and experiences. Providing opportunities for learners to connect new information with their prior experiences can enhance the relevance of the content and support deeper learning. For example, case studies that reflect real-world entrepreneurial challenges and successes can help learners relate theoretical concepts to practical scenarios, making the learning experience more meaningful.

5.0 PROFESSIONAL DEVELOPMENT FOR EDUCATORS IN THE INTEGRATION OF DIGITAL TECHNOLOGIES IN ENTREPRENEURSHIP EDUCATION

The successful integration of digital technologies in entrepreneurship education hinges not only on the availability of advanced tools and resources but also on the preparedness and capability of educators to effectively utilize these technologies. Professional development for educators is crucial in this regard, as it empowers them to seamlessly incorporate digital tools into their teaching practices, thereby enhancing the quality of education delivered. To achieve this, educators must be equipped with the necessary skills and knowledge to navigate and integrate digital technologies into their curriculum. This includes building their proficiency with digital tools and understanding how to leverage these technologies to create a more engaging and effective learning environment.

5.1 Empowering Educators to Integrate Digital Technologies

Empowering educators to effectively integrate digital technologies into entrepreneurship education is crucial for enhancing the learning experience and maximizing the benefits of digital tools. Comprehensive training and ongoing support are essential to help educators transition from traditional teaching methods to digital platforms.

5.1.1 Training Programs: Effective training programs are foundational for equipping educators with the skills necessary to integrate digital technologies into their teaching. According to Kearns (2012), these programs should cover several key areas:

1. **Basic Technical Skills:** Educators need to become familiar with using digital devices and navigating online platforms. This includes understanding the functionalities of various digital tools and how to use them efficiently in an educational context.

2. **Educational Technologies:** Training should also include the use of Learning Management Systems (LMS), digital content creation tools, and interactive multimedia resources. LMS platforms, for example, facilitate the organization of course materials, assignment submissions, and communication with students.
3. **Virtual Classroom Management:** Proficiency in managing virtual classrooms is essential. This involves facilitating online discussions, engaging students through digital platforms, and using technology to assess and monitor student performance.

5.1.2 Ongoing Support: Continuous support is equally important to ensure that educators remain up-to-date with technological advancements and evolving pedagogical strategies. Kearns (2012) emphasizes that this support can take several forms:

1. **Regular Workshops:** Hosting workshops that focus on new technologies and pedagogical approaches helps educators stay current with best practices. These workshops can provide hands-on experience with emerging tools and techniques.
2. **Online Tutorials:** Access to online tutorials and resources enables educators to learn at their own pace and revisit materials as needed. These resources should cover both technical skills and pedagogical strategies.
3. **Peer Mentoring:** Creating opportunities for educators to collaborate and share insights with colleagues can foster a supportive learning community. Peer mentoring allows educators to learn from each other's experiences and strategies.
4. **Technical Support Teams:** Access to technical support teams ensures that educators can get assistance with troubleshooting and technical issues. This support helps prevent disruptions in teaching and ensures that educators can focus on delivering quality instruction.

5.1.3 Professional Development: Beyond initial training and ongoing support, professional development opportunities should be available to help educators continually refine their skills and adapt to new technologies. As digital technologies rapidly evolve, ongoing learning and adaptation are necessary to maintain effective teaching practices.

5.2 Building Educators' Proficiency with Digital Tools

Developing digital literacy among educators is a critical aspect of professional development in the digital age. As technology becomes increasingly integral to educational practices, it is essential that educators not only acquire basic computer skills but also develop a comprehensive understanding of various digital tools and platforms to enhance teaching and learning. Ribble (2015) emphasizes that digital literacy goes beyond the ability to operate computers; it involves the effective use of digital technologies to create engaging and interactive learning environments.

5.2.1 Comprehensive Training Programs: To ensure that educators are well-equipped to integrate digital technologies into their teaching, training programs must be both comprehensive and targeted. Ribble (2015) suggests that educators need to be familiar with a range of digital tools, including those for:

1. **Content Creation:** This includes tools such as video editing software, presentation tools, and digital storytelling platforms. These tools enable educators to produce dynamic content that caters to diverse learning styles, thereby enhancing student engagement and understanding.
2. **Communication:** Educators must be proficient in using email, instant messaging platforms, and discussion boards. These communication tools are essential for maintaining effective interactions with students, facilitating group discussions, and providing timely feedback.
3. **Collaboration:** Cloud-based document sharing and project management tools, such as Google Drive and Microsoft Teams, are crucial for fostering collaboration among students.

5.2.2 Digital Research Methods: Educators also need to be adept at digital research methods. Frydenberg (2016) emphasizes that educators must be capable of accessing, evaluating, and integrating digital resources into their curricula. This includes:

1. **Accessing Information:** Educators should be proficient in navigating digital libraries, academic databases, and online resources to find relevant materials for their lessons.
2. **Evaluating Sources:** It is crucial for educators to assess the credibility and relevance of digital resources. This involves scrutinizing the authority of the sources, the accuracy of the information, and its relevance to the educational objectives.
3. **Integrating Resources:** Once resources are selected, educators need to integrate them effectively into their teaching plans. This means aligning the resources with educational goals and ensuring that they complement the existing curriculum.

5.2.3 Critical Assessment and Selection of Tools: As digital technologies evolve rapidly, educators must develop the ability to critically assess and select the most appropriate tools for their educational needs. Kimmons (2018) highlights that this involves evaluating factors such as usability, compatibility with existing systems, and the potential to enhance learning outcomes.

5.2.4 Enhancing Teaching Practices: Developing digital literacy enables educators to create more adaptable and engaging learning environments. By effectively utilizing digital tools, educators can offer a variety of instructional methods and resources that meet the diverse needs of students. This proficiency also helps educators prepare students for the digital economy, where technological skills are increasingly essential for career success.

5.2.5 Ongoing Professional Development: Given the rapid pace of technological advancements, continuous professional development is vital for maintaining and expanding digital literacy skills. Educators should have access to ongoing training, workshops, and resources to keep abreast of new technologies and pedagogical strategies. This ongoing support ensures that educators remain current with technological trends and can continuously improve their teaching practices.

5.3 Leveraging Digital Technologies for Enhanced Teaching

Pedagogical innovation is crucial for effectively harnessing the potential of digital technologies in education. As technology continues to evolve, educators must be encouraged and supported in adopting new teaching methods and strategies that leverage these digital tools.

5.3.1 Interactive Teaching Models: One prominent example of pedagogical innovation is the transition from traditional lecture-based methods to more interactive models, such as flipped classrooms. McMurtrie (2020) highlights that flipped classrooms can significantly improve student engagement and learning outcomes. In this model, instructional content is delivered online, allowing students to engage with materials at their own pace outside of class. Class time is then used for interactive activities such as discussions, group work, and hands-on projects.

5.3.2 Blended Learning: Another effective pedagogical approach is blended learning, which combines online and face-to-face instruction. Tucker and Beth (2021) emphasize the flexibility and personalization that blended learning offers. This model allows educators to cater to diverse learning styles and needs by integrating digital tools with traditional teaching methods. Through blended learning, educators can track student progress more efficiently, provide personalized feedback, and adjust instructional content and pacing to meet individual student needs.

5.3.3 Professional Development for Educators: To implement these innovative teaching methods effectively, educators require access to comprehensive professional development resources. Hodges et al. (2020) argue that professional development programs should emphasize the pedagogical advantages of digital technologies, equipping educators with the necessary skills and knowledge to adopt and integrate new strategies.

5.3.4 Shifting Mindsets: Supporting educators in embracing pedagogical innovation involves more than just providing training; it also requires a shift in mindset. Educators must be encouraged to view digital technologies not merely as supplementary tools but as integral components of effective teaching strategies. This shift involves recognizing the potential of digital tools to enhance student engagement, foster collaboration, and facilitate personalized learning experiences.

5.3.5 Impact on Student Learning: Ultimately, fostering pedagogical innovation enables educators to enhance their teaching practices and better meet the needs of modern learners. By adopting interactive and blended learning models, educators can create more engaging and effective learning environments. This, in turn, prepares students more effectively for participation in the digital economy, where technological proficiency and adaptability are essential skills. Li et al. (2021) emphasize that pedagogical innovation not only improves educational outcomes but also equips students with the skills necessary for success in an increasingly digital world.

6.0 EMERGING TECHNOLOGIES AND FUTURE TRENDS

As digital technologies continue to advance, incorporating cutting-edge tools into entrepreneurship education can offer new and innovative ways to engage learners and enhance their skills. The integration of Artificial Intelligence (AI), Virtual and Augmented Reality (VR/AR), and Blockchain Technology represents a significant leap forward in educational practices, providing opportunities for more personalized, immersive, and secure learning experiences.

6.1 Artificial Intelligence (AI)

Artificial Intelligence (AI) is rapidly emerging as a transformative force in entrepreneurship education, offering innovative solutions for personalized learning and enhancing educational practices through sophisticated data analytics. This technological advancement promises to tailor educational experiences to individual needs, thereby optimizing learning outcomes and improving the overall effectiveness of instruction.

AI-driven tools are revolutionizing the way education is delivered by enabling highly personalized learning experiences. Adaptive learning platforms, as discussed by Serrano et al. (2021), utilize AI algorithms to analyze individual student performance and learning styles. These platforms adjust the educational content based on the unique needs of each learner, ensuring that the material is relevant and appropriately challenging.

Beyond personalized content delivery, AI-powered intelligent tutoring systems offer another layer of support. Roll and Wylie (2016) explain that these systems simulate one-on-one instruction by providing real-time feedback and guidance.

6.2 Virtual and Augmented Reality (VR/AR)

Virtual and Augmented Reality (VR/AR) technologies are significantly transforming entrepreneurship education by creating immersive and experiential learning environments. These technologies offer students realistic, hands-on experiences that are challenging to replicate through traditional classroom methods, thereby enhancing the educational process.

6.2.1 Virtual Reality (VR) in Entrepreneurship Education: VR technology provides an immersive experience by simulating realistic business environments. Students can engage in scenarios such as launching a startup, managing daily operations, or navigating complex negotiations within a controlled and risk-free virtual space. This simulation enables students to practice decision-making and problem-solving skills in a setting that closely mirrors real-world conditions (Freina & Ott, 2015).

Research by Bower et al. (2020) underscores the effectiveness of VR simulations in entrepreneurship education. Their study highlights that VR can enhance student engagement by providing an experiential learning platform that improves comprehension and retention of business concepts. By engaging with VR scenarios, students can better grasp the practical challenges of entrepreneurship, thereby gaining valuable skills and knowledge that are directly applicable to real-world situations.

6.2.2 Augmented Reality (AR) in Entrepreneurship Education: AR technology enriches the educational experience by overlaying digital information onto the physical world. In the context of entrepreneurship education, AR can create interactive case studies where students interact with virtual elements within their physical environment. This interaction enables students to visualize and manipulate business plans, financial models, and marketing strategies in real-time.

García et al. (2020) highlight that AR applications make complex business concepts more accessible and engaging by integrating digital information into students' physical surroundings. This technology supports a more hands-on approach to learning, enabling students to interact with business models and strategies in a dynamic and intuitive manner. By bridging the gap between theoretical knowledge and practical application, AR enhances students' ability to understand and apply business concepts effectively.

6.3 Blockchain Technology

Blockchain technology, renowned for its role in securing digital transactions and data, holds significant promise for transforming entrepreneurship education. Its decentralized and immutable nature offers several advantages, including enhanced credential verification, improved data security, and innovative methods for peer-to-peer collaboration.

One of the most impactful applications of blockchain in entrepreneurship education is its ability to verify academic credentials. The decentralized and tamper-proof characteristics of blockchain technology ensure that academic records, certificates, and degrees are securely stored and authenticated. This is crucial in the field of entrepreneurship, where the credibility of qualifications can significantly affect a graduate's ability to secure funding, form partnerships, or gain employment (Grech & Camilleri, 2017).

Blockchain technology also plays a pivotal role in enhancing data security within educational institutions. As digital platforms become increasingly integral to learning and administrative processes, protecting sensitive student data is of utmost importance. Blockchain's encryption and decentralized storage methods offer robust safeguards against data breaches, ensuring that personal information, academic records, and intellectual property are protected from unauthorized access and tampering (Li et al., 2020). This level of security is essential for maintaining the integrity and confidentiality of educational data in the digital era, providing students and institutions with greater assurance regarding data privacy and protection.

Beyond its roles in credential verification and data security, blockchain facilitates peer-to-peer learning and collaboration by enabling secure and transparent sharing of resources, ideas, and feedback among students and educators. For instance, smart contracts self-executing contracts with terms written directly into code can be employed to manage collaborative projects, allocate rewards for contributions, and track the progress of group activities (Zheng et al., 2020). This decentralized approach supports a student-centered learning environment, aligning with the core principles of entrepreneurship, where collaboration and innovation are crucial.

As blockchain technology continues to evolve, its applications in entrepreneurship education are likely to expand further. The ongoing development of blockchain solutions may introduce new methods to enhance security, transparency, and trust in the educational process (Chen et al., 2018). For example, future advancements could enable more sophisticated systems for managing intellectual property rights, streamlining administrative processes, and creating new avenues for educational content distribution and access.

7.0 CASE STUDIES

7.1 Case Study 1: A Successful Digital Entrepreneurship Program

The Lagos State Employment Trust Fund (LSETF), established under the Lagos State Employment Trust Fund Law of 2016, is a prominent digital entrepreneurship initiative in Nigeria. Launched in collaboration with the United Nations Development Programme (UNDP), LSETF is designed to tackle youth unemployment by providing digital skills training and fostering entrepreneurial mindsets among participants. LSETF offers a comprehensive curriculum that encompasses digital marketing, web development, and data analysis, all tailored to meet the specific demands of the local business environment.

Since its inception, LSETF has trained thousands of young people, many of whom have gone on to launch successful digital businesses or secure employment in tech-related fields. The program's strong emphasis on practical skills and industry-relevant knowledge has significantly enhanced the employability of its graduates, contributing to the growth of Lagos State's digital economy. However, despite its successes, LSETF has encountered challenges such as limited internet access in certain areas and difficulties in securing sustained funding. To address these issues, the project has sought to expand its partnerships with private sector companies and explore innovative funding models. LSETF's success is largely attributed to its strong alignment with market needs, effective use of digital technologies, and the government's commitment to supporting youth entrepreneurship.

7.2 Case Study 2: Addressing the Digital Divide

The Digital Access Program (DAP), spearheaded by the British Council in collaboration with the Nigerian government, ran from October 2020 to September 2022 with the goal of bridging the digital divide in Nigeria. This initiative primarily targeted underserved and rural communities, aiming to enhance digital literacy and broaden access to digital technologies. The Digital Access Program adopted several strategies to achieve its goals, including the establishment of digital hubs in remote areas, the provision of affordable internet access, and the implementation of training programs to boost digital literacy.

However, the Digital Access Program in Nigeria faced significant challenges, particularly the lack of infrastructure in rural areas, which impeded the delivery of digital services. Cultural resistance to adopting new technologies and a shortage of skilled trainers further complicated the program's implementation. Through its efforts, the Digital Access Program learned the importance of customizing digital literacy programs to meet the specific needs and contexts of different communities. Engaging local stakeholders and fostering a sense of community ownership over the initiative were also crucial in overcoming resistance and ensuring the program's sustainability.

8.0 CONCLUSION

The integration of digital technologies presents a paradigm shift for entrepreneurship education in Nigeria. By leveraging the power of online platforms, interactive tools, and emerging technologies like AI, VR/AR, and blockchain, educators can cultivate a more accessible, engaging, and impactful learning experience for aspiring entrepreneurs.

This chapter has comprehensively examined the advantages of digital transformation within entrepreneurship education. These advantages include enhanced accessibility, fostering engagement, cultivating crucial digital competencies, and seamlessly integrating real-world experiences into the curriculum.

To fully capitalize on the benefits of digital technologies and foster an innovative and inclusive entrepreneurial ecosystem in Nigeria, the chapter emphasizes the necessity of a interdisciplinary approach. This approach should encompass several key strategies:

1. The first step towards ensuring equitable access to digital education is to bridge the digital divide. This involves expanding internet access, particularly in rural and underserved areas, to ensure that all students have the opportunity to benefit

from digital learning. It also requires actively promoting digital literacy so that students are equipped with the skills needed to navigate and utilize digital tools effectively.

2. Equipping educators with the necessary skills and knowledge to effectively integrate digital technologies into their teaching practices is paramount. This requires ongoing professional development opportunities that are tailored to the specific needs of entrepreneurship educators.
3. Developing culturally sensitive and up-to-date content that aligns with the demands of the modern business environment is critical for maximizing the impact of digital education. This involves creating materials that are not only relevant to the Nigerian context but also globally competitive. Content should be regularly reviewed and updated to reflect current trends and practices in the business world, ensuring that students are receiving an education that is both practical and forward-looking.
4. Collaboration between government, private sector entities, and non-profit organizations can facilitate the development and deployment of affordable digital resources and bridge the digital divide. Public-private partnerships can also play a role in supporting educator professional development and content creation.
5. Finally, it is important to encourage educators to adopt innovative teaching strategies that leverage the power of digital tools. This could include using flipped classrooms, where students access lecture materials online and use class time for interactive activities, or incorporating gamification into the curriculum to make learning more engaging.

In conclusion, this chapter serves as a valuable resource for educators, policymakers, and stakeholders committed to fostering a vibrant and inclusive entrepreneurial ecosystem in the country.

REFERENCES

Bower, M., Howe, C., & McCredie, N. (2020). Augmented Reality in Education – Cases, places, and potentials. *Educational Media International*, 57(2), 152–169.

British Council Nigeria. (2021). Empowering Underserved Communities through Digital Hubs. DOI: 10.1002/9781119239086

Chen, C. M., & Tsai, Y. H. (2020). Interactive virtual reality for collaborative learning in higher education. *Interactive Learning Environments*, 28(2), 225–242.

Chen, G., Xu, B., Lu, M., & Chen, N.-S. (2018). Exploring blockchain technology and its potential applications for education. *Smart Learning Environments*, 5(1), 1–10. DOI: 10.1186/s40561-017-0050-x

Chen, J., Vorvoreanu, M., & Madhavan, K. (2021). A web-based learning analytics system for improving student engagement in higher education. *Journal of Educational Technology & Society*, 24(2), 31–42. https://www.j-ets.net/ets/journals/24_2/4.pdf

Clark, R. C., & Mayer, R. E. (2016). *E-Learning and the Science of Instruction: Proven Guidelines for Consumers and Designers of Multimedia Learning* (4th ed.). Wiley. DOI: 10.1002/9781119239086

Dynamic Language. (2023). The Role of Localization in Education: Bridging Cultural and Linguistic Gaps. Retrieved from https://www.dynamiclanguage.com/the-role-of-localization-in-education-bridging-cultural-and-linguistic-gaps

Eze, S. C., Chinedu-Eze, V. C. A., Okike, C. K., & Bello, A. O. (2020). Factors influencing the use of e-learning facilities by students in a private Higher Education Institution (HEI) in a developing economy. *Humanities & Social Sciences Communications*, 7(1), 133. DOI: 10.1057/s41599-020-00624-6

Freina, L., & Ott, M. (2015). Augmented reality and virtual reality in education: A review of the literature. *European Journal of Contemporary Education*, 4(3), 80–92.

Frydenberg, M. (2016). *Technology for teaching and learning: Strategies for improving classroom practice*. Springer.

García, J., García-Sánchez, J. N., & García-Sánchez, E. (2020). Augmented Reality in Education: A Systematic Review of the Literature. *Interactive Learning Environments*, 28(3), 331–346.

García Botero, G., Questier, F., & Zhu, C. (2018). Self-directed language learning in a mobile-assisted, out-of-class context: Do students walk the talk? *Computer Assisted Language Learning*, 31(2), 162–185. DOI: 10.1080/09588221.2017.1375903

Garrison, D. R. (2011). *E-Learning in the 21st Century: A Framework for Research and Practice* (2nd ed.). Routledge. DOI: 10.4324/9780203838761

Grech, A., & Camilleri, A. F. (2017). *Blockchain in Education. Joint Research Centre (JRC) Science for Policy Report*. European Commission.

Grigg, R. (2021). EntreCompEdu, a professional development framework for entrepreneurial education. *Education + Training*, 63(7/8), 1058–1072. DOI: 10.1108/ET-06-2020-0166

Guardian Nigeria. (2024, May 07). Nigeria needs more Public Private Partnerships for Digital Economy, Says U.S. Retrieved from https://guardian.ng/news/nigeria-needs-more-public-private-partnership-for-digital-economy-says-u-s/

Hodges, C., Moore, S., Lockee, B., Trust, T., & Bond, A. (2020). The difference between emergency remote teaching and online learning. Educause Review. https://er.educause.edu/articles/2020/3/the-difference-between-emergency-remote-teaching-and-online-learning

Hwang, G. J., Xie, H., Wah, B. W., & Gašević, D. (2020). Examining the impact of learning analytics and AI on education: A systematic review. *Computers & Education*, 151, 103896. DOI: 10.1016/j.compedu.2020.103896

Kearns, L. R. (2012). Student assessment in online learning: Challenges and effective practices. *Journal of Online Learning and Teaching*, 8(3), 198–208. https://jolt.merlot.org/vol8no3/kearns_0912.pdf

Kimmons, R. (2018). *Technology integration and teacher education: Social practices and the sociocultural challenges of integrating technology in classrooms*. Springer.

Lagos State Government. (2016). Lagos State Employment Trust Fund (LSETF). Retrieved from https://lsetf.ng/content/employability

Lajoie, S. P., & Azevedo, R. (2019). The role of self-regulation in learning with metacognitive tools. *Educational Psychologist*, 54(4), 322–335. DOI: 10.1080/00461520.2019.1631423

Li, C., Liu, D., & Xu, S. (2021). Implementing flipped classroom model in English language course: A meta-analysis. *Education and Information Technologies*, 26(4), 4819–4842.

Li, J., Greenwood, D., & Kassem, M. (2020). Blockchain in the built environment and property industry: A review of the use-cases in research. *Automation in Construction*, 119, 103–133.

McMurtrie, B. (2020). The agile college: How institutions are adapting to a new era. *The Chronicle of Higher Education.*

Means, B., Bakia, M., & Murphy, R. (2014). *Learning Online: What Research Tells Us About Whether, When and How*. Routledge. DOI: 10.4324/9780203095959

Merriam, S. B., & Bierema, L. L. (2014). *Adult learning: Bridging theory and practice*. Jossey-Bass.

Olanrewaju, F. O., Aluko, O. E., & Akinola, O. R. (2023). Integrating digital technologies in entrepreneurship education: The Nigerian experience. *Journal of Entrepreneurship and Innovation in Emerging Economies*, 9(4), 351–367.

Oluwakemi, O. T. (2019). Digital literacy and entrepreneurial returns among small business owners in Lagos State, Nigeria. *Education & Science Journal of Policy Review and Curriculum Development*, 9(2), 1–11.

Othman, I. W., Mokhtar, S., Tham, A., & Yong, K. (2021). The Significance of Entrepreneurship Education Literacy in the Era of Digital Transformation: Graduates of the Post-Pandemic Covid-19 Unemployment Crisis. *The International Journal of Accounting*, 6(37).

Oyeleke, O., & Adeyemi, A. (2023). The impact of digital literacy on rural communities in Nigeria: A case study of the Digital Access Program. *Journal of Digital Education and Technology*, 15(2), 75–88.

Ozgen, E. (2022). Digital Technologies for Discovering Opportunities in Entrepreneurship Education: Future Trends. *Journal of International Business Disciplines*, 17(1).

Permatasari, A., & Anggadwita, G. (2019). Digital entrepreneurship education in emerging countries: Opportunities and challenges. Opening up education for inclusivity across digital economies and societies, 156-169.

Pulse Nigeria. (2023, September 1). LSETF: Empowering Nigerian Youth with Digital Skills. Retrieved from https://www.pulse.ng/

Research, I. C. T. Africa. (2023). After Access 2023: Digital Nigeria Post the Pandemic. Retrieved from https://researchictafrica.net

Ribble, M. (2015). *Digital citizenship in schools: Nine elements all students should know. International Society for Technology in Education.* ISTE.

Rippa, P., & Secundo, G. (2019). Digital academic entrepreneurship: The potential of digital technologies on academic entrepreneurship. *Technological Forecasting and Social Change*, 146, 900–911. DOI: 10.1016/j.techfore.2018.07.013

Roll, I., & Wylie, R. (2016). Evolution and revolution in artificial intelligence in education. *International Journal of Artificial Intelligence in Education*, 26(2), 582–599. DOI: 10.1007/s40593-016-0110-3

Serrano, J. P., Moreno-Guerrero, A. J., & Torres-Gordillo, J. J. (2021). The effect of interactive learning environments on improving learning outcomes in higher education. *Journal of Educational Computing Research*, 59(4), 643–667. DOI: 10.1177/0735633120984630

TechCabal. (2022, April 22). Lagos State Government Launches Digital Entrepreneurship Program for Youth. Retrieved from https://techcabal.com/

Tucker, C. R., & Beth, P. (2021). *The Shift to Digital Learning: The New Digital Divide in Education*. Solution Tree.

UNESCO. (2023). Bridging the Digital Divides. Retrieved from https://www.unesco.org

United Nations Development Programme. (2023). UNDP Nigeria. Retrieved from https://www.undp.org/nigeria

Wahab, F. K. (2019). Entrepreneurship Education as a Tool for Reducing Unemployment Rate among Secondary School Students, An unpublished Professional Diploma in Education Certificate Project Research, Kwara State College of Education, Ilorin. Available at https://doi.org/10.13140/RG.2.2.28659.71206

Wahab, F. K. (2022). Entrepreneurship: A Career Choice for Nigerian Youth. *FU-Lafia Journal for Entrepreneurial Development*, 2(1), 254–270.

WebManager.NG. (2023, June 28). ICT Policies and Regulations in Nigeria. Retrieved from https://webmanager.ng/blog/ict-policies-and-regulations-in-nigeria/#:~:text=Nigeria's%20National%20ICT%20Policy%20provides,growth%20of%20the%20ICT%20industry

WebManager.NG. (2023, June 22). Promoting ICT in Nigeria [Key Government Initiatives and Players. Retrieved from https://webmanager.ng/blog/promoting-ict-government-initiatives-players/]. *Discover*, 8.

World Economic Forum. (2023). How public-private cooperation can advance digital inclusion in the 'Global South'. Retrieved from https://www.weforum.org

Yamin, M. (2019). Information Technologies of 21st century and their Impact on the Society. Int. j. inf. tecnol. **11**, 759–766. https://doi.org/DOI: 10.1186/s41239-019-0176-8

Zawacki-Richter, O., Marín, V. I., Bond, M., & Gouverneur, F. (2019). Systematic review of research on artificial intelligence applications in higher education: A broader perspective. *Journal of Educational Technology in Higher Education*, 16(1), 1–27. DOI: 10.1186/s41239-019-0176-8

Zheng, Z., Xie, S., Dai, H., Chen, X., & Wang, H. (2020). An overview of blockchain technology: Architecture, consensus, and future trends. *IEEE International Conference on Big Data*, 1-12.

Chapter 11
Analyzing Linguistic Differences in Academic English: A Graph-Based Machine Learning Approach

Krishna Kumari R.
https://orcid.org/0000-0002-1802-628X
Department of Mathematics, SRM Institute of Science and Technology, Kattankulathur, India

Ami Femila P.
Department of English and Foreign Languages, SRM Institute of Science and Technology, Kattankulathur, India

ABSTRACT

This study employs graph-based machine learning techniques to explore and analyze the linguistic differences between the English used by Indian and British academicians. By constructing language graphs from academic texts, we identify distinct patterns, syntactic structures, and semantic variations. These graphs represent sentences as nodes and relationships, such as co-occurrences or syntactic dependencies, as edges. Our approach leverages advanced community detection algorithms to uncover clusters of linguistically similar nodes and node centrality measures to identify key terms or structures that dominate regional writing styles. Additionally, we incorporate semantic network analysis to understand contextual nuances and word usage. By combining these techniques, we reveal underlying linguistic characteristics and trends, offering novel insights into regional variations in academic writing, which can have significant implications for cross-cultural communication, education, and

DOI: 10.4018/979-8-3693-7863-2.ch011

global academic collaborations.

1. INTRODUCTION

Linguistic variations within English, especially in academic writing, offer critical insights into how regional differences shape communication and comprehension. English, as a global language, has evolved into various forms influenced by cultural, historical, and social contexts. Among these, Indian English and British English stand out as two prominent varieties with distinctive characteristics.

Indian English has developed as a nativized variant, heavily influenced by the multilingual landscape of India. This variety reflects a blend of English with local languages, resulting in unique syntactic structures, vocabulary, and idiomatic expressions. For example, Indian English often incorporates terms and expressions derived from regional languages, and its syntax may differ from the standard British English patterns. These adaptations serve to address the specific communicative needs and cultural contexts of Indian speakers, resulting in a distinct variant that is both reflective of and adapted to its socio-linguistic environment. In contrast, British English adheres more closely to traditional norms and standards of the English language. It represents the standardized form of English used in the United Kingdom and often serves as the reference point for various aspects of English grammar, spelling, and pronunciation. British English maintains a level of uniformity that is less influenced by external languages compared to Indian English. As a result, the linguistic features of British English tend to be more consistent with historical and formal norms of English usage.

The differences between these two varieties of English are not merely academic curiosities; they have practical implications for communication, particularly in academic settings. Academic writing in Indian English may exhibit variations in clarity, tone, and readability compared to British English. These variations can affect how scholarly work is perceived, interpreted, and evaluated across different linguistic and cultural contexts. For instance, differences in idiomatic expressions or syntactic structures might influence the readability and comprehension of academic texts among international audiences. Traditional linguistic analysis has often relied on qualitative methods to study these variations, focusing on descriptive and interpretive approaches. However, the advent of machine learning and computational linguistics has introduced new opportunities for more systematic and quantitative analysis. Graph-based machine learning techniques represent a particularly promising approach for this type of analysis. By employing graph representations, these techniques enable researchers to model and analyze complex linguistic structures and patterns in a more comprehensive and scalable manner.

Graph-based machine learning techniques offer a powerful framework for understanding the intricate relationships and patterns within linguistic data. By representing linguistic elements as nodes and their relationships as edges, researchers can uncover underlying structures and dynamics that might be obscured in traditional analyses. This approach allows for a more nuanced exploration of linguistic differences, providing insights into how different varieties of English are used and how they can be effectively compared.

The primary objective of this study is to leverage graph-based machine learning techniques to analyze and compare the English used by Indian and British academicians. Through this approach, we aim to identify and elucidate the unique patterns and differences that characterize these two variants of academic English. By examining linguistic structures through graph representations, we seek to enhance our understanding of how these varieties diverge and what implications these differences have for academic communication. The significance of this study extends beyond academic analysis. Understanding the linguistic differences between Indian and British English has important implications for various aspects of academic communication and cross-cultural collaboration. Insights gained from this analysis can contribute to the development of more effective writing support tools, improve peer review processes, and enhance the overall quality of academic publications. As global academic collaboration continues to grow, appreciating and addressing linguistic differences becomes increasingly crucial for fostering clear and effective communication across diverse linguistic backgrounds.

2. LITERATURE REVIEW

2.1 Linguistic Differences in Indian and British English

Indian English, as a variety of English, has evolved distinct linguistic features shaped by India's multilingual environment and the influence of various local languages. This variety of English is often characterized by unique lexical, syntactic, and pragmatic features. Kachru (1983) describes Indian English as a creative adaptation of English, molded by local communicative needs and cultural contexts. Indian English includes vocabulary borrowed from Indian languages, distinct idiomatic expressions, and syntactic structures not typically found in British English (Bhatia, 2004; Brinton & Akimoto, 1999). For instance, common usage patterns in Indian English, such as the frequent use of phrasal verbs, have been documented through corpus studies, highlighting differences in linguistic preferences and usage frequencies (Gardner & Davies, 2007).

British English, meanwhile, retains a more standardized form, often serving as a global reference for correct usage in grammar, spelling, and pronunciation. Crystal (2012) emphasizes that British English maintains linguistic norms that are relatively stable and less influenced by external languages. This variety of English, widely recognized and used internationally, adheres to traditional standards in spelling, vocabulary, and syntax (Crystal, 2012). Studies have also examined the historical development of British English and its connection to social prestige and educational frameworks, showing how linguistic stability has been maintained over time (Sinclair, 1991; Stubbs, 2001). The sociocultural and historical factors influencing both varieties underscore the complex evolution of English as it adapts to new contexts while preserving its regional uniqueness (Kachru, 1983; Crystal, 2012; Bhatia, 2004).

2.2 Graph-Based Machine Learning in Linguistic Analysis

Graph-based machine learning has emerged as a transformative approach for linguistic analysis, allowing researchers to represent complex relationships within text. By structuring linguistic elements as nodes and their relationships as edges, graph-based methods provide a detailed view of language patterns and interconnections (Navigli & Lapata, 2010; Mihalcea & Radev, 2011). This method has been widely applied in syntactic parsing, semantic analysis, and authorship attribution, aiding in the discovery of latent structures within language. For instance, Navigli and Lapata (2010) applied graph connectivity measures to unsupervised word sense disambiguation, showcasing the potential of graph models in resolving linguistic ambiguities. Mihalcea and Radev (2011) further illustrate the applicability of graph-based methods in information retrieval and natural language processing, emphasizing the value of graph representations in analyzing textual data.

Additionally, graph-based techniques have facilitated advancements in syntactic analysis, where sentences are represented as syntactic graphs, allowing researchers to explore grammatical dependencies and hierarchical structures within language (Newman, 2010; Manning et al., 2014). Techniques such as community detection algorithms, as proposed by Blondel et al. (2008), have been employed to uncover clusters within linguistic networks, revealing how words and phrases group together contextually. This approach has proven useful in both semantic and syntactic analyses, helping to understand language complexity and improve parsing accuracy. Graph-based machine learning has also advanced authorship attribution studies by constructing stylistic and syntactic profiles for different authors, enabling precise identification based on unique linguistic traits (Mihalcea & Radev, 2011). Furthermore, graph neural networks (GNNs), as discussed by Zhou et al. (2020) and Velickovic et al. (2018), provide deep learning architectures capable of leveraging complex graph-structured data, enhancing the scope of linguistic analysis across vast textual datasets. Beyond text structure analysis, graph models have been adapted for semantic applications, such as in word sense disambiguation and information network embedding. Tang et al. (2015) introduced the LINE model for large-scale network embedding, facilitating the organization of linguistic elements by similarity and relevance within massive datasets. Kipf and Welling's (2016) work on Graph Convolutional Networks (GCNs) similarly showcases the adaptability of graph models for linguistic data, where GCNs have been used for tasks like text classification and word embedding. Linguistic variations in academic English can be effectively analyzed using AI and machine learning techniques. Kumari. R.K., (2025) highlights the role of AI in enhancing learning, which extends to analyzing textual data and identifying syntactic and semantic differences in scholarly writing. Additionally, pedagogical influences shape academic discourse, as educators impact students' writing styles over time (Kumari. R.K. 2025). Methodological rigor is essential in research design, as emphasized by (Kumari. R.K. 2025). By integrating AI, educational insights, and computational techniques, this study advances the understanding of linguistic differences between Indian and British academicians.

Overall, graph-based machine learning represents a valuable asset in linguistic research, as it enables a nuanced exploration of text structures, semantic networks, and linguistic patterns. From foundational studies in graph-based text analysis to recent advances in neural networks, graph-based methods continue to provide a robust framework for understanding and modeling the complexity of language (Navigli & Lapata, 2010; Mihalcea & Radev, 2011; Newman, 2010; Kipf & Welling, 2016; Zhou et al., 2020).

3. METHODOLOGY

In this study, we utilized a dataset of 100 academic text excerpts to explore linguistic differences between English used by Indian and British academicians. The dataset includes a diverse range of topics relevant to both academic communities. The texts were carefully selected to represent common research themes and are labeled according to their origin, with equal representation from both Indian and British sources. This approach provides a balanced and relevant foundation for analyzing linguistic variations in academic writing.

Graph Construction

Language graphs are constructed from academic texts, where nodes represent words or phrases, and edges represent syntactic or semantic relationships. Dependency parsing captures syntactic structures, and word embeddings encode semantic similarities (Manning et al., 2014).

Feature Extraction

Key features extracted from the graphs include node centrality measures (degree, betweenness, closeness), clustering coefficients, and community structures. These features provide insights into the prominence and connectivity of linguistic elements within the texts.

Figure 1. Methodology for analyzing linguistic differences

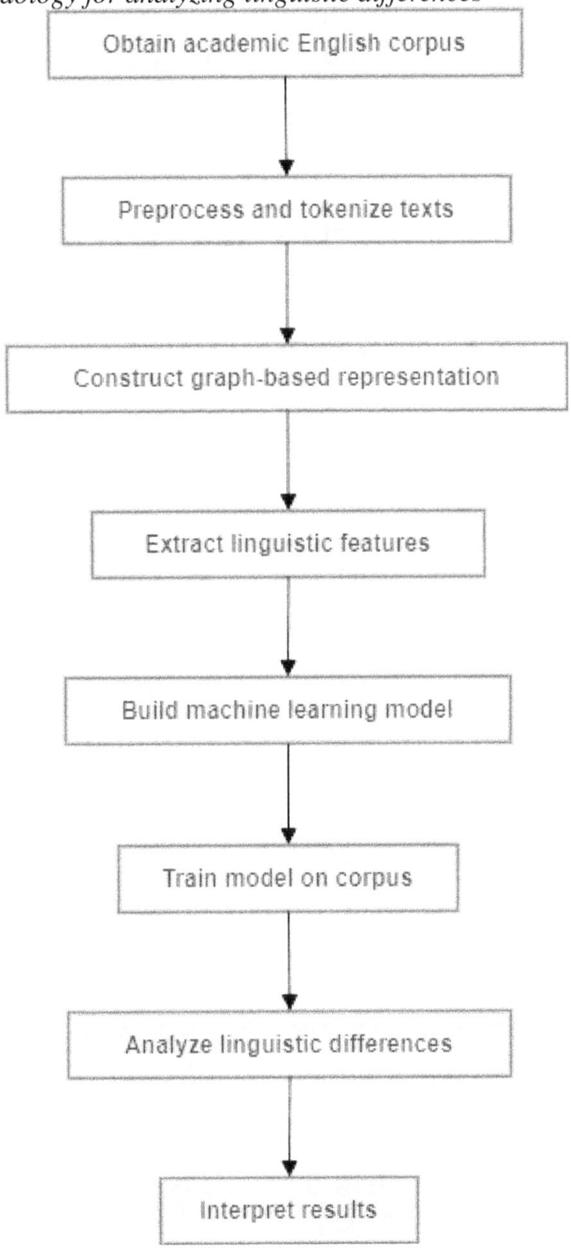

Machine Learning Techniques

Graph-based machine learning algorithms, such as community detection, hierarchical clustering, and Principal Component Analysis (PCA), are employed to analyze the constructed language graphs. Community detection algorithms like Louvain and Infomap help identify clusters of related words, while PCA aids in dimensionality reduction and visualization.

4. GRAPH-BASED MACHINE LEARNING FOR ANALYZING LINGUISTIC DIFFERENCES IN ACADEMIC ENGLISH

4.1 Extraction and Analysis of Phrasal Verbs from Text Data

In this section, we present a program designed to extract phrasal verbs from textual data contained in a CSV file and analyze their frequency of occurrence. This program utilizes Natural Language Processing (NLP) techniques, specifically leveraging the Natural Language Toolkit (NLTK) for tokenization and part-of-speech tagging. The primary objective of this tool is to identify and quantify the usage of phrasal verbs in academic texts, which can provide valuable insights into linguistic patterns and stylistic choices of authors.

4.1.1 Dataset Description

The dataset used in this program consists of textual data stored in a CSV file. Each row in the CSV file contains a sentence or a passage of text extracted from linguistic journal articles. The dataset is specifically curated to include articles published by authors using both Indian English and British English. This diverse collection of sentences and passages allows for a comparative analysis of linguistic patterns between these two varieties of English. The textual data includes a range of academic topics, ensuring that the phrasal verbs extracted represent a variety of contexts and usages. By processing these texts, the program extracts verb-particle or verb-preposition pairs, which are crucial for linguistic analysis. This analysis enables researchers to examine the syntactic and semantic variations of phrasal verbs across different dialects of English.

The dataset serves as the input for the program to identify and count phrasal verbs. Each entry is processed to extract not only the phrasal verbs themselves but also their contextual usage, which can reveal the authors' preferences and styles in academic writing. Additionally, the comparative analysis aims to highlight any significant differences in the usage of phrasal verbs between Indian and British English, contributing to a broader understanding of linguistic diversity in academic discourse.

4.1.2 Program Overview

The program is designed to read textual data from a CSV file, process each sentence to identify phrasal verbs, and calculate the frequency of each identified phrasal verb. It begins by importing necessary libraries, including pandas for data manipulation, nltk for natural language processing tasks, and defaultdict from the collections module to count occurrences of phrasal verbs. It ensures that the required NLTK resources, such as averaged_perceptron_tagger for part-of-speech tagging and punkt for tokenization, are downloaded. The core functionality lies in the extract_phrasal_verbs function, which tokenizes the input text and tags each token with its part of speech. This function identifies phrasal verbs by detecting verb-particle or verb-preposition pairs. The read_csv_and_extract_phrasal_verbs function reads text data from the specified CSV file and processes each row to extract phrasal verbs, storing them in a list. A dictionary, phrasal_verbs_count, is used to count the occurrences of each phrasal verb. Finally, the program prints each identified phrasal verb along with its count.

Algorithm for Extracting Phrasal Verbs and Counting Their Occurrences
Require: Dataset containing sentences in CSV format
Ensure: Extraction and frequency count of phrasal verbs

1. **Import Libraries:**
   - Import pandas for data manipulation.
   - Import nltk for natural language processing tasks.
   - Import defaultdict from collections for counting occurrences.
2. **Download NLTK Resources:**
   - Ensure the averaged_perceptron_tagger and punkt resources are downloaded using nltk.download.
3. **Define extract_phrasal_verbs Function:**
   - Tokenize the input text using nltk.word_tokenize.
   - Tag each token with its part of speech using nltk.pos_tag.
   - Initialize an empty list phrasal_verbs to store identified phrasal verbs.
   - Iterate over the tagged tokens:
     - Identify verb-particle or verb-preposition pairs based on their POS tags.
     - Append identified phrasal verbs to the phrasal_verbs list.
   - Return the phrasal_verbs list.
4. **Define read_csv_and_extract_phrasal_verbs Function:**
   - Read the CSV file into a pandas DataFrame using pd.read_csv.

    - Initialize an empty list phrasal_verbs_list to store phrasal verbs for each row.
    - Iterate over each row in the DataFrame:
        - Extractphrasalverbsfromthetextusingextract_phrasal_verbs.
        - Append the extracted phrasal verbs to the phrasal_verbs_list.
    - Return the phrasal_verbs_list.
5. **Define count_phrasal_verbs Function:**
    - Initialize a defaultdict of integers to count phrasal verb occurrences.
    - Iterate over the list of phrasal verbs:
        - Increment the count for each phrasal verb in the dictionary.
    - Return the defaultdict containing phrasal verb counts.
6. **Read CSV File and Extract Phrasal Verbs:**
    - Specify the path to the CSV file.
    - Call read_csv_and_extract_phrasal_verbs with the CSV file path to get the list of phrasal verbs.
7. **Count and Display Phrasal Verbs:**
    - Call count_phrasal_verbs with the list of phrasal verbs to get the count of each phrasal verb.
    - Print the phrasal verbs and their counts.
8. **Save Results to CSV:**
    - Convert the phrasal verbs count dictionary to a pandas DataFrame.
    - Save the DataFrame to a CSV file.

This program serves as a powerful tool for linguists, educators, and researchers interested in studying the use of phrasal verbs in various texts. By automating the extraction and counting process, the program saves considerable time and effort compared to manual analysis. Additionally, it can be applied to large datasets, making it suitable for extensive linguistic research.

Entity Phrasal Verbs Count
0 based on 84
1 shown in 28
2 used for 26
3 used in 20
4 proposed in 17
642 established that 1
643 improves throughout 1
644 analyzed that 1
645 made through 1
646 Working with 1

Figure 2. Top 12 phrasal verbs by frequency

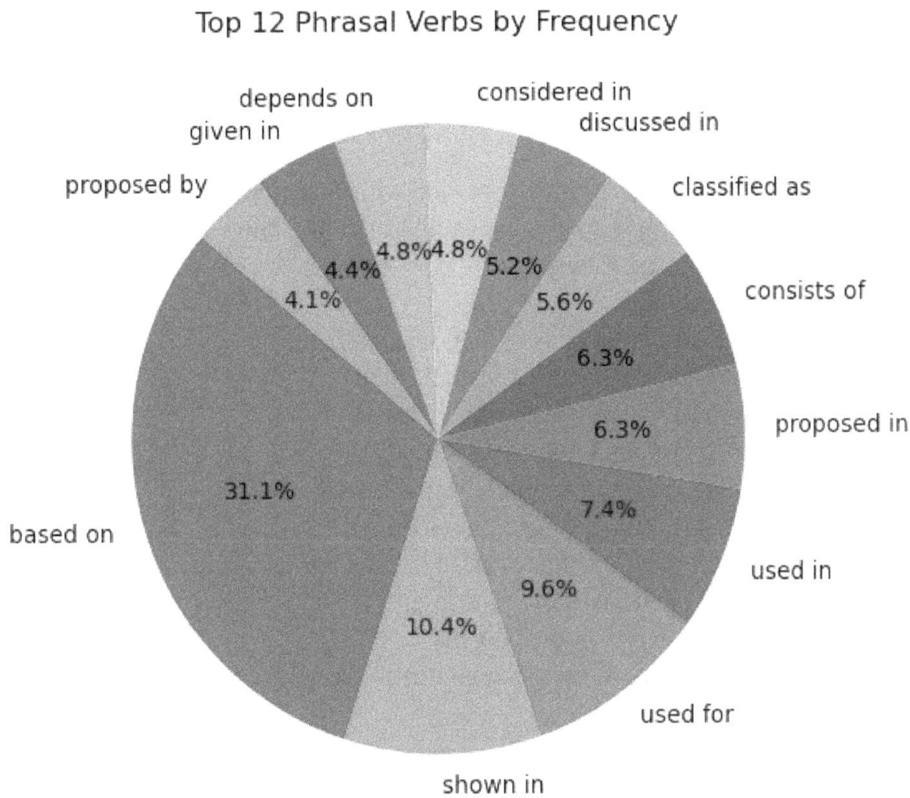

4.2 Graph-Based Visualization of Linguistic Patterns in Phrasal Verbs

To elucidate the linguistic patterns in the use of phrasal verbs by Indian and British academicians, we employed a graph-based visualization approach using the NetworkX library in Python. This section outlines the methodology used to construct, analyze, and visualize the graph, highlighting key findings and their implications.

4.2.1 Data Preparation and Graph Construction

The dataset, stored in a CSV file named phrasal_verbs.csv, contains phrasal verbs labeled based on their usage, with texts attributed to Indian (label 0), British (label 1), and both (label 2) authors. The graph GGG was initialized as an undirected graph using the nx.Graph() function. We read the CSV file and added nodes to the graph, each representing a phrasal verb. Nodes were labeled according to their origin by parsing the verb and its corresponding label from the CSV entries.

Algorithm for Graph-Based Visualization of Linguistic Patterns in Phrasal Verbs

Require: Dataset containing phrasal verbs with their usage labels in CSV format.
Ensure: Creation of a graph, application of community detection, and visualization of linguistic patterns.

1. **Import Libraries:**
    - o Import networkx for graph manipulation.
    - o Import matplotlib for visualization.
    - o Import csv for reading the dataset.
2. **Create a New Graph:**
    - o Initialize a new graph object G using networkx.
3. **Read the CSV File and Add Nodes:**
    - o Open the CSV file and read its contents using csv.reader.
    - o Skip the header row.
    - o For each row in the CSV file:
        - ▪ Split the first element of the row by commas to extract the verb and label.
        - ▪ If the verb and label are correctly identified:
        - ▪ Add a node to the graph G with the verb as the node and the label as an attribute.
4. **Add Edges Based on Co-occurrence or Syntactic Dependencies:**
    - o Iterate over all pairs of nodes in the graph.
    - o If the nodes have different names but the same label, add an edge between them.
5. **Apply the Louvain Method for Community Detection:**
    - o Import the community_louvain module.
    - o Apply the Louvain method to find the best partition of the graph.
    - o Set the community attribute for each node based on the partition.
6. **Calculate Degree Centrality:**
    - o Compute the degree centrality for each node in the graph.
    - o Set the centrality attribute for each node.
7. **Define Colors for Communities:**
    - o Create a list of colors for each community using matplotlib's color map.
8. **Draw the Graph Using Circular Layout:**
    - o Set the figure size for the plot.

- o Define the layout for the graph using the circular layout.

9. **Draw Nodes and Edges:**
    - o For each community, draw the nodes with sizes proportional to their centrality and colors based on their community.
    - o Draw edges with a specified transparency.
10. **Draw Labels with Offset:**
    - o For each node, add a label slightly offset from its position.
11. **Set Title and Legend:**
    - o Add a title to the plot.
    - o Add a legend to the plot.

Community Detection with Louvain Method

Edges were added between nodes to capture relationships based on co-occurrence or syntactic dependencies. Specifically, an edge was created between two nodes if they shared the same label, indicating common usage. This step highlighted the linguistic connections within each group, forming a basis for community detection. To identify clusters within the graph, we applied the Louvain method for community detection. This method optimizes modularity to detect densely connected communities. The community_louvain.best_partition function was used to partition the nodes into communities. Each node was assigned a community attribute based on the partition results, revealing clusters of phrasal verbs used by Indian, British, or both groups of authors.

Centrality Measures

We calculated the degree centrality for each node to measure its influence based on the number of connections. The degree centrality was computed using the nx.degree_centrality function and stored as a node attribute. This metric provided insights into the most influential phrasal verbs within the network, emphasizing their central role in the linguistic patterns of the respective groups.

Visualization

To visually represent the graph, we used a circular layout (nx.circular_layout), which arranged the nodes in a circle, facilitating the observation of community structures. Nodes were color-coded based on their community membership, with distinct colors assigned to each community. The size of the nodes was proportional to their degree centrality, highlighting the most influential nodes within each community. The graph was drawn using the nx.draw_networkx_nodes and nx.draw_networkx_edges functions, with node labels added for clarity.

Results

The Louvain method successfully identified distinct communities, representing clusters of phrasal verbs frequently used together by Indian, British, or both groups of authors. Degree centrality analysis revealed the most influential phrasal verbs, characterized by their high number of connections. These findings highlighted the linguistic patterns and differences between the groups, offering a deeper understanding of their language use.

Figure 3. Linguistic differences between Indian and British academicians

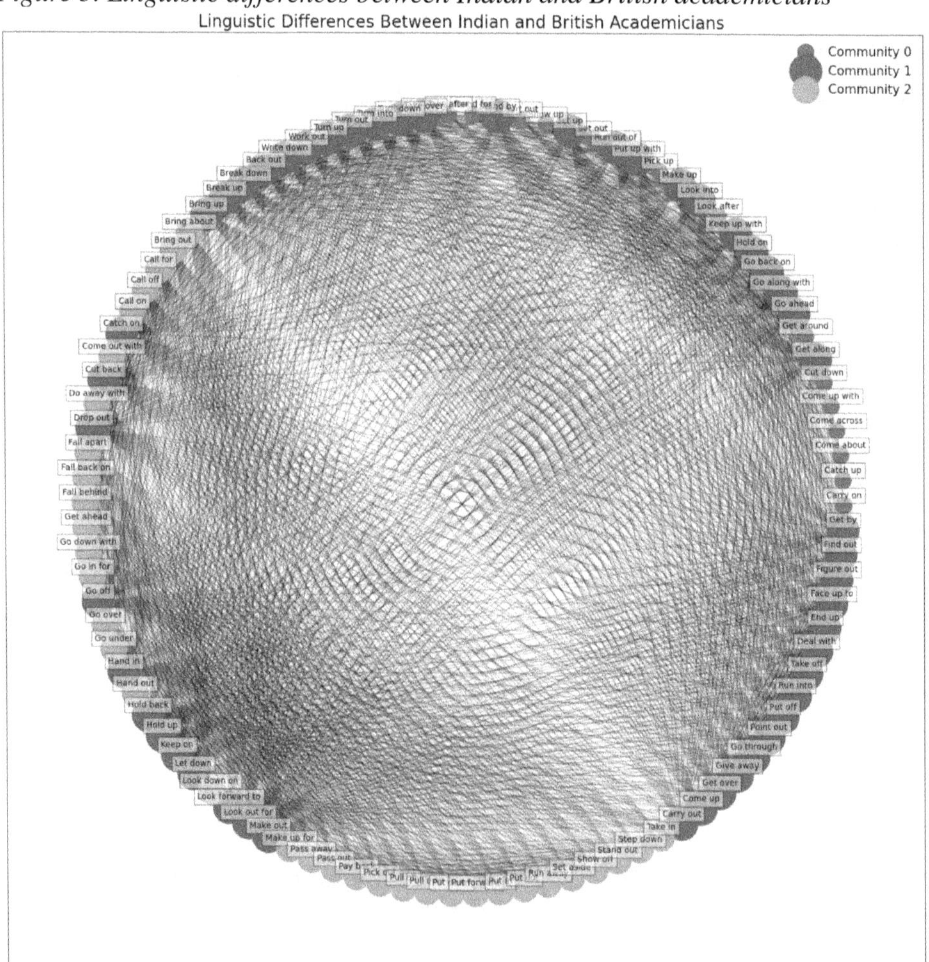

This graph-based visualization approach provided valuable insights into the linguistic patterns in the use of phrasal verbs by Indian and British academicians. The identified communities and centrality measures underscored the distinct linguistic features and influential phrasal verbs within each group. This study demonstrates the efficacy of graph-based techniques in analyzing linguistic data, contributing to a better understanding of cross-cultural communication and collaboration in academia.

5. DISCUSSION

5.1 Interpretation of Results

The results indicate that Indian English, as used by academicians, often includes localized expressions, idiomatic phrases, and syntactic variations. These differences likely arise from the influence of native languages, such as Hindi, Tamil, and Bengali, and educational practices in India that encourage a more flexible approach to English. This flexibility allows Indian English to incorporate unique linguistic structures and vocabulary, resulting in a distinct variety that caters to regional communicative needs.

British English, on the other hand, follows more standardized norms that prioritize consistency, precision, and formal structures, reflecting an institutional emphasis on adherence to established linguistic conventions. These variations between Indian and British English affect not only the style and tone of academic writing but also potentially impact how readability, professionalism, and credibility are perceived in international academic circles. The network-based approach also highlights distinct linguistic communities within each variety, identifying clusters of language patterns that correlate with specific stylistic preferences, such as informal/formal language blending in Indian English versus a more formal, concise approach in British English.

5.2 Limitations

- **Data Scope**: The dataset may not fully represent all academic disciplines, limiting the generalizability of findings to specific fields or areas of study.
- **Feature Selection Bias**: Certain linguistic features chosen for graph construction may overlook subtleties, such as tone and pragmatics, that influence the style but are difficult to quantify.
- **Algorithmic Constraints**: The use of existing community detection and graph analysis algorithms may not capture the full complexity of syntactic and stylistic variations unique to Indian or British English.

5.3 Future Work

Future research could expand in the following areas:

- **Diverse and Larger Datasets**: Analyze a wider range of academic disciplines, genres, and time periods to provide a more comprehensive view of linguistic differences in academic English.
- **Advanced NLP Techniques**: Utilize deep learning models, such as BERT or Graph Neural Networks, to capture more nuanced semantic relationships and contextual language patterns.
- **Cross-Regional Comparisons**: Extend the analysis to include other regional varieties of English (e.g., American, Australian) to understand how these compare with Indian and British English in academic contexts.
- **Genre-Based Analysis**: Investigate non-academic genres, such as journalism or policy documents, to see if these linguistic distinctions persist outside of scholarly writing.
- **Impact on Peer Review**: Study how these linguistic differences influence perceptions of professionalism and readability in peer review and publishing processes.
- **Interactive Visualization Tools**: Develop visualization tools to present the findings interactively, allowing users to explore specific language patterns or differences in syntactic structures.

6. CONCLUSION

This study has effectively showcased the application of graph-based machine learning techniques in examining the linguistic differences between Indian and British English in academic writing. By utilizing advanced computational methods to model and analyze the structures of language, we have uncovered distinct syntactic and semantic patterns that differentiate these two varieties of English. The graph-based approach has proven to be a valuable tool for revealing nuanced variations and providing a clearer understanding of how regional differences manifest in academic texts.

The analysis has not only enhanced our comprehension of the unique features of Indian and British English but also demonstrated the power of graph-based methods in the field of computational linguistics. By representing linguistic elements as nodes and their relationships as edges, the study has illustrated how these techniques can be used to capture complex language structures and identify patterns that might be less apparent through traditional qualitative methods. The contributions of this research extend beyond theoretical insights. The findings offer practical implications for academicians, language educators, and researchers who are engaged in cross-cultural communication and academic writing. Understanding the linguistic differences highlighted by this study can aid in developing better writing support tools, improving the peer review process, and enhancing the quality of academic publications across diverse linguistic backgrounds. As global academic collaboration continues to expand, the ability to navigate and appreciate linguistic variations becomes increasingly important, and this research provides valuable guidance for achieving effective and clear communication in international academic contexts.

REFERENCES

Bhatia, V. K. (2004). *Worlds of Written Discourse: A Genre-Based View*. Continuum.

Blondel, V. D., Guillaume, J. L., Lambiotte, R., & Lefebvre, E. (2008). Fast unfolding of communities in large networks. *Journal of Statistical Mechanics*, 2008(10), P10008. DOI: 10.1088/1742-5468/2008/10/P10008

Brinton, L. J., & Akimoto, M. (Eds.). (1999). *Collocational and Idiomatic Aspects of Composite Predicates in the History of English*. John Benjamins Publishing Company. DOI: 10.1075/slcs.47

Crystal, D. (2012). *English as a Global Language*. Cambridge University Press. DOI: 10.1017/CBO9781139196970

Ellis, R. (1994). *The Study of Second Language Acquisition*. Oxford University Press.

Gardner, D., & Davies, M. (2007). Pointing out frequent phrasal verbs: A corpus-based analysis. *TESOL Quarterly*, 41(2), 339–359. DOI: 10.1002/j.1545-7249.2007.tb00062.x

Granger, S. (1998). *Learner English on Computer*. Longman.

Hagberg, A. A., Schult, D. A., & Swart, P. J. (2008). Exploring network structure, dynamics, and function using NetworkX. *Proceedings of the 7th Python in Science Conference (SciPy2008)*, 11-15. DOI: 10.25080/TCWV9851

Halliday, M. A. K., & Matthiessen, C. M. I. M. (2014). *Halliday's Introduction to Functional Grammar*. Routledge. DOI: 10.4324/9780203783771

Hoffmann, T., & Trousdale, G. (Eds.). (2013). *The Oxford Handbook of Construction Grammar*. Oxford University Press. DOI: 10.1093/oxfordhb/9780195396683.001.0001

Hyland, K. (2000). *Disciplinary Discourses: Social Interactions in Academic Writing*. Longman.

Kachru, B. B. (1983). *The Indianization of English: The English Language in India*. Oxford University Press.

Kipf, T. N., & Welling, M. (2016). Semi-Supervised Classification with Graph Convolutional Networks. arXiv preprint arXiv:1609.02907.

Kumari, R. K. (2025). Artificial Intelligence in Special Education: Enhancing Learning Outcomes for Students With Disabilities. In Walters, A. G. (Ed.), *Transforming Special Education Through Artificial Intelligence* (pp. 79–112). IGI Global., DOI: 10.4018/979-8-3693-5538-1.ch003

Kumari, R. K. (2025). The Lasting Legacy of Educators: Stories and Strategies from Former Teachers. In Former Educators' Roles in Supporting Student Growth and Learning (pp. 28). IGI Global. https://doi.org/DOI: 10.4018/979-8-3693-6427-7.ch006

Kumari, R. K. (2025). Crafting an Effective Research Proposal. In Mdikana, A. A. (Ed.), *Enhancing Research Output in Higher Education: Research Proposals, Profiles, and Publishing* (pp. 291–320). IGI Global., DOI: 10.4018/979-8-3373-0806-7.ch012

Manning, C. D., Surdeanu, M., Bauer, J., Finkel, J., Bethard, S., & McClosky, D. (2014). The Stanford CoreNLP natural language processing toolkit. *Proceedings of 52nd Annual Meeting of the Association for Computational Linguistics: System Demonstrations*, 55-60. DOI: 10.3115/v1/P14-5010

McEnery, T., & Wilson, A. (2001). *Corpus Linguistics: An Introduction.* Edinburgh University Press.

Meyer, C. F. (2002). *English Corpus Linguistics: An Introduction.* Cambridge University Press. DOI: 10.1017/CBO9780511606311

Mihalcea, R., & Radev, D. (2011). *Graph-based Natural Language Processing and Information Retrieval.* Cambridge University Press. DOI: 10.1017/CBO9780511976247

Moon, R. (1998). *Fixed Expressions and Idioms in English: A Corpus-Based Approach.* Clarendon Press. DOI: 10.1093/oso/9780198236146.001.0001

Navigli, R., & Lapata, M. (2010). An Experimental Study of Graph Connectivity for Unsupervised Word Sense Disambiguation. *IEEE Transactions on Pattern Analysis and Machine Intelligence*, 32(4), 678–692. DOI: 10.1109/TPAMI.2009.36 PMID: 20224123

Newman, M. E. J. (2010). *Networks: An Introduction.* Oxford University Press. DOI: 10.1093/acprof:oso/9780199206650.001.0001

Rosvall, M., & Bergstrom, C. T. (2008). Maps of random walks on complex networks reveal community structure. *Proceedings of the National Academy of Sciences of the United States of America*, 105(4), 1118–1123. DOI: 10.1073/pnas.0706851105 PMID: 18216267

Sinclair, J. (1991). *Corpus, Concordance, Collocation*. Oxford University Press.

Stubbs, M. (2001). *Words and Phrases: Corpus Studies of Lexical Semantics*. Blackwell Publishers.

Tang, J., Qu, M., Wang, M., Zhang, M., Yan, J., & Mei, Q. (2015). LINE: Large-scale Information Network Embedding. *Proceedings of the 24th International Conference on World Wide Web*, 1067-1077. DOI: 10.1145/2736277.2741093

Velickovic, P., Cucurull, G., Casanova, A., Romero, A., Lio, P., & Bengio, Y. (2018). Graph Attention Networks. arXiv preprint arXiv:1710.10903.

Zhou, J., Cui, G., Hu, S., Zhang, Z., Yang, C., Liu, Z., Wang, L., Li, C., & Sun, M. (2020). Graph Neural Networks: A Review of Methods and Applications. *AI Open*, 1, 57–81. DOI: 10.1016/j.aiopen.2021.01.001

Chapter 12
Using AI–Powered Grammar Correction Tools to Support ESL Students' Writing Skills Development

Kawkab Al Balushi
University Technology and Applied Sciences, Sohar, Oman

ABSTRACT

The purpose of this study is to examine how AI grammar correction tools can improve the writing abilities of GFP students at the University of Technology and Applied Sciences-Suhar. A focus group discussion and classroom observations were conducted as part of the study. We observed two classes, one in the classroom and one in the computer lab, where students used AI grammar tools. During the focus group, students discussed both traditional instruction and artificial intelligence tools. Combining both approaches led to students becoming more engaged with their writing, moving from passive acceptance of AI suggestions to critical engagement. Despite some technical challenges, students reported increased confidence and independence in their writing. Additionally, teacher guidance was found to be crucial alongside the use of AI tools. Using artificial intelligence grammar tools in conjunction with traditional instruction results in an effective learning environment, however proper support and training are required for implementation to be successful.

DOI: 10.4018/979-8-3693-7863-2.ch012

INTRODUCTION

There has been a significant change in the way education is delivered, including the way languages are taught due to advancement in Technology (Afendi et al., 2022). This research looks at how students, in the General Foundation Program at the University of Technology and Applied Sciences - Suhar Branch, perceive the use of AI grammar correction tools and the traditional way of learning grammar in order to improve their writing skills. At UTAS-Suhar, students must demonstrate strong writing abilities to succeed in their academic programs, whether in Engineering or Information Technology departments. In addition to traditional grammar instruction, AI-powered tools offer new opportunities for developing writing skills. Using these tools in combination with conventional teaching methods, this study explores how to help students become more independent learners who can correctly identify and correct their writing errors. In this study, we aim to understand how AI grammar tools contribute to ESL students' writing development by examining students' experiences, challenges, and perceptions.

Nowadays, English has become the lingua franca of international communication, academia, and business (Jaramillo et al., 2020). English proficiency has become more than just a personal goal for non-native speakers; it is often a requirement for academic and professional success. According to research, while English proficiency is attainable, writing is a particularly challenging part of the process (Baharudin et al., 2023). It is common for ESL learners to have ideas for an important essay in their minds, but the fear of making grammar mistakes looms large. Globally, ESL writers face this challenge every day, indicating the urgent need for effective support systems.

Language learning has undergone a technological revolution over the last decade, as AI-powered tools have transformed the experience. One of the most fascinating innovations is the AI-powered grammar correction tools which stand out as particularly promising for ESL writers. With these tools, ESL learners can receive real-time, personalized grammar advice, ranging from writing assistants to integrated word processors (Rebolledo Font de la Vall & González Araya, 2023).

The question is, what exactly are these AI grammar tools, and how do they work? A key feature of these systems is the use of natural language processing and machine learning algorithms to analyze text, identify errors, and suggest corrections. Park (2019) mentioned that AI grammar tools are different from traditional spell-checkers as they can understand context, detect nuanced language errors, and even suggest style changes.

For students learning English as a second language, these tools have the potential to be very beneficial. This would be like having a tireless writing teacher available 24/7, offering immediate feedback on grammar, word choice, and sentence structure.

As a result, students are more likely to focus on content and creativity rather than getting stuck due to their fear of making grammatical mistakes. This can accelerate learning, boost confidence, and enable learners to learn more quickly (Park, 2019)

However, Dugosija (2024) believes that using AI grammar tools to teach ESL can be challenging just as like any technological innovation in education. He added that there are many concerns regarding the accuracy of the information and the risk of over-reliance which can jeopardize learning. There have been debates among educators and researchers about the potential for these tools to hinder natural language acquisition (Dugosija, 2024).

At UTAS-Suhar, one of eleven UTAS campuses across Oman, students must demonstrate strong writing abilities to succeed in their academic programs within the Engineering and Information Technology departments. Students take placement tests in English, Mathematics, and IT before enrollment. Passing the placement test qualifies them for a waiver test, success in which allows direct entry into their chosen academic department. Students who do not pass enroll in the Preparatory Studies Centre's General Foundation Program (GFP), where they are placed in one of four English levels.

Traditional teaching methods often struggle to provide students with immediate, personalized feedback to improve their writing. Many students submit assignments without understanding their recurring errors, and teachers find it challenging to provide detailed feedback to every student in large classes. While modern tools offer potential solutions to support both learners and teachers through immediate feedback and suggestions, questions remain about their effective integration with traditional instruction methods.

This case study examines the combined use of traditional and modern grammar correction approaches. It seeks to understand how students interpret and apply corrections, develop self-editing strategies, and balance tool suggestions with teacher guidance.

This research aims to study the effectiveness and impact of grammar correction tools on ESL writing skills through the following objectives:

1. To explore ESL students' perceptions and interpretations of their learning experiences with both grammar tools and traditional instruction methods.
2. To examine how ESL students develop their self-editing strategies when combining grammar tools with traditional grammar instruction.
3. To analyze ESL students' developmental journey in error correction abilities through the dual approach.
4. To identify and analyze the challenges ESL students face when incorporating grammar tools in their writing development.

5. To assess ESL students' perceptions of the value and effectiveness of these tools in their writing development journey.

Primary: **How do ESL students enhance their writing skills when traditional grammar instruction is improved with modern grammar tools?**

Secondary:

1. How do ESL students describe and make meaning of their learning experiences with grammar tools and traditional instruction?
2. How do ESL students develop their self-editing strategies when using grammar tools alongside traditional grammar instruction?
3. How do ESL students narrate their journey of developing error correction abilities through both methods?
4. How do ESL students describe their challenges when using grammar tools in their writing development?
5. How do ESL students perceive the value of grammar tools in their writing journey?

This research will contribute valuable insights into using grammar tools to support students in the General Foundation Program at UTAS-Suhar in their writing process. Furthermore, this research will assist learners in developing autonomous learning skills, allowing them to take a more active

TECHNOLOGY IN EDUCATION

The use of technologies in education has been researched for more than 30 years. According to Holmes et al., (2019), it has become evident that technology is transforming the teaching and learning processes in education as there have been a number of studies demonstrating that technology-powered tools have significant potential to improve learning outcomes in educational settings.

In recent years, technology has developed and spread rapidly all around the world (Holmes et al., 2019). Everyone is currently using technology for different purposes. As a result, it plays a more and more important role in our daily lives. As technology continues to gain popularity, its use in different devices, applications, and services is also spreading widely (Holmes et al., 2019). Thus, in education, the importance of technology cannot be overstated.

M Al-Bahrani, Gombos, & Cree (2018) agree that technology has enormous potential in education despite these challenges. By providing interactive and engaging learning opportunities, technology can improve student engagement and enable educators to make data-driven decisions.

Grammar Teaching and Learning

There has been debate in the field of English Language Teaching (ELT) regarding how grammar ought to be incorporated into language learning, for example, explicitly, implicitly, or classically (Swan & Widdowson, 2005). According to some scholars, grammar is the most significant aspect of the English language (Cook, 2013). A student's ability to comprehend grammar ensures that he or she is learning the language correctly Effendi et al. (2017).

In general, students spend a lot of time learning and analyzing grammar rules. According to Fithriani (2018) many English teachers in foreign language context still teach grammar theoretically. In other words, learners are presented with grammar rules and examples and are instructed to memorize them and apply them. According to Gayanti & Satriani (2020), students should be taught grammar through fun, interactive methods to avoid boredom and ineffective learning.

Technology Integration in Language Learning

According to Kannan & Munday, (2018), using technology in language learning has advantages and disadvantages, such as not being able to replicate cultural and contextual differences in language learning. Grammatical checking tools are designed to enhance the structure of sentences in documents. Additionally, there is the option of adjusting the tone to fit the writer's intended audience.

The study by Li and Hegelheimer (2013) showed that students who used grammar tools along with traditional instruction improved their writing accuracy more than those who only received traditional instruction. By providing immediate feedback, grammar correction tools promote learner autonomy and allow them to identify and correct errors independently (Chen & Cheng, 2022).

Students can master and complete grammar exercises using technology tools. According to Bikoswki (2018), using technology in grammar instruction presents challenges as well as opportunities for students and teachers. Grammar tools are increasingly being integrated into language learning platforms. According to Kaur et al., (2023) adaptive systems facilitate language acquisition more efficiently than static online exercises.

According to Ellis, R. (2019), presenting realistic contexts such as dialogues rather than teaching rules without regard to context is recommended for teaching grammar. Thus, there is no doubt that the concept of context-based learning plays an important role in modern grammar integration. This approach will help learners understand grammar functions in real-world communication.

Teacher Roles and Pedagogical Implications

The role of teachers is increasingly shifting from solely focusing on error correction to guiding students in using tools effectively (Brown & Lee, 2020). A shift to constructivist learning theories emphasizes learner autonomy and metacognitive skills development. Despite being smart, technology lacks emotional intelligence. In contrast, teachers are capable of providing empathy, understanding, and support. Educators are responsible for celebrating students' successes, helping them through failure, and understanding their unique social and emotional needs. The importance of this emotional connection to a student's development and well-being cannot be overstated.

Facilitating Autonomous Learning

Despite linguistics and educationalists' attempts to reach consensus on what autonomy is, the term has sparked considerable controversy. The goal of autonomy in language learning serves philosophical, pedagogical, and practical purposes. The role of the teacher, however, is not oppressed. It would be ludicrous to treat autonomous learning as an unbridled learning process, just like assuming that a baby can grow up without its mother's assistance. To facilitate students' development of autonomy, teachers scaffold students towards independence through a variety of strategies.

Implementation Challenges

Policy debates and regulatory frameworks have not resolved these concerns or challenges. Technology tools cannot identify errors and provide explanations as accurately as human teachers would. This may result in students repeating errors or developing inappropriate language learning habits (Rebolledo Font de la Vall & González Araya, 2023). Furthermore, English language teachers are facing the challenge of keeping up with the latest trends and technologies and learning how to use them to produce innovative and engaging learning materials (Dugosija, 2024).

Research Approach

In this study, data collection is based on a qualitative approach. This approach has been selected because it provides in-depth understanding of learners' experiences and perceptions. A qualitative study does not employ statistical techniques in order to generate its findings (Fischer & Guzel, 2022). In qualitative research, feelings, ideas, or experiences are examined. The primary goal of collecting data, which is often done in narrative form, is to identify insights that can be used to test hypotheses.

During the exploratory phases of a study, educators use qualitative research to find patterns or fresh perspectives. Qualitative research gathers non-numerical data to produce insights (Ugwu & Eze, 2023). There is no statistical analysis and it is either semi-structured or unstructured. Based on data gathered through a research methodology, it provides an explanation of why (Ugwu & Eze, 2023). Qualitative research was selected for this study for several reasons. To begin with, it can provide understanding of the feelings and experiences students have with these tools. Moreover, qualitative research allows us to determine whether these tools are more or less useful under different classroom circumstances. The importance of qualitative research in observing unusual or unexpected events can't be overstated, as it reflects people's perspectives and experiences (Ugwu & Eze, 2023).

This study was conducted at the University of Technology and Applied Sciences Suhar branch specifically within the General Foundation Program (GFP). The General Foundation Program offers three courses for the students which are English, Math and IT. Students are placed into four levels for English: level 4 for those with the highest placement scores and level 1 for beginners. There are three modules in the English curriculum: Reading and Writing (8 hours per week), Listening and Speaking (7 hours per week), and Research Project (3 hours per week). Two hours are dedicated to grammar under the reading and writing block.

This study will be conducted over 8 weeks in order to allow the students sufficient time to experience both approaches and to determine the development in their writing skills. Regular writing classes will serve as the primary setting for the research. In a typical writing class, students use a computer lab as well as regular classrooms. It will be ensured that students' normal learning routines will not be disrupted. In order to conduct observations and focus group discussion, permission has been obtained from the head of the English unit and relevant instructors. An illustration of the methodology and thematic analysis process used in this study is shown in Figure 1.

Figure 1. The study design and the data collection method

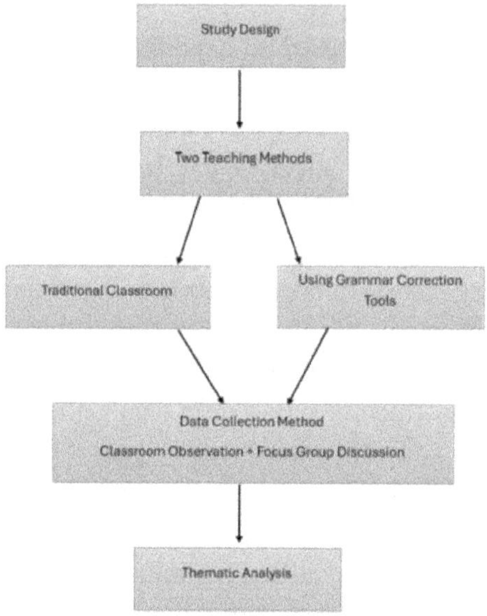

Sampling and Data Collection

A purposive sampling approach was used in this study. A sample size of ten is suggested by some commentators for qualitative sampling among homogeneous populations (Sandelowski, 1995). Therefore, 10 students were selected to participate as per the below criteria:

- The student is enrolled in level 4
- The student has not repeated the course
- Willing to participate in focus group discussion

In qualitative studies, interviews and focus groups are commonly used methods to gain insight into the perceptions of the participants (Kvale & Brinkmann, 2009). Two focus group discussions will be conducted. There were six students in each focus group who will share their experiences. As part of these sessions, participants will have an opportunity to share their writing journey, challenges, and successes with both learning methods. Semi-structured questions will be used. The semi-structured interview consists of a mix of predetermined and open-ended questions. In addition to asking the planned questions, the researcher may ask additional questions based on the participant's responses.

In order to collect data for a research study, university management approval is required. Whenever human participants are involved, data collection raises ethical considerations that must be addressed. For the protection of the participants' rights and welfare, university management approval of data collection is required. Following approval, data collection would begin with defining the observation objectives. Observing classes is the first step in collecting data. Classes will be observed in a real classroom setting.

The purpose of the observation is to monitor and observe student writing using modern tools and through getting teacher's feedback. This would be helpful to develop the focus group discussion questions. After taking the participants' approval, a phone was used to record the focus group discussion. Afterwards, the recording was transcribed and analyzed thematically.

Data Analysis

To analyze data using a thematic approach, the following steps must be taken: The first step is to listen to the recording, process it, and become familiar with its contents. Secondly, coding is accomplished by establishing codes that represent relevant information. As a third step, it is crucial to review the data, codes, and other information to identify patterns, similarities, and differences. A fourth step involves reviewing and analyzing the themes. The fifth step is to name and map the themes by arranging them logically. Choosing quotes from the interview transcripts to illustrate each concept is the sixth step. Finally, after examining the themes in relation to the objectives and research questions, we examine their importance, implications, and meanings.

Ethical Considerations

The following ethical considerations have been taken into account. To start, the participation is voluntary, and participants have the right to withdraw at any time. Additionally, pseudonyms are used to maintain confidentiality. Furthermore, participant privacy was protected during data collection and reporting. Moreover, there was clear communication about time commitments and expectations. Finally, participants will also be checked in regularly to ensure they are comfortable with the process.

Classroom Observations Analysis

The observation data revealed several key patterns in traditional classroom writing instruction. During Week 4, a detailed observation was conducted in two different settings: a regular classroom and a computer lab. This analysis focuses first on the regular classroom session, which demonstrated the traditional approach to writing instruction.

My second observation was in a computer lab in week 4. There were 25 computers in the lab. The class had 20 students. This was a follow-up session to the previous class. Students' essays from last time were marked by the teacher. On the screen, the teacher displayed a scanned copy of an essay that she had marked. The teacher highlighted the grammar errors and asked the students to identify them. Then, she elicited the answers from the students by asking them to discuss in groups.

For forty minutes, the students typed quietly without seeking assistance. Within 20 minutes, five students sent the teacher the second draft via email. The second draft was submitted by seven students in 30 minutes. Four students submitted their draft on time after 40 minutes. Four students struggled with typing, so the second draft could not be submitted on time. The teacher told the students to save their work and submit the second draft by the end of the day. Students were instructed to work during break in the college's Free Lab.

Focus Group Analysis

An email was sent to 12 students inviting them to the college library for a 30-minute focus group discussion. The purpose of the meeting was explained to the participants. The students were informed that participation is voluntary and that they can withdraw anytime. Two groups of students were formed. Each group consisted of six students. Using a thematic approach, the discussion was recorded, transcribed, and analyzed.

Theme 1: Students' Experiences with Grammar Tools and Traditional Instruction

Participants in the focus group discussed how grammar tools were encountered and incorporated into their learning process. These tools were introduced to students through a variety of channels, some in formal settings. *"My first experience with Grammarly was this semester during when my teacher talked about it in class"*. My teacher encouraged us to use it in class. Students also discovered these tools informally, as one student said: *"I learned about Grammarly from a Youtube advertisement but I was not sure if I should try it but when my teacher told us about it in class, I because more interested."* Students all agreed that grammar correction tools improved their writing skills.

Theme 2: Development of Self-Editing Strategies

Through the use of both tools and traditional methods, students demonstrated evolving approaches to self-editing. A student explained this dual approach: *"My teacher was very supportive and always provided timely feedback.* She helped me structure my essays correctly... Using grammar correction tools made me improve my writing skills. Now, when I correct the mistakes, I try not to make them again." Another student reflected on their learning journey: *"I noticed that when I first started using Grammarly, I used to accept the changes without looking at correction or understanding why, on the other hand, when it comes to getting the feedback from the teacher, she always explains to me so I have to listen and learn even if I didn't want to".*

Theme 3: Challenges in Using Grammar Tools

Students explained that receiving feedback through Grammarly can be challenging. Some of them encountered various challenges when using the tools. Some struggled with understanding corrections: *"Sometimes, I don't understand the changes that I need to make."* Others faced technical limitations: *"Sometimes the tool shows suggestions, but it cannot be viewed unless if I subscribe, so free features are limited. Another student said, "sometimes the tool provides suggestions which I don't know if I need to accept or not* " Decision-making also posed challenges, as one student noted: *"Sometimes, too many suggestions appear, and I don't know which one to go for and I don't know if my original sentence is correct or not."*

Theme 4: Student Perceptions of Tool Value

Students generally expressed positive perceptions about combining tools with traditional instruction. One student emphasized the complementary nature: *"I think it is great to have multiple support sources".* The teacher explains and then we get to learn on our own and learn from our mistakes. This makes me a confident writer. Another student noted the impact on their independence: "I used to worry whenever I had a writing assignment now, I feel that I can work on my own." However, students also recognized limitations, as expressed by one participant: *"We still need to think before making changes. We need to understand why we are making changes."*

Discussion

The integration of grammar tools with traditional instruction proved beneficial for writing skill development. Students demonstrated improved confidence and self-editing abilities while maintaining the benefits of teacher guidance. The research revealed that success depends on proper training, maintained teacher guidance, structured writing practice, and a balanced approach to feedback.

CONCLUSION

The research examined how grammar tools are integrated into the General Foundation Program at UTAS-Suhar. It aimed to understand how traditional grammar instruction and modern grammar tools can enhance ESL students' writing skills. In the study, classroom observations and focus group discussions revealed several key insights into students' experiences.

The study found that using grammar correction tools along with traditional instruction improved students' confidence in writing and helped them develop independent learning skills. The research shared students' learning experiences and revealed that they found both methods very beneficial, completing each other. Modern tools provided immediate feedback and correction suggestions in contrast to traditional instruction that provided structured learning and detailed explanations. By combining the two, students gained a deeper understanding and a more effective application of grammar rules.

Students developed their writing skills from passively accepting suggestions to critically engaging with them. Additionally, the research revealed that students faced three primary challenges: understanding explanations, managing multiple correction suggestions, and dealing with limited access to premium features. These challenges affected their learning process but did not diminish the overall value they found in using the tools.

Recommendations

The following recommendations were drawn from the research findings:

1.Technical Preparation Before implementing AI grammar tools, students should receive proper training on how to use them.

2.Establish a peer support system where experienced students can assist others, following the successful model observed where three experienced students helped their classmates with Grammarly.

3.Maintain a balance between traditional classroom instruction and AI tool use, as evidenced by classroom observations and student responses, in which students benefitted both from teacher explanations and AI feedback.
4.Teacher Development Equip teachers with the necessary skills to integrate AI tools effectively in their writing instruction, as the classroom observations showed teachers need to balance between traditional instruction and technical facilitation roles.
5.Regular Assessment of Tool Effectiveness Implement periodic evaluations to monitor the impact of AI grammar tools on student writing progress.

REFERENCES

Afendi, A., Sholihah, N., Mutmainah, F., Ishak, K., & Lubis, A. (2022). *Penggunaan Microsoft Office untuk Meningkatkan Motivasi dan Hasil Belajar Siswa Sekolah Dasar*. Jurnal PGSD., DOI: 10.32534/jps.v8i1.2949

Baharudin, F., Ramli, N. H. L., Habali, A. H. M., Azmi, A. A., & Rahmat, N. H. (2023). Process of Writing: The Challenges in Writing Skill Among ESL Learners. *International Journal of Academic Research in Business & Social Sciences*, 13(10), 32–50. DOI: 10.6007/IJARBSS/v13-i10/18649

Bikowski, D. (2018). Technology for teaching grammar. In Teaching and Technology. DOI: 10.1002/9781118784235.eelt0441

Brown, D., & Lee, H. (2020). Metacognition in EFL: The role of reflective practices. *TESOL Quarterly*, 54(1), 65–87. DOI: 10.2307/3587508

Chen, J., & Cheng, T. (2022). Review of research on teacher emotion during 1985-2019: A descriptive quantitative analysis of knowledge production trends. *European Journal of Psychology of Education*, 37(3), 417–438. DOI: 10.1007/s10212-021-00537-1

Cook, V. (2013). *Second Language Learning and Language Teaching*. Routledge. DOI: 10.4324/9780203770511

Dugosija, T. (2024). Benefits and challenges of artificial intelligence in English language teaching. *Knowledge International Journal*, 62(2), 275–280.

Effendi, M. S.. (2017). English as a second language learning and grammar accuracy: A case study. *Journal of Language Teaching and Research*, 8(4), 52–58.

Ellis, R. (2019). *Understanding Second Language Acquisition*. Oxford University Press.

Fischer, E., & Guzel, G. T. (2022). The case for qualitative research. *Journal of Consumer Psychology*, 33(1), 259–272. DOI: 10.1002/jcpy.1300

Fithriani, R. (2018). Communicative game-based learning in EFL grammar class: Suggested activities and students' perception. [Journal of English Education and Linguistics Studies]. *JEELS*, 5(2), 171–188. DOI: 10.30762/jeels.v5i2.509

Gayanti, R., & Satriani, I. (2020). Teaching students' vocabulary through total physical response. [Professional Journal of English Education]. *PROJECT*, 3(3), 414–419. DOI: 10.22460/project.v3i3.p414-419

Holmes, W., Bialik, M., & Fadel, C. (2019). *Artificial intelligence in education: Promise and implications for teaching and learning*. Center for Curriculum Redesign.

Jaramillo, M. G., Dávila, A. M., & Jarquín, E. V. E. (2020). English as a Lingua Franca: Perspectives from International MA TESOL Students in the United States. *Universal Journal of Educational Research*, 8(4), 1605–1619. DOI: 10.13189/ujer.2020.080454

Kannan, J., & Munday, P. (2018). New trends in second language learning and teaching through the lens of ICT, networked learning, and artificial intelligence. *Círculo de Lingüística Aplicada a la Comunicación*, 76, 13–30. DOI: 10.5209/CLAC.62495

Kaur, J., Lavuri, R., Parida, R., & Singh, S. V. (2023). Exploring the impact of gamification elements in brand apps on the purchase intention of consumers. *Journal of Global Information Management*, 31(1), 1–30. DOI: 10.4018/JGIM.317216

Kvale, S., & Brinkmann, S. (2009). *InterViews: Learning the craft of qualitative research interviewing*. Sage Publications.

Li, Z., & Hegelheimer, V. (2013). Mobile-assisted grammar exercises: Effects on self-editing in L2 writing. *Language Learning & Technology*, 17(3), 135–156.

Rebolledo Font de la Vall, R., & González Araya, F. (2023). Exploring the benefits and challenges of AI-language learning tools. *International Journal of Social Sciences and Humanities Invention*, 10(1), 7569–7576. DOI: 10.18535/ijsshi/v10i01.02

Sandelowski, M. (1995). Sample size in qualitative research. *Research in Nursing & Health*, 18(2), 179–183. DOI: 10.1002/nur.4770180211 PMID: 7899572

Swan, M., & Widdowson, H. G. (2005). *Grammar*. Oxford University Press.

Ugwu, C. N., & Eze, H. U. (2023). Qualitative research. *IDOSR Journal of Computer and Applied Sciences*, 8(1), 20–35.

Chapter 13
Effects of the Animation Infographic on Learning Retention and Motivation

Mitha Obaid Al-Khazimi
Independent Researcher, Oman

ABSTRACT

In spite of a huge library of technological materials available for teachers of Information Technology courses in most tertiary institutions, there are truly limited scholastic resources available on the use of animation Infographics as a pedagogical tool. The challenges of communicating complex ideas of technical nature to students have been exacerbated by the proliferation of information in the golden era of information and communication technology (ICT); hence, the need for developing an effective tool of communication to aid the process of information sharing between teachers and students.

1.0 INTRODUCTION

The study stems from the recognition of gaps in current educational practices, particularly within IT education. Traditional methods often fail to fully engage students or simplify complex technical concepts, which animated infographics aim to resolve. This investigation offers a solution by examining how dynamic, visually rich tools can improve understanding and retention in challenging IT courses, such as Networking and Browsing.

In today's educational landscape, the integration of technology into teaching methodologies is increasingly essential, particularly in Information Technology (IT) education. This study examines the impact of animated infographics as a ped-

DOI: 10.4018/979-8-3693-7863-2.ch013

agogical tool to enhance both learning retention and motivation among students at academic universities. The rapid advancement of Information and Communication Technology (ICT) has increased the demand for effective communication strategies. These strategies should simplify complex technical concepts, especially for students who often struggle with conventional teaching methods. This research is based on the observation that many students find IT subjects, such as 'Networking and Browsing,' challenging to grasp. This difficulty is further intensified by the lack of engaging educational resources that enhance understanding and retention. Animated infographics, recognized for their visual appeal and interactivity, are suggested as a potential solution. By transforming traditional course content into dynamic visual formats, the study aims to assess whether these tools can improve student motivation and learning outcomes. A quasi-experimental design was used in the study, which involved comparing an experimental group exposed to animated infographics with a control group receiving traditional instruction. It was particularly suitable for this approach for this context, as it reflects real-world classroom settings where random assignment is not always feasible. The study utilized various instruments-including achievement tests, motivation scales, and satisfaction checklists-to assess the intervention's impact on students' learning experiences.

The literature review highlights the importance of animated infographics as dynamic visual tools that integrate graphics, text, and multimedia elements to convey complex information more effectively. Several studies support the effectiveness of infographics in improving both student motivation and learning retention. For instance, Hassan (2016) and Lankow et al. (2012) emphasized that animation infographics simplify intricate subjects by transforming static content into visually stimulating material, making complex concepts more accessible. Similarly, Afify (2018) and Peters (2014) demonstrated that animated infographics enhance understanding by catering to diverse learning styles, making the learning experience more enjoyable and engaging for students. These visual tools encourage students to actively engage with the material, thus increasing motivation, as noted by Bicen and Beheshti (2017) and Cifçi (2016). Rezaei and Sayadian (2015) and Gallagher et al. (2017) also found that animated infographics improve information retention by organizing and presenting content in structured, visually engaging formats, aiding students' ability to recall information over time. Despite these advantages, literature reveals gaps in the research, particularly concerning the long-term effects of animated infographics on higher education. There have been few studies exploring this topic impact in higher education, especially in Arab countries like Oman, which presents Research is critical in this area (Afify, 2018; Singh & Jain, 2017). While the current body of research affirms the effectiveness of animated infographics in enhancing motivation and short-term learning retention, more research is needed to explore their role in long-term retention and their application applied to higher education contexts (Chianson, Kurumeh, & Obida, 2010).

This study seeks to fill some of these gaps by providing new insights into the potential benefits of animated infographics for IT education. It aims to inform educators and policymakers on how innovative teaching strategies, such as the use of animated infographics, can contribute to improved academic performance, increased student motivation, and enhanced satisfaction in higher education settings.

The study provides a comprehensive introduction that highlights the growing importance of innovative tools, such as animated infographics, in enhancing the learning process, especially in complex IT subjects like 'Networking and Browsing. The study acknowledges that globalization and the rapid development of technology have transformed educational methods. However, students at Academic University, like many others, face challenges in understanding complex IT content. So, this research explores the potential of animation infographics to simplify technical information and make learning more interactive and engaging. These tools are expected to positively influence students' motivation and retention of knowledge by converting static learning materials into dynamic visual aids. Despite the growing use of such tools, lack of research on their application in higher education, especially in the Arabian context and specifically in Oman. The problem identified in the study is that students struggle with the complexities of the 'Networking and Browsing' subject. Therefore, this research aims to determine if using animation infographics can improve student motivation and performance in learning. The study's main objectives include evaluating the impact of these infographics on students' motivation, achievement, and learning retention. Also discusses the significance of the research for higher education in Oman. The findings could help enhance teaching methods in IT courses and provide for future research in similar educational contexts. Additionally, the study may guide decision-makers in incorporating effective learning tools like animation infographics into the curriculum.

2.0 ANIMATION INFOGRAPHIC DEFINITION

The animation Infographics examine to be presented on graphic animation video screens at video websites like TV ads, YouTube, or the animation presentations on smartphones, etc. In the animation type, the data and the elements are in a state of incessant movement; also, it is described by much creativity during the expressive movements' selection that helps design the animation enjoyable and interesting. Besides, this type needs an entire scenario to make the final form with essential software programs (Hassan, 2016; Lankow et al., 2012). Infographic animation is defined as a visual knowledge and data representation in the form of pictures, video, graphs, charts, text boxes, and tables. They are created through combining different animations to generate a mean, which helps in the information explanation by engaging these animations that aim to improve the perspective of the learners on the subject (Naparin and Saad, 2017).In this study, animation Infographic is defined as a visually engaging representation of data to enhance the way that information could be reached to the students as the aim is to investigate about the effect of animation Infographics on the students' motivation and learning retention.

2.1 Teaching and Learning With Animation Infographics

The animation Infographics offered a continuous motion to the subject. Moreover, they emphasized that this animation Infographic was successful in every other situation or subjects, scenarios, or settings where animation makes understanding and comprehension easier (Afify, 2018). Peters (2014) affirmed that when learning multifaceted scientific processes and cognitive tasks, animation gives the learners over what they require. The results of a lot of preceding studies have confirmed that the employment of Infographics in education influences the learners who have diverse thinking ways. Furthermore, they have confirmed that Infographics present strong arguments in addition to presenting them to further than one sensory organ, also helps learners to connect effectively within the learning procedure, resulting in continuous learning as well as higher scores (Lee and Kim, 2016). Additionally, Infographics contribute to rising students' success while used as a choice to texts, making learning easy compared to normal texts (Dick, 2014). Moreover, Infographics help teachers to display and develop learning activities in an appealing way which attracts students' consideration, in addition to raising awareness to the subject substance as well as making it simpler to be memorized. This can be thanks to the educating ability of efficient visual images that provide an obvious message (Lee and Kim, 2016). Separately with this, the employ of Infographics in education is affecting the learning results of learners too (Çifçi, 2016). As well as they are extremely efficient for teaching multifaceted subjects that involve both temporal and quantitative data that makes them simple to learn. In addition, Infographics are measured as a useful tool to develop several students' social and moral values. They can be used to assist them to understand the values obtainable in the lessons, therefore, contributing to the advance of the learners' personality as well as providing teachers with new opportunities for identifying students' mental and moods states to get their behavior better (Islamoglu et al., 2015). Another characteristic of Infographics is participation in breaking boredom and monotony for students, resulting from the huge number of verbal presentations. Also, as an alternative, Infographics is drawing the attention of people during visual attractiveness of the visual designing basics that enhances positive orientation to the learning content (Martix and Hodson, 2014).

2.2 Students' Motivation

Motivation concept is considered a crucial factor which affects human performance and behavior (Kian, Yusoff, and Rajah, 2014; Turan, 2015). Particularly educational researchers besides practitioner's state that motivation is one of the principal factors in ensuring incessant achievement and in student achievement (Alkış, 2015; Alucdibi and Ekici, 2012; Guay, Ratelle, Roy, and Litalien, 2010). Lin (2012) explained motivation the same as intrinsic desires that are previously present within the individual or that are reflected within the individual as acquiring new learning and information.

2.3 Learning Retention

Retention of learned information can be defined as having the information stored in long-term memory in such a way that it can be readily retrieved, for example, in response to standard prompts. The transfer is Described as the procedure by which learning in one context is applied to solve a problem or make sense of a situation in a different context (Detterman and Sternberg, 1993). Lankow et al., (2012) in his study "Infographics: The Power of visual story telling" identified three primary provisions that should exist in any visual communication methods including Appeal that should engage a voluntary audience, Comprehension that should effectively provide knowledge that enables a clear comprehension of the details.

2.4 Effect of Animation Infographics on Learning Retention

Rezaei and Sayadian (2015) study intended to discover the effect of Infographics instruction on the Iranian EFL learners' grammar learning rooted in the researcher's incentive to find experimental evidence in Iranian English language learners. Grammar teaching was provided during two processes: the first one, during the Infographics instruction, and the second, during traditional and routine techniques. Because of the consequence of paired sample t-test, it was established that Infographic instruction was an effectual instrument to assist EFL learners studying foreign language grammar.

Afify (2018) study aimed at studying the impact of the divergence between Infographic designing forms, animation versus static, on raising the designing skills in addition to making visual learning materials, plus the appreciation of the design elements as well as its principles. The study was performed on a sample of college students of the Education at Imam Abdu Rahman bin Faisal University (IAU) in the Kingdom of Saudi Arabia. The sample consisted of 36 students; also, they were amongst the students who are registered to study production and design of instructional media courses (EDU195N) within the 2nd semester of the year 2016/2017. The students involved were separated into two experimental groups. Group one contained 19 students who had studied the learning content during static Infographics using WhatsApp platform. Moreover, group two consisted of 17 students who studied the learning content during animation Infographics using WhatsApp platform. In general, the results showed that Infographics result in the advance of several learning outcomes. In addition, the results confirmed that static Infographic form has more results on enhancing abilities in design alongside creating visual educational resources recognizing its principles and elements matched up to the animation form.

Chianson, Kurumeh, and Obida (2010) study investigated the consequence of the cooperative learning process compared with the conservative learning method to find out the preservation level of students within circle geometry. The study was approved on senior secondary II students during the 3 education zones (Zone A, Zone B plus Zone C) within Benue State, Nigeria. The aptitude of students to memorize and grasp a mathematical topic or concept which was educated has become an essential problem in secondary schools. These problems may perhaps arise because of inappropriate teaching processes being used to clarify these topics. Therefore, this study approved the cooperative learning strategy for teaching 358 senior secondary two (SSII) students circle geometry, plus to see how the learning process may effectively get better on students' capability to retain mathematics concepts in comparison to the teaching conservative learning method. An independent T-test analysis was utilized to determine if a statistically significant difference presented between the conventional learning approach and the cooperative learning approach in terms of students' preservation of the taught concept. The answers to the study show that students who were exposed to cooperative learning strategy could retain the circle geometry concepts over students who shared similar characteristics educated using the conventional learning process. Thus, the suggestions were that students would be capable of retaining learned and taught mathematics concepts for a longer phase of time if the mathematics teachers used the cooperative learning strategy within teaching.

2.5 Effect of Animation Infographics on Student's Motivation

Within Singh and Jain (2017) studied, 48 dyscalculic students at the junior schools were chosen from Agra city through uncomplicated random sampling. Mathematical Comprehension Scale, Mathematics Academic Achievement Test, Achievement Motivation Scale, Image Processing Ability Test tools were employed to gather the data. These dyscalculic students were not different in their ability of image processing and motivation achievement on the base of urban and rural areas.

The dyscalculic students had different abilities in their achievement motivation and image processing attributed to the gender.

Bicen and Beheshti (2017) study aimed at investigating the perceptions of students regarding applying Infographics in learning. The research was designed as a quantitative study. The number of undergraduate students in this study was 163. Data accumulated with close-ended questions during this study. The gathered data were analyzed via the descriptive analysis approach. The results showed that applying Infographics in learning can increase the perceptions of students regarding learning.

Çifçi (2016) study was designed as a quasi-experimental study that is a quantitative study method. "Solomon Four Group Design" was used. The results showed that using Infographics within geography lessons enhances the attitude levels and academic achievement of the students. Also, enhancing verbal and visual learning levels. Furthermore, the results found that Infographics can be widely and effectively used in geography lessons in various grade levels and learning fields. It is also recommended to apply Infographics when students' attitudes and achievement in geography lessons are relatively low.

Long-Term Retention: Studies indicate that while animated infographics significantly improve short-term learning, their effects on long-term retention remain uncertain. Gallagher et al. (2017) suggest that combining animated infographics with spaced repetition and active recall strategies could enhance retention. Moreover, integrating interactive elements such as quizzes and feedback loops within the infographic design may help reinforce learning and support long-term memory consolidation (Rezaei & Sayadian, 2015).

Cross-Disciplinary Application: Animated infographics have demonstrated effectiveness in simplifying complex concepts in technical disciplines, but their application in non-technical fields remains underexplored. According to Bicen and Beheshti (2017), disciplines like arts, humanities, and social sciences could benefit from using infographics to visualize abstract concepts such as historical timelines, cultural narratives, and philosophical arguments. Future research should evaluate their adaptability and impact across diverse fields.

Personalized Learning: Adaptive learning technologies, powered by artificial intelligence, can customize animated infographics to meet individual learning needs. Naparin and Saad (2017) highlight the potential of personalized infographics in catering to varying cognitive styles and learning speeds. For instance, incorporating user-specific data and preferences into infographic designs can create more engaging and effective learning experiences.

Integration with Emerging Technologies: The integration of animated infographics with AI-driven platforms, such as intelligent tutoring systems, can enhance interactivity and user engagement. Afify (2018) notes that technologies like augmented reality (AR) and virtual reality (VR) can be used to create immersive infographic experiences, providing learners with a multisensory approach to education.

Large-Scale Implementation: To generalize the findings of this study, large-scale trials in diverse educational settings are essential. Alrwele (2017) emphasizes the importance of testing animated infographics in varying cultural and institutional contexts to assess their scalability and efficacy. Such studies could inform policymaking and curriculum design, enabling widespread adoption of this innovative tool.

2.6 Summary and Research Gap

While most of the studies focused on the advantages of applying Infographics in the education process, there is an apparent lack in studies that criticize this kind of teaching technique. Moreover, most of the studies focused on the effect of the applying of Infographics on the students' attitude and motivation; however, few of them investigated learning retention as one of the key pillars of academic achievement. Few studies were found in the Arabian world that investigates on the effect of applying Infographics on the earning process while no such studies were found in Oman. The majority of the conducted studies in this field dealt with the school student level, while the focus on higher education seemed to be rare. Therefore, this study came to fill those gaps in the related literature.

3.0 RESEARCH METHODOLOGY

3.1 Introduction

This is a quasi-experimental study that was designed to measure the effectiveness of using animation Infographics in the teaching of IT complex subjects at Academic University. This study was conducted through controlled pre-test and post-test to explore the effects of using animation Infographics on the students' motivation, learning retention. Quantitative method was used to examine the effect of animation Infographics on developing the content or material of Information Technology Subject "Networking and Browsing" course at Academic University. More specifically, it investigates whether using animation Infographics as a tool can affect the students' motivation and learning retention. The tools of this study include the achievement test, satisfaction checklist, and motivation scale to collect the data related to using animation Infographics in the "Networking and Browsing" course that may result in a more profound insight into the student's experiences with animated infographics. The (Figure 1) below shows the phases of the research design.

Figure 1. The figure phases of (Quasi-experimental) research design

1. PLANNING & PREPARATION

- ├── Define Objectives: Measure retention & motivation.
- ├── Select Sample: IT students at Academic University.
- └── Divide into Groups:
- ├── Experimental Group (Animated Infographics).
- └── Control Group (Traditional Methods).

2. DESIGN TOOLS

- ├── Pre/Post Knowledge Tests.
- ├── Motivation Survey.
- └── Satisfaction Checklist.

3. IMPLEMENTATION

- ├── Pre-Test (Both Groups).
- ├── Intervention:
- ├── Experimental Group: Teach with animated infographics.
- └── Control Group: Teach with lectures/static materials.
- └── Duration: 4 Weeks.

4. DATA COLLECTION

- ├── Post-Test (Both Groups).
- ├── Collect Scores: Knowledge retention.
- ├── Motivation Survey Results.
- └── Satisfaction Feedback.

5. DATA ANALYSIS

- ├── T-Test: Compare experimental vs. control group.
- ├── ANOVA: Assess motivation differences.
- └── Correlation Analysis: Retention vs. animation use.

6. CONCLUSIONS

- ├── Interpret Results:
- ├── Does animation improve retention?
- └── Does animation boost motivation?
- └── Report Limitations & Recommendations.

7. DISSEMINATION

3.2 Research Design

This study applied a quasi-experimental, nonequivalent control group design that is an appropriate alternative to an experimental design when randomization is not feasible (Cook & Campbell, 1979; Gall, Borg, & Gall, 1996; Huck, Cormier, & Bounds, 1974). The nonequivalent control group design can be applied as a nonequivalent comparison group design in which two treatments are applied (Huck et al., 1974). Since the subjects in this type of design were not randomly assigned, intact classes of students were randomly assigned to either the experimental group or the control group where both intact groups took a pretest and a posttest.

The research design is used to examine motivation and retention in learning of design animation Infographics on developing the content or material of Information Technology Subject "Networking and Browsing" course at Academic University. Following the selection of research methodology and research type, this study has selected quasi-experimental research design for investigating causal relationships as well as for studying the relationship between one construct and another (Bell, Bryman, and Harley, 2018; Kuehl and Kuehl, 2000). The selection of quasi-experimental research design is usually based on three fundamental attributes, (1) nonrandom selection and assignment to groups, (2) administration of a pre-test for capturing the initial differences between the groups; and (3) the presence of a control group (Creswell, 2002, 2014; Creswell and Creswell, 2017). In this study, the selection of quasi-experimental research the design relies on the inclusion of design animation Infographics, selection of students based on their cultural level, previous knowledge, retention, and motivation, in the information technology subject, and identification and designing of graphics based on content analysis. This research used a quasi-experimental research design to measure the effects of animation Infographics in student's motivation and learning retention through achievement test, satisfaction checklist and motivation scale. The one-group pre-test and post-test design were adopted for control achievement test while the satisfaction checklist and motivation scale were repeated before and after the treatment in this study.

The case is observed at two time points, one before the application of animation Infographics and one after the application of animation Infographics in the "Networking and Browsing" course.

The selected "Networking and Browsing" course include two parts; Networking, which includes USB -internet connection - topology - Ethernet - Protocol - LAN & WAN - connected network, serve s- Domain- Types of Computer Network-networking Security - Internet Terminologies, Server Protocol, Server Name, Organization Name, and Domain Category, while the Browsing part include URL – Linked - Web Browser Web page - Web Search Engine. This course was selected primarily because of the course instructor as she is the researcher of the current study, among other reasons including the low achievement of students in this course and low motivation toward it as observed by the researcher. Moreover, this course is one of the hard courses that students find difficult to comprehend. Therefore, Infographics could help in increasing students' motivation toward it and hence their achievement by implementing a quantitative research method, control' inevitably has become the key element of this research design. For the purpose of this study, the environment of the test will be controlled and manipulated as much as possible where the concentration will be on the study variables in order to come up with the desired outcomes. However, as the aim is to seek at the effects of animation Infographics as a tool for teaching a fairly complex technical subject in this study, an experimental group will be presented to make a comparison with the control group on the template of pre-test-post-test experiment by using the achievement test and the repeating of the satisfaction checklist and motivation scales before and after the treatment.

3.3 Population and Sample of the Study

The population of this study consisted of all students registered in the Information Technology course 'Networking and Browsing' as a university requirement at Academic University in Oman during the second semester of the academic year 2018/2019, totaling 230 male and female students. Since it was practically impossible to include the entire population who are registered in the Information Technology course in the study sample, the snowball sampling technique was used as those members were convenient sources as they haven't taken a course with animation Infographics before. Based on the selected sampling technique, 99 students were selected; the demographics of the selected sample are presented in Table 1). As shown in the table, participants ages ranged between 22 and 23 years and their gender distribution were close as the male percentage was (51.5%) of the total sample. Although the selection of the sample was based on their registration on the same course, their distribution on the classes was not taken into consideration as their access to the Schoology platform was the criteria. All the participants were provided with the introduction to Infographics before sampling into the study during the first week of the study. The selection of the study was based on their sufficient computer skills such as hardware, software, file management and familiarity with good quality documentation software services, spreadsheet features, presentation software skills, communication networks since they were studying computer and instructional technologies in the university and these skills were tested through their achievement in the previous similar courses. Similar selection criteria have been previously adopted by (Afify, 2018; Fadzil, 2018b; Ozdamli and Ozdal, 2018; Yildirim, 2016).

The selected sample (n=99) was divided into two groups; one group was called the control group where the normal lesson was given to them (n=33) and the other group is the experimental group where the animation Infographic was implemented as a source in the lessons (n=66). The selection of the control and experimental group was based on a consent form that was distributed on the study sample where they have chosen in which group they prefer to participate in. The differences in the numbers of the experimental and control groups are caused due to the fact that there are two available classes at the time of the study teaching the target course and that is why the researcher had to deal with them. It is worth mentioning that both groups had access to the Schoology platform; however, the use of the animation Infographics as an external source for the case of the experimental group is what makes the difference. The "Networking and browsing" course was selected purposively from IT department center foundation Language. This course was introduced in the spring semester; therefore, the implementation process of measuring animation Infographics effects began in conjunction with the start of the next semester in February until the end of April 2019.

Table 1. Distribution of the study sample members according to the demographic variables (age and gender)

Demographic variables	Sub-variables	Whole sample	Control group	Experimental group
Gender	Male	51	17	34
	Female	48	16	32
Total		**99**	**33**	**66**
Age	22	62	18	44
	23	37	15	22
Total		**99**	**33**	**66**

3.4 The Research Instruments

To answer the research questions, three tools were used through the study to collect the primary data: (1) Achievement Test, (2) Motivation Scale and (3) Satisfaction Checklist (See Appendixes). In both the motivation and satisfaction checklist scales, the Likert scale was used; see (Appendices B and C). The three tools were administered to the participants before the treatment as a pre-test, and after the treatment as a post-test, to identify the effect of animation Infographics on participants' motivation and retention. After two weeks from the first tests, the tests were administered again for both groups. (control and experimental) to compare the motivation and learning retention of them in both tests.

The study has conducted a 4-week experiment, which includes the introduction of Infographics to the participants; engage them in learning activities and using the given Infographics among their learning preferences. All the participants in the experimental group were informed regarding their features and types of Infographics and the ways to access the Infographics and their design procedures.

3.4.1 Likert Scale

The Likert scale is a rating tool designed to assess attitudes or opinions. Using this scale, respondents evaluate items based on a degree of agreement. In this study, the Likert Scale used in motivation tests and checklist scale by the following rating scale.

Table 2. Motivation scale

Statement	From	to
Not At All True	1	1.8
Somewhat True	1.81	2.6
TRUE	2.61	3.4
Very True	3.41	4.2
Extremely True	4.21	5

Table 3. Satisfaction checklist scale

Statement	from	To
Excellent	1	1.66
Good	1.67	2.33
Satisfactory	2.34	3

3.4.2 Validity of the Motivation Scale, Satisfaction Checklist and Achievement Test

Before discussing the validation process of the study tools, it is worth mentioning that the achievement test and the satisfaction checklist were initially built by the researcher based on her experience in the course as an instructor and her experience in teaching the course using the Schoology platform.

3.4.2.1 Validity of the Motivation Scale

The quasi-experimental research design is used to examine motivation and retention in learning of design animation Infographics on developing the content or material of Information Technology Subject "Networking and Browsing" course at academic university. Following the selection of research methodology and research type, this study has selected quasi-experimental research design for investigating causal relationships as well as for studying the relationship between one construct and another (Bell, Bryman, and Harley, 2018; Kuehl and Kuehl, 2000). The selection of quasi-experimental research design is usually based on three fundamental attributes, (1) random selection and assignment to groups, (2) administration of a pre-test for capturing the initial differences between the groups; and (3) the presence of a control group (Creswell, 2002, 2014; Creswell and Creswell, 2017). In this study, the selection of quasi-experimental research design is based on the presence of design animation Infographics, selection of students based on their cultural level, previous knowledge, retention, and motivation, in the information technology subject, and identification and designing of graphics based on content analysis.

3.4.2.2 Validity of the Achievement Test

The achievement test was initially developed by the researcher as an instructor for the course in collaboration with other instructors in the department. To validate the achievement test, it was presented in its initial form to a panel of five specialized arbitrators in the design and converting the content of animation Infographic of lectures and designers to make their observations on the relevance, clarity of the contents. Based on their recommendation, some changes were made. To test the clarity of the content, the checklist was distributed to a sample of (5) students from outside the sample members with similar characteristics to check the clarity. Then, the checklist was rephrased in its final form.

3.4.2.3 Validity of the Satisfaction Checklist

The satisfaction checklist was initially developed by the researcher as an instructor for the course in collaboration with other instructors in the department. To validate the satisfaction checklist, it was presented in its initial form to a panel of five specialized arbitrators in the design and converting the content of animation Infographic of lectures and designers to make their observations on the relevance, clarity of the contents. Based on their recommendation, some changes were made. To test the clarity of the content, the test was distributed to a sample of (5) students from outside the sample members with similar characteristics to check the clarity. Then, the test was rephrased in its final form.

3.4.3 Reliability of the Motivation Scale, Satisfaction Checklist and Achievement Test

The reliability of the motivation scale, satisfaction checklist, and achievement test were confirmed for each one by the test-retest method, where the pilot study was resent with one week on the same sample of (5) students. The reliability of the motivation scale, satisfaction checklist and achievement test were (0.95), (0.85) and (0.85) Respectively, this signifies a very high level of reliability.

3.5 Procedures of the Study and Experiment

3.5.1 Design Process of the Browsing and Networking Topics

The implementation process of the design Infographic was initiated in the second week of the research with an animation Infographic to convert the content of the Information technology subject "Networking and Browsing" course in the IT department at Academic University. The lessons for the "Networking and Browsing" course was converted to the different animation Infographic that was assigned to the students along the course. The animation Infographic indicated the purpose of the information and provided the visual content. The application A process that was started with Infographic provided a solid structure and enriched or expanded the visual material presented in line with their readings or requirements. The researcher, who is the designer, began to convert the content to some lectures of various types of animation Infographics. Figures 2 and 3 show the "Browsing and Networking" lessons which the researcher converted them into animation Infographic.

Figure 2. "Browsing" infographic design via Illustrator

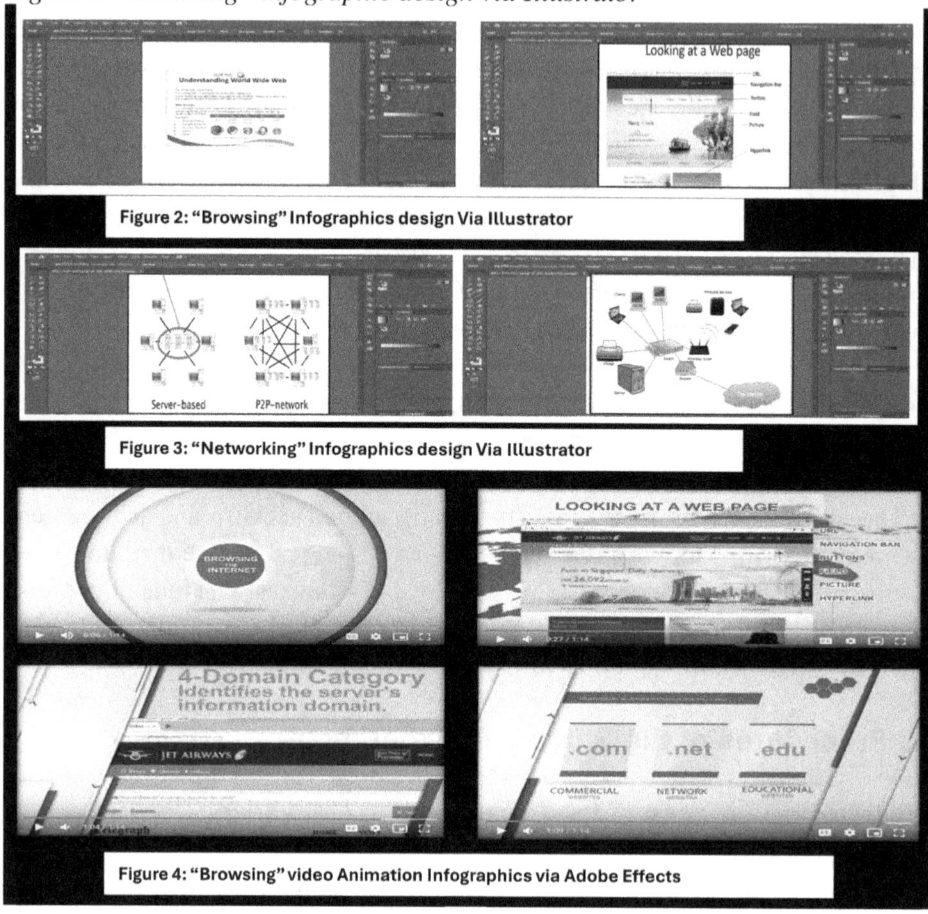

Figure 3. "Browsing" video animation infographics via Adobe effects

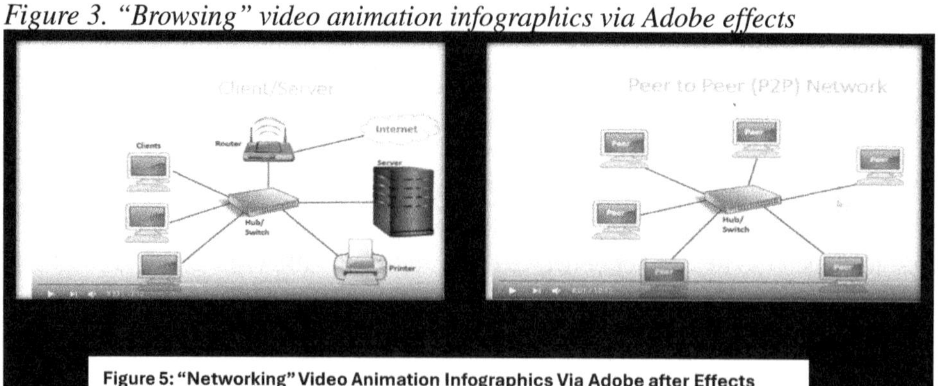

The animation Infographics were developed according to (Shaltout and Fatani, 2017) model. It contained five steps within one week as follows:

1. Study and analysis to analyze learner's characteristics and the Browsing content.
2. Design steps, in which the educational goals were determined, and lines, diagrams and other representations were designed.
3. Production step involved producing the initial model for Infographics, Adobe Illustrator CC was used to design static Infographics, and Adobe After Effects was utilized to design animation Infographics. In this stage, the following points were checked: the representation of entire Browsing and Networking content, logical sequence of information and linguistic integrity.
4. Evaluation step involves administrating the Infographics by a group of expert arbitrators; and
5. Finally, the publishing and application step in which the designed animation Infographics were administrated to the sample of the study.

Figure (5) shows a diagram that represents the outline that has been used to design the "Animation Infographic" for the "Networking and Browsing" course in this study.

3.5 Applying Post-Tests and Pre-Tests

After a week, in the first phase of the procedure, the control group took two regular normal lectures of "Browsing" and "Networking" with a normal teaching approach and procedures without any convert of using animation Infographics. Then, the students were subjected to the achievement test, satisfaction checklist and motivation scale where the students' responses were collected to test the rate of students' assimilation of the topic taught.

The experimental group in this study received the experimental group taking two animation Infographics " Browsing" and " Networking" lectures; while the control group, on the other hand, will not be presented with any 'treatment' at all (i.e., some lectures on a highly complex technical subject in Networking and Browsing course but without any visually engaging animation Infographics and digital visualization materials and designs). Both groups will receive a pre-test and post-test on the 'instrument' (achievement test) and the satisfaction checklist and motivation scales repeated before and after treatment and given as a means to assess the effect of the experiment before and after the treatment is given, Table (4) shows the two-group pre-test-post-test experimental design.

Table 4. The two-group pre-test-post-test experimental design

	Pre-test	**Treatment**	**Post-test**
Experimental Group	X	X	X
Control Group	X		X

The researcher opened the Schoology platform and added two groups (control and experimental) separately to be sure there is no intervention or overleap between two groups. The platform is provided with content of animation Infographics with three tools (achievement test, motivation scale and satisfaction checklist). After creating the Through the Networking and Browsing course and inserting it into the Schoology platform, "Normal lessons" option was selected for the control group that was created by the researcher and instructor and within this option, the linked exams that are available to test the achievement are "chat interaction, motivation scale, checklist and achievement test); however, in this study, the chat interaction option was excluded. The other created group was the experimental group where the "Sources" option was selected and the "Animation Infographics" was selected as an external source with the previous lined exams (achievement test, motivation scale and satisfaction checklist).

3.5.1 Technical Process for Creating and Setting Up Animation Infographics in This Study

First, the important components of the course were converted into visually engaging graphic elements (Figure 6) and then the lessons were developed into full video material with background music. Then, the rate of student motivation and response were measured using the research instrument of pre-test and post-test analysis and motivation scale and checklist. A series of lectures on "networks and Browsing the Internet" were chosen as they are considered the most complex content in the Networking and Browsing course as confirmed by the researcher. However, the Schoology platform was created then two groups; control and experimental were created separately from each other in giving each group their content of the material. As part of the research procedure, lessons of Information Technology course were adopted, as a research tool to be used for training the sample students through the three tools of quasi-experimental research. The course was presented to the sample students (control) without any addition of graphic design, Infographics or any audio-visual media conversion and then the rate of student's motivation through pre-test-post-test achievement test, checklist and Motivation scale were measured. Then, the approach was different as the same course was presented (InfoTech Networking and Browsing) to sample students (experimental) but this time it was converted to the animation video with fully developed audio-visual contents and with colorful video, pictures and some animation Infographic images and 3D movement (Figure 7). The response and rate of students' motivation were measured next time using the same instrument (i.e., pre-test-post-test motivation scale and checklist). Finally, after two weeks (inconsistent with several studies (Kosar, 2003; Ta'amneh, 2014)) the same experiment was repeated to the same sample (control and experimental) to measure the learning retention by using the same tools pre-test-post-test test, checklist and Motivation scale.

Figure 4. (a) "Browsing the Internet" with fully designed graphics and video presentation (b) "Networking" with fully designed graphics and video presentation

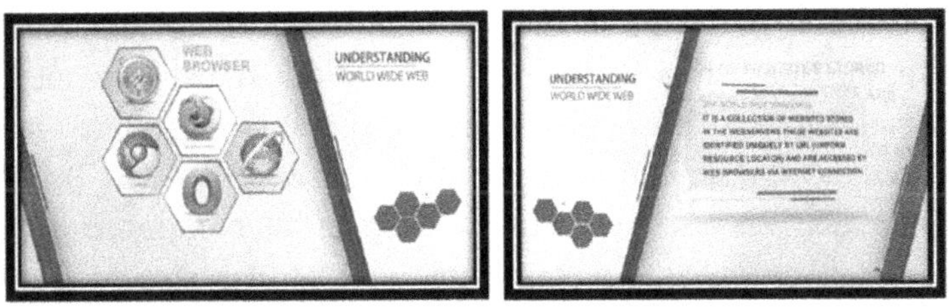

Figure 3.5 Browsing the Internet" with fully designed graphics and video presentation

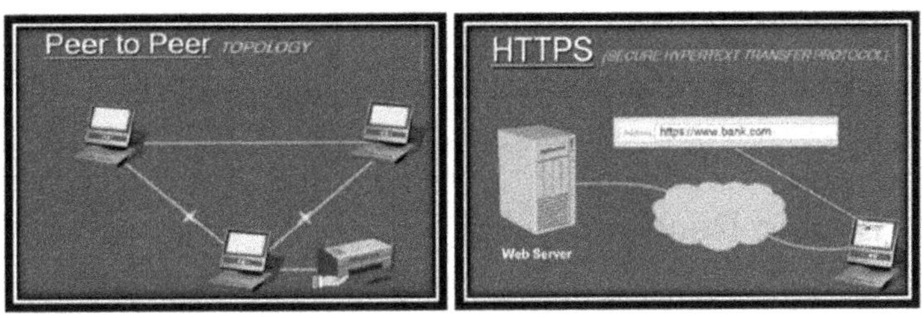

Figure 3.6 'Networking" with fully designed graphics and video presentation

3.6 Data Analysis

The first step was entering the data into a spreadsheet where they were coded in a way that gives them meaning. The next step was using the descriptive statistics in order to describe the data through the frequencies, mean and standard deviation values. Then, predictions were performed about the population where inferential statistics were used to examine the differences between the experimental and control groups. This kind of analysis aims at finding significant differences between the sample groups of the population. In this study, the Paired-Sample T-Test was used to look at the pre-test and post-test scores for the students. It is worth mentioning that the data related to the participants' responses on these instruments were analyzed using the Statistical Package for the Social Sciences (SPSS) software.

4.0 RESULT

The study results indicate that the use of animation infographics significantly improved student motivation and achievement but did not show a clear effect on long-term learning retention. The achievement test analysis revealed that students in the experimental group, who were taught using animated infographics, performed significantly better on the post-test than those in the control group, who received traditional instruction ($p = 0.001$), indicating improved learning outcomes (Afify, 2018). Likewise, the motivation scale results demonstrated a significant increase in motivation levels among students in the experimental group, while the control group experienced a decrease in motivation (Bicen & Beheshti, 2017). However, when learning retention was assessed for two weeks post-intervention, no significant differences were found between the experimental and control groups, suggesting that while animated infographics may enhance immediate learning and motivation, their effect on long-term retention remains unclear (Gallagher et al., 2017). In conclusion, the study supports the effectiveness of animation infographics for boosting short-term learning and motivation, although further research is necessary to evaluate their impact on long-term retention.

4.1 Discussion and Recommendation

Since this study is the first to investigate the effect of animation infographics on students' motivation and learning retention in the Omani context, some recommendations are forwarded for further research considering its findings. This study recommends conducting further research on the impact of animated infographics on student attitudes across various educational levels and subjects. Moreover, studies should be implemented to highlight the setbacks and challenges facing applying animation Infographics in the educational system and the opportunities they have. For the practical recommendations, this study suggests that Academic University should work on enhancing the students' experience on the Schoology platform by implementing the different external sources on the educational process. Training campaigns and educational courses should be provided to teachers and instructors of the different subjects in order to enhance their skills in handling animated Infographics within the class effectively. As this study tested only students' motivation and learning retention differences for short-term effects, further research is in demand to evaluate the long-term effects of animated infographics. More reports on how animation infographics are contextualized in their research would help inform the wise adoption of animation infographics. The current study focused on investigating animation infographics on students' motivation and learning retention Achievement and performance might play a key role as variables in maximizing the positive effect of animated infographics. Further research should consider conducting tests of achievements and performance before and after animation infographics treatment. Generally, learners love to study animation infographics. Research in the future can also examine what factors make learners want to study them, such as motivation differences and achievement differences.

5.0 SUMMARY

This study demonstrates the significant positive impact of animated infographics on student motivation in the Networking and Browsing course. The findings reveal that traditional teaching methods often fail to engage students effectively, leading to a lack of excitement in the learning process. In contrast, the use of animated infographics enhances motivation by making learning more accessible and visually stimulating. This aligns with previous research indicating that infographics can foster greater student engagement and create a more interactive educational experience.

Despite the positive effects on motivation, the study found no significant improvement in long-term learning retention associated with the use of animated infographics. The lack of statistical differences in pre-test and post-test scores among the control group suggests that traditional methods still play a role in knowledge acquisition, albeit limited. This finding contrasts with earlier studies suggesting that infographics could enhance memory retention. The results imply that retention may be more closely related to individual cognitive abilities and memory skills rather than the teaching methods employed. Therefore, while animated infographics effectively boost motivation, further research is necessary to assess their impact on long-term retention of knowledge.

REFERENCES

Ada, N. (2013). Implementation challenges of emerging reforms in teacher education in the 21st century Nigeria. A convocation lecture delivered at the 2005-2011 combined convocation ceremonies of the College of Education, Katsina-Ala, Benue State held at the New College Auditorium, 17th May, 2013.Benue State Nigeria. DOI: 10.3991/ijet.v13i09.8541

Afify, M. K. (2018). The effect of the difference between infographic designing types (static vs animation) on developing visual learning designing skills and recognition of its elements and principles. [iJET]. *International Journal of Emerging Technologies in Learning*, 13(09), 204–223. DOI: 10.3991/ijet.v13i09.8541

Al-Mohammadi, N. (2017). Effectiveness of using infographics as an approach for teaching programming fundamentals on developing analytical thinking skills for high school students in the city of Makkah in Saudi Arabia. *Global Journal of Educational Studies*, 3(1), 22–42. DOI: 10.5296/gjes.v3i1.10854

Alkış, N. (2015). The influence of personality traits, motivation and persuasion principles on academic performance. (Unpublished Doctoral Dissertation). Middle East Technical University, Ankara.

Alrwele, N. S. (2017). Effects of Infographics on Student Achievement and Students' Perceptions of the Impacts of Infographics. *Journal of Education and Human Development*, 6(3), 104–117. DOI: 10.15640/jehd.v6n3a12

Altin, N. C. (2016). Use of Interactive Infographics in News Sites. Scholars Journal of Arts. *Humanities and Social Sciences*, 5(11C), 1749–1754.

Alucdibi, F., & Ekici, G. (2012). The effect of biology teachers' classroom management profiles on the biology course motivation level of the high school students. *Hacettepe University Journal of Education*, 43, 25–36.

Angura, M. T., & Abakpa, V. O. (2018). Impact of Cooperative Instructional Strategies and Conventional Teaching Methods on Students Achievement and Interest in Upper Basic Education Science and Technology in Nigeria. *International Journal of Innovative Research and Development*, 7(2), 38–45. DOI: 10.24940/ijird/2018/v7/i2/JAN18085

Bell, E., Bryman, A., & Harley, B. (2018). *Business research methods* (5th ed.). Oxford university press.

Bicen, H., & Beheshti, M. (2017). The Psychological Impact of Infographics in Education. BRAIN. *Broad Research in Artificial Intelligence and Neuroscience*, 8(4), 99–108.

Çifçi, T. (2016). Effects of infographics on students achievement and attitude towards geography lessons. *Journal of Education and Learning*, 5(1), 154–166. DOI: 10.5539/jel.v5n1p154

Creswell, J. W. (2014). *A concise introduction to mixed methods research.* Sage Publications.

Creswell, J. W., & Creswell, J. D. (2017). *Research design: Qualitative, quantitative, and mixed methods approaches*. Sage publications.

Davis, M., & Quinn, D. (2013). Visualizing text: The new literacy of infographics. *Reading Today*, 31(3), 16–18.

Dick, M. (2014). Interactive infographics and news values. *Digital Journalism (Abingdon, England)*, 2(4), 490–506. DOI: 10.1080/21670811.2013.841368

Fadzil, H. M. (2018a). Designing infographics for the educational technology course: Perspectives of pre-service science teachers. *Journal of Baltic Science Education*, 17(1), 8–18. DOI: 10.33225/jbse/18.17.08

Fadzil, H. M. (2018b). Designing infographics for the educational technology course: Perspectives of pre-service science teachers. *Journal of Baltic Science Education*, 17(1), 8–18. DOI: 10.33225/jbse/18.17.08

Gallagher, S., O'Dulain, M., O'Mahony, N., Kehoe, C., McCarthy, F., & Morgan, G. (2017). Instructor-provided summary infographics to support online learning. *Educational Media International*, 54(2), 129–147. DOI: 10.1080/09523987.2017.1362795

Gaotlhobogwe, M. (2017). The impact of lack of resources on declining students' enrolments in Design and Technology in Botswana junior secondary schools. Design and Technology Education: An International Journal, 17(1). DOI: 10.1080/09523987.2017.1362795

Gover, G. B. (2017). Teacher Thoughts on Infographics as Alternative Assessment: A Post-Secondary Educational Exploration. (Unpublished Doctoral Dissertation), Eastern Kentucky University, USA.

Guay, F., Ratelle, C. F., Roy, A., & Litalien, D. (2010). Academic self-concept, autonomous academic motivation, and academic achievement: Mediating and additive effects. *Learning and Individual Differences*, 20(6), 644–653. DOI: 10.1016/j.lindif.2010.08.001

Hassan, H. G. (2016). Designing Infographics to support teaching complex science subject: A comparison between static and animation Infographics. (Mater thesis), Iowa State University Ames, Iowa.

Hilas, C. S., & Politis, A. (2014). Motivating students' participation in a computer networks course by means of magic, drama and games. *SpringerPlus*, 3(1), 362. DOI: 10.1186/2193-1801-3-362 PMID: 25105085

Islamoglu, H., Ay, O., Ilic, U., Mercimek, B., Donmez, P., Kuzu, A., & Odabasi, F. (2015). Infographics: A new competency area for teacher candidates. *Cypriot Journal of Educational Sciences*, 10(1), 32–39.

Kian, T., Yusoff, W., & Rajah, S. (2014). Motivation for generations' cohorts: An organizational justice perspective. *International Journal of Management Sciences*, 11(2), 536–542.

Kumar, M., & Jamil, M. (2016). Enhanced learning using motion graphics in higher education. Paper presented at the International Technology, Education and Development Conference, Spain. DOI: 10.21125/iceri.2016.0157

Lankow, J., Ritchie, J., & Crooks, R. (2012). *Infographics: The power of visual storytelling. Chicago/Turabian*. John Wiley and Sons.

Lee, E.-J., & Kim, Y. W. (2016). Effects of infographics on news elaboration, acquisition, and evaluation: Prior knowledge and issue involvement as moderators. *New Media & Society*, 18(8), 1579–1598. DOI: 10.1177/1461444814567982

Lin, L.-C. (2012). *Measuring adult learners'foreign language anxiety, motivational factors, and achievement expectations: a comparative study between Chinese as a second-language students and English as a second-language students. (Doctoral Dessertation)*. Cleveland State University.

Martix, S., & Hodson, J. (2014). Teaching with infographics: practising new digital competencies and visual literacies. Journal of pedagogic development,4 (2).

Meirelles, I. (2013). *Design for information: an introduction to the histories, theories, and best practices behind effective information visualizations*. Rockport publishers.

Mol, L. (2011). The potential role for infographics in science communication. (Master Thesis), Biomedical Sciences, Vrije University, Amsterdam, Netherlands.

Mudulia, A. M. (2012). The relationship between availability of teaching/learning resources and performance in secondary school science subjects in Eldoret Municipality, Kenya. *Journal of Emerging Trends in Educational Research and Policy Studies*, 3(4), 530–536.

Naparin, H., & Saad, A. B. (2017). Infographics in education: Review on infographics design. [IJMA]. *The International Journal of Multimedia and Its Applications*, 9(4), 5. DOI: 10.5121/ijma.2017.9602

Okwuduba, E. N., & Okigbo, E. C. (2018). Effect of teaching methods on students' academic performance in chemistry in Nigeria: Meta-analytic review. *Bulgarian Journal of Science and Education Policy*, 12(2), 418–434.

Osba, S. (2015). Impact of using Infographics strategy on academic achievement among fifth grade female students and their attitudes and motivation towards learning science. (Unpublished Master thesis), Alnajah University, Nablus.

Ozdal, H., & Ozdamli, F. (2017). The Effect of Infographics in Mobile Learning: Case Study in Primary School. *J. UCS*, 23(12), 1256–1275.

Ozdamli, F., & Ozdal, H. (2018). Developing an Instructional Design for the Design of Infographics and the Evaluation of Infographic Usage in Teaching Based on Teacher and Student Opinions. *Eurasia Journal of Mathematics, Science and Technology Education*, 14(4), 1197–1219. DOI: 10.29333/ejmste/81868

Peters, D. (2014). *Interface design for learning: Design strategies for learning experiences*. Pearson Education.

Pooja, G. (2017). Study the Effect of Teaching Method on the Academic Achievement of School Going Childern of Semiurban Area, S Schools of Luckynow City. *International Journal of Home Science*, 3(2), 447–453.

Ractham, P., & Firpo, D. (2011). Using social networking technology to enhance learning in higher education: A case study using Facebook. Paper presented at the 2011 44th Hawaii International Conference on System Sciences, USA. DOI: 10.1109/HICSS.2011.479

Rezaei, N., & Sayadian, S. (2015). The impact of infographics on Iranian EFL learners' grammar learning. *Journal of Applied Linguistics and Language Research*, 2(1), 78–85.

Rueda, R. A. S. (2015). Use of infographics in virtual environments for personal learning process on Boolean algebra. *Vivat Academia*, (130), 64–74. DOI: 10.15178/va.2015.130.64-74

Schrock, K. (2014). Infographics as a creative assessment. Retrieved from https://home.edweb.net/infographics-as-a-creative-assessment/, June, 2019.

Shaltout, M., & Fatani, H. (2017). Impact of two different infographics types "interactivestatic" on developing mathematical concepts among female students at second grade intermediate in the Kingdom of Saudi Arabia. *International Journal of Research and Reviews in Education*, 4, 1–8.

Singh, N., & Jain, N. (2017). Effects of infographic designing on image processing ability and achievement motivation of dyscalculic students. Paper presented at the Proceedings of the International Conference for Young Researchers in Informatics, Mathematics and Engineering. Kaunas, Lithuania.

Ta'amneh, M. (2014). The effect of using educational websites on first year students' achievement in English grammar in Badr community college. *Journal of Emerging Trends in Educational Research and Policy Studies*, 5(2), 184–189.

Turan, Z. (2015). The evaluation of flipped classroom method and examination of its effects on academic achievement, cognitive load and motivation. (Unpublished Doctoral dissertation). Atatürk University, Erzurum.

Vanichvasin, P. (2013). Enhancing the quality of learning through the use of infographics as visual communication tool and learning tool. Paper presented at the Proceedings ICQA 2013 international conference on QA culture: Cooperation or competition. Bangkok.

Wibowo, D. C., Friana, F., & Pelipa, E. D. (2018). Effect of Recitation Method to the Students' Interest and Learning Results. Jurnal Studi Guru dan Pembelajaran, 1(1), 16-20.

Yap, W. L. (2016). Transforming conventional teaching classroom to learner-centred teaching classroom using multimedia-mediated learning module. *International Journal of Information and Education Technology (IJIET)*, 6(2), 105–112. DOI: 10.7763/IJIET.2016.V6.667

Yildirim, S. (2016). Infographics for Educational Purposes: Their Structure, Properties and Reader Approaches. *Turkish Online Journal of Educational Technology-TOJET*, 15(3), 98–110.

Compilation of References

Abduljaber, M. F. (2024). Perceived influence of artificial intelligence on educational leadership's decision-making, teaching, and learning outcomes: A transcendental phenomenological study. DOI: 10.30935/cedtech/13152

Abt, C. C. (1970). *Serious games*. Viking Press.

Acevedo-Duque, Á., Jiménez-Bucarey, C., Prado-Sabido, T., Fernández-Mantilla, M. M., Merino-Flores, I., Izquierdo-Marín, S. S., & Valle-Palomino, N. (2023). Education for sustainable development: Challenges for postgraduate programmes. *International Journal of Environmental Research and Public Health*, 20(3), 1759. DOI: 10.3390/ijerph20031759 PMID: 36767126

Adams, H., & Hall, D. (2022). Innovations in artificial intelligence research fueled by big data analytics. *European Journal of Business and Innovation Research*, 10(2), 96–104.

Ada, N. (2013). Implementation challenges of emerging reforms in teacher education in the 21st century Nigeria. A convocation lecture delivered at the 2005-2011 combined convocation ceremonies of the College of Education, Katsina-Ala, Benue State held at the New College Auditorium, 17th May, 2013.Benue State Nigeria. DOI: 10.3991/ijet.v13i09.8541

Adeleye,, Olabisi Oluwakemi, Eden,, Chima Abimbola, & Adeniyi, Idowu Sulaimon (2024). Innovative teaching methodologies in the era of artificial intelligence: A review of inclusive educational practices. *World Journal of Advanced Engineering Technology and Sciences, 11*(2), 069–079. DOI: 10.5539/ijel.v10n6p40

Afendi, A., Sholihah, N., Mutmainah, F., Ishak, K., & Lubis, A. (2022). *Penggunaan Microsoft Office untuk Meningkatkan Motivasi dan Hasil Belajar Siswa Sekolah Dasar*. Jurnal PGSD., DOI: 10.32534/jps.v8i1.2949

Afzal, M., Farooq, M. S., & Ahmad, H. K. (2010). Relationship between School Education and Economic Growth in Pakistan ARDL Bounds Testing Approach to Cointegration. *School Education and Economic Growth in Pakistan*, 48(1), 39–61.

Afzal, M., Shafique, M., Ahmad, N., & Qasim, H. (2016). Education, Poverty and Economic Growth in South Asia: A Panel Data Analysis. *Journal of Quality and Technology Management*, 9(1), 131–154.

Agrawal, K., & Nargund, N. (2024, January). Deep learning in Industry 4.0: Transforming manufacturing through data-driven innovation. In *International Conference on Distributed Computing and Intelligent Technology* (pp. 222-236). Cham: Springer Nature Switzerland. DOI: 10.1007/978-3-031-50583-6_15

Ahel, O., & Schirmer, M. (2023). Education for sustainable development through research-based learning in an online environment. *International Journal of Sustainability in Higher Education*, 24(1), 118–140. DOI: 10.1108/IJSHE-07-2021-0305

Ahir, K., Govani, K., Gajera, R., & Shah, M. (2020). Application on virtual reality for enhanced education learning, military training and sports. *Augmented Human Research*, 5(1), 1–9. DOI: 10.1007/s41133-019-0025-2

Ahlquist, J. (2020). *Digital leadership in higher education: Purposeful social media in a connected world*. Routledge.

Ahmadi, A., & RabieNezhad Ganji, N. (2023). AI-driven medical innovations: Transforming healthcare through data intelligence. [IJBLS]. *International Journal of BioLife Sciences*, 2(2), 132–142.

Ahmad, K., Iqbal, W., El-Hassan, A., Qadir, J., Benhaddou, D., Ayyash, M., & Al-Fuqaha, A. (2023). Data-driven artificial intelligence in education: A comprehensive review. *IEEE Transactions on Learning Technologies*.

Akçayır, M., & Akçayır, G. (2017). Advantages and challenges associated with augmented reality for education: A systematic review of the literature. *Educational Research Review*, 20, 1–11. DOI: 10.1016/j.edurev.2016.11.002

Akhmedov, J., Jurayev, U., Kosimova, S., Rakhimova, G., Tursunov, Q., & Kosimov, L. (2024, May). The significant technical mantle of AI in the field of secular engineering: An innovative design. In *2024 4th International Conference on Advance Computing and Innovative Technologies in Engineering (ICACITE)* (pp. 601-606). IEEE.

Akyuz, E., & Celik, E. (2018). The role of human factor in maritime environment risk assessment: A practical application on Ballast Water Treatment (BWT) system in ship. *Human and Ecological Risk Assessment*, 24(3), 653–666. DOI: 10.1080/10807039.2017.1396184

Al Hajri, M. (2020). A cloud-based collaborative virtual learning environment for the higher education institutions in the Sultanate of Oman [Unpublished doctoral dissertation]. Bournemouth University.

Al Harrasi, N., El Din, M. S., & Al Balushi, B. (2021). Towards an artificial intelligence (AI)-driven government in the Sultanate of Oman: Transforming and augmenting leadership competencies. In *Managerial Issues in Digital Transformation of Global Modern Corporations* (p. 13). IGI Global., DOI: 10.4018/978-1-7998-2402-2.ch016

Al Matari, A. S., Mukit, A., Al Saadi, S., Balushi, W. A., & Al-Abri, J. S. Artificial intelligence and the future of teaching in higher education at A'Sharqiyah University (ASU) in Oman. DOI: 10.1007/s10833-021-09448-w PMID: 38624840

Alenezi, M. (2023). Digital learning and digital institution in higher education. *Education Sciences*, 13(2), 88. DOI: 10.3390/educsci13010088

Alkış, N. (2015). The influence of personality traits, motivation and persuasion principles on academic performance. (Unpublished Doctoral Dissertation). Middle East Technical University, Ankara.

Allen, I. E., & Seaman, J. (2007). *Online nation: Five years of growth in online learning*. Retrieved from ERIC.

Almarzooq, Z., Lopes, M., & Kochar, A. (2020). Virtual learning during the COVID-19 pandemic: A disruptive technology in graduate medical education. *Journal of the American College of Cardiology*, 75(20), 2635–2638. DOI: 10.1016/j.jacc.2020.04.015 PMID: 32304797

Al-Mohammadi, N. (2017). Effectiveness of using infographics as an approach for teaching programming fundamentals on developing analytical thinking skills for high school students in the city of Makkah in Saudi Arabia. *Global Journal of Educational Studies*, 3(1), 22–42. DOI: 10.5296/gjes.v3i1.10854

Al-Omoush, K., & McDowell, W. C. (2023). The impact of digital corporate social responsibility on social entrepreneurship and organizational resilience. *Management Decision*. Advance online publication. DOI: 10.1108/MD-11-2022-1613

Alonso-Fernández, C., Calvo-Morata, A., Freire, M., Martínez-Ortiz, I., & Fernández-Manjón, B. (2019). Applications of data science to game learning analytics data: A systematic literature review. *Computers & Education*, 141, 103612. DOI: 10.1016/j.compedu.2019.103612

Alonso-Fernández, C., Calvo-Morata, A., Freire, M., Martínez-Ortiz, I., & Fernández-Manjón, B. (2023). Evidence-based evaluation of a serious game to increase bullying awareness. *Interactive Learning Environments*, 31(2), 644–654. DOI: 10.1080/10494820.2020.1799031

Alqahtani, S. M., Bhaskar, C. V., Vadakalur Elumalai, K., & Abumelha, M. (2018). WhatsApp: An online platform for university-level English language education. *Arab World English Journal*, 9(4), 108–121. DOI: 10.24093/awej/vol9no4.7

Alrwele, N. S. (2017). Effects of Infographics on Student Achievement and Students' Perceptions of the Impacts of Infographics. *Journal of Education and Human Development*, 6(3), 104–117. DOI: 10.15640/jehd.v6n3a12

Altan, B., & Milson, S. (2024). *AI-powered data revolution: Navigating the big data landscape (No. 11898)*. EasyChair.

Altin, N. C. (2016). Use of Interactive Infographics in News Sites. Scholars Journal of Arts. *Humanities and Social Sciences*, 5(11C), 1749–1754.

Alucdibi, F., & Ekici, G. (2012). The effect of biology teachers' classroom management profiles on the biology course motivation level of the high school students. *Hacettepe University Journal of Education*, 43, 25–36.

Alyaz, Y., Spaniel-Weise, D., & Gursoy, E. (2017). A study on using serious games in teaching German as a foreign language. *Journal of Education and Learning*, 6(3), 250–264. https://eric.ed.gov/?id=EJ1141668. DOI: 10.5539/jel.v6n3p250

Anderson, T. (2013). Digital Resilience in Higher Education, *European Journal of Open, Distance and E-Learning*, 16 (1), pp. 53-66. https://eric.ed.gov/?id=EJ1017457

Angura, M. T., & Abakpa, V. O. (2018). Impact of Cooperative Instructional Strategies and Conventional Teaching Methods on Students Achievement and Interest in Upper Basic Education Science and Technology in Nigeria. *International Journal of Innovative Research and Development*, 7(2), 38–45. DOI: 10.24940/ijird/2018/v7/i2/JAN18085

Appiah, E. N. (2017). The Effect of Education Expenditure on Per Capita GDP in Developing Countries. *International Journal of Economics and Finance*, 9(10), 136–144. DOI: 10.5539/ijef.v9n10p136

Arbaugh, J. B., & Duray, R. (2002). Technology and the transformation of higher education: A comparative study of online and traditional courses. *Journal of Education for Business*, 77(6), 335–342.

Ayed, I. A. H. (2022). *Oman higher education institutions dealing with artificial intelligence* [Doctoral dissertation, Universidade do Minho]. ProQuest Dissertations & Theses. https://doi.org/DOI: 30227343

Ayeni, O. O., Al Hamad, N. M., Chisom, O. N., Osawaru, B., & Adewusi, O. E. (2024). AI in education: A review of personalized learning and educational technology. *GSC Advanced Research and Reviews*, 18(2), 261–271. DOI: 10.30574/gscarr.2024.18.2.0062

Baharudin, F., Ramli, N. H. L., Habali, A. H. M., Azmi, A. A., & Rahmat, N. H. (2023). Process of Writing: The Challenges in Writing Skill Among ESL Learners. *International Journal of Academic Research in Business & Social Sciences*, 13(10), 32–50. DOI: 10.6007/IJARBSS/v13-i10/18649

Bah, I. A. (2023). The relationship between education and economic growth: A cross-country analysis. *Research. Social Development*, 12(5), 13. DOI: 10.33448/rsd-v12i5.40522

Bai, S., Hew, K. F., & Huang, B. (2020). Does gamification improve student learning outcome? Evidence from a meta-analysis and synthesis of qualitative data in educational contexts. *Educational Research Review*, 30, 100322. DOI: 10.1016/j.edurev.2020.100322

Bandara, D., Woodward, M., Chin, C., & Jiang, D. (2020). Augmented reality lights for compromised visibility navigation. *Journal of Marine Science and Engineering*, 8(12), 1014. DOI: 10.3390/jmse8121014

Bandura, A. (1977). *Social learning theory*. Prentice-Hall.

Bappy, M. A., Ahmed, M., & Rauf, M. A. (2024). Exploring the integration of informed machine learning in engineering applications: A comprehensive review. *Manam and Rauf, Md Abdur, Exploring the Integration of Informed Machine Learning in Engineering Applications: A Comprehensive Review* (February 19, 2024).

Barnett, M., Gatfield, D., & Pekcan, C. (2006, March). Non-technical skills: the vital ingredient in world maritime technology. In *Proceedings of the International Conference on world maritime technology*. Institute of Marine Engineering, Science and Technology, London, UK, pp. 1–11.

Barnosky, Anthony (2016). Toward a digital resilience. *Elementa: Science of the Anthropogenic.* . DOI: 10.12952/journal.elementa.000082

Basak, S. K. (2017). A framework on the factors affecting to implement maritime education and training system in educational institutions: A review of the literature. *Procedia Engineering*, 194, 345–350. DOI: 10.1016/j.proeng.2017.08.155

Baskara, F. R. (2023). AI-Driven Dynamics: ChatGPT Transforming ELT Teacher-Student Interactions. *Lensa: Kajian Kebahasaan, Kesusastraan. Dan Budaya*, 13(2), 261–275. DOI: 10.26714/lensa.13.2.2023.261-275

Bedwell, W. L., Pavlas, D., Heyne, K., Lazzara, E. H., & Salas, E. (2012). Toward a taxonomy linking game attributes to learning: An empirical study. *Simulation & Gaming*, 43(6), 729–760. DOI: 10.1177/1046878112439444

Bekbolatova, M., Mayer, J., Ong, C. W., & Toma, M. (2024). Transformative Potential of AI in Healthcare: Definitions, Applications, and Navigating the Ethical Landscape and Public Perspectives. *Healthcare (Basel)*, 12(2), 1–31. DOI: 10.3390/healthcare12020125 PMID: 38255014

Bell, E., Bryman, A., & Harley, B. (2018). *Business research methods* (5th ed.). Oxford university press.

Bender, S. M. (2024). Awareness of Artificial Intelligence as an Essential Digital Literacy: ChatGPT and Gen-AI in the Classroom. *Changing English*, 31(2), 161–174. DOI: 10.1080/1358684X.2024.2309995

Bergeron, B. (2005). *Developing serious games (game development series)*. Charles River Media, Inc.

Bernacki, M. L., Greene, J. A., & Crompton, H. (2020). Mobile technology, learning, and achievement: Advances in understanding and measuring the role of mobile technology in education. *Contemporary Educational Psychology*, 60, 101827. DOI: 10.1016/j.cedpsych.2019.101827

Berns, A., Gonzàlez-Pardo, A., & Camacho, D. (2011). Implementing the use of virtual worlds in the teaching of foreign languages (level A1). *Proceedings of Learning a Language in Virtual Worlds: A Review of Innovation and ICT in Language Teaching Methodology. 2011. Warsaw*, 33-40.

Bhatia, V. K. (2004). *Worlds of Written Discourse: A Genre-Based View*. Continuum.

Bhattacharyya, P. (2019). Public Expenditure on Education and Economic Growth: A state-level analysis in India, Humanities & Social. *Scientific Review (Singapore)*, 7(6), 533–539. DOI: 10.18510/hssr.2019.7683

Bicen, H., & Beheshti, M. (2017). The Psychological Impact of Infographics in Education. BRAIN. *Broad Research in Artificial Intelligence and Neuroscience*, 8(4), 99–108.

Biggs, J. (1993). From theory to practice: A cognitive systems approach. *Higher Education Research & Development*, 12(1), 73–85. DOI: 10.1080/0729436930120107

Biggs, J., & Collis, K. F. (1982). *Evaluating the quality of learning: The SOLO taxonomy*. Academic Press.

Bikowski, D. (2018). Technology for teaching grammar. In Teaching and Technology. DOI: 10.1002/9781118784235.eelt0441

Blender. (2021). *Blender 2.93 Reference Manual.* Blender Documentation. Retrieved March 13, 2021, from https://docs.blender.org/manual/en/latest/

Blondel, V. D., Guillaume, J. L., Lambiotte, R., & Lefebvre, E. (2008). Fast unfolding of communities in large networks. *Journal of Statistical Mechanics*, 2008(10), P10008. DOI: 10.1088/1742-5468/2008/10/P10008

Bloom, B. S. (1956). *Taxonomy of educational objectives: The classification of educational goals*. David McKay Company, Inc.

Borenstein, J., & Howard, A. (2021). Emerging challenges in AI and the need for AI ethics education. *AI and Ethics*, 1(1), 61–65. DOI: 10.1007/s43681-020-00002-7 PMID: 38624388

Bower, M., Howe, C., & McCredie, N. (2020). Augmented Reality in Education – Cases, places, and potentials. *Educational Media International*, 57(2), 152–169.

Brinton, L. J., & Akimoto, M. (Eds.). (1999). *Collocational and Idiomatic Aspects of Composite Predicates in the History of English*. John Benjamins Publishing Company. DOI: 10.1075/slcs.47

British Council Nigeria. (2021). Empowering Underserved Communities through Digital Hubs. DOI: 10.1002/9781119239086

Brown, D., & Lee, H. (2020). Metacognition in EFL: The role of reflective practices. *TESOL Quarterly*, 54(1), 65–87. DOI: 10.2307/3587508

Brown, J. S., Collins, A., & Duguid, P. (1989). Situated cognition and the culture of learning. *Educational Researcher*, 18(1), 32–42. DOI: 10.3102/0013189X018001032

Brunetti, F., & Orzes, G. (2020). Digital transformation challenges: Strategies emerging from a multi-stakeholder approach. *The TQM Journal*, 32(4), 697–724. DOI: 10.1108/TQM-12-2019-0309

Brunton, S. L., Nathan Kutz, J., Manohar, K., Aravkin, A. Y., Morgansen, K., Klemisch, J., & McDonald, D. (2021). Data-driven aerospace engineering: Reframing the industry with machine learning. *AIAA Journal*, 59(8), 2820–2847. DOI: 10.2514/1.J060131

Bruzzone, A. G., Massei, M., Solis, A. O., Poggi, S., Bartolucci, C., & Capponi, L. D. A. (2013, July). Serious games as enablers for training and education on operations on ships and off-shore platforms. In *Proceedings of the 2013 summer computer simulation conference* (pp. 1-8).

Bryant, J., Heitz, C., Sanghvi, S., & Wagle, D. (2020). How artificial intelligence will impact K-12 teachers. McKinsey & Company. Retrieved September 8, 2020, from https://www.mckinsey.com/industries/social-sector/our-insights/how-artificial-intelligence-will-impact-k-12-teachers

Bryman, A. (2021). *Social research methods* (5th ed.). Oxford University Press.

Bulathwela, S., Pérez-Ortiz, M., & Sánchez, J. M. (2023). Smart learning environments in education: A systematic review and future directions. *Educational Technology Research and Development*, 71, 887–907.

Cabauatan, R. R. (2016). Analysing the effects of selected economic indicators on education and on the causality between education and economic growth of the Philippines. *Science and Technology Development Journal*, 19(3), 57–69. DOI: 10.32508/stdj.v19i3.479

Calderón, A., & Ruiz, M. (2015). A systematic literature review on serious games evaluation: An application to software project management. *Computers & Education*, 87, 396–422. DOI: 10.1016/j.compedu.2015.07.011

Cano, A. R., Fernández-Manjón, B., & García-Tejedor, Á. J. (2018). Using game learning analytics for validating the design of a learning game for adults with intellectual disabilities. *British Journal of Educational Technology*, 49(4), 659–672. DOI: 10.1111/bjet.12632

Carrión-Toro, M., Santorum, M., Acosta-Vargas, P., Aguilar, J., & Pérez, M. (2020). iPlus a user-centered methodology for serious games design. *Applied Sciences (Basel, Switzerland)*, 10(24), 9007. DOI: 10.3390/app10249007

Carter, R. (2019, January 8). Microsoft Kaizala: App for comms & work management. *Uctoday.com*. https://www.uctoday.com/collaboration/microsoft-kaizala-review-mobile-app-for-comms-work-management

Carvalho, M. B., Bellotti, F., Berta, R., De Gloria, A., Sedano, C. I., Hauge, J. B., Hu, J., & Rauterberg, M. (2015). An activity theory-based model for serious games analysis and conceptual design. *Computers & Education*, 87, 166–181. DOI: 10.1016/j.compedu.2015.03.023

Cavanaugh, D. (2005). Teaching online – A time comparison. *Online Journal of Distance Learning Administration*, 8, 1–9.

Celik, I., Dindar, M., Muukkonen, H., & Järvelä, S. (2022). The promises and challenges of artificial intelligence for teachers: A systematic review of research. *TechTrends*, 66(5), 616–630. DOI: 10.1007/s11528-022-00715-y

Chae, C. J., Kim, D., & Lee, H. T. (2021). A study on the analysis of the effects of passenger ship abandonment training using VR. *Applied Sciences (Basel, Switzerland)*, 11(13), 5919. DOI: 10.3390/app11135919

Chaiyakun, S., & Yang, J. W. L. (2024). Digital Renaissance: A comprehensive exploration of education transformation - hotspots, models, and strategic approaches. *International Journal of Current Educational Practice*, 12(2), 86–95. DOI: 10.5281/zenodo.10954537

Chan, K., & Zary, N. (2019). Knowledge, use and barriers to Serious Games in undergraduate medical education. OSF Preprints. Retrieved October 9, 2022 from https://osf.io/2f7rw/download DOI: 10.31219/osf.io/2f7rw

Chang, A. H., Lin, P. C., Lin, P. C., Lin, Y. C., Kabasawa, Y., Lin, C. Y., & Huang, H. L. (2022). Effectiveness of virtual reality-based training on oral healthcare for disabled elderly persons: A randomized controlled trial. *Journal of Personalized Medicine*, 12(2), 218. DOI: 10.3390/jpm12020218 PMID: 35207706

Chatterjee, R., Bandyopadhyay, A., Chakraborty, S., & Dutta, S. (2023). Digital education: The basics with slant to digital pedagogy—An overview. In *Digital Learning Based Education: Transcending Physical Barriers* (pp. 63–80). Springer.

Chaudhry, I. S., Sarwary, S. A. M., El Refae, G. A., & Chabchoub, H. (2023). Time to revisit existing student's performance evaluation approach in higher education sector in a new era of ChatGPT — A case study. *Cogent Education*, 10(1), 2210461. DOI: 10.1080/2331186X.2023.2210461

Chen, K. and Xue, F. (2022). The renaissance of augmented reality in construction: history, present status and future directions, *Smart and Sustainable Built Environment*, 11 (3), pp. 575 592. .DOI: 10.1108/SASBE-08-2020-0124

Chen, C. M., & Tsai, Y. H. (2020). Interactive virtual reality for collaborative learning in higher education. *Interactive Learning Environments*, 28(2), 225–242.

Chen, G., Xu, B., Lu, M., & Chen, N.-S. (2018). Exploring blockchain technology and its potential applications for education. *Smart Learning Environments*, 5(1), 1–10. DOI: 10.1186/s40561-017-0050-x

Chen, J., & Cheng, T. (2022). Review of research on teacher emotion during 1985-2019: A descriptive quantitative analysis of knowledge production trends. *European Journal of Psychology of Education*, 37(3), 417–438. DOI: 10.1007/s10212-021-00537-1

Chen, J., Vorvoreanu, M., & Madhavan, K. (2021). A web-based learning analytics system for improving student engagement in higher education. *Journal of Educational Technology & Society*, 24(2), 31–42. https://www.j-ets.net/ets/journals/24_2/4.pdf

Chernov, A., & Chernova, V. (2019) Artificial intelligence in management: challenges and opportunities. In Hammes, K., Machrafi, M., & Samodol, A. (Eds.) The proceedings of the 38th international scientific conference on economic and social development (pp. 133-140). Varazdin Development and Entrepreneurship Agency.

Choi, K.-S. (2020). Opportunities for higher education of artificial intelligence in Korea. *International Journal of Engineering Research & Technology (Ahmedabad)*, 13(11), 3428–3430. DOI: 10.37624/IJERT/13.11.2020.3428-3430

Chow, C. Y., Riantiningtyas, R. R., Kanstrup, M. B., Papavasileiou, M., Liem, G. D., & Olsen, A. (2020). Can games change children's eating behaviour? A review of gamification and serious games. *Food Quality and Preference*, 80, 103823. DOI: 10.1016/j.foodqual.2019.103823

Chuckedmonson, SuPotter, Pebaum, & MaabSaleem. (2019, May). Kaizala mobile app. *Docs.microsoft.com*.https://docs.microsoft.com/en-us/office365/kaizala/kaizala-mobile-app

Cichosz, M., & Knemeyer, A. M. (2020). Digital transformation at logistics service providers: Barriers, success factors and leading practices. *International Journal of Logistics Management*, 31(2), 209–238. DOI: 10.1108/IJLM-08-2019-0229

Çifçi, T. (2016). Effects of infographics on students achievement and attitude towards geography lessons. *Journal of Education and Learning*, 5(1), 154–166. DOI: 10.5539/jel.v5n1p154

Coker, H., & Mercieca, D. (2023). Digital technology for inclusive education: Reflecting on the role of teachers. In *Inclusion, Equity, Diversity, and Social Justice in Education: A Critical Exploration of the Sustainable Development Goals* (pp. 233–243). Springer Nature.

Cook, V. (2013). *Second Language Learning and Language Teaching*. Routledge. DOI: 10.4324/9780203770511

Cooper, G. (2023). Examining science education in ChatGPT: An exploratory study of generative artificial intelligence. *Journal of Science Education and Technology*, 32(3), 444–452. DOI: 10.1007/s10956-023-10039-y

Cope, B., Kalantzis, M., & Searsmith, D. (2021). Artificial intelligence for education: Knowledge and its assessment in AI-enabled learning ecologies. *Educational Philosophy and Theory*, 53(11), 1229–1245. DOI: 10.1080/00131857.2020.1728732

Cresswell, J. W. (2014). *Research design: Qualitative, quantitative, and mixed methods approaches* (4th ed.). Sage Publications.

Creswell, J. W. (2014). *A concise introduction to mixed methods research*. Sage Publications.

Crompton, H., & Burke, D. (2023). Artificial intelligence in higher education: The state of the field. *International Journal of Educational Technology in Higher Education*, 20(1), 22–33. DOI: 10.1186/s41239-023-00392-8

Crystal, D. (2012). *English as a Global Language*. Cambridge University Press. DOI: 10.1017/CBO9781139196970

Csikszentmihalyi, M. (1975). *Beyond boredom and anxiety: Experiencing flow in work and play*. Jossey-Bass, https://psycnet.apa.org/record/2000-12701-000

Curry, L. (1983). An organisation of learning styles theory and its applications in the classroom. In Keefe, J. W. (Ed.), *Student learning styles and their implications for teaching* (pp. 49–59). National Association of Secondary School Principals.

Daggett, W. R., & Jones, R. D. (2010). *The Process of Change: Why Change, What to Do, and How to Do It.* International Center for Leadership in Education. Retrieved January 11 2021 from http://www.daggett.com/pdf/Process_of_Change_2014.pdf

Dangal, D. N. (2022). Tertiary Education and Economic Growth of Nepal: An ARDL-ECM Analysis. *Humanity & Social Sciences Journal*, 13(2), 25. DOI: 10.3126/hssj.v13i2.49799

Daniel, R. B., & Andrea, R. L. (2020). Learning from experience in the midst of COVID-19: Benefits, challenges, and strategies in online teaching. *Computer-Assisted Language Learning Electronic Journal*, 21(2), 176–196.

Darvishi, A., Khosravi, H., Sadiq, S., Gašević, D., & Siemens, G. (2024). Impact of AI assistance on student agency. *Computers & Education*, 210, 104967. DOI: 10.1016/j.compedu.2023.104967

Dastidar, S. G., Mohan, S., & Chatterji, M. (2013). The relationship between public education expenditure and economic growth: The case of India. *Scottish Institute for Research in Economics*, 2013(07), 14.

Davis, M., & Quinn, D. (2013). Visualizing text: The new literacy of infographics. *Reading Today*, 31(3), 16–18.

de Água, P. M. G. B., da Silva Frias, A. D., Carrasqueira, M. D. J., & Daniel, J. M. M. (2020). Future of maritime education and training: Blending hard and soft skills. *Pomorstvo*, 34(2), 345–353. DOI: 10.31217/p.34.2.15

de Freitas, S., & Jarvis, S. (2009). Towards a development approach to serious games. *Games-based learning advancements for multi-sensory human computer interfaces: Techniques and effective practices*, 215-231.

Del Vecchio, P., & Garzoni, A. (2024). Digital transformation and resilience in family business: An exploratory study of generational dynamics. *European Journal of Innovation Management*. Advance online publication. DOI: 10.1108/EJIM-02-2024-0137

Di Stefano, A. G., Ruta, M., & Masera, G. (2023). Advanced digital tools for data-informed and performance-driven design: A review of building energy consumption forecasting models based on machine learning. *Applied Sciences (Basel, Switzerland)*, 13(24), 12981. DOI: 10.3390/app132412981

Di Vaio, A., Hassan, R., & Alavoine, C. (2022). Data intelligence and analytics: A bibliometric analysis of human–artificial intelligence in public sector decision-making effectiveness. *Technological Forecasting and Social Change*, 174, 121201. DOI: 10.1016/j.techfore.2021.121201

Dicheva, D., Dichev, C., Agre, G., & Angelova, G. (2015). Gamification in education: A systematic mapping study. *Journal of Educational Technology & Society*, 18(3), 75–88. https://www.jstor.org/stable/jeductechsoci.18.3.75

Dick, M. (2014). Interactive infographics and news values. *Digital Journalism (Abingdon, England)*, 2(4), 490–506. DOI: 10.1080/21670811.2013.841368

Dix, A., Finlay, J., Abowd, G., & Beale, R. (2004). *Human-computer interaction* (3rd ed.). Pearson.

Djaouti, D., Alvarez, J., & Jessel, J. P. (2011). Classifying serious games: the G/P/S model. In *Handbook of research on improving learning and motivation through educational games: Multidisciplinary approaches* (pp. 118–136). IGI global., DOI: 10.4018/978-1-60960-495-0.ch006

Donasco, A., & Oliveros, S. T. R. (2024). AI's impact on educational leadership and learning. [IMJRISE]. *International Multidisciplinary Journal of Research for Innovation, Sustainability, and Excellence*, 1(8), 228–236.

Downes, S. (2005). E-learning 2.0. *eLearn,* 4-7.

Dugosija, T. (2024). Benefits and challenges of artificial intelligence in English language teaching. *Knowledge International Journal*, 62(2), 275–280.

Dunn, R., & Dunn, K. (1978). *Teaching students through their individual learning styles: A practical approach.* Allyn& Bacon.

Dynamic Language. (2023). The Role of Localization in Education: Bridging Cultural and Linguistic Gaps. Retrieved from https://www.dynamiclanguage.com/the-role-of-localization-in-education-bridging-cultural-and-linguistic-gaps

Effendi, M. S.. (2017). English as a second language learning and grammar accuracy: A case study. *Journal of Language Teaching and Research*, 8(4), 52–58.

Ekman, P., & Whitaker, J. (2020). Digital transformation of global business processes: The role of dual embeddedness. *Business Process Management Journal*, 26(2), 570–592. DOI: 10.1108/BPMJ-02-2019-0080

Ellis, R. (1994). *The Study of Second Language Acquisition.* Oxford University Press.

Ellis, R. (2019). *Understanding Second Language Acquisition.* Oxford University Press.

Emad, E. G. (2011). *Rethinking adult and vocational education: hauling in from maritime domain.* PhD Thesis, University of Victoria. http://hdl.handle.net/1828/3285

Emeru, G. M. (2023). Effect of Public Expenditure on Economic Growth in the Case of Ethiopia, The Scientific World Journal, vol. 2023. *TheScientificWorldJournal*, 9305196, 14. DOI: 10.1155/2023/9305196

Evans, K. H., Daines, W., Tsui, J., Strehlow, M., Maggio, P., & Shieh, L. (2015). Septris: A novel, mobile, online, simulation game that improves sepsis recognition and management. *Academic Medicine*, 90(2), 180–184. DOI: 10.1097/ACM.0000000000000611 PMID: 25517703

Eze, S. C., Chinedu-Eze, V. C. A., Okike, C. K., & Bello, A. O. (2020). Factors influencing the use of e-learning facilities by students in a private Higher Education Institution (HEI) in a developing economy. *Humanities & Social Sciences Communications*, 7(1), 133. DOI: 10.1057/s41599-020-00624-6

Fadzil, H. M. (2018a). Designing infographics for the educational technology course: Perspectives of pre-service science teachers. *Journal of Baltic Science Education*, 17(1), 8–18. DOI: 10.33225/jbse/18.17.08

Felder, R. M., & Silverman, L. K. (1988). Learning and teaching styles in engineering education. *Engineering Education*, 78(7), 674–681.

Fernando, P., & Rajapakshe, D. (2018). *Redefining FDI-Growth Relationship under Liberalized Economic Policies Empirical Evidence from Sri Lanka*. 20–39.

Fiellin, L. E., Hieftje, K. D., Pendergrass, T. M., Kyriakides, T. C., Duncan, L. R., Dziura, J. D., Sawyer, B. G., Mayes, L., Crusto, C. A., Forsyth, B. W. C., & Fiellin, D. A. (2017). Video game intervention for sexual risk reduction in minority adolescents: Randomized controlled trial. *Journal of Medical Internet Research*, 19(9), e314. DOI: 10.2196/jmir.8148 PMID: 28923788

Fischer, E., & Guzel, G. T. (2022). The case for qualitative research. *Journal of Consumer Psychology*, 33(1), 259–272. DOI: 10.1002/jcpy.1300

Fischer, G., & Lindberg, J. O. (2020). Rethinking and reinventing learning, education and collaboration in the digital age-from creating technologies to transforming cultures. *International Journal of Information and Learning Technology*, 37(5), 241–252. DOI: 10.1108/IJILT-04-2020-0051

Fithriani, R. (2018). Communicative game-based learning in EFL grammar class: Suggested activities and students' perception. [Journal of English Education and Linguistics Studies]. *JEELS*, 5(2), 171–188. DOI: 10.30762/jeels.v5i2.509

Fjeld, G. P., Tvedt, S. D., & Oltedal, H. (2018). Bridge officers' non-technical skills: A literature review. *WMU Journal of Maritime Affairs*, 17(4), 475–495. DOI: 10.1007/s13437-018-0158-z

Fleming, N. D. (2001). Teaching and learning styles: VARK strategies. *The International Journal of Innovation in Education*, 1(1), 1–6.

Fleming, N. D., & Mills, C. (1992). Not another inventory, rather a catalyst for reflection. *To Improve the Academy*, 11(1), 137–155. DOI: 10.1002/j.2334-4822.1992.tb00213.x

Flores-Vivar, J. M., & García-Peñalvo, F. J. (2023). Reflections on the ethics, potential, and challenges of artificial intelligence in the framework of quality education (SDG4). *Comunicar*, 31(72), 37–47. DOI: 10.3916/C74-2023-03

Fokides, E. (2018). Digital educational games and mathematics. Results of a case study in primary school settings. *Education and Information Technologies*, 23(2), 851–867. DOI: 10.1007/s10639-017-9639-5

Foo, Y. S., Chin, L., Chen, K. S., & Allayarov, P. (2023, December 21). Digitalization, globalization and economic growth: A panel analysis using GMM. *Proceedings of the 7th International Conference on Future Networks and Distributed Systems*. Presented at the ICFNDS '23: The International Conference on Future Networks and Distributed Systems, Dubai United Arab Emirates. https://doi.org/ DOI: 10.1145/3644713.3644790

Fotiadis, A. K., & Sigala, M. (2015). Developing a framework for designing an Events Management Training Simulation (EMTS). *Journal of Hospitality, Leisure, Sport and Tourism Education*, 16, 59–71. DOI: 10.1016/j.jhlste.2015.03.001

Frank, M. R., Autor, D., Bessen, J. E., Brynjolfsson, E., Cebrian, M., Deming, D. J., & Wang, D. (2019). Toward understanding the impact of artificial intelligence on labor. *Proceedings of the National Academy of Sciences of the United States of America*, 116(14), 6531–6539. DOI: 10.1073/pnas.1900949116 PMID: 30910965

Freina, L., & Ott, M. (2015). Augmented reality and virtual reality in education: A review of the literature. *European Journal of Contemporary Education*, 4(3), 80–92.

Frydenberg, M. (2016). *Technology for teaching and learning: Strategies for improving classroom practice*. Springer.

Fu, K., Hainey, T., & Baxter, G. (2016, October). A systematic literature review to identify empirical evidence on the use of computer games in business education and training. In *European Conference on Games Based Learning* (p. 232). Academic Conferences International Limited.

Fullan, M., Azorín, C., Harris, A., & Jones, M. (2024). Artificial intelligence and school leadership: Challenges, opportunities and implications. *School Leadership & Management*, 44(4), 339–346. DOI: 10.1080/13632434.2023.2246856

Gallagher, S., O'Dulain, M., O'Mahony, N., Kehoe, C., McCarthy, F., & Morgan, G. (2017). Instructor-provided summary infographics to support online learning. *Educational Media International*, 54(2), 129–147. DOI: 10.1080/09523987.2017.1362795

García Botero, G., Questier, F., & Zhu, C. (2018). Self-directed language learning in a mobile-assisted, out-of-class context: Do students walk the talk? *Computer Assisted Language Learning*, 31(2), 162–185. DOI: 10.1080/09588221.2017.1375903

García, J., García-Sánchez, J. N., & García-Sánchez, E. (2020). Augmented Reality in Education: A Systematic Review of the Literature. *Interactive Learning Environments*, 28(3), 331–346.

Gardner, D., & Davies, M. (2007). Pointing out frequent phrasal verbs: A corpus-based analysis. *TESOL Quarterly*, 41(2), 339–359. DOI: 10.1002/j.1545-7249.2007.tb00062.x

Gardner, H. (1983). *Frames of mind: The theory of multiple intelligences*. Basic Books.

Garrido-Iñigo, P., & Rodríguez-Moreno, F. (2015). The reality of virtual worlds: Pros and cons of their application to foreign language teaching. *Interactive Learning Environments*, 23(4), 453–470. DOI: 10.1080/10494820.2013.788034

Garrison, D. R. (2011). *E-Learning in the 21st Century: A Framework for Research and Practice* (2nd ed.). Routledge. DOI: 10.4324/9780203838761

Gayanti, R., & Satriani, I. (2020). Teaching students' vocabulary through total physical response. [Professional Journal of English Education]. *PROJECT*, 3(3), 414–419. DOI: 10.22460/project.v3i3.p414-419

Ghamrawi, N. (2024). Educational Leadership in the Age of Artificial Intelligence: Are We Ready? The 8th Annual International Educational Conference: (Visions and Ideas for Hot Issues in education in the Arab Education: reality challenges and future prospects, 18-41. Hargreaves, S. (2023). "Words are flowing out like endless rain into a paper cup": ChatGPT & law school assessments. *Legal Education Review, 33*, 69.

Gleason, A. W. (2015). RELM: Developing a serious game to teach evidence-based medicine in an academic health sciences setting. *Medical Reference Services Quarterly*, 34(1), 17–28. DOI: 10.1080/02763869.2015.986709 PMID: 25611438

Gomez, M. J., Ruipérez-Valiente, J. A., & Clemente, F. J. G. (2022). A systematic literature review of game-based assessment studies: Trends and challenges. *IEEE Transactions on Learning Technologies*, 16(4), 500–515. DOI: 10.1109/TLT.2022.3226661

Gonzalez-Pardo, A., Rosa, A., & Camacho, D. (2014). Behaviour-based identification of student communities in virtual worlds. *Computer Science and Information Systems*, 11(1), 195–213. DOI: 10.2298/CSIS130214003G

Gover, G. B. (2017). Teacher Thoughts on Infographics as Alternative Assessment: A Post-Secondary Educational Exploration. (Unpublished Doctoral Dissertation), Eastern Kentucky University, USA.

Granger, S. (1998). *Learner English on Computer*. Longman.

Gray, S. I., Robertson, J., Manches, A., & Rajendran, G. (2019). BrainQuest: The use of motivational design theories to create a cognitive training game supporting hot executive function. *International Journal of Human-Computer Studies*, 127, 124–149. DOI: 10.1016/j.ijhcs.2018.08.004

Grech, A., & Camilleri, A. F. (2017). *Blockchain in Education. Joint Research Centre (JRC) Science for Policy Report*. European Commission.

Grigg, R. (2021). EntreCompEdu, a professional development framework for entrepreneurial education. *Education + Training*, 63(7/8), 1058–1072. DOI: 10.1108/ET-06-2020-0166

Guardian Nigeria. (2024, May 07). Nigeria needs more Public Private Partnerships for Digital Economy, Says U.S. Retrieved from https://guardian.ng/news/nigeria-needs-more-public-private-partnership-for-digital-economy-says-u-s/

Guay, F., Ratelle, C. F., Roy, A., & Litalien, D. (2010). Academic self-concept, autonomous academic motivation, and academic achievement: Mediating and additive effects. *Learning and Individual Differences*, 20(6), 644–653. DOI: 10.1016/j.lindif.2010.08.001

Guilherme, A. (2019). AI and education: The importance of teacher and student relations. *AI & Society*, 34(1), 47–54. DOI: 10.1007/s00146-017-0693-8

Gull, M., & Sridadi, A. R. (2024). Resilient higher educational institutions in a world of digital transformation. *Foresight*, 26(5), 755–774. DOI: 10.1108/FS-12-2022-0186

Guo, J., Bai, L., Yu, Z., Zhao, Z., & Wan, B. (2021). An AI-application-oriented in-class teaching evaluation model by using statistical modeling and ensemble learning. *Sensors (Basel)*, 21(1), 241. Advance online publication. DOI: 10.3390/s21010241 PMID: 33401482

Guo, K., Li, Y., Li, Y., & Chu, S. K. W. (2024). Understanding EFL students' chatbot-assisted argumentative writing: An activity theory perspective. *Education and Information Technologies*, 29(1), 1–20. DOI: 10.1007/s10639-023-12230-5

Gurbuz, S. C. (2021). A conceptual approach for design and development of serious game in maritime domain [Unpublished Doctoral Dissertation Progress Report-1].Istanbul Technical University, İstanbul, Turkiye.

Gurbuz, S. C., & Celik, M. (2022). Serious games in future skills development: A systematic review of the design approaches. *Computer Applications in Engineering Education*, 30(5), 1591–1612. DOI: 10.1002/cae.22557

Hagberg, A. A., Schult, D. A., & Swart, P. J. (2008). Exploring network structure, dynamics, and function using NetworkX. *Proceedings of the 7th Python in Science Conference (SciPy2008)*, 11-15. DOI: 10.25080/TCWV9851

Halliday, M. A. K., & Matthiessen, C. M. I. M. (2014). *Halliday's Introduction to Functional Grammar*. Routledge. DOI: 10.4324/9780203783771

Hamari, J., & Sjöblom, M. (2017). What is eSports and why do people watch it? *Internet Research*, 27(2), 211–232. DOI: 10.1108/IntR-04-2016-0085

Hamka, M. (2022). Digital resilience: Opportunities and threats for adolescents in a virtual world [AIM]. *Acta Informatica Malaysia*, 6(2), 67–71. DOI: 10.26480/aim.02.2022.67.71

Hao, X., Li, Y., Ren, S., Wu, H., & Hao, Y. (2023). The role of digitalization on green economic growth: Does industrial structure optimization and green innovation matter? *Journal of Environmental Management, 325*(Pt A), 116504. https://doi.org/ DOI: 10.1016/j.jenvman.2022.116504

Harmer, J. (2007). How to teach English (New ed.). Pearson Education Limited.

Harris, A., & Jones, M. (2023). Compassionate leadership. *School Leadership & Management*, 43(3), 185–188. DOI: 10.1080/13632434.2023.2235540

Haruna, H., Zainuddin, Z., Mellecker, R. R., Chu, S. K., & Hu, X. (2019). An iterative process for developing digital gamified sexual health education for adolescent students in low-tech settings. *Information and Learning Science*, 120(11), 723–742. Advance online publication. DOI: 10.1108/ILS-07-2019-0066

Hasan, A., & Wagner, A. (1996). The school of the future. *International Journal of Emerging Technologies in Learning*, 18(199), 6–9. DOI: 10.3991/ijet.v18i09.38133

Hassan, A. (2022). The influence of artificial intelligence on smart learning: An overview. In *Technologies, artificial intelligence and the future of learning post-COVID-19: The crucial role of international accreditation* (pp. 591-615).

Hassan, H. G. (2016). Designing Infographics to support teaching complex science subject: A comparison between static and animation Infographics. (Mater thesis), Iowa State University Ames, Iowa.

Hejres, S. (2022). The impact of artificial intelligence on instructional leadership. In *Technologies, artificial intelligence and the future of learning post-COVID-19: The crucial role of international accreditation* (pp. 697–711). Springer International Publishing. DOI: 10.1007/978-3-030-93921-2_36

Henderson, K., & Loreau, M. (2023). A model of Sustainable Development Goals: Challenges and opportunities in promoting human well-being and environmental sustainability. *Ecological Modelling*, 475, 110164. DOI: 10.1016/j.ecolmodel.2022.110164

Hendrix, M., Bellamy-Wood, T., McKay, S., Bloom, V., & Dunwell, I. (2018). Implementing adaptive game difficulty balancing in serious games. *IEEE Transactions on Games*, 11(4), 320–327. DOI: 10.1109/TG.2018.2791019

He, Z., & Bilgihan, A. (2023). Building organizational resilience with digital transformation. *Journal of Service Management*, 34(1), 147–171. DOI: 10.1108/JOSM-06-2021-0216

Hickmann, T., Biermann, F., Spinazzola, M., Ballard, C., Bogers, M., Forestier, O., Kalfagianni, A., Kim, R. E., Montesano, F. S., Peek, T., Sénit, C.-A., van Driel, M., Vijge, M. J., & Yunita, A. (2023). Success factors of global goal-setting for sustainable development: Learning from the Millennium Development Goals. *Sustainable Development (Bradford)*, 31(6), 1214–1225. DOI: 10.1002/sd.2461

Hilas, C. S., & Politis, A. (2014). Motivating students' participation in a computer networks course by means of magic, drama and games. *SpringerPlus*, 3(1), 362. DOI: 10.1186/2193-1801-3-362 PMID: 25105085

Hodges, C., Moore, S., Lockee, B., Trust, T., & Bond, A. (2020). The difference between emergency remote teaching and online learning. Educause Review. https://er.educause.edu/articles/2020/3/the-difference-between-emergency-remote-teaching-and-online-learning

Hoffmann, T., & Trousdale, G. (Eds.). (2013). *The Oxford Handbook of Construction Grammar*. Oxford University Press. DOI: 10.1093/oxfordhb/9780195396683.001.0001

Holmes, W., Bialik, M., & Fadel, C. (2019). *Artificial intelligence in education: Promise and implications for teaching and learning*. Center for Curriculum Redesign.

Holmes, W., Bialik, M., & Fadel, C. (2019). *Artificial intelligence in education: Promises and implications for teaching and learning*. Center for Curriculum Redesign.

Holmes, W., & Tuomi, I. (2022). State of the art and practice in AI in education. *European Journal of Education*, 57(4), 542–570. DOI: 10.1111/ejed.12533

Honey, P., & Mumford, A. (2000). *The learning styles helper's guide*. Peter Honey Publications.

Hooi, L. W., & Chan, A. J. (2023). Does workplace digitalization matter in linking transformational leadership and innovative culture to employee engagement? *Journal of Organizational Change Management*, 36(2), 197–216. DOI: 10.1108/JOCM-06-2022-0184

Hopcan, S., Türkmen, G., & Polat, E. (2024). Exploring the artificial intelligence anxiety and machine learning attitudes of teacher candidates. *Education and Information Technologies*, 29(6), 7281–7301. DOI: 10.1007/s10639-023-12086-9

Hopfenbeck, T. N., Zhang, Z., Sun, S. Z., Robertson, P., & McGrane, J. A. (2023). Challenges and opportunities for classroom-based formative assessment and AI: A perspective article. *Frontiers in Education*, 8, 1–9. DOI: 10.3389/feduc.2023.1270700

Hunter, D., & Werbach, K. (2012). *For the win* (Vol. 2). Philadelphia, PA, USA: Wharton digital press.

Hutson, J., Plate, D., & Berry, K. (2024). Embracing AI in English Composition: Insights and Innovations in Hybrid Pedagogical Practices. *International Journal of Changes in Education*, 1(1), 19–31. DOI: 10.47852/bonviewIJCE42022290

Hwang, G. J., & Chang, C. Y. (2023). A review of opportunities and challenges of chatbots in education. *Interactive Learning Environments*, 31(7), 4099–4112. DOI: 10.1080/10494820.2021.1952615

Hwang, G. J., Xie, H., Wah, B. W., & Gašević, D. (2020). Examining the impact of learning analytics and AI on education: A systematic review. *Computers & Education*, 151, 103896. DOI: 10.1016/j.compedu.2020.103896

Hyland, K. (2000). *Disciplinary Discourses: Social Interactions in Academic Writing*. Longman.

ICS (International Chamber of Shipping). (2020). *Annual Review 2020.* International Chamber of Shipping. Retrieved April 18 2021, from https://www.ics-shipping.org/wp-content/uploads/2020/11/annual-review-2020-final-compressed.pdf

Ihsan, S. N., Kadir, T. A. A., Benedict, R., & Abdullah, A. R. (2020, February). Preventive Self-Care Serious Games for Diabetes: A Game Design. In *IOP Conference Series: Materials Science and Engineering* (Vol. 769, No. 1, p. 012058). IOP Publishing. https://iopscience.iop.org/article/10.1088/1757-899X/769/1/012058/meta

Ingkavara, T., Panjaburee, P., Srisawasdi, N., & Sajjapanroj, S. (2022). The use of a personalized learning approach to implementing self-regulated online learning. *Computers & Education: Artificial Intelligence*, 3, 100086.

Isensee, C., & Griese, K. M. (2023). Success factors of organizational resilience: A qualitative investigation of four types of sustainable digital entrepreneurs. *Management Decision*, 61(5), 1244–1273. DOI: 10.1108/MD-03-2022-0326

Islamoglu, H., Ay, O., Ilic, U., Mercimek, B., Donmez, P., Kuzu, A., & Odabasi, F. (2015). Infographics: A new competency area for teacher candidates. *Cypriot Journal of Educational Sciences*, 10(1), 32–39.

Jaramillo, M. G., Dávila, A. M., & Jarquín, E. V. E. (2020). English as a Lingua Franca: Perspectives from International MA TESOL Students in the United States. *Universal Journal of Educational Research*, 8(4), 1605–1619. DOI: 10.13189/ujer.2020.080454

Järvelä, S., Nguyen, A., & Hadwin, A. (2023). Human and artificial intelligence collaboration for socially shared regulation in learning. *British Journal of Educational Technology*, 54(5), 1057–1076. DOI: 10.1111/bjet.13325

Jiang, J. (2017). *A Surface-based Volume Haptics Approach and Applications in Surgical Simulation*. Doctoral dissertation, University of Illinois at Chicago. Published by ProQuest LLC. https://0-www-proquest-com.divit.library.itu.edu.tr/pqdtglobal/docview/2026669493/C1DC4247FD6D4386PQ/12?accountid=11638

Johnson, D., Horton, E., Mulcahy, R., & Foth, M. (2017). Gamification and serious games within the domain of domestic energy consumption: A systematic review. *Renewable & Sustainable Energy Reviews*, 73, 249–264. DOI: 10.1016/j.rser.2017.01.134

Jonassen, D. (1999). Designing constructivist learning environments. In Reigeluth, C. (Ed.), *Instructional-design theories and models: A new paradigm of instructional theory* (pp. 215–239). Pennsylvania State University., https://scirp.org/reference/referencespapers.aspx?referenceid=800372

Joshi, S., Rambola, R. K., & Churi, P. (2021). Evaluating artificial intelligence in education for next generation. *Journal of Physics: Conference Series*, 1714(1), 012039. Advance online publication. DOI: 10.1088/1742-6596/1714/1/012039

Kabuga, N. A. (2015). Government Spending on Education and Economic Growth in Nigeria: An Empirical Investigation. [KAJEST]. *Kano Journal of Educational Studies*, 4(3), 225–236.

Kachru, B. B. (1983). *The Indianization of English: The English Language in India*. Oxford University Press.

Kamalov, F., Santandreu, C. D., & Gurrib, I. (2023). New era of artificial intelligence in education: Towards a sustainable multifaceted revolution. *Sustainability (Basel)*, 15(16), 12451. DOI: 10.3390/su151612451

Kannan, J., & Munday, P. (2018). New trends in second language learning and teaching through the lens of ICT, networked learning, and artificial intelligence. *Círculo de Lingüística Aplicada a la Comunicación*, 76, 13–30. DOI: 10.5209/CLAC.62495

Kapralos, B., Fisher, S., Clarkson, J., & van Oostveen, R. (2015). A course on serious game design and development using an online problem-based learning approach. *Interactive Technology and Smart Education*, 12(2), 116–136. DOI: 10.1108/ITSE-10-2014-0033

Kasowaki, L., & Deniz, B. (2024). *Revolutionizing big data: AI algorithms and predictive analytics (No. 11685)*. EasyChair.

Katsantonis, N. M., Kotini, I., Fouliras, P., & Mavridis, I. (2019, April). Conceptual framework for developing cyber security serious games. In *2019 IEEE Global Engineering Education Conference (EDUCON)* (pp. 872-881). IEEE. DOI: 10.1109/EDUCON.2019.8725061

Kaur, J., Lavuri, R., Parida, R., & Singh, S. V. (2023). Exploring the impact of gamification elements in brand apps on the purchase intention of consumers. *Journal of Global Information Management*, 31(1), 1–30. DOI: 10.4018/JGIM.317216

Kearns, L. R. (2012). Student assessment in online learning: Challenges and effective practices. *Journal of Online Learning and Teaching*, 8(3), 198–208. https://jolt.merlot.org/vol8no3/kearns_0912.pdf

Kebritchi, M., Lipschuetz, A., & Santiague, L. (2017). Issues and challenges for teaching successful online courses in higher education: A literature review. *Journal of Educational Technology Systems*, 46(1), 4–29. DOI: 10.1177/0047239516661713

Kemelbekova, Z., Degtyareva, X., Yessenaman, S., Ismailova, D., & Seidaliyeva, G. (2024). AI in teaching English as a foreign language: Effectiveness and prospects in Kazakh higher education. *XLinguae*, 17(1), 69–83. DOI: 10.18355/XL.2024.17.01.05

Khan, M. A., Merabet, A., Alkaabi, S., & Sayed, H. E. (2022). Game-based learning platform to enhance cybersecurity education. *Education and Information Technologies*, 27(4), 1–25. DOI: 10.1007/s10639-021-10807-6

Khurana, V. (2024). Accelerating pace of scientific discovery and innovation through big data-enabled artificial intelligence and deep learning. *Emerging Trends in Machine Intelligence and Big Data*, 16(1), 38–53.

Kian, T., Yusoff, W., & Rajah, S. (2014). Motivation for generations' cohorts: An organizational justice perspective. *International Journal of Management Sciences*, 11(2), 536–542.

Kimmons, R. (2018). *Technology integration and teacher education: Social practices and the sociocultural challenges of integrating technology in classrooms*. Springer.

Kim, T. E., & Gausdal, A. H. (2020). Leaders' influence tactics for safety: An exploratory study in the maritime context. *Safety (Basel, Switzerland)*, 6(1), 8. DOI: 10.3390/safety6010008

Kim, T. E., & Mallam, S. (2020). A Delphi-AHP study on STCW leadership competence in the age of autonomous maritime operations. *WMU Journal of Maritime Affairs*, 19(2), 163–181. DOI: 10.1007/s13437-020-00203-1

Kim, T. E., Nazir, S., & Øvergård, K. I. (2016). A STAMP-based causal analysis of the Korean Sewol ferry accident. *Safety Science*, 83, 93–101. DOI: 10.1016/j.ssci.2015.11.014

Kipf, T. N., & Welling, M. (2016). Semi-Supervised Classification with Graph Convolutional Networks. arXiv preprint arXiv:1609.02907.

Kitada, M., Baldauf, M., Mannov, A., Svendsen, P. A., Baumler, R., Schröder-Hinrichs, J. U., & Lagdami, K. (2018, July). Command of vessels in the era of digitalization. In *International Conference on Applied Human Factors and Ergonomics* (pp. 339-350). Springer, Cham.

Klami, A., Damoulas, T., Engkvist, O., Rinke, P., & Kaski, S. (2024). Virtual laboratories: Transforming research with AI. *Data-Centric Engineering*, 5, e19. DOI: 10.1017/dce.2024.15

Knowles, M. S. (1980). *The modern practice of adult education: From pedagogy to andragogy*. Cambridge Adult Education.

Ko, A., & Szabó, Z. (2022). Influencing factors of digital transformation: Management or IT is the driving force? *International Journal of Innovation Science*, 14(1), 1–20. DOI: 10.1108/IJIS-01-2021-0007

Kolb, D. A. (1984). *Experience as the source of learning and development. Upper Sadle River*. Prentice Hall., DOI: 10.1016/B978-0-7506-7223-8.50017-4

Kolb, D. A. (1984). *Experiential learning: Experience as the source of learning and development*. Prentice Hall.

Kolić-Vehovec, S., Smojver-Ažić, S., Martinac Dorčić, T., & Rončević Zubković, B. (2020). Evaluation of serious game for changing students' behaviour in bullying situation. *Journal of Computer Assisted Learning*, 36(3), 323–334. DOI: 10.1111/jcal.12402

Korhonen, T., Halonen, R., Ravelin, T., Kemppainen, J., & Koskela, K. (2017, September). A Multidisciplinary Approach To Serious Game Development In The Health Sector. In *MCIS* (p. 30).

Koupritzioti, D., & Xinogalos, S. (2020). PyDiophantus maze game: Play it to learn mathematics or implement it to learn game programming in Python. *Education and Information Technologies*, 25(4), 2747–2764. DOI: 10.1007/s10639-019-10087-1

Kraft, C., & Peter, M. K. (2022). The digital transformation of Swiss small and medium-sized enterprises: Insights from digital tool adoption. *Journal of Strategy and Management*, 15(3), 468–494. DOI: 10.1108/JSMA-02-2021-0063

Krath, J., Schürmann, L., & Von Korflesch, H. F. (2021). Revealing the theoretical basis of gamification: A systematic review and analysis of theory in research on gamification, serious games and game-based learning. *Computers in Human Behavior*, 125, 106963. DOI: 10.1016/j.chb.2021.106963

Kruyen, P. M., & Helderman, J.-K. (2020). Searching for the renaissance bureaucrat: A longitudinal computer-assisted study of personality traits in government vacancies. *International Journal of Public Sector Management*, 33(1), 22–44. DOI: 10.1108/IJPSM-07-2019-0195

Kumar, M., & Jamil, M. (2016). Enhanced learning using motion graphics in higher education. Paper presented at the International Technology, Education and Development Conference, Spain. DOI: 10.21125/iceri.2016.0157

Kumar, N., & Chaudhary, P. (2019). The Relationship between Education Expenditure and Economic Growth in India. *J. Adv. Res. Appl. Math. Stat. 2016, 1*(2), 119–123.

Kumari, R. K. (2025). The Lasting Legacy of Educators: Stories and Strategies from Former Teachers. In Former Educators' Roles in Supporting Student Growth and Learning (pp. 28). IGI Global. https://doi.org/DOI: 10.4018/979-8-3693-6427-7.ch006

Kumari, R. K. (2025). Artificial Intelligence in Special Education: Enhancing Learning Outcomes for Students With Disabilities. In Walters, A. G. (Ed.), *Transforming Special Education Through Artificial Intelligence* (pp. 79–112). IGI Global., DOI: 10.4018/979-8-3693-5538-1.ch003

Kumari, R. K. (2025). Crafting an Effective Research Proposal. In Mdikana, A. A. (Ed.), *Enhancing Research Output in Higher Education: Research Proposals, Profiles, and Publishing* (pp. 291–320). IGI Global., DOI: 10.4018/979-8-3373-0806-7.ch012

Kumar, V., & Pereira, V. (2023). Modelling and analysing the enablers of digital resilience for small and medium enterprises. *Journal of Enterprise Information Management*. Advance online publication. DOI: 10.1108/JEIM-01-2023-0002

Kurkan, G., & Çetin, M. (2024). The perceptions of educational administrators towards digital leadership in the age of artificial intelligence: A qualitative study. *International Journal of Contemporary Educational Research*, 11(3), 425–439. DOI: 10.52380/ijcer.2024.11.3.602

Kvale, S., & Brinkmann, S. (2009). *InterViews: Learning the craft of qualitative research interviewing*. Sage Publications.

Lagos State Government. (2016). Lagos State Employment Trust Fund (LSETF). Retrieved from https://lsetf.ng/content/employability

Laily, F. N., Suparno, S., & Ngadiso, N. (2023). Classroom-based assessment practices during the Covid-19 outbreak in Indonesia: EFL students' perceptions and challenges. *VELES: Voices of English Language Education.*

Lajoie, S. P., & Azevedo, R. (2019). The role of self-regulation in learning with metacognitive tools. *Educational Psychologist*, 54(4), 322–335. DOI: 10.1080/00461520.2019.1631423

Landers, R. N., & Sanchez, D. R. (2022). Game-based, gamified, and gamefully designed assessments for employee selection: Definitions, distinctions, design, and validation. *International Journal of Selection and Assessment*, 30(1), 1–13. DOI: 10.1111/ijsa.12376

Lankow, J., Ritchie, J., & Crooks, R. (2012). *Infographics: The power of visual storytelling. Chicago/Turabian*. John Wiley and Sons.

Laporte, L., & Zaman, B. (2018). A comparative analysis of programming games, looking through the lens of an instructional design model and a game attributes taxonomy. *Entertainment Computing*, 25, 48–61. DOI: 10.1016/j.entcom.2017.12.005

Lee, E.-J., & Kim, Y. W. (2016). Effects of infographics on news elaboration, acquisition, and evaluation: Prior knowledge and issue involvement as moderators. *New Media & Society*, 18(8), 1579–1598. DOI: 10.1177/1461444814567982

Lee, J. (2020). Problem-based gaming via an augmented reality mobile game and a printed game in foreign language education. *Education and Information Technologies*, •••, 1–29.

Lee, S. M., & Park, M. (2020). Reconceptualization of the context in language learning with a location-based AR app. *Computer Assisted Language Learning*, 33(8), 936–959. DOI: 10.1080/09588221.2019.1602545

Legard, R., Keegan, J., & Ward, K. (2003). In-depth Interviews. In J. Richie & J. Lewis (Eds.), *Qualitative Research Practice* (pp. 139–168). Sage Publications.

Levy, R. (2019). Dynamic Bayesian network modeling of game-based diagnostic assessments. *Multivariate Behavioral Research*, 54(6), 771–794. DOI: 10.1080/00273171.2019.1590794 PMID: 30942094

Lewin, P. M. E. (2015). *Training effectiveness in maritime transport*. Master's thesis, Buskerud and Vestfold University College. https://openarchive.usn.no/usn-xmlui/handle/11250/1558681

Li, C., Liu, D., & Xu, S. (2021). Implementing flipped classroom model in English language course: A meta-analysis. *Education and Information Technologies*, 26(4), 4819–4842.

Li, F. (2020). Leading digital transformation: Three emerging approaches for managing the transition. *International Journal of Operations & Production Management*, 40(6), 809–817. DOI: 10.1108/IJOPM-04-2020-0202

Li, J., Greenwood, D., & Kassem, M. (2020). Blockchain in the built environment and property industry: A review of the use-cases in research. *Automation in Construction*, 119, 103–133.

Lin, L.-C. (2012). *Measuring adult learners' foreign language anxiety, motivational factors, and achievement expectations: a comparative study between Chinese as a second-language students and English as a second-language students. (Doctoral Dessertation)*. Cleveland State University.

Liu, Y., Guo, M., & Wang, T. (2024). Effects of digital orientation on organizational resilience: A dynamic capabilities perspective. *Journal of Manufacturing Technology Management*, 35(2), 268–290. DOI: 10.1108/JMTM-06-2023-0224

Liu, Z., Yang, C., Rüdiän, S., Liu, S., Zhao, L., & Wang, T. (2019).. . *Interactive Learning Environments*, •••, 1–30.

Li, Z., & Hegelheimer, V. (2013). Mobile-assisted grammar exercises: Effects on self-editing in L2 writing. *Language Learning & Technology*, 17(3), 135–156.

Long, P. D., Siemens, G., Conole, G., & Gašević, D. 2011. International Conference Proceeding Series (ICPS). Proc. 1st International Conference on Learning Analytics and Knowledge (LAK'11), NY, USA: ACM.

Loon, M., Evans, J., & Kerridge, C. (2015). Learning with a strategic management simulation game: A case study. *International Journal of Management Education*, 13(3), 227–236. DOI: 10.1016/j.ijme.2015.06.002

Löytömäki, J., Ohtonen, P., & Huttunen, K. (2024). Serious game the Emotion Detectives helps to improve social–emotional skills of children with neurodevelopmental disorders. *British Journal of Educational Technology*, 55(3), 1126–1144. DOI: 10.1111/bjet.13420

Luo, Z. (2024). The Application of Artificial Intelligence Technology in Music Education. *Lecture Notes in Education Psychology and Public Media*, 35(1), 305–310. DOI: 10.54254/2753-7048/35/20232155

Luu, T. M. V. (2022). Readiness for online learning: Learners' comfort and self-directed learning ability. *International Journal of TESOL & Education*, 2(1), 213–224. DOI: 10.54855/ijte.222113

Machmud, K. (2018). The smartphone use in Indonesian schools: The high school students' perspectives. *Journal of Arts and Humanities*, 7(3), 33–40. DOI: 10.18533/journal.v7i3.1354

Maher, M. (2022). Inflation and Education Expenditure: Evidence from Egypt. *Journal of Economics and Sustainable Development*, 13(4), 71–82. DOI: 10.7176/JESD/13-4-07

Majeed, A., & Hwang, S. O. (2021). Data-driven analytics leveraging artificial intelligence in the era of COVID-19: An insightful review of recent developments. *Symmetry*, 14(1), 16. DOI: 10.3390/sym14010016

Mallam, S. C., Nazir, S., & Renganayagalu, S. K. (2019). Rethinking maritime education, training, and operations in the digital era: Applications for emerging immersive technologies. *Journal of Marine Science and Engineering*, 7(12), 428. DOI: 10.3390/jmse7120428

Maneejuk, P., & Yamaka, W. (2021). The Impact of Higher Education on Economic Growth in ASEAN-5 Countries. *Sustainability (Basel)*, 13(2), 520. DOI: 10.3390/su13020520

Manning, C. D., Surdeanu, M., Bauer, J., Finkel, J., Bethard, S., & McClosky, D. (2014). The Stanford CoreNLP natural language processing toolkit. *Proceedings of 52nd Annual Meeting of the Association for Computational Linguistics: System Demonstrations*, 55-60. DOI: 10.3115/v1/P14-5010

Manuel, M. E. (2017). Vocational and academic approaches to maritime education and training (MET): Trends, challenges and opportunities. *WMU Journal of Maritime Affairs*, 16(3), 473–483. DOI: 10.1007/s13437-017-0130-3

Margoudi, M., Oliveira, M., & Waddell, G. (2016, October). Game-based learning of musical instruments: A review and recommendations. In *European Conference on Games Based Learning* (p. 426). Academic Conferences International Limited.

Martin, L., & Tapp, D. (2019). Teaching with Teams: An introduction to teaching an undergraduate law module using Microsoft Teams. *Innovative Practice in Higher Education*, 3(3), 58–66.

Martix, S., & Hodson, J. (2014). Teaching with infographics: practising new digital competencies and visual literacies. Journal of pedagogic development,4 (2).

Massaro, M. (2020). The challenges of digital transformation in healthcare: Aninter disciplinary literature review, framework, and future research agenda, volume 123. https://www.sciencedirect.com/science/article/abs/pii/S0166497223000275

Mattalo, B. (2024). Artificial Intelligence: The Future of Pedagogy. *Journal of Legal Studies Education*, 41(1), 49–71. DOI: 10.1111/jlse.12146

Matthew, N. O., Philip, O. A., & Sarhan, M. M. (2018). Online teaching and learning. *International Journal of Advanced Research in Computer Science and Software Engineering*, 8(2), 73–75. DOI: 10.23956/ijarcsse.v8i2.549

Mazhari, S. (2018). *Competency of Merchant Ship Officers in the Global Shipping Labour Market: A Study of the 'Knowing-Doing' Gap*. Doctoral dissertation, Cardiff University. Cardiff University Dissertation Archieve https://orca.cardiff.ac.uk/109737/2/Shahriar%20Mazhari%20Final%20PhD%20Thesis.pdf

Mbulawa, S., & Mehta, P. (2016). The Effect of Access and Quality of Education on Economic Development in Botswana. *International Journal of Business. Economics and Management*, 3(11), 144–159. DOI: 10.18488/journal.62/2016.3.11/62.11.144.159

McCarthy, B. (1987). *The 4MAT system: Teaching to learning styles with right/left mode techniques*. Exposition Press.

McEnery, T., & Wilson, A. (2001). *Corpus Linguistics: An Introduction*. Edinburgh University Press.

McMurtrie, B. (2020). The agile college: How institutions are adapting to a new era. *The Chronicle of Higher Education*.

Means, B., Bakia, M., & Murphy, R. (2014). *Learning Online: What Research Tells Us About Whether, When and How*. Routledge. DOI: 10.4324/9780203095959

Meirelles, I. (2013). *Design for information: an introduction to the histories, theories, and best practices behind effective information visualizations*. Rockport publishers.

Mendhe, D., Dogra, A., Nair, P. S., Punitha, S., Preetha, K. S., & Babu, S. B. T. (2024, April). AI-enabled data-driven approaches for personalized medicine and healthcare analytics. In *2024 Ninth International Conference on Science Technology Engineering and Mathematics (ICONSTEM)* (pp. 1-5). IEEE. DOI: 10.1109/ICONSTEM60960.2024.10568722

Merriam, S. B., & Bierema, L. L. (2014). *Adult learning: Bridging theory and practice*. Jossey-Bass.

Merriam, S. B., & Tisdell, E. J. (2015). *Qualitative research: A guide to design and implementation*. John Wiley & Sons.

Meyer, C. F. (2002). *English Corpus Linguistics: An Introduction*. Cambridge University Press. DOI: 10.1017/CBO9780511606311

Miao, F., Holmes, W., Huang, R., & Zhang, H. (2023). *AI and education : Guidance for policymakers*. UNESCO. https://discovery.ucl.ac.uk/id/eprint/10130180/1/Miao and Holmes - 2021 - AI and education guidance for policy-makers.pdf

Michailidis, T., Meadow, G., Barlow, C., & Rajabally, E. (2020, September). Implementing remote audio as a diagnostics tool for maritime autonomous surface ships. In *2020 27th Conference of Open Innovations Association (FRUCT)* (pp. 157-163). IEEE. DOI: 10.23919/FRUCT49677.2020.9211029

Microsoft Teams. (2020, August 26). In *Wikipedia*.https://en.wikipedia.org/wiki/Microsoft_Teams

Mihalcea, R., & Radev, D. (2011). *Graph-based Natural Language Processing and Information Retrieval*. Cambridge University Press. DOI: 10.1017/CBO9780511976247

Miles, M. B., & Huberman, A. M. (1994). *An Expanded Sourcebook: Qualitative Data Analysis* (2nd ed.). Sage Publications.

Miller, D. (2017). *Case study research: A guide for researchers and practitioners*. Cambridge University Press.

Milson, S., & Levent, K. (2024). Deep learning applications in big data: Expanding horizons with AI-driven solutions.

Milton, J., & Al-Busaidi, A. (2023). New role of leadership in the AI era: Educational sector. *SHS Web of Conferences*. https://doi.org/DOI: 10.1051/shsconf/202315609005

Mitchell, A., & Murphy, S. (2022). Unleashing the power of big data: A catalyst for advancements in artificial intelligence. *European Journal of Mechanical Engineering Research*, 9(1), 56–65.

Mitgutsch, K., & Alvarado, N. (2012, May). Purposeful by design? A serious game design assessment framework. In *Proceedings of the International Conference on the foundations of digital games* (pp. 121-128). DOI: 10.1145/2282338.2282364

Mohamad, U. H., Ahmad, M. N., Benferdia, Y., Shapi'i, A., & Bajuri, M. Y. (2021). An overview of ontologies in virtual reality-based training for healthcare domain. *Frontiers in Medicine*, 8, 698855. DOI: 10.3389/fmed.2021.698855 PMID: 34307424

Mohamed, M. Z. (2022). Artificial intelligence in mathematics education: A systematic literature review. *International Electronic Journal of Mathematics Education*, 17(3), em0694. Advance online publication. DOI: 10.29333/iejme/12132

Mohammad, A., & Mahjabeen, F. (2023). Revolutionizing solar energy with AI-driven enhancements in photovoltaic technology. *BULLET: Jurnal Multidisiplin Ilmu*, 2(4), 1174–1187.

Mohd Hussin, M. Y., & Muhammed, F. (2012). Education Expenditure and Economic Growth: A Causal Analysis for Malaysia. *Journal of Economics and Sustainable Development*, 3(7), 71–81.

Mohmmed, A. O., Khidhir, B. A., Nazeer, A., & Vijayan, V. J. (2020). Emergency remote teaching during coronavirus pandemic: The current trend and future directive at Middle East College Oman. *Innovative Infrastructure Solutions*, 5(3), 1–11. DOI: 10.1007/s41062-020-00326-7

Moinuddin, M., Usman, M., & Khan, R. (2024). Strategic insights in a data-driven era: Maximizing business potential with analytics and AI. *Revista Española de Documentación Cientifica*, 18(02), 125–149.

Mol, L. (2011). The potential role for infographics in science communication. (Master Thesis), Biomedical Sciences, Vrije University, Amsterdam, Netherlands.

Mollick, E. R., & Mollick, L. (2022). New modes of learning enabled by AI chatbots: Three methods and assignments. Available at *SSRN* 4300783. DOI: 10.2139/ssrn.4300783

Moncayo Cueva, H. L., Cuesta-Chávez, G., Ramírez, A., & Zambrano Pintado, R. N. (2024). Utilizing Emerging Technology Trends and Artificial Intelligence in Higher Education. *Journal of Higher Education Theory and Practice*, 24(3). Advance online publication. DOI: 10.33423/jhetp.v24i3.6847

Moon, R. (1998). *Fixed Expressions and Idioms in English: A Corpus-Based Approach*. Clarendon Press. DOI: 10.1093/oso/9780198236146.001.0001

Mora, A., Riera, D., González, C., & Arnedo-Moreno, J. (2017). Gamification: A systematic review of design frameworks. *Journal of Computing in Higher Education*, 29(3), 516–548. DOI: 10.1007/s12528-017-9150-4

Moulieswaran, N., & Kumar, P. N. S. (2023). Investigating ESL Learners' Perception and Problem towards Artificial Intelligence (AI) -Assisted English Language Learning and Teaching. *World Journal of English Language*, 13(5), 290–298. DOI: 10.5430/wjel.v13n5p290

Moussa, N., Bentoumi, R., & Saali, T. (2024). Promoting student success with neutrosophic sets: Artificial intelligence and student engagement in higher education context. *International Journal of Neutrosophic Science*, 23(1), 238–38. DOI: 10.54216/IJNS.230121

Mudulia, A. M. (2012). The relationship between availability of teaching/learning resources and performance in secondary school science subjects in Eldoret Municipality, Kenya. *Journal of Emerging Trends in Educational Research and Policy Studies*, 3(4), 530–536.

Mukhtarov, S., Mammadov, I., & Humbatova, S. (2020). The Relationship Between Government Expenditures on Education and Economic Growth: The Case of Azerbaijan. *Review of World Economics*, 11(1), 195. DOI: 10.5430/rwe.v11n1p195

Mulukuntla, S., & Gaddam, M. (2021). Data-driven healthcare: Trends in machine learning and AI for disease prediction and prevention. *ESP Journal of Engineering & Technology Advancements*, 1(1), 25–33.

Murawski, M., & Bick, M. (2017). Digital competences of the workforce - a research topic? *Business Process Management Journal*, 23(3), 721–734. DOI: 10.1108/BPMJ-06-2016-0126

Mutawa, A. M., & Sruthi, S. (2022). Students' perspective towards online proctoring in exams during COVID-19. *Journal of Engineering Research (Kuwait)*, 10(4), 96–113. DOI: 10.36909/jer.14749

Myers, I. B., & Myers, P. B. (1995). *Gifts differing: Understanding personality type*. Consulting Psychologists Press.

Nantwi, V. O. (2015). Education Expenditures and Economic Growth: Evidence from Ghana. *Journal of Economics and Sustainable Development*, 6(16), 69–77.

Naparin, H., & Saad, A. B. (2017). Infographics in education: Review on infographics design. [IJMA]. *The International Journal of Multimedia and Its Applications*, 9(4), 5. DOI: 10.5121/ijma.2017.9602

Naqvi, W. M., Sundus, H., Mishra, G., Muthukrishnan, R., & Kandakurti, P. K. (2024). AI in Medical Education Curriculum: The Future of Healthcare Learning. *European Journal of Therapeutics*, 30(2), e23–e25. DOI: 10.58600/eurjther1995

Navigli, R., & Lapata, M. (2010). An Experimental Study of Graph Connectivity for Unsupervised Word Sense Disambiguation. *IEEE Transactions on Pattern Analysis and Machine Intelligence*, 32(4), 678–692. DOI: 10.1109/TPAMI.2009.36 PMID: 20224123

Newman, M. E. J. (2010). *Networks: An Introduction*. Oxford University Press. DOI: 10.1093/acprof:oso/9780199206650.001.0001

Nguyen, A., Ngo, H. N., Hong, Y., Dang, B., & Nguyen, B. P. T. (2023). Ethical principles for artificial intelligence in education. *Education and Information Technologies*, 28(4), 4221–4241. DOI: 10.1007/s10639-022-11316-w PMID: 36254344

Nikitakos, N., Sirris, I., Dalaklis, D., Papachristos, D., & Tsoukalas, V. D. (2017). Game-based learning for maritime education and training: The case of Trader of the World. *WMU Journal of Maritime Affairs*, 16(2), 265–291. DOI: 10.1007/s13437-016-0119-3

Ninduwezuor-Ehiobu, N., Tula, O. A., Daraojimba, C., Ofonagoro, K. A., Ogunjobi, O. A., Gidiagba, J. O., & Banso, A. A. (2023). Tracing the evolution of AI and machine learning applications in advancing materials discovery and production processes. *Engineering Science & Technology Journal*, 4(3), 66–83. DOI: 10.51594/estj.v4i3.552

Ning, K. (2021). Data driven artificial intelligence techniques in renewable energy system (Doctoral dissertation, Massachusetts Institute of Technology).

Nugroho, A., Andriyanti, E., Widodo, P., & Mutiaraningrum, I. (2024). Students' appraisals post-ChatGPT use: Students' narrative after using ChatGPT for writing. *Innovations in Education and Teaching International*, •••, 1–13. DOI: 10.1080/14703297.2024.2319184

Nursalim, A., Judijanto, L., & Asfahani, A. (2022). Educational revolution through the application of AI in the digital era. *Journal of Artificial Intelligence and Development*, 1(1), 31–40.

Nuţă, A. C. C.. (2023). The Impact of Public Education Spending on Economic Growth in Central and Eastern Europe. An ARDL Approach with Structural Break. *Economic Research-Ekonomska Istraživanja*, 36(1), 1261–1278. DOI: 10.1080/1331677X.2022.2086147

Obi, Zita C., Ogugua, C., & Ejefobihi, U. (2020). The efficiency of Education Expenditure in Nigeria. *European Journal of Education Studies*, 7(1), 423–447. DOI: 10.5281/zenodo.3748101

Ogata, H., Flanagan, B., Takami, K., Dai, Y., Nakamoto, R., Takii, K. (2024). EXAIT: Educational eXplainable Artificial Intelligent Tools for personalized learning. *Research and Practice in Technology Enhanced Learning, 19*, 019.

Ohalete, N. C., Aderibigbe, A. O., Ani, E. C., Ohenhen, P. E., & Akinoso, A. E. (2023). Data science in energy consumption analysis: A review of AI techniques in identifying patterns and efficiency opportunities. *Engineering Science & Technology Journal*, 4(6), 357–380. DOI: 10.51594/estj.v4i6.637

Okerekeoti, C. U. (2022). Government Expenditure on Education and Economic growth in Nigeria. [IJRRCEM]. *International Journal of Recent Research in Commerce Economics and Management*, 9(2), 126–134. DOI: 10.5281/zenodo.6656411

Okwuduba, E. N., & Okigbo, E. C. (2018). Effect of teaching methods on students' academic performance in chemistry in Nigeria: Meta-analytic review. *Bulgarian Journal of Science and Education Policy*, 12(2), 418–434.

Olanrewaju, F. O., Aluko, O. E., & Akinola, O. R. (2023). Integrating digital technologies in entrepreneurship education: The Nigerian experience. *Journal of Entrepreneurship and Innovation in Emerging Economies*, 9(4), 351–367.

Oloyede, A. A., Faruk, N., Noma, N., Tebepah, E., & Nwaulune, A. K. (2023). Measuring the impact of the digital economy in developing countries: A systematic review and meta- analysis. *Heliyon*, 9(7), e17654. DOI: 10.1016/j.heliyon.2023.e17654 PMID: 37501966

Oluwakemi, O. T. (2019). Digital literacy and entrepreneurial returns among small business owners in Lagos State, Nigeria. *Education & Science Journal of Policy Review and Curriculum Development*, 9(2), 1–11.

Osba, S. (2015). Impact of using Infographics strategy on academic achievement among fifth grade female students and their attitudes and motivation towards learning science. (Unpublished Master thesis), Alnajah University, Nablus.

Othman, I. W., Mokhtar, S., Tham, A., & Yong, K. (2021). The Significance of Entrepreneurship Education Literacy in the Era of Digital Transformation: Graduates of the Post-Pandemic Covid-19 Unemployment Crisis. *The International Journal of Accounting*, 6(37).

Ouyang, F., & Jiao, P. (2021). Artificial intelligence in education: The three paradigms. *Computers and Education: Artificial Intelligence*, 2(April), 1–6. DOI: 10.1016/j.caeai.2021.100020

Oyeleke, O., & Adeyemi, A. (2023). The impact of digital literacy on rural communities in Nigeria: A case study of the Digital Access Program. *Journal of Digital Education and Technology*, 15(2), 75–88.

Ozdal, H., & Ozdamli, F. (2017). The Effect of Infographics in Mobile Learning: Case Study in Primary School. *J. UCS*, 23(12), 1256–1275.

Ozdamli, F., & Ozdal, H. (2018). Developing an Instructional Design for the Design of Infographics and the Evaluation of Infographic Usage in Teaching Based on Teacher and Student Opinions. *Eurasia Journal of Mathematics, Science and Technology Education*, 14(4), 1197–1219. DOI: 10.29333/ejmste/81868

Ozgen, E. (2022). Digital Technologies for Discovering Opportunities in Entrepreneurship Education: Future Trends. *Journal of International Business Disciplines*, 17(1).

Palmer, M. (2006). *Data is the new oil*. ANA Marketing Maestros.

Papadimitriou, I., Gialampoukidis, I., Vrochidis, S., & Kompatsiaris, I. (2024). AI methods in materials design, discovery and manufacturing: A review. *Computational Materials Science*, 235, 112793. DOI: 10.1016/j.commatsci.2024.112793

Papa, R., & Jackson, K. M. (Eds.). (2021). *Artificial intelligence, human agency and the educational leader*. Springer Nature. DOI: 10.1007/978-3-030-77610-7

Pask, G. (1975). *Conversation theory: Applications in education and epistemology*. Elsevier.

Patel, K., Beeram, D., Ramamurthy, P., Garg, P., & Kumar, S. (2024). AI-enhanced design: Revolutionizing methodologies and workflows. [IJAIRD]. *International Journal of Artificial Intelligence Research and Development*, 2(1), 135–157.

Patton, M. Q. (1990). *Qualitative Evaluation and Research Methods* (2nd ed.). Sage Publications.

Pellas, N., Fotaris, P., Kazanidis, I., & Wells, D. (2019). Augmenting the learning experience in primary and secondary school education: A systematic review of recent trends in augmented reality game-based learning. *Virtual Reality (Waltham Cross)*, 23(4), 329–346. DOI: 10.1007/s10055-018-0347-2

Permatasari, A., & Anggadwita, G. (2019). Digital entrepreneurship education in emerging countries: Opportunities and challenges. Opening up education for inclusivity across digital economies and societies, 156-169.

Peters, D. (2014). *Interface design for learning: Design strategies for learning experiences*. Pearson Education.

Petri, G., & von Wangenheim, C. G. (2017). How games for computing education are evaluated? A systematic literature review. *Computers & Education*, 107, 68–90. DOI: 10.1016/j.compedu.2017.01.004

Pham, M. T., Luu, T. T. U., Mai, T. H. U., Thai, T. T. T., & Ngo, T. C. T. (2022). EFL students' challenges of online courses at Van Lang University during the COVID-19 pandemic. *International Journal of TESOL & Education*, 2(2), 1–26. DOI: 10.54855/ijte.22221

Pham, V. P. H., & Vo, N. D. T. (2021). CALL in Asia during COVID-19 and models of e-learning. In *Proceedings of the 17th International Conference of the Asia Association of Computer-Assisted Language Learning (AsiaCALL 2021)* (Vol. 533, pp. 1-10). https://doi.org/DOI: 10.2991/assehr.k.210226.001

Philbin-Briscoe, O., Simon, B., Mudur, S., Poullis, C., Rizvic, S., Boskovic, D., . . . Skarlatos, D. (2017, September). A serious game for understanding ancient seafaring in the Mediterranean sea. In *2017 9th international conference on virtual worlds and games for serious applications (VS-games)* (pp. 1-5). IEEE. DOI: 10.1109/VS-GAMES.2017.8055804

Piaget, J. (1976). Piaget's theory. In Greenfield, P. M., & Cocking, R. R. (Eds.), *Cross-cultural roots of minority child development* (pp. 24–43). Academic Press.

Plotzky, C., Lindwedel, U., Bejan, A., König, P., & Kunze, C. (2021). Virtual reality in healthcare skills training: The effects of presence on acceptance and increase of knowledge. *I-Com*, 20(1), 73–83. DOI: 10.1515/icom-2021-0008

Pokhrel, S., & Khadka, C. B. (2019). Assessment of Long and Short Run Relationship Amongst Macroeconomic Variables and Economic Growth of Nepal. *Economic Jornal of Development Issues(2019), 27 & 28*(1). https://doi.org/DOI: 10.3126/ejdi.v28i1-2.33196

Pooja, G. (2017). Study the Effect of Teaching Method on the Academic Achievement of School Going Childern of Semiurban Area, S Schools of Luckynow City. *International Journal of Home Science*, 3(2), 447–453.

Poullis, C., Kersten-Oertel, M., Benjamin, J. P., Philbin-Briscoe, O., Simon, B., Perissiou, D., Demesticha, S., Markou, E., Frentzos, E., Kyriakidis, P., Skarlatos, D., & Rizvic, S. (2019). Evaluation of "The Seafarers": A serious game on seaborne trade in the Mediterranean sea during the Classical period. *Digital Applications in Archaeology and Cultural Heritage*, 12, e00090. DOI: 10.1016/j.daach.2019.e00090

Pradana, M., Elisa, H. P., & Syarifuddin, S. (2023). Discussing ChatGPT in education: A literature review and bibliometric analysis. *Cogent Education*, 10(2), 2243134. DOI: 10.1080/2331186X.2023.2243134

Prince, N. U., Faheem, M. A., Khan, O. U., Hossain, K., Alkhayyat, A., Hamdache, A., & Elmouki, I. (2024). AI-powered data-driven cybersecurity techniques: Boosting threat identification and reaction. *Nanotechnology Perceptions*, •••, 332–353.

Pruyn, J. (2023). The use of digital games in academic maritime education: A theoretical framework and practical applications. *Maritime Policy & Management*, •••, 1–14.

Pulse Nigeria. (2023, September 1). LSETF: Empowering Nigerian Youth with Digital Skills. Retrieved from https://www.pulse.ng/

Ractham, P., & Firpo, D. (2011). Using social networking technology to enhance learning in higher education: A case study using Facebook. Paper presented at the 2011 44th Hawaii International Conference on System Sciences, USA. DOI: 10.1109/HICSS.2011.479

Rahiman, H. U., & Kodikal, R. (2024). Revolutionizing education: Artificial intelligence empowered learning in higher education. *Cogent Education*, 11(1), 2293431. DOI: 10.1080/2331186X.2023.2293431

Raimo, N., De Turi, I., Ricciardelli, A., & Vitolla, F. (2022). Digitalization in the cultural industry: Evidence from Italian museums. *International Journal of Entrepreneurial Behaviour & Research*, 28(8), 1962–1974. DOI: 10.1108/IJEBR-01-2021-0082

Rao, M. S. (2014). Enhancing employability in engineering and management students through soft skills. *Industrial and Commercial Training*, 46(1), 42–48. DOI: 10.1108/ICT-04-2013-0023

Rausch, A. (2023). Informal learning from dealing with software-related problems in the digital workplace. *Journal of Workplace Learning*, 35(9), 291–310. DOI: 10.1108/JWL-03-2023-0042

Rawas, S. (2023). ChatGPT: Empowering lifelong learning in the digital age of higher education. *Education and Information Technologies*, 29(5), 6895–6908.

Rebolledo Font de la Vall, R., & González Araya, F. (2023). Exploring the benefits and challenges of AI-language learning tools. *International Journal of Social Sciences and Humanities Invention*, 10(1), 7569–7576. DOI: 10.18535/ijsshi/v10i01.02

Reid, J. M. (1987). The learning style preferences of ESL students. *TESOL Quarterly*, 21(1), 87–111. DOI: 10.2307/3586356

Research, I. C. T. Africa. (2023). After Access 2023: Digital Nigeria Post the Pandemic. Retrieved from https://researchictafrica.net

Rezaei, N., & Sayadian, S. (2015). The impact of infographics on Iranian EFL learners' grammar learning. *Journal of Applied Linguistics and Language Research*, 2(1), 78–85.

Ribble, M. (2015). *Digital citizenship in schools: Nine elements all students should know. International Society for Technology in Education*. ISTE.

Riding, R., & Rayner, S. (1998). *Cognitive styles and learning strategies: Understanding style differences in learning and behaviour*. David Fulton Publishers.

Rippa, P., & Secundo, G. (2019). Digital academic entrepreneurship: The potential of digital technologies on academic entrepreneurship. *Technological Forecasting and Social Change*, 146, 900–911. DOI: 10.1016/j.techfore.2018.07.013

Roll, I., & Wylie, R. (2016). Evolution and revolution in artificial intelligence in education. *International Journal of Artificial Intelligence in Education*, 26(2), 582–599. DOI: 10.1007/s40593-016-0110-3

Romero Rodríguez, L. (2022). Engaging future engineers: The case study of a serious game implementation. *Education and Information Technologies*, •••, 1–31.

Rossini, M., Cifone, F. D., Kassem, B., Costa, F., & Portioli-Staudacher, A. (2021). Being lean: How to shape digital transformation in the manufacturing sector. *Journal of Manufacturing Technology Management*, 32(9), 239–259. DOI: 10.1108/JMTM-12-2020-0467

Rosvall, M., & Bergstrom, C. T. (2008). Maps of random walks on complex networks reveal community structure. *Proceedings of the National Academy of Sciences of the United States of America*, 105(4), 1118–1123. DOI: 10.1073/pnas.0706851105 PMID: 18216267

Roulston, K. (2023). *Interviews in education research.* Sage Publications.

Rueda, R. A. S. (2015). Use of infographics in virtual environments for personal learning process on Boolean algebra. *Vivat Academia*, (130), 64–74. DOI: 10.15178/va.2015.130.64-74

Ryan, R. M., & Deci, E. L. (2017). *Self-determination theory: Basic psychological needs in motivation, development, and wellness.* Guilford Publications., DOI: 10.1521/978.14625/28806

Sağın, F. G., Özkaya, A. B., Tengiz, F., Geyik, Ö. G., & Geyik, C. (2024). Current evaluation and recommendations for the use of artificial intelligence tools in education. *Türk Biyokimya Dergisi*, 48(6), 620–625. DOI: 10.1515/tjb-2023-0254

Sandelowski, M. (1995). Sample size in qualitative research. *Research in Nursing & Health*, 18(2), 179–183. DOI: 10.1002/nur.4770180211 PMID: 7899572

Sardi, L., Idri, A., & Fernández-Alemán, J. L. (2017). A systematic review of gamification in e-Health. *Journal of Biomedical Informatics*, 71, 31–48. DOI: 10.1016/j.jbi.2017.05.011 PMID: 28536062

Sari, T., Nayír, F., & Bozkurt, A.SARI. (2024). Reimagining education: Bridging artificial intelligence, transhumanism, and critical pedagogy. *Journal of Educational Technology and Online Learning*, 7(1), 102–115. Advance online publication. DOI: 10.31681/jetol.1308022

Sartini, S. (2020). Kahoot in Maritime English Teaching: Its Impact on Nautical Science Cadet's Oral Reproduction and Vocabulary. *English Language Teaching Educational Journal*, 3(1), 41–51. DOI: 10.12928/eltej.v3i1.1667

Sasmal, S. (2023). Next-gen data engineering: The AI revolution.

Schiff, D. (2022). Education for AI, not AI for education: The role of education and ethics in national AI policy strategies. *International Journal of Artificial Intelligence in Education*, 32(3), 527–563. DOI: 10.1007/s40593-021-00270-2

Schiff, D. S. (2023). Looking through a policy window with tinted glasses: Setting the agenda for US AI policy. *The Review of Policy Research*, 40(5), 729–756. DOI: 10.1111/ropr.12535

Schneider, W., & Pressley, M. (1989). *Memory development between two and twenty*. Springer-Verlag. DOI: 10.1007/978-1-4613-9717-5

Schrock, K. (2014). Infographics as a creative assessment. Retrieved from https://home.edweb.net/infographics-as-a-creative-assessment/, June, 2019.

Schroeder, K. T., Hubertz, M., Van Campenhout, R., & Johnson, B. G. (2022). Teaching and Learning with AI-Generated Courseware: Lessons from the Classroom. *Online Learning : the Official Journal of the Online Learning Consortium*, 26(3), 73–87. DOI: 10.24059/olj.v26i3.3370

Sellberg, C., Lindmark, O., & Lundin, M. (2019). Certifying navigational skills: A video-based study on assessments in simulated environments. *TransNav: International Journal on Marine Navigation and Safety of Sea Transportation*, 13(4), 881–886. DOI: 10.12716/1001.13.04.23

Serrano, J. P., Moreno-Guerrero, A. J., & Torres-Gordillo, J. J. (2021). The effect of interactive learning environments on improving learning outcomes in higher education. *Journal of Educational Computing Research*, 59(4), 643–667. DOI: 10.1177/0735633120984630

Shaltout, M., & Fatani, H. (2017). Impact of two different infographics types "interactivestatic" on developing mathematical concepts among female students at second grade intermediate in the Kingdom of Saudi Arabia. *International Journal of Research and Reviews in Education*, 4, 1–8.

Sharifuddin, N. S., & Hashim, H. (2024). Benefits and Challenges in Implementing Artificial Intelligence in Education (AIED) in ESL Classroom: A Systematic Review (2019-2022). *International Journal of Academic Research in Business & Social Sciences*, 14(1), 1–19. DOI: 10.6007/IJARBSS/v14-i1/20422

Sharma, A., Kim, T. E., & Nazir, S. (2021). Implications of Automation and Digitalization for Maritime Education and Training. In *Sustainability in the Maritime Domain* (pp. 223–233). Springer., DOI: 10.1007/978-3-030-69325-1_11

Silva, F. G. (2020). Practical methodology for the design of educational serious games. *Information (Basel)*, 11(1), 1–13. DOI: 10.3390/info11010014

Sinclair, J. (1991). *Corpus, Concordance, Collocation*. Oxford University Press.

Singh, N., & Jain, N. (2017). Effects of infographic designing on image processing ability and achievement motivation of dyscalculic students. Paper presented at the Proceedings of the International Conference for Young Researchers in Informatics, Mathematics and Engineering. Kaunas, Lithuania.

Singh, A., Kanaujia, A., Singh, V. K., & Vinuesa, R. (2024). Artificial intelligence for Sustainable Development Goals: Bibliometric patterns and concept evolution trajectories. *Sustainable Development (Bradford)*, 32(1), 1–31. DOI: 10.1002/sd.2706

Sousa-Zomer, T. T., & Martinez, V. (2020). Digital transforming capability and performance: A micro foundational perspective. *International Journal of Operations & Production Management*, 40(7/8), 1095–1128. DOI: 10.1108/IJOPM-06-2019-0444

Stecuła, K., & Wolniak, R. (2022). Advantages and disadvantages of e-learning innovations during COVID-19 pandemic in higher education in Poland. *Journal of Open Innovation*, 8(3), 159–180. DOI: 10.3390/joitmc8030159

Steenbeek, J., Romagnoni, G., Bentley, J., Heymans, J. J., Serpetti, N., Gonçalves, M., Santos, C., Warmelink, H., Mayer, I., Keijser, X., Fairgrieve, R., & Abspoel, L. (2020). Combining ecosystem modeling with serious gaming in support of transboundary maritime spatial planning. *Ecology and Society*, 25(2), art21. DOI: 10.5751/ES-11580-250221

Stojanovic, V., Falconer, R., Isaacs, J., Gilmour, D., & Blackwood, D. (2013). Interactive visualisation to support sustainability assessment in land use scenario planning. Proceedings of the 29th Annual ARCOM Conference (S. D. Smith and D. D. Ahiaga-Dagbui eds.), Association of Researchers in Construction Management, Reading, UK, 2- 4 September 2013, pp. 1373-1382.

Storyals. (2020, March). What is Microsoft Teams. *Storyals.*https://storyals.com/blog/what-is-microsoft-teams

Stubbs, M. (2001). *Words and Phrases: Corpus Studies of Lexical Semantics.* Blackwell Publishers.

Su, J., & Yang, W. (2023). A systematic review of integrating computational thinking in early childhood education. *Computers and Education Open*, 4(100122), 1–12. DOI: 10.1016/j.caeo.2023.100122

Su, J., & Zhong, Y. (2022). Artificial Intelligence (AI) in early childhood education: Curriculum design and future directions. *Computers and Education: Artificial Intelligence*, 3(100072), 1–12. DOI: 10.1016/j.caeai.2022.100072

Suwandru, A., Alghamdi, T., & Nurwantu, N. (2021). Empirical Analysis on Public Expenditure for Education and Economic Growth: Evidence from Indonesia. *Economies*, 9(4), 146. DOI: 10.3390/economies9040146

Swan, M., & Widdowson, H. G. (2005). *Grammar.* Oxford University Press.

Sweller, J. (1988). Cognitive load during problem solving: Effects on learning. *Cognitive Science*, 12(2), 257–285. DOI: 10.1207/s15516709cog1202_4

Sysoyev, P. V. (2023). Artificial Intelligence in Education: Awareness, Readiness and Practice of Using Artificial Intelligence Technologies in Professional Activities by University Faculty. *Vysshee Obrazovanie v Rossii = Higher Education in Russia, 32*(10), 9–33. DOI: 10.31992/0869-3617-2023-32-10-9-33

Ta'amneh, M. (2014). The effect of using educational websites on first year students' achievement in English grammar in Badr community college. *Journal of Emerging Trends in Educational Research and Policy Studies*, 5(2), 184–189.

Tahiru, F. (2021). AI in education: A systematic literature review. *Journal of Cases on Information Technology*, 23(1), 1–20. DOI: 10.4018/JCIT.2021010101

Tamang, P. (2011). The Impact of Education Expenditure on India's Economic Growth. *Journal of International Academic Research*, 11(3), 14–21.

Tang, J., Qu, M., Wang, M., Zhang, M., Yan, J., & Mei, Q. (2015). LINE: Large-scale Information Network Embedding. *Proceedings of the 24th International Conference on World Wide Web*, 1067-1077. DOI: 10.1145/2736277.2741093

Tariq, M. U. (2024). Harnessing Persuasive Technologies for Enhanced Learner Engagement and Motivation. In M. Sanmugam, D. Lim, N. Mohd Barkhaya, W. Wan Yahaya, & Z. Khlaif (Eds.), *Power of Persuasive Educational Technologies in Enhancing Learning* (pp. 30-62). IGI Global. https://doi.org/DOI: 10.4018/979-8-3693-6397-3.ch002

Tariq, M. U. (2024). Generative AI in Curriculum Development in Higher Education. In Fields, Z. (Ed.), *Impacts of Generative AI on Creativity in Higher Education* (pp. 227–258). IGI Global., DOI: 10.4018/979-8-3693-2418-9.ch009

Tariq, M. U. (2024). Navigating the Personalization Pathway: Implementing Adaptive Learning Technologies in Higher Education. In Minh Tung, T. (Ed.), *Adaptive Learning Technologies for Higher Education* (pp. 265–291). IGI Global., DOI: 10.4018/979-8-3693-3641-0.ch012

Tariq, M. U. (2025). *AI-Driven Learning and Engagement in Higher Education*. IGI Global., DOI: 10.4018/979-8-3693-4074-5

Tariq, M. U. (2025). The Belmont Report: Guiding Ethical Principles in Human Research. In Throne, R. (Ed.), *IRB, Human Research Protections, and Data Ethics for Researchers* (pp. 245–268). IGI Global Scientific Publishing., DOI: 10.4018/979-8-3693-3848-3.ch010

Tariq, M. U., & Sergio, R. P. (2025). Nurturing Digital Citizenship in Society 5.0 Through AI and Computational Intelligence Education. In Pandey, R., Srivastava, N., Prasad, R., Prasad, J., & Garcia, M. (Eds.), *Open AI and Computational Intelligence for Society 5.0* (pp. 59–84). IGI Global Scientific Publishing., DOI: 10.4018/979-8-3693-4326-5.ch003

Tayo, D. Lionel, Fouda, A., & Olivier, M. (2016). Government spending in education and economic growth in Cameroon. A Vector error Correction Model approach. *Munich Personal RePEc Archive*, 16 pages.

TechCabal. (2022, April 22). Lagos State Government Launches Digital Entrepreneurship Program for Youth. Retrieved from https://techcabal.com/

Tenhunen, M.-L. (2022). Digitalisation innovation in university education. In *Proceedings of the EL 2022 Proceedings* (pp. 85-92). Lisbon, Portugal. ISBN 978-989-8704-39-9

Teschner, J. (2016). *Serious Games in Medical Education: As Learning Tools*. Master's Thesis, University of Twente, Netherlands. https://purl.utwente.nl/essays/69684

Thomson, R., & Anderson, J. (2021). Bridging the gap: Big data's influence on AI algorithms and models. *EPH-International Journal of Science and Engineering*, 7(4), 52–56.

Tien, J. M. (2017). Internet of things, real-time decision making, and artificial intelligence. *Annals of Data Science*, 4(2), 149–178. DOI: 10.1007/s40745-017-0112-5

Timms, M. J. (2016). Letting artificial intelligence in education out of the box: Educational cobots and smart classrooms. *International Journal of Artificial Intelligence in Education*, 26(2), 701–712. DOI: 10.1007/s40593-016-0095-y

Tim, Y., Cui, L., & Sheng, Z. (2020). Digital resilience: How rural communities leapfrogged into sustainable development. *Information Systems Journal*, 31(2), 323–345. DOI: 10.1111/isj.12312

Tim, Y., & Leidner, D. E. (2023). Digital Resilience: A Conceptual Framework for Information Systems Research. *Journal of the Association for Information Systems*, 24(5), 1184–1198. DOI: 10.17705/1jais.00842

Torrente, J., Borro-Escribano, B., Freire, M., del Blanco, Á., Marchiori, E. J., Martínez-Ortiz, I., Moreno-Ger, P., & Fernández-Manjón, B. (2013). Development of game-like simulations for procedural knowledge in healthcare education. *IEEE Transactions on Learning Technologies*, 7(1), 69–82. DOI: 10.1109/TLT.2013.35

Towey, D., & Pike, M. (2021). Not a silver bullet, but a silver lining: Metamorphic marking administration. In *2021 IEEE Global Engineering Education Conference (EDUCON)* (pp. 928-935). Vienna, Austria. https://doi.org/DOI: 10.1109/EDUCON46332.2021.9454074

Trabelsi, S.SALWA TRABELSI. (2018, March). Public Education Spending and Economic Growth: The Governance Threshold Effect. *Journal of Economic Development*, 43(1), 99–122. DOI: 10.35866/caujed.2018.43.1.005

Tucker, C. R., & Beth, P. (2021). *The Shift to Digital Learning: The New Digital Divide in Education*. Solution Tree.

Turan, Z. (2015). The evaluation of flipped classroom method and examination of its effects on academic achievement, cognitive load and motivation. (Unpublished Doctoral dissertation). Atatürk University, Erzurum.

Türkistanli, T. T., & Kuleyin, B. (2022). Game-based learning for better decision-making: A collision prevention training for maritime transportation engineering students. *Computer Applications in Engineering Education*, 30(3), 917–933. DOI: 10.1002/cae.22494

Turner, P. E., Johnston, E., Kebritchi, M., Evans, S., & Heflich, D. A. (2018). Influence of online computer games on the academic achievement of non-traditional undergraduate students. *Cogent Education*, 5(1), 1437671. DOI: 10.1080/2331186X.2018.1437671

Udeozor, C., Russo Abegão, F., & Glassey, J. (2022). An evaluation of the relationship between perceptions and performance of students in a serious game. *Journal of Educational Computing Research*, 60(2), 322–351. DOI: 10.1177/07356331211036989

Ugwu, C. N., & Eze, H. U. (2023). Qualitative research. *IDOSR Journal of Computer and Applied Sciences*, 8(1), 20–35.

UNESCO. (2023). Bridging the Digital Divides. Retrieved from https://www.unesco.org

UNESCO. (2023). *Global Education Monitoring Report. Technology in Education: A Tool on Whose Terms?* UNESCO.

United Nations Development Programme. (2023). UNDP Nigeria. Retrieved from https://www.undp.org/nigeria

Unity Technologies. (2020). *Unity User Manual 2020.3 (LTS)*. Unity 3D Documentation. Retrieved February 23, 2021, from https://docs.unity3d.com/Manual/index.html

Usman, F. K., & Adeyinka, O. B. (2018). Effect of Human Capital Development on Economic Growth of Ecowas Member States. *Advances in Sciences and Humanities*, 5(1), 27–42. DOI: 10.11648/j.ash.20190501.14

Vaioleti, T. (2016). Talanoa: A transformative research method. *New Zealand Journal of Educational Studies*, 51(2), 191–202. DOI: 10.1007/s40841-016-0001-1

Van Quaquebeke, N., & Gerpott, F. H. (2023). The now, new, and next of digital leadership: How artificial intelligence (AI) will take over and change leadership as we know It. *Journal of Leadership & Organizational Studies*, 30(3), 265–275. DOI: 10.1177/15480518231181731

Vanichvasin, P. (2013). Enhancing the quality of learning through the use of infographics as visual communication tool and learning tool. Paper presented at the Proceedings ICQA 2013 international conference on QA culture: Cooperation or competition. Bangkok.

Vázquez-Cano, E. (2021). Artificial intelligence and education: A pedagogical challenge for the 21st century. In *Educational Process: International Journal* (Vol. 10, Issue 3, pp. 7–12). Universitepark. DOI: 10.22521/edupij.2021.103.1

Velickovic, P., Cucurull, G., Casanova, A., Romero, A., Lio, P., & Bengio, Y. (2018). Graph Attention Networks. arXiv preprint arXiv:1710.10903.

Veronica, R., & Calvano, G. (2020). Promoting sustainable behavior using serious games: Seadventure for ocean literacy. *IEEE Access : Practical Innovations, Open Solutions*, 8, 196931–196939. DOI: 10.1109/ACCESS.2020.3034438

Vygotsky, L. S. (1978). *Mind in society: The development of higher psychological processes*. Harvard University Press.

Wahab, F. K. (2019). Entrepreneurship Education as a Tool for Reducing Unemployment Rate among Secondary School Students, An unpublished Professional Diploma in Education Certificate Project Research, Kwara State College of Education, Ilorin. Available at https://doi.org/10.13140/RG.2.2.28659.71206

Wahab, F. K. (2022). Entrepreneurship: A Career Choice for Nigerian Youth. *FU-Lafia Journal for Entrepreneurial Development*, 2(1), 254–270.

Wang, F., & Hannafin, M. (2020). Design-based implementation research: An emerging model for transforming education. *Educational Technology Research and Development*, 68(1), 1–25. DOI: 10.1007/s11423-019-09714-1

Wang, F., & Hannafin, M. J. (2005). Design-based research and technology-enhanced learning environments. *Educational Technology Research and Development*, 53(4), 5–23. DOI: 10.1007/BF02504682

Wang, Q., & Abbas, M. (2018). Designing web-games for transportation engineering education. *Computer Applications in Engineering Education*, 26(5), 1699–1710. DOI: 10.1002/cae.22031

Wang, T., & Cheng, E. C. K. (2021). An investigation of barriers to Hong Kong K-12 schools incorporating Artificial Intelligence in education. *Computers and Education: Artificial Intelligence*, 2, 100031. Advance online publication. DOI: 10.1016/j.caeai.2021.100031

Wang, Y. (2021). When artificial intelligence meets educational leaders' data-informed decision-making: A cautionary tale. *Studies in Educational Evaluation*, 69, 100872. DOI: 10.1016/j.stueduc.2020.100872

WebManager.NG. (2023, June 22). Promoting ICT in Nigeria [Key Government Initiatives and Players. Retrieved from https://webmanager.ng/blog/promoting-ict-government-initiatives-players/]. *Discover*, 8.

WebManager.NG. (2023, June 28). ICT Policies and Regulations in Nigeria. Retrieved from https://webmanager.ng/blog/ict-policies-and-regulations-in-nigeria/#:~:text=Nigeria's%20National%20ICT%20Policy%20provides,growth%20of%20the%20ICT%20industry

Weng, J., & Li, G. (2019). Exploring shipping accident contributory factors using association rules. *Journal of Transportation Safety & Security*, 11(1), 36–57. DOI: 10.1080/19439962.2017.1341440

Westera, W., Prada, R., Mascarenhas, S., Santos, P. A., Dias, J., Guimarães, M., Georgiadis, K., Nyamsuren, E., Bahreini, K., Yumak, Z., Christyowidiasmoro, C., Dascalu, M., Gutu-Robu, G., & Ruseti, S. (2020). Artificial intelligence moving serious gaming: Presenting reusable game AI components. *Education and Information Technologies*, 25(1), 351–380. DOI: 10.1007/s10639-019-09968-2

Wibowo, D. C., Friana, F., & Pelipa, E. D. (2018). Effect of Recitation Method to the Students' Interest and Learning Results. Jurnal Studi Guru dan Pembelajaran, 1(1), 16-20.

Wood, D., Bruner, J. S., & Ross, G. (1976). The role of tutoring in problem solving. *Journal of Child Psychology and Psychiatry, and Allied Disciplines*, 17(2), 89–100. DOI: 10.1111/j.1469-7610.1976.tb00381.x PMID: 932126

World Economic Forum. (2023). How public-private cooperation can advance digital inclusion in the 'Global South'. Retrieved from https://www.weforum.org

Wu, W., & Kaushik, I. (2015, June). Design for aging with BIM and game engine integration. In *2015 ASEE Annual Conference & Exposition* (pp. 26-461). DOI: 10.18260/p.23799

Xiao, Y., Zhang, T., & He, J. (2024). The promises and challenges of AI-based chatbots in language education through the lens of learner emotions. *Heliyon*, 10(18), 1–14. DOI: 10.1016/j.heliyon.2024.e37238 PMID: 39309898

Xu, Z. (2024). AI in education: Enhancing learning experiences and student outcomes. *Applied Computational Engineering*, 51(1), 104–111. DOI: 10.54254/2755-2721/51/20241187

Yamin, M. (2019). Information Technologies of 21st century and their Impact on the Society. Int. j. inf. tecnol. **11**, 759–766. https://doi.org/DOI: 10.1186/s41239-019-0176-8

Yani, B. S. H. (2019). Developing students' critical thinking through assessing evidence by utilizing Microsoft Kaizala. In *Committee of the 16th Jeta International Conference 2019 Patron.*https://www.researchgate.net/publication/335824689_Adapting_Authentic_Texts_for_Reading_Material

Yap, W. L. (2016). Transforming conventional teaching classroom to learner-centred teaching classroom using multimedia-mediated learning module. *International Journal of Information and Education Technology (IJIET)*, 6(2), 105–112. DOI: 10.7763/IJIET.2016.V6.667

Yeh, H. C., & Tseng, S. S. (2020). Enhancing multimodal literacy using augmented reality.

Yetişensoy, O., & Karaduman, H. (2024). The effect of AI-powered chatbots in social studies education. *Education and Information Technologies*, 29(13), 17035–17069. Advance online publication. DOI: 10.1007/s10639-024-12485-6

Yıldırım, İ., & Şen, S. (2021). The effects of gamification on students' academic achievement: A meta-analysis study. *Interactive Learning Environments*, 29(8), 1301–1318. DOI: 10.1080/10494820.2019.1636089

Yildirim, S. (2016). Infographics for Educational Purposes: Their Structure, Properties and Reader Approaches. *Turkish Online Journal of Educational Technology-TOJET*, 15(3), 98–110.

Yue, M., Jong, M. S. Y., & Dai, Y. (2022). Pedagogical Design of K-12 Artificial Intelligence Education: A Systematic Review. In *Sustainability (Switzerland)* (Vol. 14, Issue 23, pp. 1–29). DOI: 10.3390/su142315620

Yu, Y., Li, G., & Weng, J. (2022). A three-step methodology to complement under-reporting maritime accident records. *Journal of Transportation Safety & Security*, 14(9), 1451–1469. DOI: 10.1080/19439962.2021.1928353

Zaid, A., & Milson, S. (2024). *Precision analytics: AI-driven solutions for big data challenges (No. 11895)*. EasyChair.

Zainuddin, Z., Shujahat, M., Haruna, H., & Chu, S. K. W. (2020). The role of gamified e-quizzes on student learning and engagement: An interactive gamification solution for a formative assessment system. *Computers & Education*, 145, 103729. DOI: 10.1016/j.compedu.2019.103729

Zarei, M., Eftekhari Mamaghani, H., Abbasi, A., & Hosseini, M. S. (2024). Application of artificial intelligence in medical education: A review of benefits, challenges, and solutions. *Medicina Clinica Practica*, 7(2), 7–11. DOI: 10.1016/j.mcpsp.2023.100422

Zawacki-Richter, O., Bai, J. Y. H., Lee, K., Slagter van Tryon, P. J., & Prinsloo, P. (2024). New advances in artificial intelligence applications in higher education? *International Journal of Educational Technology in Higher Education*, 21(32), 1–4. DOI: 10.1186/s41239-024-00464-3

Zawacki-Richter, O., Marín, V. I., Bond, M., & Gouverneur, F. (2019). Systematic review of research on artificial intelligence applications in higher education–where are the educators? *International Journal of Educational Technology in Higher Education*, 16(1), 39. DOI: 10.1186/s41239-019-0171-0

Zeira, J. (2018). Workers, machines, and economic growth. *The Quarterly Journal of Economics*, 113(4), 1091–1117. DOI: 10.1162/003355398555847

Zhai, X., Chu, X., Chai, C. S., Jong, M. S. Y., Istenic, A., Spector, M., Liu, J. B., Yuan, J., & Li, Y. (2021). A review of artificial intelligence (AI) in education from 2010 to 2020. *Complexity*, 2021(1), 8812542. DOI: 10.1155/2021/8812542

Zhang, B., & Mao, J. (2023, July). On the teaching and learning in the information age of "Big Data + Internet?"—Some thoughts on the application of ChatGPT in teaching. In *2023 2nd International Conference on Educational Innovation and Multimedia Technology (EIMT 2023)* (pp. 1005-1016). Atlantis Press.

Zhang, D., & Zhang, L. J. (2019). Metacognition and self-regulated learning (SRL) in second/foreign language teaching. In Gao, X. (Ed.), *Second Handbook of English Language Teaching* (pp. 883–897). Springer., DOI: 10.1007/978-3-030-02899-2_47

Zhang, R., & Zou, D. (2022). Self-regulated second language learning: A review of types and benefits of strategies, modes of teacher support, and pedagogical implications. *Computer Assisted Language Learning*, 37(4), 720–765. DOI: 10.1080/09588221.2022.2055081

Zhao, T., Wang, S., Ouyang, C., Chen, M., Liu, C., Zhang, J., & Wang, L. (2024). Artificial intelligence for geoscience: Progress, challenges and perspectives. *Innovation (Cambridge (Mass.))*, 5(5), 100691. DOI: 10.1016/j.xinn.2024.100691 PMID: 39285902

Zhao, X. (2023). The impact on higher education under COVID-19 pandemic prevention and control in China. *The International Conference on Interdisciplinary Humanities and Communication Studies, 7*, 226-232. https://doi.org/DOI: 10.54254/2753-7048/7/20220808

Zheng, Z., Xie, S., Dai, H., Chen, X., & Wang, H. (2020). An overview of blockchain technology: Architecture, consensus, and future trends. *IEEE International Conference on Big Data*, 1-12.

Zhou, J., Cui, G., Hu, S., Zhang, Z., Yang, C., Liu, Z., Wang, L., Li, C., & Sun, M. (2020). Graph Neural Networks: A Review of Methods and Applications. *AI Open*, 1, 57–81. DOI: 10.1016/j.aiopen.2021.01.001

Ziberi, B. F., Rexha, D., Ibraimi, X., & Avdiaj, B. (2022). Empirical Analysis of the Impact of Education on Economic Growth. *Economies*, 10(4), 89. DOI: 10.3390/economies10040089

Zulaikha, M. B., Azlin, N. M., Khairul, A. J., & Bity, S. A. (2021). The effectiveness and challenges of online learning for secondary school students – A case study. *Asian Journal of University Education*, 17(3), 119–129. DOI: 10.24191/ajue.v17i3.14514

Zull, J. E. (2002). *The art of changing the brain: Enriching the practice of teaching by exploring the biology of learning*. Stylus Publishing.

About the Contributors

Sadhik Basha J. obtained his Doctorate Degree in Mechanical Engineering at the National Institute of Technology, Trichy, India in the year 2011. He is currently working as a Professor & Head, National University of Science & Technology, IMCO, Sohar, Oman. Dr. Basha is an experienced educator and researcher for more than two decades. His current research interests include water-diesel/biodiesel emulsions as alternative fuels, thermal desalination, combustion modeling, spray combustion, nano-additive emulsion fuels, thermal sciences, and renewable energy. He has received various research supported & consultancy projects totaling over $1,00,000 in the fields of thermal desalination, waste plastic oil synthesis, alternative fuels, nano-additive fuel catalysts, renewable energy, etc. He is an expert referee, editorial board member, and advisory board member for more than fifty reputed international journals in the fields of energy, combustion, and power engineering. He has published ten patents and eighty research articles, and participated in several national and international conferences. He has been the chief editor for three books in the area of IC Engines, Digital Optimization, etc. Further, the contents of his research work have been cited more than two thousand times in various technical articles, magazines, and international journals. He has more than fifty professional memberships (such as Combustion Institute, USA; IFPASA, etc.). He is a Recipient of "Best Supervisor Award" by MEDRC & GPCA in the year 2021 & 2023 respectively, and "Best Researcher Award" by IMCO in the year 2021. He has won "Best Teaching Cash Awards" several times. He is one of the top 2% of the academically cited researchers as per the global Stanford University Ranking for the past three years (2022, 2023, 2024). Dr. Sadhik is currently working in the area of zero-emission techniques, CCUS, and thermal desalination techniques to produce potable water from waste heat recovery systems.

Taofeek Olanrewaju Alade is an esteemed Assistant Professor of Mathematics at the National University of Science and Technology, Oman. He obtained his BSc in

Mathematics from Ladoke Akintola University of Technology, Nigeria (2007), followed by an MSc in Mathematics from the University of Ibadan, Nigeria (2012). In recognition of his academic excellence, he was awarded a PhD scholarship at King Abdulaziz University, Saudi Arabia, where he earned his doctorate in Applied Mathematics (2019). With over a decade of teaching and research experience, Dr. Alade specializes in Mathematical Biology, Infectious Disease Modeling, Virus Dynamics, Optimal Control Theory, Computational Mathematics, Population Dynamics, and Nonlinear Dynamics. He has published extensively in high-impact journals, accumulating over 200 citations. Additionally, he is an active reviewer for several Scopus- and Web of Science-indexed journals, contributing significantly to the advancement of mathematical research.

***

Akintade Elizabeth Abidemi is a research, and senior technologist in the Department of Ecotourism and Wildlife Management, Federal University of Technology Akure, Ondo State, Nigeria.

Hala Al-Ruheili is an assistant professor at Sohar University. Her research interests include educational leadership and technology integration into educational leadership.

Sheikha Al-Buraiki is currently an assistant professor at Sohar University. Her research interests include second language acquisition and learning, classroom interaction and the incorporation of technology into education.

Metin Celik is a Professor of Maritime Faculty at ITU and co-founder of Blueanalytica Maritime established in 2021. He has published 4 book chapters, 70+ SCI/SSCI indexed journal papers (h-index 30; 2500+ citations in Wos/WoK) and 70+ international conference papers. He has conducted granted 18 different maritime research and technology projects. He has completed the supervision of 7 PhD dissertations and 12 MSc theses in the maritime era. Professor Celik has been featured among the World's Top 2% Scientists List, according to a Stanford University ranking study, published in 2020-2024. His main research topic includes marine engineering, maritime skills, compliance management, safety engineering, human reliability and operations modelling.

Meenakshi Gupta is working as an Assistant Professor in the School of Economics, at Shri Mata Vaishno Devi University, Katra. She has teaching and research experience of almost 16 years. She has been a part of many academic and non- academic committees of the university since 2007. Her main areas of interest are

Agricultural Economics, Environmental Economics and Development Economics. Her research work has been published in various national and international journals. She has contributed to various books also. She has also presented various articles at National and International Conferences. She is also awarded with many prestigious national and international awards. She is a life Member of Indian Economic Association, Indian Society of Agri- business and Management, Indian Society of Agricultural Economics, TIES, AERA, etc.

Süleyman Gürbüz is a Naval Officer in Türkiye. He earned his BSc (2016) in Meteorology and Physical Oceanography in Naval Post Graduate School California/ USA and PhD (2024) in Maritime Transportation Engineering in Istanbul Technical University. His research interests include Technology-enhanced Maritime Education and Training, Serious Gaming, Maritime Safety and Security, and future maritime solutions

P. Ami Femila is an Assistant Professor in SRM Institute of Science and Technology (SRMIST), Kattankulathur, Chennai. With over 26 years of experience in the field of education, she has made significant contributions to teaching and training, particularly in verbal aptitude, communication skills, and soft skills development.

Krishna Kumari is a distinguished academic and career development expert at SRM Institute of Science and Technology (SRM IST), Kattankulathur, where she serves as a key faculty member at the Department of Mathematics. With a strong background in career counseling and professional development, Dr. Kumari has become a vital resource for students and professionals seeking to advance their careers. Dr. Kumari holds a Ph.D. in Mathematics and has a rich academic and professional background. Her research and publications focus on [Formal languages and Automata Theory, Graph based machine learning, Educational Pedagogy], and she has authored several papers in peer-reviewed journals that contribute to her field.

Deepa Sharma has done Ph.D., MBA in Human Resource Management, currently working as Assistant Professor at MMIM, Maharishi Markandeshwar (Deemed to be University), NAAC Accredited Grade 'A++' University, Mullana, Ambala (Haryana). She has more than 9 years of experience in academics. She has written 61+ research papers for various Scopus and UGC listed referred National & International Journals and 13 papers appear on SCOPUS Preview.

Muhammad Usman Tariq has more than 16+ year's experience in industry and academia. He has authored more than 200+ research articles, 110+ case studies, 105+ book chapters and several books other than 4 patents. He is founder and CEO of The Case HQ, a unique repository for courses, narrative and video case studies. He has been working as a consultant and trainer for industries representing six sigma, quality, health and safety, environmental systems, project management, and information security standards. His work has encompassed sectors in aviation, manufacturing, food, hospitality, education, finance, research, software and transportation. He has diverse and significant experience working with accreditation agencies of ABET, ACBSP, AACSB, WASC, CAA, EFQM and NCEAC. Additionally, Dr. Tariq has operational experience in incubators, research labs, government research projects, private sector startups, program creation and management at various industrial and academic levels. He is Certified Higher Education Teacher from Harvard University, USA, Certified Online Educator from HMBSU, Certified Six Sigma Master Black Belt and has been awarded PFHEA, SFSEDA, SMIEEE, and CMBE.

Wahab Fatai Kayode is a lecturer of entrepreneurship at Ahman Pategi University, Kwara State, Nigeria. He is an interdisciplinary researcher and educationist with a proven track record in the field. With academic qualifications from Kwara State University, Malete, and the National Open University of Nigeria, Abuja, among other institutions, Kayode has made significant contributions to the academic community through his published research in reputable journals.

Seema Yadav has academic qualifications of M. Sc. (Chemistry), M Ed (RIE), UGC-NET, and PhD in Education. Presently she is working as an Assistant Professor, in the Department of Education at The Bhopal School of Education, Bhopal. She has almost 18 years of teaching experience. Her areas of specialization are educational psychology, environmental education, digital learning, and curriculum development.

Index

A

B

C

D

Q

S

T

U

V

W

www.ingramcontent.com/pod-product-compliance
Lightning Source LLC
LaVergne TN
LVHW080609300926
849162LV00005B/1088